A NEW

Omnibus of Crime

EDITED BY

Tony Hillerman and Rosemary Herbert

CONTRIBUTING EDITORS

Sue Grafton and Jeffery Deaver

OXFORD

UNIVERSITY PRESS

OXFORD
UNIVERSITY PRESS

Oxford University Press, Inc., publishes works that further
Oxford University's objective of excellence
in research, scholarship, and education.

Oxford   New York
Auckland   Cape Town   Dar es Salaam   Hong Kong   Karachi
Kuala Lumpur   Madrid   Melbourne   Mexico City   Nairobi
New Delhi   Shanghai   Taipei   Toronto

With offices in
Argentina   Austria   Brazil   Chile   Czech Republic   France   Greece
Guatemala   Hungary   Italy   Japan   Poland   Portugal   Singapore
South Korea   Switzerland   Thailand   Turkey   Ukraine   Vietnam

Published by Oxford University Press, Inc.
198 Madison Avenue, New York, New York, 10016

www.oup.com

First issued as an Oxford University Press paperback, 2010

Oxford is a registered trademark of Oxford University Press.

Library of Congress Cataloging-in-Publication Data
A new omnibus of crime/edited by Tony Hillerman and Rosemary Herbert; contributing
editors Sue Grafton and Jeffery Deaver.
p.   cm.
ISBN 978-0-19-537071-3
1. Detective and mystery stories, American.   2. Detective and mystery stories, English.
3. Crime—Fiction.
I. Hillerman, Tony.   II. Herbert, Rosemary.   III. Grafton, Sue.   IV. Deaver, Jeffery.
PS374.D4N45 2005
813'.087208—dc22   2005011606

1   3   5   7   9   8   6   4   2

Printed in the United States of America
on acid-free paper

For
Daisy and Jeremy Ruggiero
with love,
wishing you a happy journey

For
Marie Hillerman
with love

ACKNOWLEDGMENTS

Tony Hillerman and Rosemary Herbert would like to thank the following people for their support of this project: Barbara Herbert, Marie Hillerman, Justin A. Kraft, Richard Layman, Tom Libby, Cara Nissman, Elaine M. Ober, Juliet Partington, Linda Robbins, Todd Sawyer, Tim Squires, Dr. Barbara Tagg, and Cybele Tom.

Special thanks go to our contributing editors, Sue Grafton and Jeffery Deaver, for their taste and judgment.

We note our gratitude to Catherine Aird, Jeffery Deaver, and Alexander McCall Smith, who contributed new stories to this anthology.

PREFACE

Three-quarters of a century have passed since the publication of Dorothy L. Sayers's landmark anthology of mystery writing, *The Omnibus of Crime*. That book was, and is, a masterwork and a treasure. But, as Bob Dylan musically warned us, "The times, they are a changin'."

And so has crime, and the nature of the detective and mystery fiction Miss Sayers educated us about. Therefore, after seventy-five years which have included global warfare, the rise and fall of nations, the advent of space flight, motorized roller skates, crack cocaine, political correctness, and all sorts of other innovations, Rosemary Herbert and I feel the time is ripe for another look at what has become the most read form of printed literature on the planet.

Miss Sayers took a well-informed look at this genre in 1928 and gave us an astute account of what she saw. If she took the same look in 2005, some of the basics would be about the same. But some would surprise her. For example, she found little effort on the part of pre-1928 writers to make the characters who moved through their fiction seem to be real, genuine people recognizable as humans. She wanted them to be interesting and lively, but not so real that they provoked emotions which interfered with the crime-solving plot. She also saw the introduction of the love element as a distraction with disastrous results on the detective story. And she was preoccupied with the need for ingenuity in the criminal's modus operandi. In fact, Sayers worried that detective fiction's longevity was doomed, unless writers could keep coming up with more and more ingenious and surprising methods of murder.

What she didn't anticipate was the ingenuity future crime writers would apply to characterization. In her day, characters were subservient to the plot. And now character is king.

If she were alive today to read the short stories we have selected to represent crime writing in our time, she would note that many of them make every effort to show their characters complete with human emotions and imperfections. She would also notice that the policy of earlier writers of crime fiction to avoid, or minimize, allowing any love interests to interfere with the plot has pretty well faded away.

Miss Sayers would be absolutely delighted to see how later writers have taken the detective story out of the drawing room and English village and put it into the real world. Like Raymond Chandler, Dashiell Hammett moved crime writing into the "mean streets." We are publishing a Hammett story that does just that, in these pages. And, as our book proves, city streets are not the only turf that crime writers have claimed as their own.

For a fine example of what can be done away from imaginary places like Gotham City, take a look at "By the Scruff of the Soul," in which Dorothy Salisbury Davis provides a gripping example of what a crime writer can do with a rural, very regional setting. Or, to give myself a pat on the back, how about "Chee's Witch," in which I make Navajo Reservation landscape and tribal witchcraft mythology crucial to the plot?

With Miss Sayers—and readers of today and tomorrow—in mind, we put together *A New Omnibus of Crime*. We think it does a fair job of representing the strengths of the crime writing genre in our time. Like her book, we hope it will also stand the test of time.

—*Tony Hillerman, Albuquerque, New Mexico, April 2005*

CONTENTS

A NEW OMNIBUS OF CRIME

INTRODUCTION

It's a tall order to walk in the footsteps of Dorothy L. Sayers. Not only is she the creator of two of the more highly memorable characters in detective fiction—Lord Peter Wimsey and Harriet Vane—but her landmark volume, *The Omnibus of Crime*, is coveted, to this day, by mystery lovers and scholars of the genre. In that definitive collection, which has stood the test of time for seventy-five years, Sayers brings together stories that have crime at their hearts, from the Apocryphal Scriptures to whodunits from the 1920s. To underline the fact that her book contained a mix of stories traveling together in one vehicle, she called her volume an "Omnibus." It is a term that was far more commonly used in her day, but one we are happy to make current again with this compendium, which we see as a conveyance for crime stories selected to take the reader forward through three quarters of a century.

In Sayers's book, her choice of stories reveals a great deal about the editor's taste in reading. In addition, her substantial introduction tells readers much about developments in crime writing as Sayers saw them. Now, Tony Hillerman and I have the honor and the challenge of bringing together another one-volume collection of stories that represents further developments in the genre we love. To do so, we did four things: (1) We looked for stories from the 1930s to the 1970s that were groundbreaking in their day and influential on later writers. (2) We identified stories published since 1980 that show the range of crime writing in our time. (3) We invited Sue Grafton and Jeffery Deaver to help us cull the collected stories to pick out the best of the bunch. (4) We packed them into another "omnibus"—a conveyance that speeds along with all the urgency and attitude our times demand.

That four-point list rather simplifies the process, of course, especially if you scrutinize point number two. That's because, in the years following 1928, there has been explosive growth in the genre, not only in the numbers of writers who are producing crime fiction, but in their approaches and intent. The only way to get a good sense of just what's out there was to read broadly to see if patterns or trends presented themselves. We did that and we found some.

In his preface, Tony points to the most important change of them all, the emphasis on complex characterization. He also speculates on how Sayers might react to developments in crime writing, if she could be here to see how the genre evolved in the latter part of the twentieth century and the first years of the twenty-first. Now, it is my pleasure to point out more of what Sayers had to say about crime writing in her day, and to tell readers more about how we think the genre has changed since then.

In her introduction to *The Omnibus of Crime*, Sayers writes about detective stories as entertaining fare that ultimately comforts the reader: "It may be that in them he finds a sort of catharsis or purging of his fears and self-questionings," Sayers writes. "These mysteries made only to be solved, these horrors which he knows to be mere figments of the creative brain, comfort him by subtly persuading that life is a mystery which death will solve, and whose horrors will pass away as a tale that is told."

This is one area in which crime writing has changed profoundly. It was once possible for W. H. Auden—in his influential 1942 essay "The Guilty Vicarage"—to write of the crime story as one in which an idyllic way of life is shattered by the intrusion of violent crime. According to Auden, the mystery writer must then introduce an omniscient sleuth who would sort out the puzzle, identify the culprit, and reestablish order. By and large, this is what Sayers, her contemporaries, and numerous authors writing today set out to do. However, since Sayers's day, more and more mystery writers look at crime as something a sleuth may solve factually, and lay to rest legally but not necessarily set to rights emotionally. In other words, while a perpetrator may be identified and brought to justice, the emotional ramifications of the crime remain troublesome, like a stain that cannot be eradicated. In the work of P. D. James and others, the effects of the crime on the innocent are disturbing and long-lasting enough to leave readers feeling there can be no return to the idyll.

In fact, in crime writing that postdates the Golden Age of detective fiction (largely published between the two World Wars), the image of an idyll is often quickly revealed to have been false to begin with. An exemplar of this is Margaret Millar's short story "The Couple Next Door," anthologized here. In Millar's story, a neighbor is stunned when it is revealed that the apparently perfect marriage of his neighbors is not at all what it seemed to be. Neither does the pampered life equal paradise in Elmore Leonard's disturbing story "When the Women Come Out to Dance," a powerful piece, in which a new domestic worker learns the miserable truth that lurks behind the life of leisure led by her employer.

And then there's the question of the criminal psyche. Everyone knows that in Sayers's day the whodunit held sway. With its emphasis on identifying the person who perpetrated a crime, this form of fiction was preoccupied with material motive rather than with psychological motivation. According to Sayers, authors of mystery stories and novels dared not delve too deeply into the criminals' or any other characters' psyches, lest they give away so much information that readers could identify the innocent and the guilty.

She also thought detective fiction should shun high emotion. "Though it deals with the most desperate acts of rage, jealousy, and revenge, it rarely touches the heights and depths of human passion," Sayers writes. "It presents us only with the *fait accompli*, and looks upon death and mutilation with a dispassionate eye. It does not show us the inner workings of the murderer's mind—it must not; for the identity of the murderer is hidden until the end of the book. The victim is shown rather as a subject for the dissecting-table than as a husband and father. A too violent emotion flung into the glittering mechanism of the detective-story jars the movement by disturbing its delicate balance." It needs to be noted that Sayers herself broke this rule in her 1931 novel, *The Five Red Herrings*, and again in 1935, in *Gaudy Night*. In the former, spousal abuse is revealed in a scene chock full of violent emotion effectively used to underline the background of a crime. In the latter, a woman in a jealous rage flings verbal abuse at a group of privileged scholars.

In *A New Omnibus of Crime* we take a look at several stories in which the criminal's uncertain psyche is the balance point on which everything is precariously poised. Leave it to Patricia Highsmith, creator of sociopath Tom Ripley and other unbalanced characters, to get us into the head of oddball Clive Wilkes in her short story, "Woodrow Wilson's Necktie." This socially inept man, who lives with his mother, takes to a criminal extreme his fascination with figures in a wax museum. Another outcast wreaks havoc on many in Donald E. Westlake's breathtaking short story, "Breathe Deep," set in a gambling casino. Sayers's own entry here, "The Man Who Knew How," takes another tack by showing how paranoia can lead a person to perpetrate crime.

As Tony has already noted, Sayers also wrote—in her introduction to *The Omnibus of Crime*—about the need for mystery writers to shun the love interest in order to avoid "distracting" the reader from the all-important puzzle element. Indeed, Dashiell Hammett does not let love get in the way of his detective's work in "The Girl with the Silver Eyes," anthologized here. That approach contrasts with several other stories we've brought together here, in which love is central.

In fact, it was Sayers herself who proved, in her 1930 novel, *Strong Poison*, and three more novels featuring Wimsey and Vane, that love can add to, rather than detract from, a tale of mystery. Following Sayers's lead, many writers have used love and what P. D. James has termed "thwarted love" as essential elements of their work. Millar's aforementioned "The Couple Next Door" is one. Dorothy Salisbury Davis's "By the Scruff of the Soul" is another. Here a lovesick traveling salesman tragically veers off course when he pursues a wild country gal.

Lovelessness is at the heart of Tony Hillerman's poignant "First Lead Gasser." Perhaps more than any other story in this book, this tale of a reporter's interview with a murderer who is about to be executed proves it is possible to, as Sayers put it, "make the transition from the detached to the human point of view." This task, Sayers writes, "is especially hard when the murderer has been made human and sympathetic." She may have overlooked how powerful can be the evocation of pity.

Long-lasting love for a beautiful woman is richly evoked in Michael Malone's "Red Clay," a story that is also strong on setting. A question of mother-daughter love is the crux of Sue Grafton's "The Poison That Leaves No Trace," while filial devotion leads to crime in Sara Paretsky's "Photo Finish." The love between a mother and her adult son creates a howler (literally) in Ruth Rendell's disquieting

"Loopy"—a short story that is also notable as one that hinges on the mental health of a pair of characters. "Loopy" and many of the stories mentioned here in the context of love depend upon the interactions that occur between duos who duel or fool around, function or dysfunction, behave as helpmates or try to checkmate one another. It should be noted that the portrayal of couples in crime writing has also been a notable trend during the last seventy-five years.

In recent decades, love of another kind—for pets—has taken center stage in many mysteries. In this *Omnibus*, we've represented the pet element with Ed McBain's "Barking at Butterflies," a misogynistic tale of a man and a perfectly insufferable pooch that is overindulged and over-adored by the protagonist's wife. In Dennis Lehane's "Running Out of Dog," dead dogs strewn along the highway irk the mayor of Eden, South Carolina, who hopes to put his town on the map as a tourist paradise. It seems this Eden's canines have discovered a passion for procreation, fouling the garden in the process.

Passion of different sort is shown in Peter Lovesey's "The Crime of Miss Oyster Brown." Here the eponymous spinster's shame about a secret vice causes her to magnify a small transgression out of all proportion. Lovesey's story exemplifies another much-loved approach to detective fiction that has been sustained, if not invented, since Sayers's time: the delivery of humor in the context of a crime story. Catherine Aird has been producing this kind of writing for almost four decades. In her "The Holly and the Poison Ivy"—a story first published in this volume—she shows how humor arising in dialogue works like a sleight of hand to disguise the delivery of clues that are also embedded in the characters' conversation.

Aird also proves Sayers need not have worried—as Sayers does in her *Omnibus* introduction—about the end of ingenuity in the crime plot. "There are signs, however," Sayers writes, "that the possibilities of the formula are becoming exhausted." Aird is also playful with an aspect of mystery writing that was unconsciously incorporated in crime writing by Sayers and her contemporaries: the importance of class. Consciousness of class and its implications in an earlier era is also at the heart of P. D. James's "Great Aunt Allie's Fly Papers," another story that might lay to rest Sayers's concerns about the loss of ingenuity in the genre.

A passion for peeping underlies Julian Symons's gem, "Flowers That Bloom in the Spring." Like Lovesey's Miss Oyster Brown, Symons's Bertie Mays is a Goody Two-shoes. He finds excitement in spying on his neighbors in search of scandal. But what's a meek man to do when he observes something that might mean murder has been done? Mays decides to search his conscience before proceeding. Meanwhile, John Mortimer's Horace Rumpole forces those who have no conscience to behave as if they do in "Rumpole and the Bubble Reputation." In a story rich with humor delivered in dialogue and in Rumpole's memorable interior monologues, Mortimer bursts the bubbles not only of overblown reputations but of pretentiousness and more. Along the way, Mortimer leads the reader to think about the meanings of justice and true friendship, while raising questions about freedom of expression, too. In this, he exemplifies another development in the genre: crime writing as conveyer of social consciousness.

Far away from Rumpole's haunts in the London law courts, Hillerman shows how insight into cultural attitudes can explain a crime and more in his story, "Chee's Witch," set on the Navajo reservation in the American Southwest. His work epitomizes a major thrust of crime writing that became particularly important over the last few decades: the locating of crimes in distinctly regional settings, and the narrating of them in voices that arise from the cultural and ethnic heritages and socioeconomic circumstances of the characters.

Of course, this had been done before, notably by pulp writers. An early example of this in *A New Omnibus of Crime* is Frederic Brown's "The Wench Is Dead." Despite the Elizabethan-sounding title—which is taken from a line from Christopher Marlowe's 1589 play, *The Jew of Malta*—Brown's piece is steeped in the voice of an alcoholic. This boozer drowns his sorrows—but not his investigative instincts—in drink. With lines like "Most of the windowfronts were as empty as a fool's laugh," Crumley's period piece is as dry a depiction of tragedy as the desiccated town in which his bank robbery occurs.

The sense of place is also strong in Ian Rankin's "The Hanged Man," set in a carnival in Kircaldy, Scotland. Like Mortimer, Rankin mulls the meaning of justice, but in this case the victim acts as judge and jury—the verdict is founded on poetic justice. Alexander McCall Smith's "He Loved to Go for Drives with His Father"—a story first published here—begins by pinpointing locale, in Swaziland, Africa. As is the case in Smith's mystery series about Mma. "Precious" Ramotswe, founder of *The No. 1 Ladies Detective Agency* in Botswana, the physical landscape is intimately tied in with the crime here. Similarly, insights into attitudes are also essential to understanding the truth of the matter in this thought-provoking tale.

Over the years, some mystery writers have used the form to work out feelings and answer questions that haunt them. After surviving a difficult childhood and youth, Ross Madonald spent his writing career wrestling with themes concerning emotional and physical abandonment. We're representing his work with the 1953 story "Gone Girl" here. In "Copy Cat," a story first printed in this volume, Jeffery Deaver chews on the question of how far a writer should go in imagining scenes of violence and horror. It is a question he is asked often, especially since his 1997 novel, *The Bone Collector,* and the film of it have given the shivers to millions.

If we are to stand tall in the footsteps of Dorothy L. Sayers, there is one more task to accomplish, and that is to predict where the genre will proceed from here. With the continued development of technologies in many areas, especially in communication devices and in the medical and forensic arenas, it seems obvious there will always be plenty of room in the genre for ingenuity based on new technologies. In addition, as Aird and James prove in this book, writers can still surprise us with inventive methods of murder that do not depend upon high-tech wizardry. Therefore, we have no worries about ingenuity fading out in the future. We also predict that distinctly regional milieus, light and black humor, socially conscious themes, and crimes tied in with terrorism and other developments in the world at large will all show up in crime writing. We would like to see writers cast their nets wider to include more children and youths in the company of characters they portray.

The real excitement lies in the realm of characterization. Where Sayers could claim the mystery writer must hold back in this department, contemporary crime writers are already daring to tell much more about character, while still constructing satisfying crime stories. Sometimes they do this by letting us know whodunit and concentrating on if and how the character will get away with a crime. But many are proving characterization need not be subservient to plot, even in novels and stories that succeed as true puzzlers.

Thanks to crime writers' willingness to take risks with characterization, we have to say we are far more sanguine than Sayers about the levels to which this genre can aspire. While she writes, "It does not, and by hypothesis never can, attain the loftiest level of literary achievement," we say a crime novel that does not play coy with the reader regarding characterization can and should reach the highest levels of literary achievement. To achieve this, the crime writer must work in the same manner as does the so-called novelist of character. He or she must make plot subservient to character, rather than the reverse. This means revealing secrets of character for reasons of art rather than for reasons of plot or formula.

That does not mean plotting in crime writing should not remain strong. After all, strong plotting has always been a great attribute of works in this genre and a great draw to countless readers. We think crime writers of the future would be well advised to remember this, even as they wow us with insights into what makes their characters tick.

—*Rosemary Herbert, Newtonville, Massachusetts, April 2005*

DOROTHY L. SAYERS

We are celebrating, with this volume, seventy-five years since the publication of Dorothy L. Sayers's *The Omnibus of Crime*, so of course it makes sense to lead off *A New Omnibus of Crime* with a short story by her. We wish to honor Sayers and to showcase her work, too. But that is not all. We knew we should include a story by Sayers only if it served to set the stage for what is to come in this anthology—stories that represent developments in the crime and mystery genre during the last three quarters of a century. Fortunately, Sayers wrote such a story in "The Man Who Knew How."

Readers know Dorothy L. Sayers was an editor, classical scholar, translator, writer of radio plays, and literary critic, as well as a mystery writer. Particularly at the start of her crime-writing career, her fiction revealed her as a product of her reading and of her times. Eventually, she became a groundbreaker, too.

When she first created Lord Peter Wimsey, he was a character whose name and early persona epitomized the aristocratic sleuth. In fact, Sayers claimed the character arrived in her imagination, "complete with spats." A man of means, good breeding, and taste, Wimsey possessed in abundance the time and inclination to dabble in crime solving. He first appeared in the 1923 novel *Whose Body?*—a classic whodunit, which places emphasis on the detective's step-by-step procedure in identifying the perpetrator of a crime. Sayers wrote ten more novels and twenty-three short stories featuring a sleuth whose character deepened as the years went by, and as Sayers grew as a writer. In 1930, Sayers broke a convention of the genre, which held that a love element would be too distracting in a detective novel, by introducing Harriet Vane, a woman who would fascinate and ultimately marry Wimsey.

Two years later, Sayers published "The Man Who Knew How," in which the author describes the classic detective story as one "that crowds all its exciting incidents into the first chapter, and proceeds thereafter by a long series of deductions to a scientific solution at the last." Here her character, a man called Pender, can hardly keep his attention tuned in on such a story. While riding in a train car with a total stranger seated across from him and a whodunit in hand, Pender finds he is more fascinated by the mystery of character that his traveling companion presents than he is with the puzzling book. In "The Man Who Knew How," Sayers anticipates major developments in the crime and mystery genre by showing how a chance encounter can have life-changing consequences, thanks to the power one character exerts over another's psyche. Like most of the writers whose work you will find in this book, Sayers dares to go beyond asking "Whodunit?" to inquire, "Who is it?" And she doesn't stop there. By getting under her protagonist's skin, she causes the reader to ask, "Who am I?"—with chilling effect.

The Man Who Knew How

1932

FOR the twentieth time since the train had left Carlisle, Pender glanced up from *Murder at the Manse* and caught the eye of the man opposite.

He frowned a little. It was irritating to be watched so closely, and always with that faint, sardonic smile. It was still more irritating to allow oneself to be so much disturbed by the smile and the scrutiny. Pender wrenched himself back to his book with a determination to concentrate upon the problem of the minister murdered in the library.

But the story was of the academic kind that crowds all its exciting incidents into the first chapter, and proceeds thereafter by a long series of deductions to a scientific solution in the last. Twice Pender had to turn back to verify points that he had missed in reading. Then he became aware that he was not thinking about the murdered minister at all—he was becoming more and more actively conscious of the other man's face. A queer face, Pender thought.

There was nothing especially remarkable about the features in themselves; it was their expression that daunted Pender. It was a secret face, the face of one who knew a great deal to other people's disadvantage. The mouth was a little crooked and tightly tucked in at the corners, as though savoring a hidden amusement. The eyes, behind a pair of rimless pincenez, glittered curiously; but that was possibly due to the light reflected in the glasses. Pender wondered what the man's profession might be. He was dressed in a dark lounge suit, a raincoat and a shabby soft hat; his age was perhaps about forty.

Pender coughed unnecessarily and settled back into his corner, raising the detective story high before his face, barrier-fashion. This was worse than useless. He gained the impression that the man saw through the manoeuvre and was secretly entertained by it. He wanted to fidget, but felt obscurely that his doing so would in some way constitute a victory for the other man. In his self-consciousness he held himself so rigid that attention to his book became a sheer physical impossibility.

There was no stop now before Rugby, and it was unlikely that any passenger would enter from the corridor to break up this disagreeable *solitude à deux*. Pender could, of course, go out into the corridor and not return, but that would be an acknowledgement of defeat. Pender lowered *Murder at the Manse* and caught the man's eye again.

"Getting tired of it?" asked the man.

"Night journeys are always a bit tedious," replied Pender, half relieved and half reluctant. "Would you like a book?"

He took *The Paper-Clip Clue* from his briefcase and held it out hopefully. The other man glanced at the title and shook his head.

"Thanks very much," he said, "but I never read detective stories. They're so—inadequate, don't you think so?"

"They are rather lacking in characterization and human interest, certainly," said Pender, "but on a railway journey—"

"I don't mean that," said the other man. "I am not concerned with humanity. But all these murderers are so incompetent—they bore me."

"Oh, I don't know," replied Pender. "At any rate they are usually a good deal more imaginative and ingenious than murderers in real life."

"Than the murderers who are found out in real life, yes," admitted the other man.

"Even some of those did pretty well before they got pinched," objected Pender. "Crippen, for instance; he need never have been caught if he hadn't lost his head and run off to America. George Joseph Smith did away with at least two brides quite successfully before fate and the *News of the World* intervened."

"Yes," said the other man, "but look at the clumsiness of it all; the elaboration, the lies, the paraphernalia. Absolutely unnecessary."

"Oh come!" said Pender. "You can't expect committing a murder and getting away with it to be as simple as shelling peas."

"Ah!" said the other man. "You think that, do you?"

Pender waited for him to elaborate this remark, but nothing came of it. The man leaned back and smiled in his secret way at the roof of the carriage; he appeared to think the conversation not worth going on with. Pender found himself noticing his companion's hands. They were white and surprisingly long in the fingers. He watched them gently tapping upon their owner's knee—then resolutely turned a page—then put the book down once more and said:

"Well, if it's so easy, how would *you* set about committing a murder?"

"I?" repeated the man. The light on his glasses made his eyes quite blank to Pender, but his voice sounded gently amused. "That's different; *I* should not have to think twice about it."

"Why not?"

"Because I happen to know how to do it."

"Do you indeed?" muttered Pender, rebelliously.

"Oh yes; there's nothing to it."

"How can you be sure? You haven't tried, I suppose?"

"It isn't a case of trying," said the man. "There's nothing uncertain about my method. That's just the beauty of it."

"It's easy to say that," retorted Pender, "but what *is* this wonderful method?"

"You can't expect me to tell you that, can you?" said the other man, bringing his eyes back to rest on Pender's. "It might not be safe. You look harmless enough, but who could look more harmless than Crippen? Nobody is fit to be trusted with *absolute* control over other people's lives."

"Bosh!" exclaimed Pender. "I shouldn't think of murdering anybody."

"Oh yes you would," said the other man, "if you really believed it was safe. So would anybody. Why are all these tremendous artificial barriers built up around murder by the Church and the law? Just because it's everybody's crime and just as natural as breathing."

"But that's ridiculous!" cried Pender, warmly.

"You think so, do you? That's what most people would say. But I wouldn't trust 'em. Not with sulphate of thanatol to be bought for two pence at any chemist's."

"Sulphate of what?" asked Pender sharply.

"Ah! you think I'm giving something away. Well, it's a mixture of that and one or two other things—all equally ordinary and cheap. For nine pence you could make up enough to poison the entire Cabinet. Though of course one wouldn't polish off the whole lot at once; it might look funny if they all died simultaneously in their baths."

"Why in their baths?"

"That's the way it would take them. It's the action of the hot water that brings on the effect of the stuff, you see. Any time from a few hours to a few days after administration. It's quite a simple chemical reaction and it couldn't possibly be detected by analysis. It would just look like heart failure."

Pender eyed him uneasily. He did not like the smile; it was not only derisive, it was smug, it was almost gloating, triumphant! He could not quite put the right name to it.

"You know," pursued the man, pulling a pipe from his pocket and beginning to fill it, "it is very odd how often one seems to read of people being found dead in their baths. It must be a very common accident. Quite temptingly so. After all, there is a fascination about murder. The thing grows upon one—that is, I imagine it would, you know."

"Very likely," said Pender.

"I'm sure of it. No, I wouldn't trust anybody with that formula—not even a virtuous young man like yourself."

The long white fingers tamped the tobacco firmly into the bowl and struck a match.

"But how about you?" said Pender, irritated. (Nobody cares to be called a virtuous young man.) "If nobody is fit to be trusted—"

"I'm not, eh?" replied the man. "Well, that's true, but it can't be helped now, can it? I know the thing and I can't unknow it again. It's unfortunate, but there it is. At any rate you have the comfort of knowing that nothing disagreeable is likely to happen to *me*. Dear me! Rugby already. I get out here. I have a little bit of business to do at Rugby."

He rose and shook himself, buttoned his raincoat about him, and pulled the shabby hat more firmly down about his enigmatic glasses. The train slowed down and stopped. With a brief good night and a crooked smile the man stepped on to the platform. Pender watched him stride quickly away into the drizzle beyond the radius of the gas light.

"Dotty or something," said Pender, oddly relieved. "Thank goodness, I seem to be going to have the compartment to myself."

He returned to *Murder at the Manse*, but his attention still kept wandering from the book he held in his hand.

"What was the name of that stuff the fellow talked about? Sulphate of what?"

For the life of him he could not remember.

It was on the following afternoon that Pender saw the news item. He had bought the *Standard* to read at lunch, and the word "Bath" caught his eye; otherwise he would probably have missed the paragraph altogether, for it was only a short one.

WEALTHY MANUFACTURER DIES IN BATH
WIFE'S TRAGIC DISCOVERY

A distressing discovery was made early this morning by Mrs. John Brittlesea, wife of the well-known head of Brittlesea's Engineering Works at Rugby. Finding that her husband, whom she had seen alive and well less than an hour previously, did not come down in time for his breakfast, she searched for him in the bathroom, where the engineer was found lying dead in his bath; life having been extinct, according to the medical men, for half an hour. The cause of the death is pronounced to be heart failure. The deceased manufacturer . . .

"That's an odd coincidence," said Pender. "At Rugby. I should think my unknown friend would be interested—if he is still there, doing his bit of business. I wonder what his business is, by the way."

It is a very curious thing how, when once your attention is attracted to any particular set of circumstances, that set of circumstances seems to haunt you. You get appendicitis: immediately the newspapers are filled with paragraphs about statesmen suffering from appendicitis and victims dying of it; you learn that all your acquaintances have had it, or know friends who have had it and either died of it, or recovered from it with more surprising and spectacular rapidity than yourself; you cannot open a popular magazine without seeing its cure mentioned as one of the triumphs of modern surgery, or dip into a scientific treatise without coming across a comparison of the vermiform appendix in men and monkeys. Probably these references to appendicitis are equally frequent at all times, but you only notice them when your mind is attuned to the subject. At any rate, it was in this way that Pender accounted to himself for the extraordinary frequency with which people seemed to die in their baths at this period.

The thing pursued him at every turn. Always the same sequence of events: the hot bath, the discovery of the corpse, the inquest. Always the same medical opinion: heart failure following immersion in too hot water. It began to seem to

Pender that it was scarcely safe to enter a hot bath at all. He took to making his own bath cooler and cooler each day, until it almost ceased to be enjoyable.

He skimmed his paper each morning for headlines about baths before settling down to read the news; and was at once relieved and vaguely disappointed if a week passed without a hot-bath tragedy.

One of the sudden deaths that occurred in this way was that of a young and beautiful woman whose husband, an analytical chemist, had tried without success to divorce her a few months previously. The coroner displayed a tendency to suspect foul play, and put the husband through a severe cross-examination. There seemed, however, to be no getting behind the doctor's evidence. Pender, brooding over the improbable possible, wished, as he did every day of the week, that he could remember the name of that drug the man in the train had mentioned.

Then came the excitement in Pender's own neighborhood. An old Mr. Skimmings, who lived alone with a housekeeper in a street just around the corner, was found dead in his bathroom. His heart had never been strong. The housekeeper told the milkman that she had always expected something of the sort to happen, for the old gentleman would always take his bath so hot. Pender went to the inquest.

The housekeeper gave her evidence. Mr. Skimmings had been the kindest of employers, and she was heartbroken at losing him. No, she had not been aware that Mr. Skimmings had left her a large sum of money, but it was just like his goodness of heart. The verdict of course was accidental death.

Pender, that evening, went out for his usual stroll with the dog. Some feeling of curiosity moved him to go around past the late Mr. Skimmings' house. As he loitered by, glancing up at the blank windows, the garden gate opened and a man came out. In the light of a street lamp, Pender recognized him at once.

"Hullo!" he said.

"Oh, it's you, is it?" said the man. "Viewing the site of the tragedy, eh? What do *you* think about it all?"

"Oh, nothing very much," said Pender. "I didn't know him. Odd, our meeting again like this."

"Yes, isn't it? You live near here, I suppose."

"Yes," said Pender; and then wished he hadn't. "Do you live in these parts too?"

"Me?" said the man. "Oh no. I was only here on a little matter of business."

"Last time we met," said Pender, "you had business at Rugby." They had fallen into step together, and were walking slowly down to the turning Pender had to take in order to reach his house.

"So I had," agreed the other man. "My business takes me all over the country. I never know where I may be wanted next, you see."

"It was while you were at Rugby that old Brittlesea was found dead in his bath, wasn't it?" remarked Pender carelessly.

"Yes. Funny thing, coincidence." The man glanced up at him sideways through his glittering glasses. "Left all his money to his wife, didn't he? She's a rich woman now. Good-looking girl—a lot younger than he was."

They were passing Pender's gate. "Come in and have a drink," said Pender, and again immediately regretted the impulse.

The man accepted, and they went into Pender's bachelor study.

"Remarkable lot of these bath deaths lately," observed Pender as he squirted soda into the tumblers.

"You think it's remarkable?" said the man, with his irritating trick of querying everything that was said to him. "Well, I don't know. Perhaps it is. But it's always a fairly common accident."

"I suppose I've been taking more notice on account of that conversation we had in the train." Pender laughed, a little self-consciously. "It just makes me wonder—you know how one does—whether anybody else had happened to hit on that drug you mentioned—what was its name?"

The man ignored the question.

"Oh, I shouldn't think so," he said. "I fancy I'm the only person who knows about that. I only stumbled on the thing by accident myself when I was looking for something else. I don't imagine it could have been discovered simultaneously in so many parts of the country. But all these verdicts just show, don't they, what a safe way it would be of getting rid of a person."

"You're a chemist, then?" asked Pender, catching at the one phrase which seemed to promise information.

"Oh, I'm a bit of everything. Sort of general utility man. I do a good bit of studying on my own, too. You've got one or two interesting books here, I see."

Pender was flattered. For a man in his position—he had been in a bank until he came into that little bit of money—he felt that he had improved his mind to some purpose, and he knew that his collection of modern first editions would be worth money some day. He went over to the glass-fronted bookcase and pulled out a volume or two to show his visitor.

The man displayed intelligence, and presently joined him in front of the shelves.

"These, I take it, represent your personal tastes?" He took down a volume of Henry James and glanced at the fly-leaf. "That your name? E. Pender?"

Pender admitted that it was. "You have the advantage of me," he added.

"Oh! I am one of the great Smith clan," said the other with a laugh, "and work for my bread. You seem to be very nicely fixed here."

Pender explained about the clerkship and the legacy.

"Very nice, isn't it?" said Smith. "Not married? No. You're one of the lucky ones. Not likely to be needing any sulphate of . . . any useful drugs in the near future. And you never will, if you stick to what you've got and keep off women and speculation."

He smiled up sideways at Pender. Now that his hat was off, Pender saw that he had a quantity of closely curled grey hair, which made him look older than he had appeared in the railway carriage.

"No, I shan't be coming to you for assistance yet a while," said Pender, laughing. "Besides, how should I find you if I wanted you?"

"You wouldn't have to," said Smith, "*I* should find *you*. There's never any difficulty about that." He grinned, oddly. "Well, I'd better be getting on. Thank you for your hospitality. I don't expect we shall meet again—but we may, of course. Things work out so queerly, don't they?"

When he had gone, Pender returned to his own armchair. He took up his glass of whisky, which stood there nearly full.

"Funny!" he said to himself. "I don't remember pouring that out. I suppose I got interested, and did it mechanically." He emptied his glass slowly, thinking about Smith.

What in the world was Smith doing at Skimmings' house?

An odd business altogether. If Skimmings' housekeeper had known about that money . . . But she had not known, and if she had, how could she have found out about Smith and his sulphate of . . . the word had been on the tip of his tongue, then.

"You would not need to find me. *I* should find *you*." What had the man meant by that? But this was ridiculous. Smith was not the devil, presumably. But if he really had this secret—if he liked to put a price upon it—nonsense.

"Business at Rugby—a little bit of business at Skimmings' house." Oh, absurd!

"Nobody is fit to be trusted. *Absolute* power over another man's life . . . it grows on you. That is, I imagine it would."

Lunacy! And, if there was anything in it, the man was mad to tell Pender about it. If Pender chose to speak he could get the fellow hanged. The very existence of Pender would be dangerous.

That whisky!

More and more, thinking it over, Pender became persuaded that he had never poured it out. Smith must have done it while his back was turned. Why that sudden display of interest in the bookshelves? It had had no connection with anything that had gone before. Now Pender came to think of it, it had been a very stiff whisky. Was it imagination, or had there been something about the flavor of it?

A cold sweat broke out on Pender's forehead.

A quarter of an hour later, after a powerful dose of mustard and water, Pender was downstairs again, very cold and shivering, huddling over the fire. He had had a narrow escape—if he had escaped. He did not know how the stuff worked, but he would not take a hot bath again for some days. One never knew.

Whether the mustard and water had done the trick in time, or whether the hot bath was an essential part of the treatment, at any rate Pender's life was saved for the time being. But he was still uneasy. He kept the front door on the chain and warned his servant to let no strangers into the house.

He ordered two more morning papers and the *News of the World* on Sundays, and kept a careful watch upon their columns. Deaths in baths became an obsession with him. He neglected his first editions and took to attending inquests.

Three weeks later he found himself at Lincoln. A man had died of heart failure in a Turkish bath—a fat man, of sedentary habits. The jury added a rider to their verdict of accidental death to the effect that the management should exercise a stricter supervision over the bathers and should never permit them to be left unattended in the hot room.

As Pender emerged from the hall he saw ahead of him a shabby hat that seemed familiar. He plunged after it, and caught Mr. Smith about to step into a taxi.

"Smith," he cried, gasping a little. He clutched him fiercely by the shoulder.

"What, you again?" said Smith. "Taking notes of the case, eh? *Can I do anything for you?*"

"You devil!" said Pender. "You're mixed up in this! You tried to kill me the other day."

"Did I? Why should I do that?"

"You'll swing for this," shouted Pender menacingly.

A policeman pushed his way through the gathering crowd.

"Here!" said he. "What's all this about?"

Smith touched his forehead significantly.

"It's all right, Officer," said he. "The gentleman seems to think I'm here for no good. Here's my card. The coroner knows me. But he attacked me. You'd better keep an eye on him."

"That's right," said a bystander.

"This man tried to kill me," said Pender.

The policeman nodded.

"Don't you worry about that, sir," he said. "You think better of it. The 'eat in there has upset you a bit. All right, *all* right."

"But I want to charge him," said Pender.

"I wouldn't do that if I was you," said the policeman.

"I tell you," said Pender, "that this man Smith has been trying to poison me. He's a murderer. He's poisoned scores of people."

The policeman winked at Smith.

"Best be off, sir," he said. "I'll settle this. Now, my lad"—he held Pender firmly by the arms—"just you keep cool and take it quiet. That gentleman's name ain't Smith nor nothing like it. You've got a bit mixed up like."

"Well, what is his name?" demanded Pender.

"Never mind," replied the constable. "You leave him alone, or you'll be getting yourself into trouble."

The taxi had driven away. Pender glanced around at the circle of amused faces and gave in.

"All right, Officer," he said. "I won't give you any trouble. I'll come round with you to the police station and tell you about it."

"What do you think o' that one?" asked the inspector of the sergeant when Pender had stumbled out of the station.

"Up the pole an' 'alfway round the flag, if you ask me," replied his subordinate. "Got one o' them ideez fix what they talk about."

"H'm!" replied the inspector. "Well, we've got his name and address. Better make a note of 'em. He might turn up again. Poisoning people so as they die in their baths, eh? That's a pretty good 'un. Wonderful how these barmy ones thinks it all out, isn't it?"

The spring that year was a bad one—cold and foggy. It was March when Pender went down to an inquest at Deptford, but a thick blanket of mist was hanging over the river as though it were November. The cold ate into your bones. As he sat in the dingy little court, peering through the yellow twilight of gas and fog, he could scarcely see the witnesses as they came to the table. Everybody in the place seemed to be coughing. Pender was coughing too. His bones ached, and he felt as though he were about due for a bout of influenza.

Straining his eyes, he thought he recognized a face on the other side of the room, but the smarting fog which penetrated every crack stung and blinded him. He felt in his overcoat pocket, and his hand closed comfortably on something thick and heavy. Ever since that day in Lincoln he had gone about armed for protection. Not a revolver—he was no hand with firearms. A sandbag was much better. He had bought one from an old man wheeling a pushcart. It was meant for keeping out draughts from the door—a good, old-fashioned affair.

The inevitable verdict was returned. The spectators began to push their way out. Pender had to hurry now, not to lose sight of his man. He elbowed his way along, muttering apologies. At the door he almost touched the man, but a stout woman intervened. He plunged past her, and she gave a little squeak of indignation. The man in front turned his head, and the light over the door glinted on his glasses.

Pender pulled his hat over his eyes and followed. His shoes had crêpe rubber soles and made no sound on the pavement. The man went on, jogging quietly up one street and down another, and never looking back. The fog was so thick that Pender was forced to keep within a few yards of him. Where was he going? Into the lighted streets? Home by bus or tram? No. He turned off to the left, down a narrow street.

The fog was thicker here. Pender could no longer see his quarry, but he heard the footsteps going on before him at the same even pace. It seemed to him that they were two alone in the world—pursued and pursuer, slayer and avenger. The street began to slope more rapidly. They must be coming out somewhere near the river.

Suddenly the dim shapes of the houses fell away on either side. There was an open space, with a lamp vaguely visible in the middle. The footsteps paused.

Pender, silently hurrying after, saw the man standing close beneath the lamp, apparently consulting something in a notebook.

Four steps, and Pender was upon him. He drew the sandbag from his pocket.

The man looked up.

"I've got you this time," said Pender, and struck with all his force.

Pender was quite right. He did get influenza. It was a week before he was out and about again. The weather had changed, and the air was fresh and sweet. In spite of the weakness left by the malady he felt as though a heavy weight had been lifted from his shoulders. He tottered down to a favorite bookshop of his in the Strand, and picked up a D. H. Lawrence "first" at a price which he knew to be a bargain. Encouraged by this, he turned into a small chop-house chiefly frequented by newspaper men, and ordered a grilled cutlet and a half-tankard of bitter.

Two journalists were seated by the next table.

"Going to poor old Buckley's funeral?" asked one.

"Yes," said the other. "Poor devil! Fancy his getting bashed on the head like that. He must have been on his way down to interview the widow of that fellow who died in a bath. It's a rough district. Probably one of Jimmy the Card's crowd had it in for him. He was a great crime-reporter—they won't get another like Bill Buckley in a hurry."

"He was a decent sort, too. Great old sport. No end of a practical joker. Remember his great stunt sulphate of thanatol?"

Pender started. *That* was the word that had eluded him for so many months. A curious dizziness came over him.

". . . looking at you as sober as a judge," the journalist was saying. "No such stuff, of course, but he used to work off that wheeze on poor boobs in railway carriages to see how they'd take it. Would you believe that one chap actually offered him—"

"Hullo!" interrupted his friend. "That bloke over there has fainted. I thought he was looking a bit white."

DASHIELL HAMMETT

There is no doubt Dashiell Hammett (1894–1961), who had worked as a private eye himself, endowed the detective story with far more realism than did his crime-writer predecessors. He is credited with taking the detective story out of the English drawing room and into American offices, alleyways, and more. More important, he brought a strong, masculine, declarative voice to the genre, and he was not afraid of spelling out his stories of crime and detection in the American vernacular. Fans and scholars alike love to point out these innovations, and to remind us of how influential Hammett's work was upon writers who followed him.

Less celebrated is Hammett's indebtedness to conventions of the genre that had been established before he arrived on the scene. Like Dorothy L. Sayers, a writer with whom he is rarely paired, Hammett was a product of his times and profoundly influenced by writers who came before him. To say this is not to denigrate his accomplishments and innovations. They stand out precisely because his work is anchored in those established conventions.

Hammett's short story "The Girl with the Silver Eyes" is a case in point. Narrated in the first person by a character called the Continental Op, it contains a number of statements that reveal the author's private eye experience. For instance, Hammett writes, "The two great bugaboos of the reputable detective agency are the persons who bring in a crooked plan or piece of divorce work all dressed up in the garb of a legitimate operation, and the irresponsible person who is laboring under wild and fanciful delusions—who wants a dream run out." At another juncture, the Op tells readers, in a parenthesized aside, "(A detective, if he is wise, takes pains to make and keep as many friends as possible among transfer company, express company and railroad employees.)" Such statements, delivered in a confidential tone, convince us the Op knows his game and is willing to share tips about his business with the intelligent reader. This is a far cry from the Sherlock Holmes model of the omniscient sleuth who places himself on a loftier level than the reader, or the Lord Peter Wimsey type who may confide a bit more to his sidekick, and therefore to the reader, but still holds back a good deal along the way.

Still, the story's structure follows a pattern Sayers describes in her introduction to *The Omnibus of Crime*: The story delivers at its start "excitement"—in this case, alarm over a beautiful woman's disappearance. The sleuth then "follows up quietly from clue to clue until the problem is solved" and his deductions are proved to be true. In addition, Hammett here makes it clear love is a complication that the effective private eye should shun. More remarkable are the economy of language and straightforward delivery of colorful detail with which Hammett builds and makes memorable character and place as he delivers a baffling mystery.

Armchair detectives may notice that this story predates Sayer's *Omnibus of Crime*. Because permissions for later Hammett stories were not as readily available, we include this piece here.

The Girl with the Silver Eyes

1924

I

A BELL jangled me into wakefulness. I rolled to the edge of my bed and reached for the telephone. The neat voice of the Old Man—the Continental Detective Agency's San Francisco manager—came to my ears:

"Sorry to disturb you, but you'll have to go up to the Glenton Apartments on Leavenworth Street. A man named Burke Pangburn, who lives there, phoned me a few minutes ago asking to have someone sent up to see him at once. He seemed rather excited. Will you take care of it? See what he wants."

I said I would and, yawning, stretching and cursing Pangburn—whoever he was—got my fat body out of pajamas and into street clothes.

The man who had disturbed my Sunday morning sleep—I found when I reached the Glenton—was a slim, white-faced person of about twenty-five, with big brown eyes that were red-rimmed just now from either sleeplessness or crying, or both. His long brown hair was rumpled when he opened the door to admit me; and he wore a mauve dressing-robe spotted with big jade parrots over wine-colored silk pajamas.

The room into which he led me resembled an auctioneer's establishment just before the sale—or maybe one of these alley tea-rooms. Fat blue vases, crooked red vases, lanky yellow vases, vases of various shapes and colors; marble statuettes, ebony statuettes, statuettes of any material; lanterns, lamps and candlesticks; draperies, hangings and rugs of all sorts; odds and ends of furniture that were all somehow queerly designed; peculiar pictures hung here and there in unexpected places. A hard room to feel comfortable in.

"My fiancée," be began immediately in a high-pitched voice that was within a notch of hysteria, "has disappeared! Something has happened to her! Foul play of some horrible sort! I want you to find her—to save her from this terrible thing that. . . ."

I followed him this far and then gave it up. A jumble of words came out of his mouth—"spirited away . . . mysterious something . . . lured into a trap"—but they were too disconnected for me to make anything out of them. So I stopped trying to understand him, and waited for him to babble himself empty of words.

I have heard ordinarily reasonable men, under stress of excitement, run on even more crazily than this wild-eyed youth; but his dress—the parroted robe and gay pajamas—and his surroundings—this deliriously furnished room—gave him too theatrical a setting; made his words sound utterly unreal.

He himself, when normal, should have been a rather nice-looking lad: his features were well spaced and, though his mouth and chin were a little uncertain, his broad forehead was good. But standing there listening to the occasional melo-dramatic phrase that I could pick out of the jumbled noises he was throwing at me, I thought that instead of parrots on his robe he should have had cuckoos.

Presently he ran out of language and was holding his long, thin hands out to me in an appealing gesture, saying,

"Will you?" over and over. "Will you? Will you?"

I nodded soothingly, and noticed that tears were on his thin cheeks.

"Suppose we begin at the beginning," I suggested, sitting down carefully on a carved bench affair that didn't look any too strong.

"Yes! Yes!" He was standing legs apart in front of me, running his fingers through his hair. "The beginning. I had a letter from her every day until—"

"That's not the beginning," I objected. "Who is she? What is she?"

"She's Jeanne Delano!" he exclaimed in surprise at my ignorance. "And she is my fiancée. "And now she is gone, and I know that—"

The phrases "victim of foul play," "into a trap" and so on began to flow hys-terically out again.

Finally I got him quieted down and, sandwiched in between occasional emotional outbursts, got a story out of him that amounted to this:

This Burke Pangburn was a poet. About two months before, he had received a note from a Jeanne Delano—forwarded from his publishers—prais-ing his latest book of rhymes. Jeanne Delano happened to live in San Francisco, too, though she hadn't known that he did. He had answered her note, and had received another. After a little of this they met. If she really was as beautiful as he claimed, then he wasn't to be blamed for falling in love with her. But whether or not she was really beautiful, he thought she was, and he had fallen hard.

This Delano girl had been living in San Francisco for only a little while, and when the poet met her she was living alone in an Ashbury Avenue apartment. He did not know where she came from or anything about her former life. He suspected—from certain indefinite suggestions and peculiarities of conduct which he couldn't put in words—that there was a cloud of some sort hanging over the girl; that neither her past nor her present were free from difficulties. But he hadn't the least idea what those difficulties might be. He hadn't cared. He knew absolutely nothing about her, except that she was beautiful, and he loved her, and she had promised to marry him.

Then, on the third of the month—exactly twenty-one days before this Sunday morning—the girl had suddenly left San Francisco. He had received a note from her, by messenger.

This note, which he showed me after I had insisted point blank on seeing it, read:

Burkelove:

Have just received a wire, and must go East on next train. Tried to get you on the phone, but couldn't. Will write you as soon as I know what my address will be.

If anything. (*These two words were erased and could be read only with great difficulty.*)
Love me until I'm back with you forever.

Your JEANNE.

Nine days later he had received another letter from her, from Baltimore, Maryland. This one, which I had a still harder time getting a look at, read:

Dearest Poet:

It seems like two years since I have seen you, and I have a fear that it's going to be between one and two months before I see you again.

I can't tell you now, beloved, about what brought me here. There are things that can't be written. But as soon as I'm back with you, I shall tell you the whole wretched story.

If anything should happen—I mean to me—you'll go on loving me forever, won't you, beloved? But that's foolish. Nothing is going to happen. I'm just off the train, and tired from traveling.

Tomorrow I shall write you a long, long letter to make up for this.

My address here is 215 N. Stricker St. Please, Mister, at least one letter a day!

Your own JEANNE.

For nine days he had had a letter from her each day—with two on Monday to make up for the none on Sunday—and then her letters had stopped. And the daily letters he had sent to the address she gave—215 N. Stricker Street—had begun to come back to him, marked "Not known."

He had sent a telegram, and the telegraph company had informed him that its Baltimore office had been unable to find a Jeanne Delano at the North Stricker Street address.

For three days he had waited, expecting hourly to hear from the girl, and no word had come. Then he had bought a ticket for Baltimore.

"But," he wound up, "I was afraid to go, I know she's in some sort of trouble—I can feel that—but I'm a silly poet. I can't deal with mysteries. Either I would find nothing at all or, if by luck I did stumble on the right track, the probabilities are that I would only muddle things; add fresh complications, perhaps endanger her life still further. I can't go blundering at it in that fashion, without knowing whether I am helping or harming her. It's a task for an expert in that sort of thing. So I thought of your agency. You'll be careful, won't you? It may be—I don't know—that she won't want assistance. It may be that you can help her without her knowing anything about it. You are accustomed to that sort of thing; you can do it, can't you?"

II

I turned the job over and over in my mind before answering him. The two great bugaboos of a reputable detective agency are the persons who bring in a crooked plan or a piece of divorce work all dressed up in the garb of a legitimate operation, and the irresponsible person who is laboring under wild and fanciful delusions—who wants a dream run out.

This poet—sitting opposite me now twining his long, white fingers nervously together—was, I thought, sincere; but I wasn't so sure of his sanity.

"Mr. Pangburn," I said after a while, "I'd like to handle this thing for you, but I'm not sure that I can. The Continental is rather strict, and, while I believe this thing is on the level, still I am only a hired man and have to go by the rules. Now if you could give us the endorsement of some firm or person of standing—a reputable lawyer, for instance, or any legally responsible party—we'd be glad to go ahead with the work. Otherwise, I am afraid—"

"But I know she's in danger!" he broke out. "I know that—And I can't be advertising her plight—airing her affairs—to everyone."

"I'm sorry, but I can't touch it unless you can give me some such endorsement." I stood up. "But you can find plenty of detective agencies that aren't so particular."

His mouth worked like a small boy's, and he caught his lower lip between his teeth. For a moment I thought he was going to burst into tears. But instead he said slowly:

"I dare say you are right. Suppose I refer you to my brother-in-law, Roy Axford. Will his word be sufficient?"

"Yes."

Roy Axford—R. F. Axford—was a mining man who had a finger in at least half of the big business enterprises of the Pacific Coast; and his word on anything was commonly considered good enough for anybody.

"If you can get in touch with him now," I said, "and arrange for me to see him today, I can get started without much delay."

Pangburn crossed the room and dug a telephone out from among a heap of his ornaments. Within a minute or two he was talking to someone whom he called "Rita."

"Is Roy home? . . . Will he be home this afternoon? . . . No, you can give him a message for me, though. . . . Tell him I'm sending a gentleman up to see him this afternoon on a personal matter—personal with me—and that I'll be very grateful if he'll do what I want. . . . Yes. . . . You'll find out, Rita. . . . It isn't a thing to talk about over the phone. Yes, thanks!"

He pushed the telephone back into its hiding place and turned to me.

"He'll be at home until two o'clock. Tell him what I told you and if he seems doubtful, have him call me up. You'll have to tell him the whole thing; he doesn't know anything at all about Miss Delano."

"All right. Before I go, I want a description of her."

"She's beautiful!" he exclaimed. "The most beautiful woman in the world!"

That would look nice on a reward circular.

"That isn't exactly what I want," I told him. "How old is she?"

"Twenty-two."

"Height?"

"About five feet eight inches, or possibly nine."

"Slender, medium or plump?"

"She's inclined toward slenderness, but she—"

There was a note of enthusiasm in his voice that made me fear he was about to make a speech, so I cut him off with another question.

"What color hair?"

"Brown—so dark that it's almost black—and it's soft and thick and—"

"Yes, yes. Long or bobbed?"

"Long and thick and—"

"What color eyes?"

"You've seen shadows on polished silver when—"

I wrote down *grey eyes* and hurried on with the interrogation.

"Complexion?"

"Perfect!"

"Uh-huh. But is it light, or dark, or florid, or sallow, or what?"

"Fair."

"Face oval, or square, or long and thin, or what shape?"

"Oval."

"What shaped nose? Large, small, turned-up—"

"Small and regular!" There was a touch of indignation in his voice.

"How did she dress? Fashionably? And did she favor bright or quiet colors?"

"Beaut—" And then as I opened my mouth to head him off he came down to earth with:

"Very quietly—usually dark blues and browns,"

"What jewelry did she wear?"

"I've never seen her wear any."

"Any scars, or moles?" The horrified look on his white face urged me on to give him a full shot. "Or warts, or deformities that you know?"

He was speechless, but he managed to shake his head.

"Have you a photograph of her?"

"Yes, I'll show you."

He bounded to his feet, wound his way through the room's excessive furnishings and out through a curtained doorway. Immediately he was back with a large photograph in a carved ivory frame. It was one of these artistic photographs—a thing of shadows and hazy outlines—not much good for identification purposes. She was beautiful—right enough—but that meant nothing; that's the purpose of an artistic photograph.

"This the only one you have?"

"Yes."

"I'll have to borrow it, but I'll get it back to you as soon as I have my copies made."

"No! No!" he protested against having his ladylove's face given to a lot of gumshoes. "That would be terrible!"

I finally got it, but it cost me more words than I like to waste on an incidental.

"I want to borrow a couple of her letters, or something in her writing, too," I said.

"For what?"

"To have photostatic copies made. Handwriting specimens come in handy—give you something to go over hotel registers with. Then, even if going under fictitious names, people now and then write notes and make memorandums."

We had another battle, out of which I came with three envelopes and two meaningless sheets of paper, all bearing the girl's angular writing.

"She have much money?" I asked, when the disputed photograph and handwriting specimens were safely tucked away in my pocket.

"I don't know. It's not the sort of thing that one would pry into. She wasn't poor; that is, she didn't have to practice any petty economies; but I haven't the faintest idea either as to the amount of her income or its source. She had an account at the Golden Gate Trust Company, but naturally I don't know anything about its size."

"Many friends here?"

"That's another thing I don't know. I think she knew a few people here, but I don't know who they were. You see, when we were together we never talked about anything but ourselves. You know what I mean: there was nothing we were interested in but each other. We were simply—"

"Can't you even make a guess at where she came from, who she was?"

"No. Those things didn't matter to me, She was Jeanne Delano, and that was enough for me."

"Did you and she ever have any financial interests in common? I mean, was there ever any transaction in money or other valuables in which both of you were interested?"

What I meant, of course, was had she got into him for a loan, or had she sold him something, or got money out of him in any other way.

He jumped to his feet, and his face went fog-grey. Then he sat down again—slumped down—and blushed scarlet.

"Pardon me," he said thickly. "You didn't know her, and of course you must look at the thing from all angles. No, there was nothing like that. I'm afraid you are going to waste time if you are going to work on the theory that she was an adventuress. There was nothing like that! She was a girl with something terrible hanging over her; something that called her to Baltimore suddenly; something that has taken her away from me. Money? What could money have to do with it? I love her!"

III

R. F. Axford received me in an office-like room in his Russian Hill residence: a big blond man, whose forty-eight or -nine years had not blurred the outlines of an athlete's body. A big, full-blooded man with the manner of one whose self-confidence is complete and not altogether unjustified.

"What's our Burke been up to now?" he asked amusedly when I told him who I was. His voice was a pleasant vibrant bass.

I didn't give him all the details.

"He was engaged to marry a Jeanne Delano, who went East about three weeks ago and then suddenly disappeared. He knows very little about her; thinks something has happened to her; and wants her found."

"Again?" His shrewd blue eyes twinkled. "And to a Jeanne this time! She's the fifth within a year, to my knowledge, and no doubt I missed one or two who were current while I was in Hawaii. But where do I come in?"

"I asked him for responsible endorsement. I think he's all right, but he isn't, in the strictest sense, a responsible person. He referred me to you."

"You're right about his not being, in the strictest sense, a responsible person." The big man screwed up his eyes and mouth in thought for a moment. Then: "Do you think that something has really happened to the girl? Or is Burke imagining things?"

"I don't know, I thought it was a dream at first. But in a couple of her letters there are hints that something was wrong."

"You might go ahead and find her then," Axford said. "I don't suppose any harm will come from letting him have his Jeanne back. It will at least give him something to think about for a while."

"I have your word for it then, Mr. Axford, that there will be no scandal or anything of the sort connected with the affair?"

"Assuredly! Burke is all right, you know. It's simply that he is spoiled. He has been in rather delicate health all his life; and then he has an income that suffices to keep him modestly, with a little over to bring out books of verse and buy doo-daws for his rooms. He takes himself a little too solemnly—is too much the poet—but he's sound at bottom."

"I'll go ahead with it, then," I said, getting up. "By the way, the girl has an account at the Golden Gate Trust Company, and I'd like to find our as much about it as possible, especially where her money came from. Clement, the cashier, is a model of caution when it comes to giving out information about depositors. If you could put in a word for me it would make my way smoother."

"Be glad to."

He wrote a couple of lines across the back of a card and gave it to me; and, promising to call on him if I needed further assistance, I left.

IV

I telephoned Pangburn that his brother-in-law had given the job his approval. I sent a wire to the agency's Baltimore branch, giving what information I had. Then I went up to Ashbury Avenue, to the apartment house in which the girl had lived.

The manager—an immense Mrs. Clute in rustling black—knew little, if any, more about the girl than Pangburn. The girl had lived there for two and a half months; she had had occasional callers, but Pangburn was the only one that the manager could describe to me. The girl had given up the apartment on the third of the month, saying that she had been called East, and she had asked the manager to hold her mail until she sent her new address. Ten days later Mrs. Clute had received a card from the girl instructing her to forward her mail to 215 N. Stricker Street, Baltimore, Maryland. There had been no mail to forward.

The single thing of importance that I learned at the apartment house was that the girl's two trunks had been taken away by a green transfer truck. Green was the color used by one of the city's largest transfer companies.

I went then to the office of this transfer company, and found a friendly clerk on duty. (A detective, if he is wise, takes pains to make and keep as many friends as possible among transfer company, express company and railroad employees.) I left the office with a memorandum of the transfer company's check numbers and the Ferry baggage-room to which the two trunks had been taken.

At the Ferry Building, with this information, it didn't take me many minutes to learn that the trunks had been checked to Baltimore. I sent another wire to the Baltimore branch, giving the railroad check numbers.

Sunday was well into night by this time, so I knocked off and went home.

V

Half an hour before the Golden Gate Trust Company opened for business the next morning I was inside, talking to Clement, the cashier. All the traditional caution and conservatism of bankers rolled together wouldn't be one-two-three to the amount usually displayed by this plump, white-haired old man. But one look at Axford's card, with *"Please give the bearer all possible assistance"* inked across the back of it, made Clement even eager to help me.

"You have, or have had, an account here in the name of Jeanne Delano," I said. "I'd like to know as much as possible about it: to whom she drew checks, and to what amounts; but especially all you can tell me about where her money came from."

He stabbed one of the pearl buttons on his desk with a pink finger, and a lad with polished yellow hair oozed silently into the room. The cashier scribbled with a pencil on a piece of paper and gave it to the noiseless youth, who disappeared. Presently he was back, laying a handful of papers on the cashier's desk.

Clement looked through the papers and then up at me.

"Miss Delano was introduced here by Mr. Burke Pangburn on the sixth of last month, and opened an account with eight hundred and fifty dollars in cash. She made the following deposits after that: four hundred dollars on the tenth; two hundred and fifty on the twenty-first; three hundred on the twenty-sixth; two hundred on thirtieth; and twenty thousand dollars on the second of this month. All of these deposits except the last were made with cash. The last one was a check—which I have here."

He handed it to me: a Golden Gate Trust Company check.

Pay to the order of Jeanne Delano, twenty thousand dollars.
                                    (Signed) BURKE PANGBURN.

It was dated the second of the month.

"Burke Pangburn!" I exclaimed, a little stupidly. "Was it usual for him to draw checks to that amount?"

"I think not. But we shall see."

He stabbed the pearl button again, ran his pencil across another slip of paper, and the youth with the polished yellow hair made a noiseless entrance, exit, entrance, and exit.

The cashier looked through the fresh batch of papers that had been brought to him.

"On the first of the month, Mr. Pangburn deposited twenty thousand dollars—a check against Mr. Axford's account here."

"Now how about Miss Delano's withdrawals?" I asked.

He picked up the papers that had to do with her account again.

"Her statement and canceled checks for last month haven't been delivered to her yet. Everything is here. A check for eighty-five dollars to the order of H. K. Clute on the fifteenth of last month; one 'to cash' for three hundred dollars on the twentieth, and another of the same kind for one hundred dollars on the twenty-fifth. Both of these checks were apparently cashed here by her. On the third of month she closed out her account, with a check to her own order for twenty-one thousand, five hundred and fifteen dollars."

"And that check?"

"Was cashed here by her."

I lighted a cigarette, and let these figures drift around in my head. None of them—except those that were fixed to Pangburn's and Axford's signatures—seemed to be of any value to me. The Clute check—the only one the girl had drawn in anyone else's favor—had almost certainly been for rent.

"This is the way of it," I summed up aloud. "On the first of the month, Pangburn deposited Axford's check for twenty thousand dollars. The next day he gave a check to that amount to Miss Delano, which she deposited. On the following day she closed her account, taking between twenty-one and twenty-two thousand dollars in currency."

"Exactly," the cashier said.

VI

Before going up to the Glenton Apartments to find out why Pangburn hadn't come clean with me about the twenty thousand dollars, I dropped in at the agency, to see if any word had come from Baltimore. One of the clerks had just finished decoding a telegram.

It read:

Baggage arrived Mt. Royal Station on eighth. Taken away same day. Unable to trace. 215 North Stricker Street is Baltimore Orphan Asylum. Girl not known there. Continuing our efforts to find her.

The Old Man came in from luncheon as I was leaving. I went back into his office with him for a couple of minutes. "Did you see Pangburn?" he asked.

"Yes. I'm working on his job now—but I think it's a bust."

"What is it?"

"Pangburn is R. F. Axford's brother-in-law. He met a girl a couple of months ago, and fell for her. She sizes up as a worker. He doesn't know anything about her. The first of the month he got twenty thousand dollars from his brother-in-law and passed it over to the girl. She blew, telling him she had been called to Baltimore, and giving him a phoney address that turns out to be an orphan asylum. She sent her trunks to Baltimore, and sent him some letters from there—but a friend could have taken care of the baggage and could have remailed her letters for her. Of course, she would have needed a ticket to check the trunks on, but in a twenty-thousand-dollar game that would be a small expense. Pangburn held out on me; he didn't tell me a word about the money. Ashamed of being easy pickings, I reckon. I'm going to the bat with him on it now."

The Old Man smiled his mild smile that might mean anything, and I left.

VII

Ten minutes of ringing Pangburn's bell brought no answer. The elevator boy told me he thought Pangburn hadn't been in all night. I put a note in his box and went down to the railroad company's offices, where I arranged to be notified if an unused Baltimore–San Francisco ticket was turned in for redemption.

That done, I went up to the *Chronicle* office and searched the files for weather conditions during the past month, making a memorandum of four dates upon which it had rained steadily day and night. I carried my memorandum to the offices of the three largest taxicab companies.

That was a trick that had worked well for me before. The girl's apartment was some distance from the street car line, and I was counting upon her having gone out—or having had a caller—on one of those rainy dates. In either case, it was very likely that she—or her caller—had left in a taxi in preference to walking through the rain to the car tine. The taxicab companies' daily records would show any calls from her address, and the fares' destinations.

The ideal trick, of course, would have been to have the records searched for the full extent of the girl's occupancy of the apartment; but no taxicab company would stand for having that amount of work thrust upon them, unless it was a matter of life and death. It was difficult enough for me to persuade them to turn clerks loose on the four days I had selected.

I called up Pangburn again after I left the last taxicab office, but he was not at home. I called up Axford's residence, thinking that the poet might have spent the night there, but was told that he had not.

Late that afternoon I got my copies of the girl's photograph and handwriting, and put one of each in the mail for Baltimore. Then I went around to the three taxicab companies' offices and got my reports. Two of them had nothing for me. The third's records showed two calls from the girl's apartment.

On one rainy afternoon a taxi had been called, and one passenger had been taken to the Glenton Apartments. That passenger, obviously, was either the girl or Pangburn. At half-past twelve one night another call had come in, and this passenger had been taken to the Marquis Hotel.

The driver who had answered this second call remembered it distinctly when I questioned him, but he thought that his fare had been a man. I let the matter rest there for the time; the Marquis isn't a large hotel as San Francisco hotels go, but it is too large to make canvassing its guests for the one I wanted practicable.

I spent the evening trying to reach Pangburn, with no success. At eleven o'clock I called up Axford, and asked him if he had any idea where I might find his brother-in-law.

"Haven't seen him for several days," the millionaire said. "He was supposed to come up for dinner last night, but didn't. My wife tried to reach him by phone a couple times today, but couldn't."

VIII

The next morning I called Pangburn's apartment before I got out of bed, and got no answer. Then I telephoned Axford and made an appointment for ten o'clock at his office.

"I don't know what he's up to now," Axford said good-naturedly when I told him that Pangburn had apparently been away from his apartment since Sunday, "and I suppose there's small chance of guessing. Our Burke is nothing if not erratic. How are you progressing with your search for the damsel in distress?"

"Far enough to convince me that she isn't in a whole lot of distress. She got twenty thousand dollars from your brother-in-law the day before she vanished."

"Twenty thousand dollars from Burke? She must be a wonderful girl! But wherever did he get that much money?"

"From you."

Axford's muscular body straightened in his chair.

"From me?"

"Yes—your check."

"He did not."

There was nothing argumentative in his voice; it simply stated a fact.

"You didn't give him a check for twenty thousand dollars on the first of the month?"

"No."

"Then," I suggested, "perhaps we'd better take a run over to the Golden Gate Trust Company."

Ten minutes later we were in Clement's office.

"I'd like to see my cancelled checks," Axford told the cashier.

The youth with the polished yellow hair brought them in presently—a thick wad of them—and Axford ran rapidly through them until he found the one he wanted. He studied that one for a long while, and when he looked up at me he shook his head slowly but with finality.

"I've never seen it before."

Clement mopped his head with a white handkerchief, and tried to pretend that he wasn't burning up with curiosity and fears that his bank had been gypped.

The millionaire turned the check over and looked at the endorsement.

"Deposited by Burke," he said in the voice of one who talks while he thinks of something entirely different, "on the first."

"Could we talk to the teller who took in the twenty-thousand-dollar check that Miss Delano deposited?" I asked Clement.

He pressed one of his desk's pearl buttons with a fumbling pink finger, and in a minute or two a little sallow man with a hairless head came in.

"Do you remember taking a check for twenty thousand from Miss Jeanne Delano a few weeks ago?" I asked him.

"Yes, sir! Yes, sir! Perfectly."

"Just what do you remember about it?"

"Well, sir, Miss Delano came to my window with Mr. Burke Pangburn. It was his check. I thought it was a large check for him to be drawing, but the bookkeepers said he had enough money in his account to cover it. They stood there—Miss Delano and Mr. Pangburn—talking and laughing while I entered the deposit in her book, and then they left, and that was all."

"This check," Axford said slowly, after the teller had gone back to his cage, "is a forgery. But I shall make it good, of course. That ends the matter, Mr. Clement, and there must be no more to-do about it."

"Certainly, Mr. Axford. Certainly."

Clement was all enormously relieved smiles and head-noddings, with this twenty-thousand-dollar load lifted from his bank's shoulders.

Axford and I left the bank then and got into his coupé, in which we had come from his office. But he did not immediately start the engine. He sat for a while staring at the traffic of Montgomery Street with unseeing eyes.

"I want you to find Burke," he said presently, and there was no emotion of any sort in his bass voice. "I want you to find him without risking the least whisper of scandal. If my wife knew of all this—She mustn't know. She thinks her brother is a choice morsel. I want you to find him for me. The girl doesn't matter any more, but I suppose that where you find one you will find the other. I'm not interested in the money, and I don't want you to make any special attempt to recover that; it could hardly be done, I'm afraid, without publicity. I want you to find Burke before he does something else."

"If you want to avoid the wrong kind of publicity," I said, "your best bet is to spread the right kind first. Let's advertise him as missing, fill the papers up with his pictures and so forth. They'll play him up strong. He's your brother-in-law and he's a poet. We can say that he has been ill—you told me that he had been in delicate health all his life—and that we fear he has dropped dead somewhere or is suffering under some mental derangement. There will be no necessity of mentioning the girl or the money, and our explanation may keep people—especially your wife—from guessing the truth when the fact that he is missing leaks out. It's bound to leak out somehow."

He didn't like my idea at first, but I finally won him over.

We went up to Pangburn's apartment then, easily securing admittance on Axford's explanation that we had an engagement with him and would wait there for him. I went through the rooms inch by inch, prying into each hole and hollow and crack; reading everything that was written anywhere, even down to his manuscripts; and I found nothing that threw any light on his disappearance.

I helped myself to his photographs—pocketing five of the dozen or more that were there. Axford did not think that any of the poet's bags or trunks were missing from the pack-room. I did not find his Golden Gate Trust Company deposit book.

I spent the rest of the day loading the newspapers up with what we wished them to have; and they gave my ex-client one grand spread: first-page stuff with photographs and all possible trimmings. Anyone in San Francisco who didn't know that Burke Pangburn—brother-in-law of R. F. Axford and author of *Sandpatches and Other Verse*—was missing, either couldn't read or wouldn't.

IX

This advertising brought results. By the following morning, reports were rolling in from all directions, from dozens of people who had seen the missing poet in dozens of places. A few of these reports looked promising—or at least possible—but the majority were ridiculous on their faces.

I came back to the agency from running out one that had—until run out—looked good, to find a note on my desk asking me to call up Axford.

"Can you come down to my office now?" he asked when I got him on the wire.

There was a lad of twenty-one or -two with Axford when I was ushered into his office: a narrow-chested, dandified lad of the sporting clerk type.

"This is Mr. Fall, one of my employees," Axford told me. "He says he saw Burke Sunday night."

"Where?" I asked Fall.

"Going into a roadhouse near Halfmoon Bay."

"Sure it was him?"

"Absolutely! I've seen him come in here to Mr. Axford's office to know him. It was him all right."

"How'd you come to see him?"

"I was coming up from further down the shore with some friends, and we stopped in at the roadhouse to get something to eat. As we were leaving, a car drove up and Mr. Pangburn and a girl or woman—I didn't notice her particularly—got out and went inside. I didn't think anything of it until I saw in the paper last night that he hadn't been seen since Sunday. So then I thought to myself that—"

"What roadhouse was this?" I cut in, not being interested in his mental processes.

"The White Shack."

"About what time?"

"Somewhere between eleven-thirty and midnight, I guess."

"He see you?"

"No. I was already in our car when he drove up. I don't think he'd know me anyway."

"What did the woman look like?"

"I don't know. I didn't see her face, and I can't remember how she was dressed or even if she was short or tall."

That was all Fall could tell me.

We shooed him out of the office, and I used Axford's telephone to call up "Wop" Healey's dive in North Beach and leave word that when "Porky" Grout came in he was to call up "Jack." That was a standing arrangement by which I got word to Porky whenever I wanted to see him, without giving anybody a chance to tumble to the connection between us.

"Know the White Shack?" I asked Axford, when I was through phoning.

"I know where it is, but I don't know anything about it."

"Well, it's a tough hole. Run by 'Tin-Star' Joplin, an ex-yegg who invested his winnings in the place when Prohibition made the roadhouse game good. He makes more money now than he ever heard of in his piking safe-ripping days. Retailing liquor is a side-line with him; his real profit comes from acting as a relay station for the booze that comes through Halfmoon Bay for points beyond; and the dope is that half the booze put ashore by the Pacific rum fleet is put ashore in Halfmoon Bay.

"The White Shack is a tough hole, and it's no place for your brother-in-law to be hanging around. I can't go down there myself without stirring things up; Joplin and I are old friends. But I've got a man I can put in there for a few nights. Pangburn may be a regular visitor, or he may even be staying there. He wouldn't be the first one Joplin had ever let hide out there. I'll put this man of mine in the place for a week, anyway, and see what he can find."

"It's all in your hands," Axford said. "Find Burke without scandal—that's all I ask."

X

From Axford's office I went straight to my rooms, left the outer door unlocked, and sat down to wait for Porky Grout. I had waited an hour and a half when he pushed the door open and came in.

"'Lo! How's tricks?"

He swaggered to a chair, leaned back in it, put his feet on the table and reached for a pack of cigarettes that lay there.

That was Porky Grout. A pasty-faced man in his thirties, neither large nor small, always dressed flashily—even if sometimes dirtily—and trying to hide an enormous cowardice behind a swaggering carriage, a blustering habit of speech, and an exaggerated pretense of self-assurance.

But I had known him for three years; so now I crossed the room and pushed his feet roughly off the table, almost sending him over backward.

"What's the idea?" He came to his feet, crouching and snarling. "Where do you get that stuff? Do you want a smack in the—"

I took a step toward him. He sprang away, across the room.

"Aw, I didn't mean nothin'. I was only kiddin'!"

"Shut up and sit down," I advised him.

I had known this Porky Grout for three years, and had been using him for nearly that long, and I didn't know a single thing that could be said in his favor. He was a coward. He was a liar. He was a thief, and a hophead. He was a traitor to his kind and, if not watched, to his employers. A nice bird to deal with! But detecting is a hard business, and you use whatever tools come to hand. This Porky was an effective tool if handled right, which meant keeping your hand on his throat all the time and checking up every piece of information he brought in.

His cowardice was—for my purpose—his greatest asset. It was notorious throughout the criminal Coast; and though nobody—crook or not—could possibly think him a man to be trusted, nevertheless he was not actually distrusted. Most of his fellows thought him too much the coward to be dangerous; they thought he would be afraid to betray them; afraid of the summary vengeance that crookdom visits upon the squealer. But they didn't take into account Porky's gift for convincing himself that he was a lion-hearted fellow, when no danger was near. So he went freely where he desired and where I sent him, and brought me otherwise unobtainable bits of information upon matters in which I was interested.

For nearly three years I had used him with considerable success, paying him well, and keeping him under my heel. *Informant* was the polite word that designated him in my reports; the underworld has even less lovely names than the common *stool-pigeon* to denote his kind.

"I have a job for you," I told him, now that he was seated again, with his feet on the floor.

His loose mouth twitched up at the left corner, pushing that eye into a knowing squint.

"I thought so."

He always says something like that.

"I want you to go down to Halfmoon Bay and stick around Tin-Star Joplin's joint for a few nights. Here are two photos"—sliding one of Pangburn and one of the girl across the table. "Their names and descriptions are written on the backs. I want to know if either of them shows up down there, what they're doing, and where they're hanging out. It may be that Tin-Star is covering them up."

Porky was looking knowingly from one picture to the other.

"I think I know this guy," he said out of the corner of his mouth that twitches.

That's another thing about Porky. You can't mention a name or give a description that won't bring that same remark, even though you make them up.

"Here's some money." I slid some bills across the table. "If you're down there more than a couple of nights, I'll get some more to you. Keep in touch with me, either over this phone or the under-cover one at the office. And—remember this—lay off the stuff! If I come down there and find you all snowed up, I promise that I'll tip Joplin off to you."

He had finished counting the money by now—there wasn't a whole lot to count—and he threw it contemptuously back on the table.

"Save that for newspapers," he sneered. "How am I goin' to get anywheres if I can't spend no money in the joint?"

"That's plenty for a couple of days' expenses; you'll probably knock back half of it. If you stay longer than a couple of days, I'll get more to you. And you get your pay when the job is done, and not before."

He shook his head and got up.

"I'm tired of pikin' along with you. You can turn your own jobs. I'm through!"

"If you don't get down to Halfmoon Bay tonight, you *are* through," I assured him, letting him get out of the threat whatever he liked.

After a little while, of course, he took the money and left.

The dispute over expense money was simply a preliminary that went with every job I sent him out on.

XI

After Porky had cleared out, I leaned back in my chair and burned half a dozen Fatimas over the job. The girl had gone first with the twenty thousand dollars, and then the poet had gone; and both had gone, whether permanently or not, to the White Shack. On its face, the job was an obvious affair. The girl had given Pangburn the *work* to the extent of having him forge a check against his brother-in-law's account; and then, after various moves whose value I couldn't determine at the time, they had gone into hiding together.

There were two loose ends to be taken care of. One of them—the finding of the confederate who had mailed the letters to Pangburn and who had taken care of the girl's baggage—was in the Baltimore branch's hands. The other was: Who had ridden in the taxicab that I had traced from the girl's apartment to the Marquis Hotel?

That might not have any bearing upon the job, or it might. Suppose I could find a connection between the Marquis Hotel and the White Shack. That would make a completed chain of some sort. I searched the back of the telephone directory and found the roadhouse number. Then I went up to the Marquis Hotel.

The girl on duty at the hotel switchboard, when I got there, was one with whom I had done business before.

"Who's been calling Halfmoon Bay numbers?" I asked her.

"My God!" She leaned back in her chair and ran a pink hand gently over the front of her rigidly waved red hair. "I got enough to do without remembering every call that goes through. This ain't a boarding-house. We have more'n one call a week."

"You don't have many Halfmoon Bay calls," I insisted, leaning an elbow on the counter and letting a folded five-spot peep out between the fingers of one hand. "You ought to remember any you've had lately."

"I'll see," she sighed, as if willing to do her best on a hopeless task.

She ran through her tickets.

"Here's one—from room 522, a couple weeks ago."

"What number was called?"

"Halfmoon Bay 51."

That was the roadhouse number. I passed over the five-spot.

"Is 522 a permanent guest?"

"Yes. Mr. Kilcourse. He's been here three or four months."

"What is he?"

"I don't know. A perfect gentleman, if you ask me."

"That's nice. What does he look like?"

"Tall and elegant."

"Be yourself," I pleaded. "What does he look like?"

"He's a young man, but his hair is turning gray. He's dark and handsome. Looks like a movie actor."

"Bull Montana?" I asked, as I moved off toward the desk.

The key to 522 was in its place in the rack. I sat down where I could keep an eye on it. Perhaps an hour later a clerk took it out and gave it to a man who did look somewhat like an actor. He was a man of thirty or so, with dark skin, and dark hair that showed grey around the ears. He stood a good six feet of fashionably dressed slenderness.

Carrying the key, he disappeared into an elevator.

I called up the agency then and asked the Old Man to send Dick Foley over. Ten minutes later Dick arrived. He's a little shrimp of a Canadian—there isn't a hundred and ten pounds of him—who is the smoothest shadow I've ever seen, and I've seen most of them.

"I have a bird in here I want tailed," I told Dick. "His name is Kilcourse and he's in room 522. Stick around outside, and I'll give you the spot on him."

I went back to the lobby and waited some more.

At eight o'clock Kilcourse came down and left the hotel. I went after him for half a block—far enough to turn him over to Dick—and then went home, so that I would be within reach of a telephone if Porky Grout tried to get in touch with me. No call came from him that night.

XII

When I arrived at the agency the next morning, Dick was waiting for me.

"What luck?" I asked.

"Damndest!" The little Canadian talks like a telegram when his peace of mind is disturbed, and just now he was decidedly peevish. "Took me two blocks. Shook me. Only taxi in sight."

"Think he made you?

"No. Wise head. Playing safe."

"Try him again, then. Better have a car handy, in case he tries the same trick again."

My telephone jingled as Dick was going out. It was Porky Grout, talking over the agency's unlisted line.

"Turn up anything?" I asked.

"Plenty," he bragged.

"Good! Are you in town?"

"Yes."

"I'll meet you in my rooms in twenty minutes," I said.

The pasty-faced informant was fairly bloated with pride in himself when he came through the door I had left unlocked for him. His swagger was almost a cake-walk; and the side of his mouth that twitches was twisted into a know-ing leer that would have fit a Solomon.

"I knocked it over for you, kid," he boasted. "Nothin' to it—for me! I went down there and talked to ever'body that knowed anything, seen ever'thing there was to see, and put the X-ray on the whole dump. I made a—"

"Uh-huh," I interrupted. "Congratulations and so forth. But just what did you turn up?"

"Now le'me tell you." He raised a dirty hand in a traffic-cop sort of gesture, and blew a stream of cigarette smoke at the ceiling. "Don't crowd me. I'll give you all the dope."

"Sure," I said. "I know. You're great, and I'm lucky to have you to knock off my jobs for me, and all that! But is Pangburn down there?"

"I'm gettin' around to that. I went down there and—"

"Did you see Pangburn?"

"As I was sayin', I went down there and—"

"Porky," I said, "I don't give a damn what you did! Did you see Pangburn?"

"Yes. I seen him."

"Fine! Now what did you see?"

"He's camping down there with Tin-Star. Him and the broad that you give me a picture of are both there. She's been there a month. I didn't see her, but one of the waiters told me about her. I seen Pangburn myself. They don't show themselves much—stick back in Tin-Star's part of the joint—where he lives—most of the time. Pangburn's been there since Sunday. I went down there and—"

"Learn who the girl is? Or anything about what they're up to?"

"No. I went down there and—"

"All right! *Went down there* again tonight. Call me up as soon as you know positively Pangburn is there—that he hasn't gone out. Don't make any mistakes. I don't want to come down there and scare them up on a false alarm. Use the agency's under-cover line, and just tell whoever answers that you won't be in town until late. That'll mean that Pangburn is there; and it'll let you call up from Joplin's without giving the play away."

"I got to have more dough," he said, as he got up. It costs—"

"I'll file your application," I promised. "Now beat it, and let me hear from you tonight, the minute you're sure Pangburn is there."

Then I went up to Axford's office.

"I think I have a line on him," I told the millionaire. "I hope to have him where you can talk to him tonight. My man says he was at the White Shack last night, and is probably living there. If he's there tonight, I'll take you down, if you want."

"Why can't we go now?"

"No. The place is too dead in the daytime for my man to hang around without making himself conspicuous, and I don't want to take any chances on either you or me showing ourselves there until we're sure we're coming face to face with Pangburn."

"What do you want me to do then?"

"Have a fast car ready tonight, and be ready to start as soon as I get word to you."

"Righto. I'll be at home after five-thirty. Phone me as soon as you're ready to go, and I'll pick you up."

XIII

At nine-thirty that evening I was sitting beside Axford on the front seat of a powerfully engined foreign car, and we were roaring down a road that led to Halfmoon Bay. Porky's telephone call had come.

Neither of us talked much during that ride, and the imported monster under us made it a rather short ride. Axford sat comfortable and relaxed at the wheel, but I noticed for the first time that he had a rather heavy jaw.

The White Shack is a large building, square-built, of imitation stone. It is set away back from the road, and is approached by two curving driveways, which, together, make a semi-circle whose diameter is the public road. The center of this semi-circle is occupied by sheds under which Joplin's patrons stow their cars, and here and there around the sheds are flower-beds and clumps of shrubbery.

We were still going at a fair clip when we turned into one end of this semi-circular driveway, and—

Axford slammed on his brakes, and the big machine threw us into the windshield as it jolted into an abrupt stop—barely in time to avoid smashing into a cluster of people who had suddenly loomed up before us.

In the glow from our headlights faces stood sharply out; white, horrified faces, furtive faces, faces that were callously curious. Below the faces, white arms and shoulders showed and bright gowns and jewelry, against the duller background of masculine clothing.

This was the first impression I got, and then, by the time I had removed my face from the windshield, I realized that this cluster of people had a core, a thing about which it centered I stood up, trying to look over the crowd's heads, but I could see nothing.

Jumping down to the driveway, I pushed through the crowd.

Face down on the white gravel a man sprawled—a thin man in dark clothes—and just above his collar, where the head and neck join, was a hole. I knelt to peer into his face.

Then I pushed through the crowd again, back to where Axford was just getting out of the car, the engine of which was still running.

"Pangburn is dead—shot!"

XIV

Methodically, Axford took off his gloves, folded them and put them in a pocket. Then he nodded his understanding of what I had told him, and walked toward where the crowd stood around the dead poet. I looked after him until he had vanished in the throng. Then I went winding through the outskirts of the crowd, hunting for Porky Grout.

I found him standing on the porch, leaning against a pillar. I passed where he could see me, and went on around to the side of the roadhouse that afforded most shadow.

In the shadows Porky joined me. The night wasn't cool, but his teeth were chattering.

"Who got him?" I demanded.

"I don't know," he whined, and that was the first thing of which I had ever known him to confess complete ignorance. "I was inside, keepin' an eye on the others."

"What others?"

"Tin-Star, and some guy I never seen before, and the broad. I didn't think the kid was going out. He didn't have no hat."

"What *do* you know about it?"

"A little while after I phoned you, the girl and Pangburn came out from Joplin's part of the joint and sat down at a table around on the other side of the porch, where it's fairly dark. They eat for a while and then this other guy comes over and sits down with 'em. I don't know his name, but I think I've saw him around town. He's a tall guy, all rung up in fancy rags."

That would be Kilcourse.

"They talk for a while and then Joplin joins 'em. They sit around the table laughin' and talkin' for maybe a quarter of a hour. Then Pangburn gets up and goes indoors. I got a table that I can watch 'em from, and the place is crowded, and I'm afraid I'll lose my table if I leave it, so I don't follow the kid. He ain't got no hat; I figure he ain't goin' nowhere. But he must of gone through the house and out front, because pretty soon there's a noise that I thought was a auto backfire, and then the sound of a car gettin' away quick. And then some guy squawks that there's a dead man outside. Ever'body runs out here, and it's Pangburn."

"You dead sure that Joplin, Kilcourse and the girl were all at the table when Pangburn was killed?"

"Absolutely," Porky said, "if this dark guy's name is Kilcourse."

"Where are they now?"

"Back in Joplin's hang-out. They went up there as soon as they seen Pangburn had been croaked."

I had no illusions about Porky. I knew he was capable of selling me out and furnishing the poet's murderer with an alibi. But there was this about it: if Joplin, Kilcourse or the girl had fixed him, and had fixed my informant, then it was hopeless for me to try to prove that they weren't on the rear porch when the shot was fired. Joplin had a crowd of hangers-on who would swear to anything he told them without batting eye. There would be a dozen supposed witnesses to their presence on the rear porch.

Thus the only thing for me to do was to take it for granted that Porky was coming clean with me.

"Have you seen Dick Foley?" I asked, since Dick had been shadowing Kilcourse.

"No."

"Hunt around and see if you can find him. Tell him I've gone up to talk to Joplin, and tell him to come on up. Then you can stick around where I can get hold of you if I want you."

I went in through a French window, crossed an empty dance-floor and went up the stairs that lead to Tin-Star Joplin's living quarters in the rear second story. I knew the way, having been up there before. Joplin and I were old friends.

I was going up now to give him and his friends a shakedown on the off-chance that some good might come of it, though I knew that I had nothing on any of them. I could have tied something on the girl, of course, but not without advertising the fact that the dead poet had forged his brother-in-law's signature to a check. And that was no go.

"Come in," a heavy, familiar voice called when I rapped on Joplin's living-room door.

I pushed the door open and went in.

Tin-Star Joplin was standing in the middle of the floor: a big-bodied ex-yegg with inordinately thick shoulders and an expressionless horse face. Beyond him Kilcourse sat dangling one leg from the corner of a table, alertness hiding behind an amused half-smile on his handsome dark face. On the other side of a room a girl whom I knew for Jeanne Delano sat on the arm of a big leather chair. And the poet hadn't exaggerated when he told me she was beautiful.

"You!" Joplin grunted disgustedly as soon as he recognized me. "What the hell do *you* want?"

"What've you got?"

My mind wasn't on this sort of repartee, however; I was studying the girl. There was something vaguely familiar about' her—but I couldn't place her. Perhaps I hadn't seen her before; perhaps much looking at the picture Pangburn had given me was responsible for my feeling of recognition. Pictures will do that.

Meanwhile, Joplin had said:

"Time to waste is one thing I ain't got."

And I had said:

"If you'd saved up all the time different judges have given you, you'd have plenty."

I had seen the girl somewhere before. She was a slender girl in a glistening blue gown that exhibited a generous spread of front, back and arms that were worth showing. She had a mass of dark brown hair above an oval face of the color that pink ought to be. Her eyes were wide-set and of a grey shade that wasn't alto-gether unlike the shadows on polished silver that the poet had compared them to.

I studied the girl, and she looked back at me with level eyes, and still I couldn't place her. Kilcourse still sat dangling a leg from the table corner.

Joplin grew impatient.

"Will you stop gandering at the girl, and tell me what you want of me?" he growled.

The girl smiled then, a mocking smile that bared the edges of razor-sharp little animal teeth. And with the smile I knew her!

Her hair and skin had fooled me. The last time I had seen her—the only time I had seen her before—her face had been marble-white, and her hair had been short and the color of fire. She and an older woman and three men and I had played hide-and-seek one evening in a house in Turk Street over a matter of the murder of a bank messenger and the theft of a hundred thousand dollars' worth of Liberty Bonds. Through her intriguing three of her accomplices had died that evening, and the fourth—the Chinese—had eventually gone to the gallows at Folsom prison. Her name had been Elvira then, and since her escape from the house that night we had been fruitlessly hunting her from border to border, and beyond.

Recognition must have shown in my eyes in spite of the effort I made to keep them blank, for, swift as a snake, she had left the arm of the chair and was coming forward, her eyes more steel than silver.

I put my gun in sight.

Joplin took a half-step toward me.

"What's the idea?" he barked.

Kilcourse slid off the table, and one of his thin dark hands hovered over his necktie.

"This is the idea," I told them. "I want the girl for a murder a couple months back, and maybe—I'm not sure—for tonight's. Anyway, I'm—"

The snapping of a light-switch behind me, and the room went black.

I moved, not caring where I went so long as I got away from where I had been when the lights went out.

My back touched a wall and I stopped, crouching low.

"Quick, kid!" A hoarse whisper that came from where I thought the door should be.

But both of the room's doors, I thought, were closed, and could hardly be opened without showing gray rectangles. People moved in the blackness, but none got between me and the lighter square of windows.

Something clicked softly in front of me—too thin a click for the cocking of a gun—but it could have been the opening of a spring-knife, and I remembered that Tin-Star Joplin a fondness for that weapon.

"Let's go! Let's go!" A harsh whisper that cut through the dark like a blow.

Sounds of motion, muffled, indistinguishable . . . one sound not far away. . . .

Abruptly a strong hand clamped one of my shoulders, a hard-muscled body strained against me. I stabbed out with my gun, and heard a grunt.

The hand moved up my shoulder toward my throat.

I snapped up a knee, and heard another grunt.

A burning point ran down my side.

I stabbed again with my gun—pulled it back until the muzzle was clear of the soft obstacle that had stopped it, and squeezed the trigger.

The crash of the shot. Joplin's voice in my ear—a curiously matter-of-fact voice:

"God damn! That got me."

XV

I spun away from him then, toward where I saw the dim yellow of an open door. I had heard no sounds of departure. I had been too busy. But I knew that Joplin had tied into me while the others made their get-away.

Nobody was in sight as I jumped, slid, tumbled down the steps—any number at a time. A waiter got in my path as I plunged toward the dance-floor. I don't know whether his interference was intentional or not. I didn't ask. I slammed the flat of my gun in his face and went on. Once I jumped a leg that came out to trip me; and at the outer door I had to smear another face.

Then I was out in the semi-circular driveway, from one end of which a red tail-light was turning east into the county road.

While I sprinted for Axford's car I noticed that Pangburn's body had been removed. A few people still stood around the spot where he had lain, and they gaped at me now with open mouths.

The car was as Axford had left it, with idling engine. I swung it through a flower-bed and pointed it east on the public road. Five minutes later I picked up the red point of a tail-light again.

The car under me had more power than I would ever need, more than I would have known how to handle. I don't know how fast the one ahead was going, but I closed in as if it had been standing still.

A mile and a half, or perhaps two—

Suddenly a man was in the road ahead—a little beyond the reach of my lights. The lights caught him, and I saw that it was Porky Grout!

Porky Grout standing facing me in the middle of the road, the dull metal of an automatic in each hand.

The guns in his hands seemed to glow dimly red and then go dark in the glare of my headlights—glow and then go dark, like two bulbs in an automatic electric sign.

The windshield fell apart around me.

Porky Grout—the informant whose name was a synonym for cowardice the full length of the Pacific Coast—stood in the center of the road shooting at a metal comet that rushed down upon him. . . .

I didn't see the end.

I confess frankly that I shut my eyes when his set white face showed close over my radiator. The metal monster under me trembled—not very much—and the road ahead was empty except for the fleeing red light. My windshield was gone. The wind tore at my uncovered hair and brought tears to my squinted-up eyes.

Presently I found that I was talking to myself, saying, "That was Porky. That was Porky." It was an amazing fact. It was no surprise that he had double-crossed me. That was to be expected. And for him to have crept up the stairs behind me and turned off the lights wasn't astonishing. But for him to have stood straight up and died—

An orange streak from the car ahead cut off my wonderment. The bullet didn't come near me—it isn't easy to shoot accurately from one moving car into another—but at the pace I was going it wouldn't be long before I was close enough for good shooting.

I turned on the searchlight above the dashboard. It didn't quite reach the car ahead, but it enabled me to see that the girl was driving, while Kilcourse sat screwed around beside her, facing me. The car was a yellow roadster.

I eased up a little. In a duel with Kilcourse here I would have been at a disadvantage, since I would have had to drive as well as shoot. My best play seemed to be to hold my distance until we reached a town, as we inevitably must. It wasn't midnight yet. There would be people on the streets of any town, and policemen. Then I could close in with a better chance of coming off on top.

A few miles of this and my prey tumbled to my plan. The yellow roadster slowed down, wavered, and came to rest with its length across the road. Kilcourse and the girl were out immediately and crouching in the road on the far side of their barricade.

I was tempted to dive pell-mell into them, but it was a weak temptation, and when its short life had passed I put on the brakes and stopped. Then I fiddled with my searchlight until it bore full upon the roadster.

A flash came from somewhere near the roadster's wheels, and the searchlight shook violently, but the glass wasn't touched. It would be their first target, of course, and . . .

Crouching in my car, waiting for the bullet that would smash the lens, I took off my shoes and overcoat.

The third bullet ruined the light.

I switched off the other lights, jumped to the road, and when I stopped running I was squatting down against the near side of the yellow roadster. As easy and safe a trick as can be imagined.

The girl and Kilcourse had been looking into the glare of a powerful light. When that light suddenly died, and the weaker ones around it went, too, they were left in pitch unseeing blackness, which must last for the minute or longer that their eyes would need to readjust themselves to the gray-black of the night. My stockinged feet had made no sound on the macadam road, and now there was only a roadster between us; and I knew it and they didn't.

From near the radiator Kilcourse spoke softly:

"I'm going to try to knock him off from the ditch. Take a shot at him now and then to keep him busy."

"I can't see him," the girl protested.

"Your eyes'll be all right in a second. Take a shot at the car anyway."

I moved, toward the radiator as the girl's pistol barked at the empty touring car.

Kilcourse, on hands and knees, was working his way toward the ditch that ran along the south side of the road. I gathered my legs under me, intent upon a spring and a blow with my gun upon the back of his head. I didn't want to kill him, but I wanted to put him out of the way quick. I'd have the girl to take care of, and she was at least as dangerous as he.

As I tensed for the spring, Kilcourse, guided perhaps by some instinct of the hunted, turned his head and saw me—saw a threatening shadow.

Instead of jumping I fired.

I didn't look to see whether I had hit him or not. At that range there was little likelihood of missing. I bent double and slipped back to the rear of the roadster, keeping on my side of it.

Then I waited.

The girl did what I would perhaps have done in her place. She didn't shoot or move toward the place the shot had come from. She thought I had forestalled Kilcourse in using the ditch and that my next play would be to circle around behind her. To offset this, she moved around the rear of the roadster, so that she could ambush me from the side nearest Axford's car.

Thus it was that she came creeping around the corner and poked her delicately chiseled nose plunk into the muzzle of the gun that I held ready for her.

She gave a little scream.

Women aren't always reasonable: they are prone to disregard trifles like guns held upon them. So I grabbed her gun hand, which was fortunate for me. As my hand closed around the weapon, she pulled the trigger, catching a chunk of my forefinger between hammer and frame. I twisted the gun out of her hand; released my finger.

But she wasn't done yet.

With me standing there holding a gun not four inches from her body, she turned and bolted off toward where a clump of trees made a jet-black blot to the north.

When I recovered from my surprise at this amateurish procedure, I stuck both her gun and mine in my pockets, and set out after her, tearing the soles of my feet at every step.

She was trying to get over a wire fence when I caught her.

XVI

"Stop playing, will you?" I said crossly, as I set the fingers of my left hand around her wrist and started to lead her back to the roadster. "This is a serious business. Don't be so childish!"

"You are hurting my arm."

I knew I wasn't hurting her arm, and I knew this girl for the direct cause of four, or perhaps five, deaths; yet I loosened my grip on her wrist until it wasn't much more than a friendly clasp. She went back willingly enough to the roadster, where, still holding her wrist, I switched on the lights.

Kilcourse lay just beneath the headlight's glare, huddled on his face, with one knee drawn up under him.

I put the girl squarely in the line of light.

"Now stand there," I said, "and behave. The first break you make, I'm going to shoot a leg out from under you," and I meant it.

I found Kilcourse's gun, pocketed it, and knelt beside him.

He was dead, with a bullet-hole above his collar-bone.

"Is he—" her mouth trembled.

"Yes."

She looked down at him, and shivered a little.

"Poor Fag," she whispered.

I've gone on record as saying that this girl was beautiful, and, standing there in the dazzling white of the headlights, she was more than that. She was a thing to start crazy thoughts even in the head of an unimaginative middle-aged thief catcher. She was—

Anyhow, I suppose that is why I scowled at her and said:

"Yes, poor Fag, and poor Hook, and poor Tai, and poor kind of a Los Angeles bank messenger, and poor Burke," calling the roll, so far as I knew it, of men who had died loving her.

She didn't flare up. Her big grey eyes lifted, and she looked at me with a gaze that I couldn't fathom, and her lovely oval face under the mass of brown hair—which I knew was phoney—was sad.

"I suppose you do think—" she began.

But I had had enough of this; I was uncomfortable along the spine.

"Come on," I said. "We'll leave Kilcourse and the roadster here for the present."

She said nothing, but went with me to Axford's big machine, and sat in silence while I laced my shoes. I found a robe on the back seat and gave it to her.

"Better wrap this around your shoulders. The windshield is gone. It'll be cool."

She followed my suggestion without a word, but when I had edged our vehicle around the rear of the roadster, and had straightened out in the road again, going east, she laid a hand on my arm.

"Aren't we going back to the White Shack?"

"No. Redwood City—the county jail."

A mile perhaps, during which, without looking at her, I knew she was studying my rather lumpy profile. Then her hand was on my forearm again and she was leaning toward me so that her breath was warm against my cheek.

"Will you stop for a minute? There's something—some things I want to tell you."

I brought the car to a halt in a cleared space of hard soil off to one side of the road, and screwed myself a little around in the seat to face her more directly.

"Before you start," I told her, "I want you to understand that we stay here for just so long as you talk about the Pangburn affair. When you get off on any other line—then we finish our trip to Redwood City."

"Aren't you even interested in the Los Angeles affair?"

"No. That's closed. You and Hook Riordan and Tai Choon Tau and the Quarres were equally responsible for the messenger's death, even if Hook did the actual killing. Hook and the Quarres passed out the night we had our party in Turk Street. Tai was hanged last month. Now I've got you. We had enough evidence to swing the Chinese, and we've even more against you. That is done—finished—completed. If you want to tell me anything about Pangburn's death, I'll listen. Otherwise—"

I reached for the self-starter.

A pressure of her fingers on my arm stopped me.

"I do want to tell you about it," she said earnestly. "I want you to know the truth about it. You'll take me to Redwood City, I know. Don't think that I expect—that I have any foolish hopes. But I'd like you to know the truth about this thing. I don't know why I should care especially what you think, but—"

Her voice dwindled off to nothing.

XVII

Then she began to talk very rapidly—as people talk when they fear interruptions before their stories are told—and she sat leaning slightly forward, so that her beautiful oval face was very close to mine.

"After I ran out of the Turk Street house that night—while you were struggling with Tai—my intention was to get away from San Francisco. I had a couple of thousand dollars, enough to carry me any place. Then I thought that going away would be what you people would expect me to do, and that the safest thing for me to do would be to stay right here. It isn't hard for a woman to change her appearance. I had bobbed red hair, white skin, and wore gay clothes. I simply dyed my hair, bought these transformations to make it look long, put color on my face, and bought some dark clothes. Then I took an apartment on Ashbury Avenue under the name of Jeanne Delano, and I was an altogether different person.

"But, while I knew I was perfectly safe from recognition anywhere, I felt more comfortable staying indoors for a while, and, to pass the time, I read a good deal. That's how I happened to run across Burke's book. Do you read poetry?"

I shook my head. An automobile going toward Halfmoon Bay came into sight just then—the first one we'd seen since we left the White Shack. She waited until it had passed before she went on, still talking rapidly.

"Burke wasn't a genius, of course, but there was something about some of his things that—something that got inside me. I wrote him a little note, telling him how much I had enjoyed these things, and sent it to his publishers. A few days later I had a note from Burke, and I learned that he lived in San Francisco. I hadn't known that.

"We exchanged several notes, and then he asked if he could call, and we met. I don't know whether I was in love with him or not, even at first. I did like him, and, between the ardor of his love for me and the flattery of having a fairly well-known poet for a suitor, I really thought that I loved him. I promised to marry him.

"I hadn't told him anything about myself, though now I know that it wouldn't have made any difference to him. But I was afraid to tell him the truth, and I wouldn't lie to him, so I told him nothing.

"Then Fag Kilcourse saw me one day on the street, and knew me in spite of my new hair, complexion and clothes. Fag hadn't much brains, but he had eyes that could see through anything. I don't blame Fag. He acted according to his code. He came up to my apartment, having followed me home; and I told him that I was going to marry Burke and be a respectable housewife. That was dumb of me. Fag was square. If I had told him that I was ribbing Burke up for a trimming, Fag would have let me alone, would have kept his hands off. But when I told him that I was through with the graft, had 'gone queer,' that made me his meat. You know how crooks are: everyone in the world is either a fellow crook or a prospective victim. So if I was no longer a crook, then Fag considered me fair game.

"He learned about Burke's family connections, and then he put it up to me— twenty thousand dollars, or he'd turn me up. He knew about the Los Angeles job, and he knew how badly I was wanted. I was up against it then. I knew I couldn't hide from Fag or run away from him. I told Burke I had to have twenty thousand dollars. I didn't think he had that much, but I thought he could get it. Three days later he gave me a check for it. I didn't know at the time how he had raised it, but it wouldn't have mattered if I had known. I had to have it.

"But that night he told me where he got the money; that he had forged his brother-in-law's signature. He told me because, after thinking it over, he was afraid that when the forgery was discovered I would be caught with him and considered equally guilty. I'm rotten in spots, but I wasn't rotten enough to let him put himself in the pen for me, without knowing what it was all about. I told him the whole story. He didn't bat an eye. He insisted that the money be paid Kilcourse, so that I would be safe, and began to plan for my further safety.

"Burke was confident that his brother-in-law wouldn't send him over for forgery, but, to be on the safe side, he insisted that I move and change my name again and lay low until we knew how Axford was going to take it. But that night, after he had gone, I made some plans of my own. I did like Burke— I liked him too much to let him be the goat without trying to save him, and I didn't have a great deal of faith in Axford's kindness. This was the second of the month. Barring accidents, Axford wouldn't discover the forgery until he got his cancelled checks early the following month. That gave me practically a month to work in.

"The next day I drew all my money out of the bank, and sent Burke a letter, saying that I had been called to Baltimore and I laid a clear trail to Baltimore, with baggage and letters and all, which a pal there took care of for me. Then I went down to Joplin's and got him to put me up. I let Fag know I was there, and when he came down I told him I expected to have the money for him in a day or two.

"He came down nearly every day after that, and I stalled him from day to day, and each time it got easier. But my time was getting short. Pretty soon Burke's letters would be coming back from the phoney address I had given him, and I wanted to be on hand to keep him from doing anything foolish. And I didn't want to get in touch with him until I could give him the twenty thousand, so he could square the forgery before Axford learned of it from his cancelled checks.

"Fag was getting easier and easier to handle, but I still didn't have him where I wanted him. He wasn't willing to give up the twenty thousand dollars—which I was, of course, holding all this time—unless I'd promise to stick with him for good. And I still thought I was in love with Burke, and I didn't want to tie myself up with Fag, even for a little while.

"Then Burke saw me on the street one Sunday night. I was careless, and drove into the city in Joplin's roadster—the one back there. And, as luck would have it, Burke saw me. I told him the truth, the whole truth. And he told me that he had just hired a private detective to find me. He was like a child in some ways: it hadn't occurred to him that the sleuth would dig up anything about the money. But I knew the forged check would be found in a day or two at the most. I knew it!

"When I told Burke that he went to pieces. All his faith in his brother-in-law's forgiveness went. I couldn't leave him the way he was. He'd have babbled the whole thing to the first person he met. So I brought him back to Joplin's with me. My idea was to hold him there for a few days, until we could see how things were going. If nothing appeared in the papers about the check, then we could take it for granted that Axford had hushed the matter up, and Burke could go home and try to square himself. On the other hand, if the papers got the whole story, then Burke would have to look for a permanent hiding-place, and so would I.

"Tuesday evening's and Wednesday morning's papers were full of the news of his disappearance, but nothing was said about the check. That looked good, but we waited another day for good measure. Fag Kilcourse was in on the game by this time, of course, and I had had to pass over the twenty thousand dollars, but I still had hopes of getting it—or most of it—back, so I continued to string him along. I had a hard time keeping him off Burke, though, because he had begun to think he had some sort of right to me, and jealousy made him wicked. But I got Tin-Star to throw a scare into him, and I thought Burke was safe.

"Tonight one of Tin-Star's men came up and told us that a man named Porky Grout, who had been hanging around the place for a couple of nights, had made a couple of cracks that might mean he was interested in us. Grout was pointed out to me, and I took a chance on showing myself in the public part of the place, and sat at a table close to his. He was plain rat—as I guess you know—and in less than five minutes I had him at my table, and half an hour later I knew that he had tipped you off that Burke and I were in the White Shack. He didn't tell me all this right out, but he told me more than enough for me to guess the rest.

"I went up and told the others. Fag was for killing both Grout and Burke right away. But I talked him out of it. That wouldn't help us any, and I had Grout where he would jump in the ocean for me. I thought I had Fag convinced, but—We finally decided that Burke and I would take the roadster and leave, and that when you got here Porky Grout was to pretend he was hopped up, and point out a man and a woman—any who happened to be handy—as the ones he had taken for us. I stopped to get a cloak and gloves, and Burke went on out to the car alone—and Fag shot him. I didn't know he was going to! I wouldn't have let him! Please believe that! I wasn't as much in love with Burke as I had thought, but please believe that after all he had done for me I wouldn't have let them hurt him!

"After that it was a case of stick with the others whether I liked it or not, and I stuck. We ribbed Grout to tell you that all three of us were on the back porch when Burke was killed, and we had any number of others primed with the same story. Then you came up and recognized me. Just my luck that it had to be you—the only detective in San Francisco who knew me!

"You know the rest: how Porky Grout came up behind you and turned off the lights, and Joplin held you while we ran for the car; and then, when you closed in on us, Grout offered to stand you off while we got clear, and now. . . ."

XVIII

Her voice died, and she shivered a little. The robe I had given her had fallen away from her white shoulders. Whether or not it was because she was so close against my shoulder, I shivered, too. And my fingers, fumbling in my pocket for a cigarette, brought it out twisted and mashed.

"That's all there is to the part you promised to listen to," she said softly, her face turned half away. "I wanted you to know. You're a hard man, but somehow I—"

I cleared my throat, and the hand that held the mangled cigarette was suddenly steady.

"Now don't be crude, sister," I said. "Your work has been too smooth so far to be spoiled by rough stuff now."

She laughed—a brief laugh that was bitter and reckless and just a little weary, and she thrust her face still closer to mine, and the grey eyes were soft and placid.

"Little fat detective whose name I don't know"—her voice had a tired huskiness in it, and a tired mockery—"you think I am playing a part, don't you? You think I am playing for liberty. Perhaps I am. I certainly would take it if it were offered me. But— Men have thought me beautiful, and I have played with them. Women are like that. Men have loved me and, doing what I liked with them, I have found men contemptible. And then comes this little fat detective whose name I don't know, and he acts as if I were a hag—an old squaw. Can I help then being piqued into some sort of feeling for him? Women are like that. Am I so homely that any man has a right to look at me without even interest? Am I ugly?"

I shook my head.

"You're quite pretty," I said, struggling to keep my voice as casual as the words.

"You beast!" she spat, and then her smile grew gentle again. "And yet it is because of that attitude that I sit here and turn myself inside out for you. If you were to take me in your arms and hold me close to the chest that I am already learning against, and if you were to tell me that there is no jail ahead for me just now, I would be glad, of course. But, though for a while you might hold me, you would then be only one of the men with which I am familiar: men who love and are used and are succeeded by other men. But because you do none of these things, because you are a wooden block of a man, I find myself wanting you. Would I tell you this, little fat detective, if I were playing a game?"

I grunted noncommittally, and forcibly restrained my tongue from running out to moisten my dry lips.

"I'm going to this jail tonight if you are the same hard man who has goaded me into whining love into his uncaring ear, but before that, can't I have one whole-hearted assurance that you think me a little more than 'quite pretty'? Or at least a hint that if I were not a prisoner your pulse might beat a little faster when I touch you? I'm going to this jail for a long while—perhaps to the gallows. Can't I take my vanity there not quite in tatters to keep me company? Can't you do some slight thing to keep me from the afterthought of having bleated all this out to a man who was simply bored?"

Her lids had come down half over the silver-grey eyes; her head had tilted back so far that a little pulse showed throbbing in her white throat; her lips were motionless over slight parted teeth, as the last word had left them. My fingers went deep into the soft white flesh of her shoulders. Her head went further back, her eyes closed, one hand came up to my shoulder.

"You're beautiful as all hell!" I shouted crazily into her face, and flung her against the door.

It seemed an hour that I fumbled with starter and gears before I had the car back in the road and thundering toward the San Mateo County jail. The girl had straightened herself up in the seat again, and sat huddled within the robe I had given her. I squinted straight ahead into the wind that tore at my hair and face, and the absence of the windshield took my thoughts back to Porky Grout.

Porky Grout, whose yellowness was notorious from Seattle to San Diego, standing rigidly in the path of a charging metal monster, with an inadequate pistol in each hand. She had done that to Porky Grout—this woman beside me! She had done that to Porky Grout, and he hadn't even been human. A slimy reptile whose highest thought had been a skinful of dope had gone grimly to death that she might get away—she—this woman whose shoulders I had gripped, whose mouth had been close under mine!

I let the car out another notch, holding the road somehow.

We went through a town: a scurrying of pedestrians for safety, surprised faces staring at us, street lights glistening off the moisture the wind had whipped from my eyes. I passed blindly by the road I wanted, circled back to it, and we were out in the country again.

XIX

At the foot of a long, shallow hill I applied the brakes and we snapped to motionlessness.

I thrust my face close to the girl's.

"Furthermore, you are a liar!" I knew I was shouting foolishly, but I was powerless to lower my voice. "Pangburn never put Axford's name on that check. He never knew anything about it. You got in with him because you knew his brother-in-law was a millionaire. You pumped him, finding out everything he knew about his brother-in-law's account at the Golden Gate Trust. You stole Pangburn's bank book—it wasn't in his room when I searched it—and deposited the forged Axford check to his credit, knowing that under those circumstances the check wouldn't be questioned. The next day you took Pangburn into the bank, saying you were going to make a deposit. You took him in because with him standing beside you the check to which *his* signature had been forged wouldn't be questioned. You knew that, being a gentleman, he'd take pains not to see what you were depositing.

"Then you framed the Baltimore trip. He told the truth to me—the truth so far as he knew it. Then you met him Sunday night—maybe accidentally, maybe not. Anyway, you took him down to Joplin's, giving him some wild yarn that he would swallow and that would persuade him to stay there for a few days. That wasn't hard, since he didn't know anything about either of the twenty-thousand-dollar checks. You and your pal Kilcourse knew that if Pangburn disappeared nobody would ever know that he hadn't forged the Axford check, and nobody would ever suspect that the second check was phoney. You'd have killed him quietly, but when Porky tipped you off that I was on my way down you had to move quick—so you shot him down. That's the truth of it!" I yelled.

All this while she had watched me with wide grey eyes that were calm and tender, but now they clouded a little and a pucker of pain drew her brows together.

I yanked my head away and got the car in motion.

Just before we swept into Redwood City one of her hands came up to my forearm, rested there for a second, patted the arm twice, and withdrew.

I didn't look at her, nor, I think, did she look at me, while she was being booked. She gave her name as Jeanne Delano and refused to make any statement until she had seen an attorney. It all took a very few minutes.

As she was being led away, she stopped and asked if she might speak privately with me.

We went together to a far corner of the room.

She put her mouth close to my ear so that her breath was warm again on my cheek, as it had been in the car, and whispered the vilest epithet of which the English language is capable.

Then she walked out to her cell.

FREDERIC BROWN

Before he won the 1947 Edgar Award for the Best First Mystery novel with his book *The Fabulous Clipjoint*, Frederic Brown (1906–1972) published a few hundred mystery and science fiction stories in pulp magazines. In that short fiction and in his novels, he demonstrated a flair for titling (*Night of the Jabberwock, Mrs. Murphy's Underpants,* and *The Screaming Mimi* are examples) and a talent for producing surprise endings. He was as comfortable delivering dry humor as he was at spelling out telling details about life on the mean streets or in science fictional settings.

Born in Cincinnati, Ohio, Brown was educated at the University of Cincinnati and then employed as an office worker, reporter, and proofreader. Twice married, he was thirty before he published his first short story. Brown's fiction benefits from the author's news writing skills. Most of his stories and novels begin with strong lead paragraphs, followed by fast-moving narrative enriched with colorful detail and well-chosen lines of dialogue. In both his science fiction and his mystery writing, Brown could come across as critical of the flaws in mankind and in individual men. The careful reader will also discover Brown's penchant for believing in a personal code of honor, and in the perseverance of the ordinary man. In his pulp mysteries, even a down-and-out character might possess a glimmer of self-respect and decency. In his science fiction, Brown sometimes indicates a faith in mankind's ability to surmount some major obstacles.

Jeffery Deaver puts Brown in a class with James M. Cain, noting, "Both Brown and Cain are good at setting up atmosphere and giving us characters with all their wrinkles and flaws and passions." He recommended we include "The Wench Is Dead" in this *Omnibus* as an example of an influential "gritty noir classic." Like Chandler, who "cannibalized" his shorter work to write his novels, Brown later expanded this short story into a novel of the same title, which was published in 1955.

Brown's "Wench" proves Ross Macdonald is not the only writer who, within the structure of a crime story, could wax poetic about loneliness. In this story, Howard Perry, a Chicago scion who is on the skids in L.A., surfaces from an alcoholic haze when it looks like he might be charged with the murder of a prostitute. Perry may be habitually soused, but can't quite drown in drink a code of honor and an underlying romantic sensibility—which may have led to his alcoholism in the first place. As Perry puts it, "A gal named Honor" keeps this bum from bumming money he might never repay. Brown is at his best in this story's opening lines. With a rhythm as relentless as a pounding hangover headache, Brown's first sentence pulls the reader into the world of a man on a bender.

The Wench Is Dead

1953

I

A FUZZ is a fuzz is a fuzz when you awaken from a wino jag. God, I'd drunk three pints of muscatel that I know of and maybe more, maybe lots more, because that's when I drew a blank, that's when research stopped. I rolled over on the cot so I could look out through the dirty pane of the window at the clock in the hockshop across the way.

Ten o'clock said the clock.

Get up, Howard Perry, I told myself. Get up, you B.A.S. for bastard, rise and greet the day. Hit the floor and get moving if you want to keep that job, that all-important job that keeps you drinking and sometimes eating and sometimes sleeping with Billie the Kid when she hasn't got a sucker on the hook. That's your life, you B.A.S., you bastard. That's your life for a while. This is it, this is the McCoy, this is the way a wino meets the not-so-newborn day. You're learning, man.

Pull on a sock, another sock, pants, shirt, shoes, get the hell to Burke's and wash a dish, wash a thousand dishes for six bits an hour and a meal or two a day when you want it.

God, I thought, did I really have the habit? Nuts, not in three months. Not when you've been a normal drinker all your life. Not when, much as you've always enjoyed drinking, it's always been in moderation and you've always been able to handle the stuff. This was just temporary.

And I had only a few weeks to go. In a few weeks I'd be back in Chicago, back at my desk in my father's investment company, back wearing white shirts, and B.A.S. would stand for Bachelor of Arts in Sociology. That was a laugh right now, that degree. Three months ago it had meant something—but that was in Chicago, and this was LA, and now all it meant was bastard. That's all it had meant ever since I started drifting.

It's funny, the way those things can happen. You've got a good family and a good education, and then suddenly, for no reason you can define, you start drifting. You lose interest in your family and your job, and one day you find yourself headed for the Coast.

You sit down one day and ask yourself how it happened. But you can't answer. There are a thousand little answers, sure, but there's no *big* answer. It's easier to worry about where the next bottle of sweet wine is coming from.

And that's when you realize your own personal B.A.S. stands for bastard.

With me, LA had been the end of the line. I'd seen the *Dishwasher Wanted* sign in Burke's window, and suddenly I'd known what I had to do. At pearl-diver's

55

wages, it would take a long time to get up the bus fare back to Chicago and family and respectability, but that was beside the point. The point was that after a hundred thousand dirty dishes there'd *be* a bus ticket to Chicago.

But it had been hard to remember the ticket and forget the dishes. Wine is cheap, but they're not giving it away. Since I'd started pearl-diving I'd had grub and six bits an hour for seven hours a day. Enough to drink on and to pay for this dirty, crumby little crackerbox of a room.

So here I was, still thinking about the bus ticket, and still on my uppers on East Fifth Street, LA. Main Street used to be the tenderloin street of Los Angeles and I'd headed for it when I jumped off the freight, but I'd found that the worst district, the real skid row, was now on Fifth Street in the few blocks east of Main. The worse the district, the cheaper the living, and that's what I'd been looking for.

Sure, by Fifth Street standards, I was being a pantywaist to hold down a steady job like that, but sleeping in doorways was a little too rugged and I'd found out quickly that panhandling wasn't for me. I lacked the knack.

I dipped water from the cracked basin and rubbed it on my face, and the feel of the stubble told me I could get by one more day without shaving. Or anyway I could wait till evening so the shave would be fresh in case I'd be sleeping with Billie.

Cold water helped a little but I still felt like hell. There were empty wine bottles in the corner and I checked to make sure they were completely empty, and they were. So were my pockets, except, thank God, for tobacco and cigarette papers. I rolled myself a cigarette and lighted it.

But I needed a drink to start the day.

What does a wino do when he wakes up broke (and how often does he wake otherwise?) and needs a drink? Well, I'd found several answers to that. The easiest one, right now, would be to hit Billie for a drink if she was awake yet, and alone.

I crossed the street to the building where Billie had a room. A somewhat newer building, a hell of a lot nicer room, but then she paid a hell of a lot more for it.

I rapped on her door softly, a little code knock we had. If she wasn't awake she wouldn't hear it and if she wasn't alone she wouldn't answer it.

But she called out, "It's not locked; come on in," and she said, "Hi, Professor," as I closed the door behind me. "Professor" she called me, occasionally and banteringly. It was my way of talking, I guess. I'd tried at first to use poor diction, bad grammar, to fit in with the place, but I'd given it up as too tough a job. Besides, I'd learned Fifth Street already had quite a bit of good grammar. Some of its denizens had been newspapermen once, some had written poetry; one I knew was a defrocked clergyman.

I said, "Hi, Billie the Kid."

"Just woke up, Howie. What time is it?"

"A little after ten," I told her. "Is there a drink around?"

"Jeez, only ten? Oh well, I had seven hours. Guy came here when Mike closed at two, but he didn't stay long."

She sat up in bed and stretched, the covers falling away from her naked body. Beautiful breasts she had, size and shape of half grapefruits and firm. Nice arms and shoulders, and a lovely face. Hair black and sleek in a pageboy bob that fell into place as she shook her head. Twenty-five, she told me once; and I believed her, but she could have passed for several years less than that, even now without make-up and her eyes still a little puffy from sleep. Certainly it didn't show that she'd spent three years as a B-girl, part-time hustler, heavy drinker. Before that she'd been married to a man who'd worked for a manufacturing jeweler; he'd suddenly left for parts unknown with a considerable portion of his employer's stock, leaving Billie in a jam and with a mess of debts.

Wilhelmina Kidder, Billie the Kid, my Billie. Any man's Billie if he flashed a roll, but oddly I'd found that I could love her a little and not let that bother me. Maybe because it had been that way when I'd first met her over a month ago; I'd come to love her knowing what she was, so why should it bother me? What she saw in me I don't know, and didn't care.

"About that drink," I said.

She laughed and threw down the covers, got out of bed and walked past me naked to the closet to get a robe. I wanted to reach for her but I didn't; I'd learned by now that Billie the Kid was never amorous early in the morning and resented any passes made before noon.

She shrugged into a quilted robe and padded barefoot over to the little refrigerator behind the screen that hid a tiny kitchenette. She opened the door and said, "God damn it."

"God damn what?" I wanted to know. "Out of liquor?"

She held up over the screen a Hiram Walker bottle with only half an inch of ready-mixed Manhattan in it. Almost the only thing Billie ever drank, Manhattans.

"As near out as matters. Honey, would you run upstairs and see if Mame's got some? She usually has."

Mame is a big blonde who works behind the bar at Mike Karas' joint, The Best Chance, where Billie works as B-girl. A tough number, Mame. I said, "If she's asleep she'll murder me for waking her. What's wrong with the store?"

"She's up by now. She was off early last night. And if you get it at the store it won't be on ice. Wait, I'll phone her, though, so if she *is* asleep it'll be me that wakes her and not you."

She made the call and then nodded. "Okay, honey. She's got a full bottle she'll lend me. Scram."

I scrammed, from the second floor rear to the third floor front. Mame's door was open; she was out in the hallway paying off a milkman and waiting for him to receipt the bill. She said, "Go on in. Take a load off." I went inside the room and sat down in the chair that was built to match Mame, overstuffed. I ran my fingers around under the edge of the cushion; one of Mame's men friends might have sat there with change in his pocket. It's surprising how much change you can pick up just by trying any overstuffed chairs or sofas you sit on. No change this time, but I came up with a fountain pen, a cheap dime-store-looking one. Mame had just closed the door and I held it up. "In the chair. Yours, Mame?"

"Nope. Keep it, Howie, I got a pen."

"Maybe one of your friends'll miss it," I said. It was too cheap a pen to sell or hock so I might as well be honest about it.

"Nope, I know who lost it. Seen it in his pocket last night. It was Jesus, and the hell with him."

"Mame, you sound sacrilegious."

She laughed. "Hay-*soos*, then. Jesus Gonzales. A Mex. But when he told me that was his handle I called him Jesus. And Jesus was *he* like a cat on a hot stove!" She walked around me over to her refrigerator but her voice kept on. "Told me not to turn on the lights when he come in and went over to watch out the front window for a while like he was watching for the heat. Looks out my side window too, one with the fire escape. Pulls down all the shades before he says okay, turn on the lights." The refrigerator door closed and she came back with a bottle.

"Was he a hot one," she said. "Just got his coat off—he threw it on that chair, when there's a knock. Grabs his coat again and goes out my side window down the fire escape." She laughed again. "Was that a flip? It was only Dixie from the next room knocking, to bum cigarettes. So if I ever see Jesus again it's no dice, guy as jumpy as that. Keep his pen. Want a drink here?"

"If you'll have one with me."

"I don't drink, Howie. Just keep stuff around for friends and callers. Tell Billie to give me another bottle like this back. I got a friend likes Manhattans, like her."

When I got back to Billie's room, she'd put on a costume instead of the robe, but it wasn't much of a costume. A skimpy Bikini bathing suit. She pirouetted in it. "Like it, Howie? Just bought it yesterday."

"Nice," I said, "but I like you better without it."

"Pour us drinks, huh? For me, just a quickie."

"Speaking of quickies," I said.

She picked up a dress and started to pull it over her head. "If you're thinking that way, Professor, I'll hide the family treasures. Say, that's a good line; I'm getting to talk like you do sometimes."

I poured us drinks and we sat down with them. She'd stepped into sandals and was dressed. I said, "You've got lots of good lines, Billie the Kid. But correct me—was that lingerie instead of a bathing suit, or am I out of date on fashions?"

"I'm going to the beach today, Howie, for a sun-soak. Won't go near the water so why not just wear the suit under and save changing? Say, why don't you take a day off and come along?"

"Broke. The one thing to be said for Burke as an employer is that he pays every day. Otherwise there'd be some dry, dry evenings."

"What you make there? A fin, maybe. I'll lend you a fin."

"That way lies madness," I said. "Drinks I'll take from you, or more important things than drinks. But taking money would make me—" I stopped and
wondered just what taking money from Billie would make me, just how con-
sistent I was being. After all, I could always send it back to her from Chicago.
What kept me from taking it, then? A gal named Honor, I guess. Corny as
it sounds, I said it lightly. "I could not love thee, dear, so much, loved I not
Honor more."

"You're a funny guy, Howie. I don't understand you."

Suddenly I wanted to change the subject. "Billie, how come Mame doesn't
drink?"

"Don't you know hypes don't like to drink?"

"Sure, but I didn't spot Mame for one."

"Hype with a big H for heroin, Howie. Doesn't show it much, though. I'll
give you that."

"I haven't known enough junkies to be any judge," I said. "The only one I
know for sure is the cook at Burke's."

"Don't ever try it, Howie. It's bad stuff. I joy-popped once just to see what
it was like, but never again. Too easy to get to like it. And Howie, it can make
things rough."

I said, "I hear your words of wisdom and shall stick to drink. Speaking of
which—" I poured myself another.

II

I got to the restaurant—it's on Main a block from Fifth—at a quarter after
eleven, only fifteen minutes late. Burke was at the stove—he does his own
cooking until noon, when Ramon comes on—and turned to glare at me but
didn't say anything.

Still feeling good from the drinks, I dived into my dishwashing.

The good feeling was mostly gone, though, by noon, when Ramon came on.
He had a fresh bandage on his forehead; I wondered if there was a new knife
wound under it. He already had two knife scars, old ones, on his cheek and on
his chin. He looked mean, too, and I decided to stay out of his way. Ramon's got
a nasty temper when he needs a jolt, and it was pretty obvious that he needed
one. He looked like a man with a kingsize monkey, and he was. I'd often wondered how he fed it. Cooks draw good money compared to other restaurant
help, but even a cook doesn't get enough to support a five or six cap a day habit,
not at a joint like Burke's anyway. Ramon was tall for a Mexican, but he was thin
and his face looked gaunt. It's an ugly face except when he grins and his teeth
flash white. But he wouldn't be grinning this afternoon, not if he needed a jolt.

Burke went front to work the register and help at the counter for the noon
rush, and Ramon took over at the stove. We worked in silence until the rush
was over, about two o'clock.

He came over to me then. He was sniffling and his eyes were running. He said, "Howie, you do me a favor. I'm burning, Howie, I need a fix, quick. I got to sneak out, fifteen minutes,"

"Okay, I'll try to watch things. What's working?"

"Two hamburg steak dinners on. Done one side, five more minutes other side. You know what else to put on."

"Sure, and if Burke comes back I'll tell him you're in the can. But you'd better hurry."

He rushed out, not even bothering to take off his apron or chef's hat. I timed five minutes on the clock and then I took up the steaks, added the trimmings and put them on the ledge, standing at an angle back of the window so Burke couldn't see that it was I and not Ramon who was putting them there. A few minutes later the waitress put in a call for stuffed peppers, a pair; they were already cooked and I didn't have any trouble dishing them.

Ramon came back before anything else happened. He looked like a different man—he would be for as long as the fix lasted. His teeth flashed. "Million thanks, Howie." He handed me a flat pint bottle of muscatel. "For you, my friend."

"Ramon," I said, "you are a gentleman and a scholar." He went back to his stove and started scraping it. I bent down out of sight to open the bottle. I took a good long drink and then hid it back out of sight under one of the tubs.

Two-thirty, and my half-hour lunch break. Only I wasn't hungry. I took another drink of the muskie and put it back. I could have killed it but the rest of the afternoon would go better if I rationed it and made it last until near quitting time.

I wandered over to the alley entrance, rolling a cigarette. A beautiful bright day out; it would have been wonderful to be at the beach with Billie the Kid.

Only Billie the Kid wasn't at the beach; she was coming toward me from the mouth of the alley. She was still wearing the dress she'd pulled on over the bathing suit but she wasn't at the beach. She was walking toward me, looking worried, looking frightened.

I walked to meet her. She grabbed my arm, tightly. "Howie. Howie, did you kill Mame?"

"Did I—*what?*"

Her eyes were big, looking up at me. "Howie, if you did, I don't care. I'll help you, give you money to get away. But—"

"Whoa," I said, "Whoa, Billie. I didn't kill Mame. I didn't even rape her. She was okay when I left. What happened? Or are you dreaming this up?"

"She's dead, Howie, murdered. And about the time you were there. They found her a little after noon and say she'd been dead somewhere around two hours. Let's go have a drink and I'll tell you what all happened."

"All right," I said. "I've got most of my lunch time left. Only I haven't been paid yet—"

"Come on, hurry." As we walked out of the alley she took a bill from her purse and stuffed it into my pocket. We took the nearest ginmill and ordered drinks at a booth at the back where we weren't near enough anyone to be heard. The bill she'd put in my pocket was a sawbuck. When the waitress brought our drinks and the change I shoved it toward Billie. She shook her head and pushed it back. "Keep it and owe me ten, Howie. You might need it in case—well, just in case." I said, "Okay, Billie, but I'll pay this back." I would, too, but it probably wouldn't be until I mailed it to her from Chicago and it would probably surprise the hell out of her to get it.

I said, "Now tell me, but quit looking so worried. I'm as innocent as new-fallen snow—and I don't mean cocaine. Let me reconstruct my end first, and then tell yours. I got to work at eleven-twenty. Walked straight there from your place, so it would have been ten after when I left you. And—let's see, from the other end, it was ten o'clock when I woke up, wouldn't have been over ten or fifteen minutes before I knocked on your door, another few minutes before I got to Mame's and I was up there only a few minutes. Say I saw her last around twenty after ten, and she was okay then. Over."

"Huh? Over what?"

"I mean, you take it. From when I left you, about ten minutes after eleven."

"Oh. Well, I straightened the room, did a couple things, and left, it must have been a little after twelve on account of the noon whistles had blown just a few minutes ago. I was going to the beach. I was going to walk over to the terminal and catch the Santa Monica bus, go to Ocean Park. Only first I stopped in the drugstore right on the corner for a cup of coffee. I was there maybe ten-fifteen minutes letting it cool enough to drink and drinking it. While I was there I heard a cop car stop near but I didn't think anything of it; they're always picking up drunks and all.

"But while I was there too I remembered I'd forgot to bring my sun glasses and sun-tan oil, so I went back to get them.

"Minute I got inside the cops were waiting and they asked if I lived there and then started asking questions, did I know Mame and when I saw her last and all."

"Did you tell them you'd talked to her on the phone?"

"Course not, Howie. I'm not a dope. I knew by then something had happened to her and if I told them about that call and what it was about, it would have brought you in and put you on the spot. 1 didn't even tell them you were with me, let alone going up to Mame's. I kept you out of it.

"They're really questioning everybody, Howie. They didn't pull me in but they kept me in *my* own room questioning me till just fifteen minutes ago. See, they really worked on me because I admitted I knew Mame—I had to admit that 'cause we work at the same place and they'd have found that out.

"And of course they knew she was a hype, her arms and all; they're checking everybody's arms and thank God mine are okay. They asked me mostly about where we worked, Mike's. I think they figure Mike Karas is a dealer, what with Mame working for him."

"Is he, Billie?"

"I don't know, honey. He's in some racket, but it isn't dope."

I said, "Well, I don't see what either of us has to worry about. It's not our—My God, I just remembered something."

"What, Howie?"

"A guy saw me going in her room, a milkman. Mame was in the hall paying him off when I went up. She told me to go on in and I did, right past him."

"Jesus, Howie, did she call you by name when she told you to go on in? If they get a name, even a first name, and you living right across the street—"

I thought hard. "Pretty sure she didn't, Billie. She told me to go in and take a load off, but I'm pretty sure she didn't add a Howie to it. Anyway, they may never find the milkman was there. He isn't likely to stick his neck out by coming to them. How was she killed, Billie?"

"Somebody said a shiv, but I don't know for sure."

"Who found her and how come?"

"I don't know. They were asking me questions, not me asking them. That part'll be in the papers, though."

"All right," I said. "Let's let it go till this evening, then. How's about this evening, Billie, are you going to The Best Chance anyway?"

"I *got* to, tonight, after that. If I don't show up, they'll want to know why and where I was and everything. And listen, don't you come around either, after hours tonight or in the morning. You stay away from that building, Howie. If they find that milkman they might even have him staked out watching for you. Don't even walk *past*. You better even stay off that block, go in and out the back way to your own room. And we better not even see each other till the heat's off or till we know what the score is."

I sighed.

I was ten minutes late reporting back and Burke glared at me again but still didn't say anything. I guess I was still relatively dependable for a dishwasher, but I was learning.

I made the rest of the wine last me till Baldy, the evening shift dishwasher, showed up to relieve me. Burke paid me off for the day then, and 1 was rich again.

III

Someone was shaking me, shaking me hard. I woke to fuzz and fog and Billie the Kid was peering through it at me, looking really scared, more scared than when she'd asked me yesterday if I'd killed Mame.

"Howie, wake up." I was in my own little shoe-box of a room, Billie standing by my cot bending over me. I wasn't covered, but the extent of my undressing had been to kick off my shoes.

"Howie, listen, you're in trouble, honey. You got to get out of here, back way like I come in. Hurry."

I sat up and wanted to know the time.

"Only nine, Howie. But hurry. Here. This will help you." She screwed off the top of a half pint bottle of whisky. "Drink some quick. Help you wake up."

I took a drink and the whisky burned rawly down my throat. For a moment I thought it was going to make me sick to my stomach, but then it decided to stay down and it did clear my head a little. Not much, but a little.

"What's wrong, Billie?"

"Put on your shoes. I'll tell you, but not here."

Luckily my shoes were loafers and I could step into them. I went to the basin of water, rubbed some on my face. While I washed and dried and ran a comb through my hair Billie was going through the dresser; a towel on the bed, everything I owned piled on it. It didn't make much of a bundle.

She handed it to me and then was pulling me out into the hallway, me and everything I owned. Apparently I wasn't coming back here, or Billie didn't think I was.

Out into the alley, through to Sixth Street and over Sixth to Main, south on Main. A restaurant with booths, mostly empty. The waitress came over and I ordered coffee, black. Billie ordered ham and eggs and toast and when the waitress left she leaned across the table. "I didn't want to argue with her in front of you, Howie, but that food I ordered is for you; you're going to eat it all. You got to be sober,"

I groaned, but knew it would be easier to eat than to argue with a Billie the Kid as vehement as this one.

"What is it, Billie? What's up?"

"Did you read the papers last night?"

I shook my head. I hadn't read any papers up to about nine o'clock and after that I didn't remember what I'd done or hadn't. But I wouldn't have read any papers. That reminded me to look in my pockets to see what money I had left, if any. No change, but thank God there were some crumpled bills. A five and two ones, when I pulled them out and looked under cover of the table. I'd had a little over nine out of the ten Billie had given me to buy us a drink with, a little under five I'd got from Burke. That made fourteen and I'd spent seven of it somehow—and God knows how since I couldn't possibly have drunk that much muskie or even that much whisky at Fifth Street prices. But at least I hadn't been rolled, so it could have been worse.

"They got that milkman, Howie," Billie was saying. "Right off. He'd given Mame a receipt and she'd dropped it on that little table by the door so they knew he'd been there and they found him and he says he'll know you if he sees you. He described you too. You thinking straight by now, Howie?"

"Sure I'm thinking straight. What if they *do* find me? Damn it, I didn't kill her. Didn't have any reason to. They can't do any more than question me."

"Howie, haven't you ever been in trouble with cops? Not on anything serious, I guess, or you wouldn't talk like that. That milkman would put you right on the scene at close to the right time and that's all they'd want. They got nobody else to work on.

"Sure they'll question you. With fists and rubber hoses they'll question you. They'll beat the hell out of you for days on end, tie you in a chair with five hundred watts in your eyes and slap you every time you close them. Sure they'll question you. They'll question you till you wish you *had* killed Mame so you could tell 'em and get it over with and get some sleep. Howie, cops are tough, mean bastards when they're trying to pin down a murder rap. This is a murder rap, Howie."

I smiled a little without meaning to. Not because what she'd been saying was funny, but because I was thinking of the headlines if they did beat the truth out of me, or if I had to tell all to beat the rap. *Chicago Scion in Heroin Murder Case.* Chicago papers please copy.

I saw the hurt look on Billie's face and straightened mine. "Sorry," I said. "I was laughing at something else. Go on."

But the waitress was coming and Billie waited till she'd left. She shoved the ham and eggs and toast in front of me. "Eat," she said. I ate.

"And that isn't all, Howie. They'll frame you on some other charge to hold you. Howie, they might even frame you on the murder rap itself if they don't find who else did it. They could do it easy, just take a few little things from her room—it had been searched—and claim you had 'em on you or they were in your room. How'd you prove they weren't? And what'd your word be against a cop's? They could put you in the little room and gas you, Howie. And there's something else, too."

"Something worse that *that*?"

"I don't mean that. I mean what they'd do to me, Howie. And that'd be for *sure*. A perjury rap, a nice long one. See, I signed a statement after they questioned me, and that'd make it perjury for me if you tell 'em the truth about why you went up to see Mame. And what else could you tell them?"

I put down my knife and fork and stared at her. I hadn't been *really* worried about the things she'd been telling me. Innocent men, I'd been telling myself, aren't framed by the cops on murder charges. Not if they're willing to tell the truth down the line. They might give me a bad time, I thought, but they wouldn't hold me long if I leveled with them. But if Billie had signed a statement, then telling them the truth was out. Billie was on the wrong side of the law already; they *would* take advantage of perjury to put her away, maybe for several years.

I said, "I'm sorry, Billie. I didn't realize I'd have to involve you if I had to tell them the truth."

"Eat, Howie. Eat all that grub. Don't worry about me; I just mentioned it. You're in worse trouble than *I* am. But I'm glad you're talking straight; you sound really awake now. Now you go on eating and I'll tell you what you've got to do.

"First, this milkman's description. Height, weight and age fairly close but not exact on any, and anyway you can't change that. But you got to change clothes, buy new ones, because Jesus, the guy got your clothes perfect. Blue denim shirt cut off above elbows, tan work pants, brown loafers. Now first thing when you leave here, buy different clothes, see?"

"All right," I said. "How else did he describe me?"

"Well, he thought you had blond hair and it's a little darker than that, not much. Said you needed a shave—you need one worse now—and said you looked like a Fifth Street bum, a wino maybe. That's all, except he's sure he could identify you if he ever saw you again. And that's bad, Howie."

"It is," I said.

"Howie, do you want to blow town? I can lend you—well, I'm a little low right now and on account of Karas' place being watched so close I won't be able to pick up any extra money for a while, but I can lend you fifty if you want to blow town. Do you?"

"No, Billie," I said. "I don't want to blow town. Not unless you want to go with me."

God, what had made me *say that?* What had I meant by it? What business had I taking Billie away from the district she knew, the place where she could make a living—if I couldn't—putting her further in a jam for disappearing when she was more or less a witness in a murder case? And when I wanted to be back in Chicago, back working for my father and being respectable, within a few weeks anyway.

What had I meant? I couldn't take Billie back with me, much as I liked—maybe loved—her. Billie the Kid as the wife of a respectable investment man? It wouldn't work, for either of us. But if I hadn't meant that, what the hell *had* I meant?

But Billie was shaking her head. "Howie, it wouldn't work. Not for us, not right now. If you could quit drinking, straighten out. But I know—I know you can't. It isn't your fault and—oh, honey, let's not talk about that now. Anyway, I'm *glad* you don't want to lam because—well, because I *am.* But listen—"

"Yes, Billie?"

"You've got to change the way you look—just a little. Buy a different colored shirt, see? And different pants, shoes instead of loafers. Get a haircut—you need one anyway so get a short one. Then get a hotel room—off Fifth Street. Main is okay if you stay away from Fifth. And shave—you had a stubble when that milkman saw you. How much money you got left?"

"Seven," I said. "But that ought to do it. I don't need *new* clothes; I can swap with uncle."

"You'll need more than that. Here." It was a twenty.

"Thanks, Billie. I owe you thirty." Owe her thirty? Hell, how much did I owe Billie the Kid already, outside of money, things money can't buy? I said, "And how'll we get in touch with one another? You say I shouldn't come to your place. Will you come to mine, tonight?"

"I—I guess they won't be suspicious if I take a night off, Howie, as long as it wasn't that first night. Right after the—after what happened to Mame. All right, Howie. You know a place called The Shoebox on Main up across from the court house?"

"I know where it is."

"I'll meet you there tonight at eight. And—and stay in your room, wherever you take one, till then. And—and try to stay sober, Howie."

IV

It shouldn't be hard, I thought, to stay sober when you're scared. And I was scared, now.

I stayed on Main Street, away from Fifth, and I did the things Billie had suggested. I bought a tan work shirt, and changed it right in the store where I bought it for the blue one I'd been wearing. I stopped in the barber school place for a four-bit haircut and, while I was at it, a two-bit shave. I had one idea Billie hadn't thought of; I spent a buck on a used hat. I hadn't been wearing one and a hat makes a man look different. At a shoe repair shop that handled used shoes I traded in my loafers and a dollar fifty for a pair of used shoes. I decided not to worry about the trousers; their color wasn't distinctive.

I bought newspapers; I wanted to read for myself everything Billie had told me about the murder, and there might be other details she hadn't mentioned. Some wine too, but just a pint to sip on. I was going to stay sober, but it would be a long boring day waiting for my eight o'clock date with Billie the Kid.

I registered double at a little walk-up hotel on Market Street around the corner from Main, less than a block from the place of my evening date. She'd be coming with me, of course, since we wouldn't dare go to her place, and I didn't want there to be even a chance of trouble in bringing her back with me. Not that trouble would be likely in a place like that but I didn't want even the minor trouble of having to change the registration from single to double if the clerk saw us coming in, not for fifty cents difference in the price of the room.

I sipped at the wine slowly and read the papers. The *Mirror* gave it the best coverage, with pictures. A picture of Mame that must have been found in her room and that had been taken at least ten years ago—she looked to be in her late teens or early twenties—a flashlight shot of the interior of her room, but taken after her body had been removed, and an exterior of The Best Chance, where she'd worked. But, even from the *Mirror*, I didn't learn anything Billie hadn't told me, except Mame's full name and just how and when the body had been discovered. The time had been 12:05, just about the time Billie was leaving from her room on the floor below. The owner of the building had dropped around, with tools, to fix a dripping faucet Mame (Miss Mamie Gaynor, 29) had complained about the day before. When he'd knocked long enough to decide she wasn't home he'd let himself in with his duplicate key. The milkman's story and the description he'd given of me was exactly as Billie had given them.

I paced up and down the little room, walked the worn and shabby carpet, wondering. Was there—short of the sheer accident of my running into that milkman—any danger of my being picked up just from that description? No, surely not. It was accurate as far as it went, but it was too vague, could fit too many men in this district, for anyone to think of me in connection with it. And now, with a change of clothes, a shave, wearing a hat outdoors, I doubted if the milkman would recognize me. I couldn't remember his face; why would he remember mine? And there was no tie-in otherwise, except through Billie. Nobody but Billie knew that I'd even met Mame. The only two times I'd ever seen her had been in Billie's place when she'd dropped in while I was there, once for only a few minutes, once for an hour or so. And one other time I'd been up to her room, that time to borrow cigarettes for Billie; it had been very late, after stores and bars were closed.

The fact that I'd disappeared from my room in that block? That would mean nothing. Tomorrow a week's rent was due; the landlord would come to collect it, find me and my few possessions gone, and rent it again. He'd think nothing of it. Why should he?

No, now that I'd taken the few precautions Billie had suggested, I was safe enough as long as I stayed away from her building.

Why was I hiding here now, then?

The wine was gone and I wanted more. But I knew what shape I'd be in by eight o'clock if I kept on drinking it, starting at this hour of the morning.

But I'd go nuts if I stayed here, doing nothing. I picked up the papers, read the funny sheets, a few other things. Back in the middle of one of them a head-line over a short item caught my eye, I don't know for what reason. *Victim in Alley Slaying Identified.*

Maybe my eye had first caught the name down in the body of the story, Jesus Gonzales. And Mame's jittery guest of the night before her death had been named Jesus Gonzales.

I read the story. Yesterday morning at dawn the body of a man had been found in an areaway off Winston Street near San Pedro Street. He had been killed with a blunt instrument, probably a blackjack. As he had been robbed of everything he was carrying, no identification had been made at first. Now he had been identified as Jesus Gonzales, 41, of Mexico City, DF. He had arrived in Los Angeles the day before on the SS Guadalajara, out of Tokyo. His passport, which had been left in his room at the Berengia Hotel, and other papers left with it, showed that he had been in the Orient on a buying trip for a Mexico City art object importing firm in which he was a partner, and that he was stopping in Los Angeles for a brief vacation on his return trip.

Mame's Jesus Gonzales? It certainly looked that way. The place and time fitted; less than two blocks from her room. So did the time, the morning after he'd been frightened by that knock at the door and had left unceremoniously via the fire escape.

But why would he have hooked up with Mame? The Berengia is a swank hotel, only people with well-lined pockets stay there. Mame was no prize; at the Berengia he could have done better through his own bellhop.

Or could it be a factor that Mame was a junkie and, stopping in at The Best Chance, he'd recognized her as one and picked her for that reason? He could have been a hype himself, in need of a jolt and in a city where he had no contacts, or—and this seemed even more likely because of his just having landed from Tokyo—he'd smuggled some dope in with him and was looking for a dealer to sell it. The simplest and safest way to find a dealer would be through an addict.

It was just a wild guess, of course, but it wasn't too wild to be possible. And damn it, Mame's Jesus Gonzales *had* acted suspiciously and he *had* been afraid of something. Maybe he'd thought somebody was following him, following him and Mame home from The Best Chance. If he was the same Jesus Gonzales who'd just been killed and robbed only two blocks from her place, then he'd been dead right in being careful. He'd made his mistake in assuming that the knocker on Mame's door was the man who'd followed him and in going down the fire escape. Maybe his *Nemesis* had still been outside the building, probably watching from across the street, and had seen him leave. And on Winston Street *Nemesis* had caught up with him.

Nice going, B.A.S., old boy, I thought. You're doing fine. It isn't every skidrow pearl-diver who can reconstruct a crime out of nothing. Sheer genius, B.A.S., sheer genius.

But it was something to pass the time, a lot better than staring at the wall and wishing I'd never left Chicago. Better than brooding.

All right, suppose it figured so far—then how did Mame's death tie in with it? I didn't see how. I made myself pace and concentrate, trying to work out an answer.

I felt sure Mame had been telling me the truth about Gonzales as far as she knew it, or else she would have had no reason for mentioning it at all. Whatever his ulterior motive in picking her up, whether to buy dope or to find a contact for selling it, he hadn't yet leveled with Mame before that knock came. Otherwise she wouldn't have told it casually, as she had, as something amusing.

But the killer wouldn't have known that. He couldn't have known that Mame was not an accomplice. If what he was looking for hadn't been on the person of the man he'd killed he could have figured that it had already changed hands. Why hadn't he gone back to Mame's the same night? I didn't know, but there could have been a reason. Perhaps he had and she'd gone out, locking the door and the fire escape window. Or maybe by that time she had other company; if he had knocked she might have opened the door on the chain—and I remembered now that there was a chain on her door—and told him so. I couldn't ask Mame now what she'd done the rest of the night after her jittery caller had left.

But if Gonzales was a stranger in town, just off the boat, how would the killer have known he had brought in heroin?—or opium or cocaine; it could have been any drug worth smuggling. And the killer must have known *something;* if it had been just a robbery kill, for whatever money Gonzales was carrying, then he wouldn't have gone back and killed Mame, searched her room. He'd have done that only if he'd known something about Gonzales that made him think Mame was his accomplice.

I killed a few more minutes worrying about that and I had the answer. Maybe not *the* answer, but at least an answer that made sense. Maybe I was just mildly cockeyed, but this off-the-cuff figuring I'd been doing *did* seem to be getting somewhere.

It was possible, I reasoned, that Mame hadn't been the first person through whom Gonzales had tried to make a contact. He could have approached another junkie on the same deal, but one who refused to tell him her contact. Her? It didn't have to be a woman, but Mame had been a woman and that made me think he'd been working that way. Say that he'd wandered around B-joints until he spotted a B-girl as an addict; he could get her in a booth and try to get information from her. She could have stalled him or turned him down. Stalled him, most likely, making a phone call or two to see if she could get hold of a dealer for him, but tipping off her boy friend instead. Killing time enough for her boy friend to be ready outside, then telling Gonzales she could-n't make a contact for him.

And if any of that had sounded suspicious to Gonzales he would have been more careful the second try, with Mame. He'd get her to her room on the obvi-ous pretext, make sure they were alone and hadn't been followed before he opened up. Only, between The Best Chance and Mame's room, he must have discovered that they were being followed.

Sure, it all fitted. But what good did it do me?

Sure, it was logical. It made a complete and perfect picture, but it was all guesswork, nothing to go to the cops with. Even if they believed me eventu-ally and could verify my guesses in the long run, I'd be getting myself and Billie the Kid into plenty of trouble in the short run. And like as not enough bad publicity—my relations with Billie would surely come out, and Billie's occu-pation—to have my father's clients in Chicago decide I wasn't fit to handle their business.

Well, was I? Worry about the fact that you want a drink so damned bad, I told myself, that soon you're going to weaken and go down and get another bottle. Well, why not? As long as I rationed it to myself so I would be drinking just enough to hold my own and not get drunk, not until after eight o'clock anyway . . .

What time was it? It seemed like I'd been in that damned room six or eight hours, but I'd checked in at around eleven and the sun was shining straight down in the dirty areaway my window opened on. Could it be only noon? I went out to the desk and past it, looking at the kitchen-type electric clock on the wall over it as I went by. It was a quarter after twelve.

I decided to walk a while before I went back to the room with a bottle, kill some time first. God, the time I had to kill before eight o'clock. I walked around the court house and over to Spring Street. I'd be safe there.

Hell, I'd be safe anywhere, I thought. Except maybe right in that one block of Fifth Street, just on the chance the police did have the milkman staked out in or near that building. And with different clothes, wearing a hat, he probably wouldn't recognize me anyway. Billie the Kid had panicked, and had panicked me. I didn't have anything to worry about. Oh, moving out of that block, changing out of the clothes I'd been wearing, those things had been sensible. But I didn't have to quit my job at Burke's—if it was still open to me. Burke's was safe for me. Nobody at Burke's knew where I'd lived and nobody in the building I'd lived in knew where I worked.

I thought, why not go to Burke's? He'd have the sign out in the window, now that I was an hour and a half late, but if nobody had taken the job, I could give him a story why I was so late and get it back. I'd gotten pretty good at washing dishes; I was probably the best dishwasher he'd ever had and I'd been steadier than the average one. Sure, I could go back there unless he'd managed to hire a new one already.

And otherwise, what? I'd either have to look for a new job of the same kind or keep on taking money from Billie for however long 1 stayed here. And taking money from Billie, except in emergency, was out. That gal named Honor back in Chicago was getting to be a pretty dim memory, but I still had some self-respect.

I cut back to Main Street and headed for Burke's. The back way, so I could see if anyone was working yet in my place, and maybe ask Ramon what the score was before I saw Burke.

From the alley doorway I could see my spot was empty, dishes piling high. Ramon was busy at the stove. He turned as I walked up to him, and his teeth flashed white in that grin. He said, "Howie! Thank God you're here. No dishwasher, everybody's going nuts."

The bandage was gone from his forehead. Under where it had been were four long scratches, downward, about an inch apart.

I stared at the scratches and thought about Ramon and his monkey and Mame and *her* monkey, and all of a sudden I had a crazy hunch. I thought about how a monkey like Ramon's could make a man do anything to get a fix. I moistened my lips. Ramon's monkey might claw the hell out of his guts, but it hadn't put those four scratches on his face. Not directly.

I didn't say it, I'd have had more sense; my mouth said it. "Mame had sharp fingernails, huh?"

V

Death can be a sudden thing. Only luck or accident kept me from dying suddenly in the next second or two. I'd never seen a face change as suddenly as Ramon's did. And before I could move, his hand had hold of the front of my shirt and his other hand had reached behind him and come up with and raised a cleaver. To step back as it started down would have put me in even better position for it to hit, so I did the only thing possible; I stepped in and pushed him backward and he stumbled and fell. I'd jerked my head but the cleaver went too wild even to scrape my shoulders. And there was a thunking sound as Ramon's head hit a sharp corner of the big stove. Yes, death can be a sudden thing.

I breathed hard a second and then—well, I don't know why I cared whether he was alive or not, but I bent forward and reached inside his shirt, held my hand over where his heart should be beating. It wasn't.

From the other side of the window Burke's voice sang out, "Two burgers, with."

I got out of there fast. Nobody had seen me there, nobody was *going* to see me there. I got out of the alley without being seen, that I knew of, and back to Main Street. I walked three blocks before I stopped into a tavern for the drink I really needed *now*. Not wine, whisky. Wine's an anodyne but it dulls the mind. Whisky sharpens it, at least temporarily. I ordered whisky, a double, straight.

I took half of it in one swallow and got over the worst of it. I sipped the rest slowly, and thought.

Damn it, Howie, I told myself, you've *got* to think.

I thought, and there was only one answer. I was in over my head now. If the police got me I was sunk. B.A.S. or not, I'd have a hell of a time convincing them I hadn't committed two murders—maybe three; if they'd tied in Jesus Gonzales, they'd pin that on me, too.

Sure, *I* knew what had really happened, but what proof did I have? Mame was dead; she wouldn't tell again what she'd told me about her little episode with Jesus. Ramon was dead; he wouldn't back up my otherwise unsupported word that I'd killed him accidentally in defending myself.

Out of this while I had a whole skin, that was the only answer. Back in Chicago, back to respectability, back to my right name—Howard Perry, B.A.S., not Howard Perry, bastard, wino, suspected soon of being a psychopathic killer. Back to Chicago, and not by freight. Too easy to get arrested that way, vagged, and maybe by that time flyers would be out with my description. Too risky.

So was waiting till eight o'clock when it was only one o'clock now. I'd have to risk getting in touch with Billie the Kid sooner. I couldn't go to her place, but I could phone. Surely they wouldn't have all the phones in that building tapped.

Just the same I was careful when I got her number. "Billie," I said, "this is the Professor." That nickname wouldn't mean anything to anybody else.

I heard her draw in her breath sharply. She must have realized I wouldn't risk calling her unless something important had come up. But she made her voice calm when she answered, "Yes, Professor?"

"Something has come up," I said. "I'm afraid I won't be able to make our eight o'clock date. Is there any chance that you can meet me now instead—same place?"

"Sure, soon as I can get there."

Click of the receiver. She'd be there. Billie the Kid, my Billie. She'd be there, and she'd make sure first that no one was following her. She'd bring money, knowing that I'd decided I had to lam after all. Money that she'd get back, damn it, if it was the last thing I ever did. Whatever money she'd lend me now, plus the other two sums and enough over to cover every drink and every cigarette I'd bummed from her. But not for the love and the trust she'd given me; you can't pay for that in money. In my case, I couldn't ever pay for it, period. The nearest I could come would be by being honest with her, leveling down the line. That much she had coming. More than that she had coming but more than that I couldn't give her.

The Shoebox is a shoebox-sized place. Not good for talking, but that didn't matter because we weren't going to talk there.

She got there fifteen minutes after I did; I was on my second drink. I ordered a Manhattan when I saw her coming in the door.

"Hello, Billie," I said.

Hello, Billie. Goodbye, Billie. This is the end for us, today. It's got to be the end. I knew she'd understand when I told her, when I told her everything.

"Howie, are you in—"

"In funds?" I cut her off. "Sure, just ordered you a drink." I dropped my voice, but not far enough to make it conspicuous. "Not here, Billie. Let's drink our drink and then I've got a room around the corner. I registered double so it'll be safe for us to go there and talk a while."

The bartender had mixed her Manhattan and was pouring it. I ordered a refill on my whisky-high. Why not? It was going to be my last drink for a long while. The wagon from here on in, even after I got back to Chicago for at least a few weeks, until I was sure the stuff couldn't get me, until I was sure I could do normal occasional social drinking without letting it start me off.

We drank our drinks and went out. Out into the sun, the warm sunny afternoon. Just before we got to the corner, Billie stopped me. "Just a minute, Howie."

She ducked into a store, a liquor store, before I could stop her. I waited. She came out with a wrapped bottle and a cardboard carton. "The ready-mixed wasn't on ice, Howie, but it's all right. I bought some ice cubes too. Are there two glasses in the room?"

I nodded; we went on. There were two glasses in the room. The wagon not yet. But it wouldn't have been right not to have a last drink or two, a stirrup cup or two, with Billie the Kid.

She took charge of the two tumblers, the drinks. Poured the drinks over ice cubes, stirred them around a while and then fished the ice cubes out when the drinks were chilled.

While I talked. While I told her about Chicago, about me in Chicago, about my family and the investment company. She handed me my drink then. She said quietly, "Go on, Howie."

I went on. I told her what Mame had told me about her guest Jesus the night before she was killed. I told her of the death of Jesus Gonzales as I'd read it in the *Mirror*. I added the two up for her.

She made us another drink while I told her about Ramon, about what had happened, about how I'd just killed him.

"Ramon," she said. "He has knife scars, Howie?" I nodded. She said, "Knife scars, a hype, a chef. I didn't know his name, but I know who his woman was, a red-headed junkie named Bess, I think it's Bess, in a place just down the block from Karas' joint. It's what happened, Howie, just like you guessed it. It must have been." She sipped her drink. "Yes, Howie, you'd better go back to Chicago, right away. It could be bad trouble for you if you don't. I brought money. Sixty. It's all I have except a little to last me till I can get more. Here."

A little roll of bills, she tucked into my shirt pocket.

"Billie," I said. "I wish—"

"Don't say it, honey. I know you can't. Take me with you, I mean. I wouldn't fit, not with the people you know there. And I'd be bad for you."

"I'd be bad for you, Billie. I'd be a square, a wet blanket. I'll have to be to get back in that rut, to hold down—" I didn't want to think about it. I said, "Billie, I'm going to send you what I owe you. Can I count on your being at the same address for another week or so?"

She sighed. "I guess so, Howie. But I'll give you my sister's name and address, what I use for a permanent address, in case you ever—in case you might not be able to send the money right away."

"I'll write it down," I said. I tore a corner off the paper the bottle had been wrapped in, looked around for something to write with; I remembered the fountain pen I'd stuck in my trousers pocket at Mame's. It was still there.

I screwed off the cap. Something glittered, falling to the carpet, a lot of somethings. Shiny little somethings that looked like diamonds. Billie gasped. Then she was scrabbling on the floor, picking them up. I stared at the pen, the hollow pen without even a point, in my hand. Hollow and empty now. But there was still something in the cap, which I'd been holding so it hadn't spilled. I emptied the cap out into my hand. Bigger diamonds, six of them, big and deep and beautifully cut.

My guess had been wrong. It hadn't been heroin Gonzales had been smuggling. Diamonds. And when he'd found himself followed to Mame's, he'd stashed them there for safety. The pen hadn't fallen from his coat pocket; he'd hidden it there deliberately.

They were in two piles on the table, Billie's hands trembling a little as she handled them one at a time. "Matched," she said reverently. "My husband taught me stones, Howie. Those six big ones—over five carats each, cut for depth, not shallow, and they're blue-white and I'll bet they're flawless, all of them, because they're matched. And the fifteen smaller ones—they're matched too, and they're almost three carats apiece. You know what Karas would give us for them, Howie?"

"Karas?"

"Fifteen grand, Howie, at least. Maybe more. These aren't ordinary; they're something special. Sure, Karas—I didn't tell you everything, because it didn't matter then, when I said I thought maybe he had some racket—not dope. He handles stones, only stones. Gonzales might have heard of him, might have been trying to contact him through Mame."

I thought about fifteen thousand dollars, and I thought about going back to Chicago. Billie said, "Mexico, Howie. In Mexico we can live like kings—like a king and queen—for five years for that much."

And stop drinking, straighten out? Billie said, "Howie, shall I take these to Karas right now so we can leave quick?" She was flushed, breathing hard, staring at me pleadingly.

"Yes," I said. She kissed me, hard, and gathered them up.

At the doorway, hand on the knob. "Howie, were you kidding when you said you were in love with a girl named Honor in Chicago? I mean, is there a real girl named that, or did you just mean—?"

"I was kidding, Billie the Kid."

The door closed.

Her heels clicked down the wooden hall. I poured myself a drink, a long one, and didn't bother to chill it with ice cubes. Yes, I'd known a girl named Honor in Chicago, once, but— . . . *but that was in another country, and besides, the wench is dead.*

I drank my drink and waited.

Twenty minutes later, I heard Billie's returning footsteps in the hall.

ROSS MACDONALD

Ross Macdonald (1915–1983) is often named, along with Dashiell Hammett and Raymond Chandler, as one of three writers who raised private eye writing out of the pulp fiction ghetto into the respectable world of literature. Certainly, like Hammett, he had grip on the American vernacular, and critics agree his penchant for penning memorable metaphors rivaled Chandler's.

All three men wrote of the sleuth as loner with great skill, but there can be a difference between going through life solo and experiencing life as a lonely enterprise. Macdonald outstripped Hammett and Chandler in conveying an aching state of loneliness again and again, not just in his portrayal of the gumshoe Lew Archer, but in numerous other characters, as well. "He spread his arms in a wide and futile embrace of emptiness" is a typical Macdonald statement.

Macdonald's empathy with misfits and disconnected characters may stem from a traumatic childhood. Born Kenneth Millar in 1915, in Los Gatos, California, he was deserted by his father when he was just three years old. Following the family breakup, he spent his childhood moving from place to place with his penniless mother, even coming close to being placed in an orphanage. Ironically, a bequest from his father made it possible for him to attend the University of Michigan, where he met and married Margaret Sturm, a woman who was destined to become a well-known mystery author under her married name, Margaret Millar. Inspired by his wife's success, and writing under the name John Macdonald and then as Ross Macdonald, he built a career as a mystery writer, too.

Macdonald took Chandler's elevated idea of the sleuth as chivalric figure and brought it down to earth in Archer, a private eye who states, "I'm a garbage collector in the moral field. It looks as if you could use me." Certainly Macdonald's detective consorts—often violently—with society's outcasts. Along the way, Macdonald proves that everything from fistfights and shootings to the existential longings of sad cases can be conveyed in a poetic turn of phrase.

The author won critical success but that did not halt the onslaught of personal tragedy in his life. After his daughter was arrested for vehicular homicide, he suffered a nervous breakdown and underwent psychoanalysis. The insights he gained during treatment seem to have underlined his view that trauma in childhood is at the heart of difficulties that haunt people later in life. While that view is nothing new to today's reader, Macdonald's delivery of that message still remains fresh, thanks to the author's choice of telling details and memorable metaphors. These are abundantly evident in the 1953 short story "Gone Girl," as Macdonald employs some of his favorite themes: loyalty, betrayal and shame. As for love, the last line says it all.

Gone Girl

1953

IT was a Friday night. I was tooling home from the Mexican border in a light blue convertible and a dark blue mood. I had followed a man from Fresno to San Diego and lost him in the maze of streets in Old Town. When I picked up his trail again, it was cold. He had crossed the border, and my instructions went no further than the United States.

Halfway home, just above Emerald Bay, I overtook the worst driver in the world. He was driving a black fishtail Cadillac as if he were tacking a sailboat. The heavy car wove back and forth across the freeway, using two of its four lanes, and sometimes three. It was late, and I was in a hurry to get some sleep. I started to pass it on the right, at a time when it was riding the double line. The Cadillac drifted towards me like an unguided missile, and forced me off the road in a screeching skid.

I speeded up to pass on the left. Simultaneously, the driver of the Cadillac accelerated. My acceleration couldn't match his. We raced neck and neck down the middle of the road. I wondered if he was drunk or crazy or afraid of me. Then the freeway ended. I was doing eighty on the wrong side of a two-lane highway, and a truck came over a rise ahead like a blazing double comet. I floorboarded the gas pedal and cut over sharply to the right, threatening the Cadillac's fenders and its driver's life. In the approaching headlights, his face was as blank and white as a piece of paper, with charred black holes for eyes. His shoulders were naked.

At the last possible second he slowed enough to let me get by. The truck went off onto the shoulder, honking angrily. I braked gradually, hoping to force the Cadillac to stop. It looped past me in an insane arc, tires skittering, and was sucked away into darkness.

When I finally came to a full stop, I had to pry my fingers off the wheel. My knees were remote and watery. After smoking part of a cigarette, I U-turned and drove very cautiously back to Emerald Bay. I was long past the hot-rod age, and I needed rest.

The first motel I came to, the Siesta, was decorated with a vacancy sign and a neon Mexican sleeping luminously under a sombrero. Envying him, I parked on the gravel apron in front of the motel office. There was a light inside. The glass-paned door was standing open, and I went in. The little room was pleasantly furnished with rattan and chintz. I jangled the bell on the desk a few times. No one appeared, so I sat down to wait and lit a cigarette. An electric clock on the wall said a quarter to one.

I must have dozed for a few minutes. A dream rushed by the threshold of my consciousness, making a gentle noise. Death was in the dream. He drove a black Cadillac loaded with flowers. When I woke up, the cigarette was starting to burn my fingers. A thin man in a gray flannel shirt was standing over me with a doubtful look on his face.

He was big-nosed and small-chinned, and he wasn't as young as he gave the impression of being. His teeth were bad, the sandy hair was thinning and receding. He was the typical old youth who scrounged and wheedled his living around motor courts and restaurants and hotels, and hung on desperately to the frayed edge of other people's lives.

"What do you want?" he said. "Who are you? What do you want?" His voice was reedy and changeable like an adolescent's.

"A room."

"Is that all you want?"

From where I sat, it sounded like an accusation. I let it pass. "What else is there? Circassian dancing girls? Free popcorn?"

He tried to smile without showing his bad teeth. The smile was a dismal failure, like my joke. "I'm sorry, sir," he said. "You woke me up. I never make much sense right after I just wake up."

"Have a nightmare?"

His vague eyes expanded like blue bubblegum bubbles. "Why did you ask me that?"

"Because I just had one. But skip it. Do you have a vacancy or don't you?"

"Yessir. Sorry, sir." He swallowed whatever bitter taste he had in his mouth, and assumed an impersonal obsequious manner. "You got any luggage, sir?"

"No luggage."

Moving silently in tennis sneakers like a frail ghost of the boy he once had been, he went behind the counter, and took my name, address, license number, and five dollars. In return, he gave me a key numbered fourteen and told me where to use it. Apparently he despaired of a tip.

Room fourteen was like any other middle-class motel room touched with the California-Spanish mania. Artificially roughened plaster painted adobe color, poinsettia-red curtains, imitation parchment lampshade on a twisted black iron stand. A Rivera reproduction of a sleeping Mexican hung on the wall over the bed. I succumbed to its suggestion right away, and dreamed about Circassian dancing girls.

Along towards morning one of them got frightened, through no fault of mine, and began to scream her little Circassian lungs out. I sat up in bed, making soothing noises, and woke up. It was nearly nine by my wristwatch. The screaming ceased and began again, spoiling the morning like a fire siren outside the window. I pulled on my trousers over the underwear I'd been sleeping in, and went outside.

A young woman was standing on the walk outside the next room. She had a key in one hand and a handful of blood in the other. She wore a wide multi-colored skirt and a low-cut gypsy sort of blouse. The blouse was distended and her mouth was open, and she was yelling her head off. It was a fine dark head, but I hated her for spoiling my morning sleep.

I took her by the shoulders and said, "Stop it."

The screaming stopped. She looked down sleepily at the blood on her hand. It was as thick as axle grease, and almost as dark in color.

"Where did you get that?"

"I slipped and fell in it I didn't see it."

Dropping the key on the walk, she pulled her skirt to one side with her clean hand. Her legs were bare and brown. Her skirt was stained at the back with the same thick fluid.

"Where? In this room?"

She faltered, "Yes."

Doors were opening up and down the drive. Half a dozen people began to converge on us. A dark-faced man about four and a half feet high came scampering from the direction of the office, his little pointed shoes dancing in the gravel.

"Come inside and show me," I said to the girl.

"I can't. I won't." Her eyes were very heavy, and surrounded by the bluish pallor of shock.

The little man slid to a stop between us, reached up and gripped the upper part of her arm. "What is the matter, Ella? Are you crazy, disturbing the guests?"

She said, "Blood," and leaned against me with her eyes closed.

His sharp glance probed the situation. He turned to the other guests, who had formed a murmuring semicircle around us.

"It is perfectly hokay. Do not be concerned, ladies and gentlemen. My daughter cut herself a little bit. It is perfectly all right."

Circling her waist with one long arm, he hustled her through the open door and slammed it behind him. I caught it on my foot and followed them in.

The room was a duplicate of mine, including the reproduction over the unmade bed, but everything was reversed as in a mirror image. The girl took a few weak steps by herself and sat on the edge of the bed. Then she noticed the blood spots on the sheets. She stood up quickly. Her mouth opened, rimmed with white teeth.

"Don't do it," I said. "We know you have a very fine pair of lungs."

The little man turned on me. "Who do you think you are?"

"The name is Archer. I have the next room."

"Get out of this one, please."

"I don't think I will."

He lowered his greased black head as if he were going to butt me. Under his sharkskin jacket, a hunch protruded from his back like a displaced elbow. He seemed to reconsider the butting gambit, and decided in favor of diplomacy.

"You are jumping to conclusions, mister. It is not so serious as it looks. We had a little accident here last night."

"Sure, your daughter cut herself. She heals remarkably fast."

"Nothing like that." He fluttered one long hand. "I said to the people outside the first thing that came to my mind. Actually, it was a little shuffle. One of the guests suffered a nosebleed."

The girl moved like a sleepwalker to the bathroom door and switched on the light. There was a pool of blood coagulating on the black and white checkerboard linoleum, streaked where she had slipped and fallen in it.

"Some nosebleed," I said to the little man. "Do you run this joint?"

"I am the proprietor of the Siesta motel hotel, yes. My name is Salanda. The gentleman is susceptible to nosebleed. He told me so himself."

"Where is he now?"

"He checked out early this morning."

"In good health?"

"Certainly in good health."

I looked around the room. Apart from the unmade bed with the brown spots on the sheets, it contained no signs of occupancy. Someone had spilled a pint of blood and vanished.

The little man opened to door wide and invited me with a sweep of his arm to leave. "If you will excuse me, sir, I wish to have this cleaned up as quickly as possible. Ella, will you tell Lorraine to get to work on it right away pronto? Then maybe you better like down for a little while, eh?"

"I'm all right now, father. Don't worry about me."

When I checked out a few minutes later, she was sitting behind the desk in the front office, looking pale but composed. I dropped my key on the desk in front of her.

"Feeling better, Ella?"

"Oh. I didn't recognize you with all your clothes on."

"That's a good line. May I use it?"

She lowered her eyes and blushed. "You're making fun of me. I know I acted foolishly this morning."

"I'm not so sure. What do *you* think happened in thirteen last night?"

"My father told you, didn't he?"

"He gave me a version, two of them in fact. I doubt that they're the final shooting script."

Her hand went to the central hollow in her blouse. Her arms and shoulders were slender and brown, the tips of her fingers carmine. "Shooting?"

"A cinema term," I said. "But there might have been a real shooting at that. Don't you think so?"

Her front teeth pinched her lower lip. She looked like somebody's pet rabbit. I restrained an impulse to pat her sleek brown head.

"That's ridiculous. This is a respectable motel. Anyway, father asked me not to discuss it with anybody."

"Why would he do that?"

"He loves this place, that's why. He doesn't want any scandal made out of nothing. If we lost our good reputation here, it would break my father's heart."

"He doesn't strike me as the sentimental type."

She stood up, smoothing her skirt. I saw that she'd changed it. "You leave him alone. He's a dear little man. I don't know what you think you're doing, trying to stir up trouble where there isn't any."

I backed away from her righteous indignation—female indignation is always righteous—and went out to my car. The early spring sun was dazzling. Beyond the freeway and the drifted sugary dunes, the bay was Prussian blue. The road cut inland across the base of the peninsula and returned to the sea a few miles north of the town. Here a wide blacktop parking space shelved off to the left of the highway, overlooking the white beach and whiter breakers. Signs at each end of the turnout stated that this was a County Park, No Beach Fires.

The beach and the blacktop expanse above it were deserted except for a single car, which looked very lonely. It was a long black Cadillac nosed into the cable fence at the edge of the beach. I braked and turned off the highway and got out. The man in the driver's seat of the Cadillac didn't turn his head as I approached him. His chin was propped on the steering wheel, and he was gazing out across the endless blue sea.

I opened the door and looked into his face. It was paper white. The dark brown eyes were sightless. The body was unclothed except for the thick hair matted on the chest, and a clumsy bandage tied around the waist. The bandage was composed of several blood-stained towels, held in place by a knotted piece of nylon fabric whose nature I didn't recognize immediately. Examining it more closely, I saw that it was a woman's slip. The left breast of the garment was embroidered in purple with a heart, containing the same name, "Fern," in slanting script. I wondered who Fern was.

The man who was wearing her purple heart had dark curly hair, heavy black eyebrows, a heavy chin sprouting black beard. He was rough-looking in spite of his anemia and the lipstick smudged on his mouth.

There was no registration on the steeringpost, and nothing in the glove compartment but a half-empty box of shells for a .38 automatic. The ignition was still turned on. So were the dash and headlights, but they were dim. The gas gauge registered empty. Curleyhead must have pulled off the highway soon after he passed me, and driven all the rest of the night in one place.

I untied the slip, which didn't look as if it would take fingerprints, and went over it for a label. It had one: Gretchen, Palm Springs. It occurred to me that it was Saturday morning and that I'd gone all winter without a week end in the desert. I retied the slip the way I'd found it, and drove back to the Siesta Motel.

Ella's welcome was a few degrees colder than absolute zero. "Well!" She glared down her pretty rabbit nose at me. "I thought we were rid of you."

"So did I. But I just couldn't tear myself away."

She gave me a peculiar look, neither hard nor soft, but mixed. Her hand went to her hair, then reached for a registration card. "I suppose if you want to rent a room, I can't stop you. Only please don't imagine you're making an impression on me. You're not. You leave me cold, mister."

"Archer," I said. "Lew Archer. Don't bother with the card. I came back to use your phone."

"Aren't there any other phones?" She pushed the telephone across the desk. "I guess it's all right, long as it isn't a toll call."

"I'm calling the Highway Patrol. Do you know their local number?"

"I don't remember." She handed me the telephone directory.

"There's been an accident," I said as I dialed.

"A highway accident? Where did it happen?"

"Right here, sister. Right here in room thirteen."

But I didn't tell that to the Highway Patrol. I told them I had found a dead man in a car on the parking lot above the county beach. The girl listened with widening eyes and nostrils. Before I finished she rose in a flurry and left the office by the rear door.

She came back with the proprietor. His eyes were black and bright like nailheads in leather, and the scampering dance of his feet was almost frenzied. "What is this?"

"I came across a dead man up the road a piece."

"So why do you come back here to telephone?" His head was in butting position, his hands outspread and gripping the corner of the desk. "Has it got anything to do with us?"

"He's wearing a couple of your towels."

"What?"

"And he was bleeding heavily before he died. I think somebody shot him in the stomach. Maybe you did."

"You're loco," he said, but not very emphatically. "Crazy accusations like that, they will get you into trouble. What is your business?"

"I'm a private detective."

"You followed him here, is that it? You were going to arrest him, so he shot himself?"

"Wrong on both accounts," I said. "I came here to sleep. And they don't shoot themselves in the stomach. It's too uncertain, and slow. No suicide wants to die of peritonitis."

"So what are you doing now, trying to make scandal for my business?"

"If your business includes trying to cover for murder."

"He shot himself," the little man insisted.

"How do you know?"

"Donny. I spoke to him just now."

"And how does Donny know?"

"The man told him."

"Is Donny your night keyboy?"

"He was. I think I will fire him, for stupidity. He didn't even tell me about this mess. I had to find it out for myself. The hard way."

"Donny means well," the girl said at his shoulder. "I'm sure he didn't realize what happened."

"Who does?" I said. "I want to talk to Donny. But first let's have a look at the register."

He took a pile of cards from a drawer and riffled through them. His large hands, hairy-backed, were calm and expert, like animals that lived a serene life of their own, independent of their emotional owner. They dealt me one of the cards across the desk. It was inscribed in block capitals: Richard Rowe, Detroit, Mich.

I said: "There was a woman with him."

"Impossible."

"Or he was a transvestite."

He surveyed me blankly, thinking of something else. "The HP, did you tell them to come here? They know it happened here?"

"Not yet. But they'll find your towels. He used them for bandage."

"I see. Yes. Of course?" He struck himself with a clenched fist on the temple. It made a noise like someone maltreating a pumpkin. "You are a private detective, you say. Now if you informed the police that you were on the trail of a fugitive, a fugitive from justice . . . He shot himself rather than face arrest . . . For five hundred dollars?"

"I'm not that private," I said. "I have some public responsibility. Besides, the cops would do a little checking and catch me out."

"Not necessarily. He *was* a fugitive from justice, you know."

"I hear you telling me."

"Give me a little time, and I can even present you with his record."

The girl was leaning back away from her father, her eyes starred with broken illusions. "Daddy," she said weakly.

He didn't hear her. All of his bright black attention was fixed on me. "Seven hundred dollars?"

"No sale. The higher you raise it, the guiltier you look. Were you here last night?"

"You are being absurd," he said. "I spent the entire evening with my wife. We drove up to Los Angeles to attend the ballet." By way of supporting evidence, he hummed a couple of bars from Tchaikovsky. "We didn't arrive back here in Emerald Bay until nearly two o'clock."

"Alibis can be fixed."

"By criminals, yes," he said. "I am not a criminal."

The girl put a hand on his shoulder. He cringed away, his face creased by monkey fury, but his face was hidden from her.

"Daddy," she said. "Was he murdered, do you think?"

"How do I know?" His voice was wild and high, as if she had touched the spring of his emotion. "I wasn't here. I only know what Donny told me."

The girl was examining me with narrowed eyes, as if I were a new kind of animal she had discovered and was trying to think of a use for.

"This gentleman is a detective," she said, "or claims to be."

I pulled out my photostat and slapped it down on the desk. The little man picked it up and looked from it to my face. "Will you go to work for me?"

"Doing what, telling little white lies?"

The girl answered for him: "See what you can find out about this—this death. On my word of honor, Father had nothing to do with it."

I made a snap decision, the kind you live to regret. "All right, I'll take a fifty-dollar advance. Which is a good deal less than five hundred. My first advice to you is to tell the police everything you know. Provided that you're innocent."

"You insult me," he said.

But he flicked a fifty-dollar bill from the cash drawer and pressed it into my hand fervently, like a love token. I had a queasy feeling that I had been conned into taking his money, not much of it but enough. The feeling deepened when he still refused to talk. I had to use all the arts of persuasion even to get Donny's address out of him.

The keyboy lived in a shack on the edge of a desolate stretch of dunes. I guessed that it had once been somebody's beach house, before sand had drifted like unthawing snow in the angles of the walls and winter storms had broken the tiles and cracked the concrete foundations. Huge chunks of concrete were piled haphazardly on what had been a terrace overlooking the sea.

On one of the tilted slabs, Donny was stretched like a long albino lizard in the sun. The onshore wind carried the sound of my motor to his ears. He sat up blinking, recognized me when I stopped the car, and ran into the house.

I descended flatstone steps and knocked on the warped door. "Open up, Donny."

"Go away," he answered huskily. His eye gleamed like a snail through a crack in the wood.

"I'm working for Mr. Salanda. He wants us to have a talk."

"You can go and take a running jump at yourself, you and Mr. Salanda both."

"Open it or I'll break it down."

I waited for a while. He shot back the bolt. The door creaked reluctantly open. He leaned against the doorpost, searching my face with his eyes, his hairless body shivering from an internal chill. I pushed past him, through a kitchenette that was indescribably filthy, littered with the remnants of old meals, and gaseous with their odors. He followed me silent on bare soles into a larger room whose spring floorboards undulated under my feet. The picture window had been broken and patched with cardboard. The stone fireplace was choked with garbage. The only furniture was an army cot in one corner where Donny apparently slept.

"Nice homey place you have here. It has that lived-in quality."

He seemed to take it as a compliment, and I wondered if I was dealing with a moron. "It suits me. I never was much of a one for fancy quarters. I like it here, where I can hear the ocean at night."

"What else do you hear at night, Donny?"

He missed the point of the question, or pretended to. "All different things. Big trucks going past on the highway. I like to hear those night sounds. Now I guess I can't go on living here. Mr. Salanda owns it, he lets me live here for nothing. Now he'll be kicking me out of here, I guess."

"On account of what happened last night?"

"Uh-huh." He subsided onto the cot, his doleful head supported by his hands. I stood over him. "Just what did happen last night, Donny?"

"A bad thing," he said. "This fella checked in about ten o'clock—"

"The man with the dark curly hair?"

"That's the one. He checked in about ten, and I gave him room thirteen. Around about midnight I thought I heard a gun go off from there. It took me a little while to get my nerve up, then I went back to see what was going on. This fella came out of the room, without no clothes on. Just some kind of bandage around his waist. He looked like some kind of a crazy Indian or something. He had a gun in his hand, and he was staggering, and I could see that he was bleeding some. He come right up to me and pushed the gun in my gut and told me to keep my trap shut. He said I wasn't to tell anybody I saw him, now or later. He said if I opened my mouth about it to anybody, that he would come back and kill me. But now he's dead, isn't he?"

"He's dead."

I could smell fear on Donny: there's an unexplained trace of canine in my chromosomes. The hairs were prickling on the back of my neck, and I wondered if Donny's fear was of the past or for the future. The pimples stood out in bas-relief against his pale lugubrious face.

"I think he was murdered, Donny. You're lying, aren't you?"

"Me lying?" But his reaction was slow and feeble.

"The dead man didn't check in alone. He had a woman with him."

"What woman?" he said in elaborate surprise.

"You tell me. Her name was Fern. I think she did the shooting, and you caught her red-handed. The wounded man got out of the room and into his car and away. The woman stayed behind to talk to you. She probably paid you to dispose of his clothes and fake a new registration card for the room. But you both overlooked the blood on the floor of the bathroom. Am I right?"

"You couldn't be wronger, mister. Are you a cop?"

"A private detective. You're in deep trouble, Donny. You'd better talk yourself out of it if you can, before the cops start on you."

"I didn't do anything." His voice broke like a boy's. It went strangely with the glints of gray in his hair.

"Faking the register is a serious rap, even if they don't hang accessory to murder on you."

He began to expostulate in formless sentences that ran together. At the same time his hand was moving across the dirty gray blanket. It burrowed under the pillow and come out holding a crumpled card. He tried to stuff it into his mouth and chew it. I tore it away from between his discolored teeth.

It was a registration card from the motel, signed in a boyish scrawl: Mr. and Mrs. Richard Rowe, Detroit, Mich.

Donny was trembling violently. Below his cheap cotton shorts, his bony knees vibrated like tuning forks. "It wasn't my fault," he cried. "She held a gun on me."

"What did you do with the man's clothes?"

"Nothing. She didn't even let me into the room. She bundled them up and took them away herself."

"Where did she go?"

"Down the highway towards town. She walked away on the shoulder of the road and that was the last I saw of her."

"How much did she pay you, Donny?"

"Nothing, not a cent. I already told you, she held a gun on me."

"And you were so scared you kept quiet until this morning?"

"That's right, I was scared. Who wouldn't be scared?"

"She's gone now," I said. "You can give me a description of her."

"Yeah." He made a visible effort to pull his vague thoughts together. One of his eyes was a little off center, lending his face a stunned, amorphous appearance. "She was a big tall dame with blondey hair."

"Dyed?"

"I guess so, I dunno. She wore it in a braid like, on top of her head. She was kind of fat, built like a lady wrestler, great big watermelons on her. Big legs."

"How was she dressed?"

"I didn't hardly notice, I was so scared. I think she had some kind of a purple coat on, with black fur around the neck. Plenty of rings on her fingers and stuff."

"How old?"

"Pretty old, I'd say. Older than me, and I'm going on thirty-nine."

"And she did the shooting?"

"I guess so. She told me to say if anybody asked me, I was to say that Mr. Rowe shot himself."

"You're very suggestible, aren't you, Donny? It's a dangerous way to be, with people pushing each other around the way they do."

"I didn't get that, mister. Come again." He batted his pale blue eyes at me, smiling expectantly.

"Skip it," I said and left him.

A few hundred yards up the highway I passed an HP car with two uniformed men in the front seat looking grim. Donny was in for it now. I pushed him out of my mind and drove across country to Palm Springs.

Palm Springs is still a one-horse town, but the horse is a Palomino with silver trappings. Most of the girls were Palomino, too. The main street was a cross-section of Hollywood and Vine transported across the desert by some unnatural force and disguised in western costumes which fooled nobody. Not even me.

I found Gretchen's lingerie shop in an expensive-looking arcade built around an imitation flagstone patio. In the patio's center a little fountain gurgled pleasantly, flinging small lariats of spray against the heat. It was late in March, and the season was ending. Most of the shops, including the one I entered, were deserted except for the hired help.

It was a small shop, faintly perfumed by a legion of vanished dolls. Stocking and robes and other garments were coiled on the glass counters or hung like brilliant treesnakes on display stands along the narrow walls. A henna-headed woman emerged from rustling recesses at the rear and came tripping towards me on her toes.

"You are looking for a gift, sir?" she cried with a wilted kind of gaiety. Behind her painted mask, she was tired and aging and it was Saturday afternoon and the lucky ones were dunking themselves in kidney-shaped swimming pools behind walls she couldn't climb.

"Not exactly. In fact, not at all. A peculiar thing happened to me last night. I'd like to tell you about it, but it's kind of a complicated story."

She looked me over quizzically and decided that I worked for a living, too. The phony smile faded away. Another smile took its place, which I liked better. "You look as if you'd had a fairly rough night. And you could do with a shave."

"I met a girl," I said. "Actually she was a mature woman, a statuesque blond to be exact. I picked her up on the beach at Laguna, if you want me to be brutally frank."

"1 couldn't bear it if you weren't. What kind of a pitch is this, brother?"

"Wait. You're spoiling my story. Something clicked when we met, in that sunset light, on the edge of the warm summer sea."

"It's always bloody cold when I go in."

"It wasn't last night. We swam in the moonlight and had a gay time and all. Then she went away. I didn't realize until she was gone that I didn't know her telephone number, or even her last name."

"Married woman, eh? What do you think I am, a lonely hearts club?" Still, she was interested, though she probably didn't believe me. "She mentioned me, is that it? What was her first name?"

"Fern."

"Unusual name. You say she was a big blonde?"

"Magnificently proportioned," I said. "If I had a classical education I'd call her Junoesque."

"You're kidding me, aren't you?"

"A little."

"I thought so. Personally I don't mind a little kidding. What did she say about me?"

Nothing but good. As a matter of fact, I was complimenting her on her—er—garments."

"I see." She was long past blushing. "We had a customer last fall some time, by the name of Fern. Fern Dee. She had some kind of a job at the Joshua Club, I think. But she doesn't fit the description at all. This one was a brunette, a middle-sized brunette, quite young. I remember the name Fern because she wanted it embroidered on all the things she bought. A corny idea if you ask me, but that was her girlish desire and who am I to argue with girlish desires."

"Is she still in town?"

"I haven't seen her lately, not for months. But it couldn't be the woman you're looking for. Or could it?"

"How long ago was she in here?"

She pondered. "Early last fall, around the start of the season. She only came in that once, and made a big purchase, stockings and nightwear and underthings. The works. I remember thinking at that time, here was a girlie who suddenly hit the chips but heavily."

"She might have put on weight since then, and dyed her hair. Strange things can happen to the female form."

"You're telling me," she said. "How old was—your friend?"

"About forty, I'd say, give or take a little."

"It couldn't be the same one then. The girl I'm talking about was twenty-five at the outside, and I don't make mistakes about women's ages. I've seen too many of them in all stages, from Quentin quail to hags, and I certainly do mean hags."

"I bet you have."

She studied me with eyes shadowed by mascara and experience. "You a policeman?"

"I have been."

"You want to tell mother what it's all about?"

"Another time. Where's the Joshua Club?"

"It won't be open yet."

"I'll try it anyway."

She shrugged her thin shoulders and gave me directions. I thanked her.

It occupied a plain-faced one-story building half a block off the main street. The padded leather door swung inward when I pushed it. I passed through a lobby with a retractable roof, which contained a jungle growth of banana trees. The big main room was decorated with tinted desert photomurals. Behind a rattan bar with a fishnet canopy, a white-coated Caribbean type was drying shot-glasses with a dirty towel. His face looked uncommunicative.

On the orchestra dais beyond the piled chairs in the dining area, a young man in shirt sleeves was playing bop piano. His fingers shadowed the tune, ran circles around it, played leapfrog with it, and managed never to hit it on the nose. I stood beside him for a while and listened to him work. He looked up finally, still strumming with his left hand in the bass. He had soft-centered eyes and frozen-looking nostrils and a whistling mouth.

"Nice piano," I said.

"I think so."

"Fifty-second Street?"

"It's the street with the beat and I'm not effete." His left hand struck the same chord three times and dropped away from the keys. "Looking for somebody, friend?"

"Fern Dee. She asked me to drop by some time."

"Too bad. Another wasted trip. She left here end of last year, the dear. She wasn't a bad little nightingale but she was no pro, Joe, you know? She had it but she couldn't project it. When she warbled the evening died, no matter how hard she tried, I don't wanna be snide."

"Where did she lam, Sam, or don't you have a damn?"

He smiled like a corpse in a deft mortician's hands. "I heard the boss retired her to private life. Took her home to live with him. That is what I heard. But I don't mix with the big boy socially, so I couldn't say for sure that she's impure. Is it anything to you?"

"Something, but she's over twenty-one."

"Not more than a couple of years over twenty-one." His eyes darkened, and his thin mouth twisted sideways angrily. "I hate to see it happen to a pretty little twist like Fern. Not that I yearn—"

I broke in on his nonsense rhymes: "Who's the big boss you mentioned, the one Fern went to live with?"

"Angel. Who else?"

"What heaven does he inhabit?"

"You must be new in these parts—" His eyes swiveled and focused on something over my shoulder. His mouth opened and closed.

A grating tenor was behind me: "Got a question you want answered, bud?"

The pianist went back to the piano as if the ugly tenor had wiped me out, annulled my very existence. I turned to its source. He was standing in a narrow doorway behind the drums, a man in his thirties with thick black curly hair and a heavy jaw blue-shadowed by closely shaven beard. He was almost the living image of the dead man in the Cadillac. The likeness gave me a jolt. The heavy black gun in his hand gave me another.

He came around the drums and approached me, bull-shouldered in a fuzzy tweed jacket, holding the gun in front of him like a dangerous gift. The pianist was doing wry things in quickened tempo with the dead march from *Saul*. A wit.

The dead man's almost-double waved his cruel chin and the crueler gun in unison. "Come inside, unless you're a government man. If you are, I'll have a look at your credentials."

"I'm a freelance."

"Inside then."

The muzzle of the automatic came into my solar plexus like a pointing iron finger. Obeying its injunction, I made my way between empty music stands and through the narrow door behind the drums. The iron finger, probing my back, directed me down a lightless corridor to a small square office containing a metal desk, a safe, a filing cabinet. It was windowless, lit by fluorescent tubes in the ceiling. Under their pitiless glare, the face above the gun looked more than ever like the dead man's face. I wondered if I had been mistaken about his deadness, or if the desert head had addled my brain.

"I'm the manager here," he said, standing so close that I could smell the piney stuff he used on his crisp dark hair. "You got anything to ask about the members of the staff, you ask me."

"Will I get an answer?"

"Try me, bud."

"The name is Archer," I said. "I'm a private detective."

"Working for who?"

"You wouldn't be interested."

"I am, though, very much interested." The gun hopped forward like a toad into my stomach again, with the weight of his shoulder behind it. "Working for who did you say?"

I swallowed anger and nausea, estimating my chances of knocking the gun to one side and taking him bare-handed. The chances seemed pretty slim. He was heavier than I was, and he held the automatic as if it had grown out of the end of his arm. You've seen too many movies, I told myself. I told him: "A motel owner on the coast. A man was shot in one of his rooms last night. I happened to check in there a few minutes later. The old boy hired me to look into the shooting."

"Who was it got himself ventilated?"

"He could be your brother," I said. "Do you have a brother?"

He lost his color. The center of his attention shifted from the gun to my face. The gun nodded. I knocked it up and sideways with a hard left uppercut. Its discharge burned the side of my face and drilled a hole in the wall. My right sank into his neck. The gun thumped the cork floor.

He went down but not out, his spread hand scrabbling for the gun, then closing on it. I kicked his wrist. He grunted but wouldn't let go of it. I threw a punch at the short hairs on the back of his neck. He took it and came up under it with the gun, shaking his head from side to side.

"Up with the hands now," he murmured. He was one of those men whose voices go soft and mild when they are in killing mood. He had the glassy impervious eyes of a killer. "Is Bart dead? My brother?"

"Very dead. He was shot in the belly."

"Who shot him?"

"That's the question."

"Who shot him?" he said in a quite white-faced rage. The single eye of the gun stared emptily at my midriff. "It could happen to you, bud, here and now."

"A woman was with him. She took a quick powder after it happened."

"I heard you say a name to Alfie, the piano-player. Was it Fern?"

"It could have been."

"What do you mean, it could have been?"

"She was there in the room, apparently. If you can give me a description of her?"

His hard brown eyes looked past me. "I can do better than that. There's a picture of her on the wall behind you. Take a look at it. Keep those hands up high."

I shifted my feet and turned uneasily. The wall was blank. I heard him draw a breath and move, and tried to evade his blow. No use. It caught the back of my head, I pitched forward against the blank wall and slid down it into three dimensions of blankness.

The blankness coagulated into colored shapes. The shapes were half human and half beast and they dissolved and reformed. A dead man with a hairy breast climbed out of a hole and doubled and quadrupled. I ran away from them through a twisting tunnel which led to an echo chamber. Under the roaring surge of the nightmare music, a rasping tenor was saying:

"I figure it like this. Vario's tip was good. Bart found her in Acapulco, and he was bringing her back from there. She conned him into stopping off at this motel for the night. Bart always went for her."

"I didn't know that," a dry old voice put in. "This is very interesting news about Bart and Fern. You should have told me before about this. Then I would not have sent him for her and this would not have happened. Would it, Gino?"

My mind was still partly absent, wandering underground in the echoing caves, I couldn't recall the voices, or who they were talking about. I had barely sense enough to keep my eyes closed and go on listening. I was lying on my back on a hard surface. The voices were above me.

The tenor said: "You can't blame Bartolomeo. She's the one, the dirty treacherous lying little bitch."

"Calm yourself, Gino. I blame nobody. But more than ever now, we want her back, isn't that right?"

"I'll kill her," he said softly, almost wistfully.

"Perhaps. It may not be necessary now. I dislike promiscuous killing—"

"Since when, Angel?"

"Don't interrupt, it's not polite. I learned to put first things first. Now what is the most important thing? Why did we want her back in the first place? I will tell you: to shut her mouth. The government heard she left me, they wanted her to testify about my income. We wanted to find her first and shut her mouth, isn't that right?"

"I know how to shut her mouth," the younger man said very quietly.

"First we try a better way, my way. You learn when you're as old as I am there is a use for everything, and not to be wasteful. Not even wasteful with somebody else's blood. She shot your brother, right? So now we have something on her, strong enough to keep her mouth shut for good. She'd get off with second degree, with what she's got, but even that is five to ten in Tehachapi. I think all I need to do is tell her that. First we have to find her, eh?"

"I'll find her. Bart didn't have any trouble finding her."

"With Vario's tip to help him, no. But I think I'll keep you here with me, Gino. You're too hot-blooded, you and your brother both. I want her alive. Then I can talk to her, and then we'll see."

"You're going soft in your old age, Angel."

"Am I?" There was a light slapping sound, of a blow on flesh. "I have killed many men, for good reasons. So I think you will take that back."

"I take it back."

"And call me Mr. Funk. If I am so old, you will treat my gray hairs with respect. Call me Mr. Funk."

"Mr. Funk."

"All right, your friend here, does he know where Fern is?"

"I don't think so."

"Mr. Funk."

"Mr. Funk," Gino's voice was a whining snarl.

"I think he's coming to. His eyelids fluttered."

The toe of a shoe prodded my side. Somebody slapped my face a number of times. I opened my eyes and sat up. The back of my head was throbbing like an engine fueled by pain. Gino rose from a squatting position and stood over me.

"Stand up."

I rose shakily to my feet. I was in a stone-walled room with a high beamed ceiling, sparsely furnished with stiff old black oak chairs and tables. The room and the furniture seemed to have been built for a race of giants.

The man behind Gino was small and old and weary. He might have been an unsuccessful grocer or a superannuated barkeep who had come to California for his health. Clearly his health was poor. Even in the stifling heat he looked pale and chilly, as if he had caught chronic death from one of his victims. He moved closer to me, his legs shuffling feebly in wrinkled blue trousers that bagged at the knees. His shrunken torso was swathed in a heavy blue turtleneck sweater. He had two days' beard on his chin, like moth-eaten gray plush.

"Gino informs me that you are investigating a shooting." His accent was Middle-European and very faint, as if he had forgotten his origins. "Where did this happen, exactly?"

"I don't think I'll tell you that. You can read it in the papers tomorrow night if you are interested."

"I am not prepared to wait. I am impatient. Do you know where Fern is?"

"I wouldn't be here if I did."

"But you know where she was last night."

"I couldn't be sure."

"Tell me anyway to the best of your knowledge."

"I don't think I will."

"He doesn't think he will," the old man said to Gino.

"I think you better let me out of here. Kidnapping is a tough rap. You don't want to die in the pen."

He smiled at me, with a tolerance more terrible than anger. His eyes were like thin stab-wounds filled with watery blood. Shuffling unhurriedly to the head of the mahogany table behind him, he pressed a spot in the rug with the toe of one felt slipper. Two men in blue serge suits entered the room and stepped towards me briskly. They belonged to the race of giants it had been built for.

Gino moved behind me and reached to pin my arms. I pivoted, landed one short punch, and took a very hard counter below the belt. Something behind me slammed my kidneys with the heft of a trailer truck bumper. I turned on weakening legs and caught a chin with my elbow. Gino's fist, or one of the beams from the ceiling, landed on my neck. My head rang like a gong. Under its clangor, Angel was saying pleasantly:

"Where was Fern last night?"

I didn't say.

The men in blue serge held me upright by the arms while Gino used my head as a punching bag. I rolled with his lefts and rights as well as I could, but his timing improved and mine deteriorated. His face wavered and receded. At intervals Angel inquired politely if I was willing to assist him now. I asked myself confusedly in the hail of fists what I was holding out for or who I was protecting. Probably I was holding out for myself. It seemed important to me not to give in to violence. But my identity was dissolving and receding like the face in front of me.

I concentrated on hating Gino's face. That kept it clear and steady for a while: a stupid square-jawed face barred by a single black brow, two close-set brown eyes staring glassily. His fists continued to rock me like an air-hammer.

Finally Angel placed a clawed hand on his shoulder, and nodded to my handlers. They deposited me in a chair. It swung on an invisible wire from the ceiling in great circles. It swung out wide over the desert, across a bleak horizon, into darkness.

I came to, cursing. Gino was standing over me again. There was an empty water-glass in his hand, and my face was dripping. Angel spoke up beside him, with a trace of irritation in his voice:

"You stand up good under punishment. Why go to all the trouble, though? I want a little information, that is all. My friend, my little girlfriend, ran away. I'm impatient to get her back."

"You're going about it the wrong way."

Gino leaned close, and laughed harshly. He shattered the glass on the arm of my chair, held the jagged base up to my eyes. Fear ran through me, cold and light in my veins. My eyes were my connection with everything. Blindness would be the end of me. I closed my eyes, shutting out the cruel edges of the broken thing in his hand.

"Nix, Gino," the old man said. "I have a better idea, as usual. There is heat on, remember."

They retreated to the far side of the table and conferred there in low voices. The young man left the room. The old man came back to me. His storm troopers stood one on each side of me, looking down at him in ignorant awe.

"What is your name, young fellow?"

I told him. My mouth was puffed and lisping, tongue tangled in ropes of blood.

"I like a young fellow who can take it, Mr. Archer. You say that you're a detective. You find people for a living, is that right?"

"I have a client," I said.

"Now you have another. Whoever he is, I can buy and sell him, believe me. Fifty times over." His thin blue hands scoured each other. They made a sound like two dry sticks rubbing together on a dead tree.

"Narcotics?" I said. "Are you the wheel in the heroin racket? I've heard of you."

His watery eyes veiled themselves like a bird's. "Now don't ask foolish questions, or I will lose my respect for you entirely."

"That would break my heart."

"Then comfort yourself with this." He brought an old-fashioned purse out of his hip pocket, abstracted a crumpled bill and smoothed it out on my knee. It was a five-hundred-dollar bill.

"This girl of mine you are going to find for me, she is young and foolish. I am old and foolish, to have trusted her. No matter. Find her for me and bring her back and I will give you another bill like this one. Take it."

"Take it," one of my guards repeated. "Mr. Funk said for you to take it."

I took it. "You're wasting your money. I don't even know what she looks like. I don't know anything about her."

"Gino is bringing a picture. He came across her last fall at a recording studio in Hollywood where Alfie had a date. He gave her an audition and took her on at the club, more for her looks than for the talent she had. As a singer she flopped. But she is a pretty little thing, about five foot four, nice figure, dark brown hair, big hazel eyes. I found a use for her." Lechery flickered briefly in his eyes and went out.

"You find a use for everything."

"That is good economics. I often think if I wasn't what I am, I would make a good economist. Nothing would go to waste." He paused and dragged his dying old mind back to the subject: "She was here for a couple of months, then she ran out on me, silly girl. I heard last week that she was in Acapulco, and the federal Grand Jury was going to subpoena her. I have tax troubles, Mr. Archer, all my life I have tax troubles. Unfortunately I let Fern help with my books a little bit. She could do me great harm. So I sent Bart to Mexico to bring her back. But I meant no harm to her. I still intend her no harm, even now. A little talk, a little realistic discussion with Fern, that is all that will be necessary. So even the shooting of my good friend Bart serves its purpose. Where did it happen, by the way?"

The question flicked out like a hook on the end of a long line.

"In San Diego," I said, "at a place near the airport: the Mission Motel."

He smiled paternally. "Now you are showing good sense."

Gino came back with a silver-framed photograph in his hand. He handed it to Angel, who passed it on to me. It was a studio portrait, of the kind intended for publicity cheesecake. On a black velvet divan, against an artificial night sky, a young woman reclined in a gossamer robe that was split to show one bent leg. Shadows accentuated the lines of her body and the fine bones in her face. Under the heavy makeup which widened the mouth and darkened the half-closed eyes I recognized Ella Salanda. The picture was signed in white, in the lower right-hand corner: "To my Angel, with all my love, Fern."

A sickness assailed me, worse than the sickness induced by Gino's fists. Angel breathed into my face: "Fern Dee is a stage name. Her real name I never learned. She told me one time that if her family knew where she was they would die of shame." He chuckled drily. "She will not want them to know that she killed a man."

I drew away from his charnel-house breath. My guards escorted me out. Gino started to follow, but Angel called him back.

"Don't wait to hear from me," the old man said after me. "I expect to hear from you."

The building stood on a rise in the open desert. It was huge and turreted, like somebody's idea of a castle in Spain. The last rays of the sun washed its wall in purple light and cast long shadows across its barren acreage. It was surrounded by a ten-foot hurricane fence topped with three strands of barbed wire.

Palm Springs was a clutter of white stones in the distance, diamonded by an occasional light. The dull red sun was balanced like a glowing cigar-butt on the rim of the hills above the town. A man with a bulky shoulder harness under his brown suede windbreaker drove me towards it. The sun fell out of sight, and darkness gathered like an impalpable ash on the desert, like a column of blue-gray smoke towering into the sky.

The sky was blue-black and swarming with stars when I got back to Emerald Bay. A black Cadillac followed me out of Palm Springs. I lost it in the winding streets of Pasadena. So far as I could see, I had lost it for good.

The neon Mexican lay peaceful under the stars. A smaller sign at his feet asserted that there was No Vacancy. The lights in the long low stucco buildings behind him shone brightly. The office door was open behind a screen, throwing a barred rectangle of light on the gravel. I stepped into it, and froze.

Behind the registration desk in the office, a woman was avidly reading a magazine. Her shoulders and bosom were massive. Her hair was blond, piled on her head in coronèted braids. There were rings on her fingers, a triple strand of cultured pearls around her thick white throat. She was the woman Donny had described to me.

I pulled the screen door open and said rudely: "Who are you?"

She glanced up, twisting her mouth in a sour grimace. "Well! I'll thank you to keep a civil tongue in your head."

"Sorry. I thought I'd seen you before somewhere."

"Well, you haven't." She looked me over coldly. "What happened to your face, anyway?"

"I had a little plastic surgery done. By an amateur surgeon."

She clucked disapprovingly. "If you're looking for a room, we're full up for the night. I don't believe I'd rent you a room even if we weren't. Look at your clothes."

"Uh-huh. Where's Mr. Salanda?"

"Is it any business of yours?"

"He wants to see me. I'm doing a job for him."

"What kind of a job?"

I mimicked her: "Is it any business of yours?" I was irritated. Under her mounds of flesh she had a personality as thin and hard and abrasive as a rasp.

"Watch who you're getting flip with, sonny boy." She rose, and her shadow loomed immense across the back door of the room. The magazine fell closed on the desk: it was *Teen-age Confessions*. "I am Mrs. Salanda. Are you a handyman?"

"A sort of one," I said. "I'm a garbage collector in the moral field. You look as if you could use me."

The crack went over her head. "Well, you're wrong. And I don't think my husband hired you, either. This is a respectable motel."

"Uh-huh. Are you Ella's mother?"

"I should say not. That little snip is no daughter of mine."

"Her stepmother?"

"Mind your own business. You better get out of here. The police are keeping a close watch on this place tonight, if you're planning any tricks."

"Where's Ella now?"

"I don't know and I don't care. She's probably gallivanting off around the countryside. It's all she's good for. One day at home in the last six months, that's a fine record for a young unmarried girl." Her face was thick and bloated with anger against her stepdaughter. She went on talking blindly, as if she had forgotten me entirely: "I told her father he was an old fool to take her back. How does he know what she's been up to? I say let the ungrateful filly go and fend for herself."

"Is that what you say, Mabel?" Salanda had softly opened the door behind her. He came forward into the room, doubly dwarfed by her blond magnitude. "I say if it wasn't for you, my dear, Ella wouldn't have been driven away from home in the first place."

She turned on him in a blubbering rage. He drew himself up tall and reached to snap his fingers under her nose. "Go back into the house. You are a disgrace to women, a disgrace to motherhood."

"I'm not *her* mother, thank God."

"Thank God," he echoed, shaking his fist at her. She retreated like a schooner under full sail, menaced by a gunboat. The door closed on her. Salanda turned to me:

"I'm sorry, Mr. Archer. I have difficulties with my wife, I am ashamed to say it. I was an imbecile to marry again. I gained a senseless hulk of flesh, and lost my daughter. Old imbecile!" He denounced himself, wagging his great head sadly. "I married in hot blood. Sexual passion has always been my downfall. It runs in my family, this insane hunger of blondeness and stupidity and size." He spread his arms in a wide and futile embrace of emptiness.

"Forget it."

"If I could." He came closer to examine my face. "You are injured, Mr. Archer. Your mouth is damaged. There is blood on your chin."

"I was in a slight brawl."

"On my account?"

"On my own. But I think it's time you leveled with me."

"Leveled with you?"

"Told me the truth. You knew who was shot last light, and who shot him, and why."

He touched my arm, with a quick, tentative grace. "I have only one daughter, Mr. Archer, only the one child It was my duty to defend her, as best as I could."

"Defend her from what?"

"From shame, from the police, from prison." He flung one arm out, indicating the whole range of human disaster. "I am a man of honor, Mr. Archer. But private honor stands higher with me than public honor. The man was abducting my daughter. She brought him here in the hope of being rescued. Her last hope."

"I think that's true. You should have told me this before."

"I was alarmed, upset. I feared your intentions. Any minute the police were due to arrive."

"But you had a right to shoot him. It wasn't even a crime. The crime was his."

"I didn't know that then. The truth came out to me gradually. I feared that Ella was involved with him." His flat black gaze sought my face and rested on it, "However, I did not shoot him, Mr. Archer. I was not even here at the time. I told you that this morning, and you may take my word for it."

"Was Mrs. Salanda here?"

"No sir, she was not. Why should you ask me that?"

"Donny described the woman who checked in with the dead man. The description fits your wife."

"Donny was lying. I told him to give a false description of the woman. Apparently he was unequal to the task of inventing one."

"Can you prove that she was with you?"

"Certainly I can. We had reserved seats at the theatre. Those who sat around us can testify that the seats were not empty. Mrs. Salanda and I, we are not an inconspicuous couple." He smiled wryly.

"Ella killed him then."

He neither assented, nor denied it. "I was hoping that you were on my side, my side and Ella's. Am I wrong?"

"I'll have to talk to her, before I know myself. Where is she?"

"I do not know, Mr. Archer, sincerely I do not know. She went away this afternoon, after the policemen questioned her. They were suspicious, but we managed to soothe their suspicions. They did not know that she had just come home, from another life, and I did not tell them. Mabel wanted to tell them. I silenced her." His white teeth clicked together.

"What about Donny?"

"They took him down to the station for questioning. He told them nothing damaging. Donny can appear very stupid when he wishes. He has the reputation of an idiot, but he is not so dumb. Donny has been with me for many years. He has a deep devotion for my daughter. I got him released tonight."

"You should have taken my advice," I said, "taken the police into your confidence. Nothing would have happened to you. The dead man was a mobster, and what he was doing amounts to kidnaping. Your daughter was a witness against his boss."

"She told me that. I am glad that it is true. Ella has not always told me the truth. She has been a hard girl to bring up, without a good mother to set her an example. Where has she been these last months, Mr. Archer?"

"Singing in a night club in Palm Springs. Her boss was a racketeer."

"A racketeer?" His mouth and nose screwed up, as if he sniffed the odor of corruption.

"Where she was isn't important, compared with where she is now. The boss is still after her. He hired me to look for her."

Salanda regarded me with fear and dislike, as if the odor originated in me. "You let him hire you?"

"It was my best chance of getting out of his place alive. I'm not his boy, if that's what you mean."

"You ask me to believe you?"

"I'm telling you. Ella is in danger. As a matter of fact, we all are." I didn't tell him about the second black Cadillac. Gino would be driving it, wandering the night roads with a ready gun in his armpit and revenge corroding his heart.

"My daughter is aware of the danger," he said. "She warned me of it"

"She must have told you where she was going."

"No. But she may be at the beach house. The house where Donny lives. I will come with you."

"You stay here. Keep your doors locked. If any strangers show and start prowling the place, call the police."

He bolted the door behind me as I went out. Yellow traffic lights cast wan reflections on the asphalt. Streams of cars went by to the north, to the south. To the west, where the sea lay, a great black emptiness opened under the stars. The beach house sat on its white margin, a little over a mile from the motel.

For the second time that day, I knocked on the warped kitchen door. There was light behind it, shining through the cracks. A shadow obscured the light.

"Who is it?" Donny said. Fear or some other emotion had filled his mouth with pebbles.

"You know me, Donny."

The door groaned on his hinges. He gestured dumbly to me to come in, his face a white blur. When he turned his head, and the light from the living room caught his face, I saw that grief was the emotion that marked it. His eyes were swollen as if he had been crying. More than ever he resembled a dilapidated boy whose growing pains had never paid off in manhood.

"Anybody with you?"

Sounds of movement in the living room answered my question. I brushed him aside and went in. Ella Salanda was bent over an open suitcase on the camp cot. She straightened, her mouth thin, eyes wide and dark. The .38 automatic in her hand gleamed dully under the naked bulb suspended from the ceiling.

"I'm getting out of here," she said, "and you're not going to stop me."

"I'm not sure I want to try. Where are you going, Fern?"

Donny spoke behind me, in his grief-thickened voice: "She's going away from me. She promised to stay here if I did what she told me. She promised to be my girl—"

"Shut up, stupid." Her voice cut like a lash, and Donny gasped as if the lash had been laid across his back.

"What did she tell you to do, Donny? Tell me just what you did."

"When she checked in last night with the fella from Detroit, she made a sign I wasn't to let on I knew her. Later on she left me a note. She wrote it with a lipstick on a piece of paper towel. I still got it hidden, in the kitchen."

"What did she write in the note?"

He lingered behind me, fearful of the gun in the girl's hand, more fearful of her anger.

She said: "Don't be crazy, Donny. He doesn't know a thing, not a thing. He can't do anything to either of us."

"I don't care what happens, to me or anybody else," the anguished voice said behind me. "You're running out on me, breaking your promise to me. I always knew it was too good to be true. Now I just don't care any more."

"I care," she said. "I care what happens to me." Her eyes shifted to me, above the unwavering gun. "I won't stay here. I'll shoot you if I have to."

"It shouldn't be necessary. Put it down, Fern. It's Bartolomeo's gun, isn't it? I found the shells to fit it in his glove compartment."

"How do you know so much?"

"I talked to Angel."

"Is he here?" Panic whined in her voice.

"No. I came alone."

"You better leave the same way then, while you can go under your own power."

"I'm staying. You need protection, whether you know it or not. And I need information. Donny, go in the kitchen and bring me that note."

"Don't do it, Donny. I'm warning you."

His sneakered feet made soft indecisive sounds. I advanced on the girl, talking quietly and steadily: "You conspired to kill a man, but you don't have to be afraid. He had it coming. Tell the whole story to the cops, and my guess is they won't even book you. Hell, you can even become famous. The government wants you as a witness in a tax case."

"What kind of a case?"

"A tax case against Angel. It's probably the only kind of rap they can pin on him. You can send him up for the rest of his life like Capone. You'll be a heroine, Fern."

"Don't call me Fern. I hate that name." There were sudden tears in her eyes. "I hate everything connected with that name. I hate myself."

"You'll hate yourself more if you don't put down that gun. Shoot me and it all starts over again. The cops will be on your trail, Angel's troopers will be gunning for you."

Now only the cot was between us, the cot and the unsteady gun facing me above it.

"This is the turning point," I said. "You've made a lot of bum decisions and almost ruined yourself, playing footsie with the evilest men there are. You can go on the way you have been, getting in deeper until you end up in a refrigerated drawer, or you can come back out of it now, into a decent life."

"A decent life? Here? With my father married to Mabel?"

"I don't think Mabel will last much longer. Anyway, I'm not Mabel. I'm on your side."

I waited. She dropped the gun on the blanket. I scooped it up and turned to Donny:

"Let me see that note."

He disappeared through the kitchen door, head and shoulders drooping on the long stalk of his body.

"What could I do?" the girl said. "I was caught. It was Bart or me. All the way up from Acapulco I planned how I could get away. He held a gun in my side when we crossed the border; the same way when we stopped for gas or to eat at the drive-ins. I realized he had to be killed. My father's motel looked like my only chance. So I talked Bart into staying there with me overnight. He had no idea who the place belonged to. I didn't know what I was going to do. I only knew it had to be some thing drastic. Once I was back with Angel in the desert, that was the end of me. Even if he didn't kill me, it meant I'd have to go on living with him. Anything was better than that. So I wrote a note to Donny in the bathroom, and dropped it out the window. He was always crazy about me."

Her mouth had grown softer. She looked remarkably young and virginal. The faint blue hollows under her eyes were dewy. "Donny shot Bart with Bart's own gun. He had more nerve than I had. I lost my nerve when I went back into the room this morning. I didn't know about the blood in the bathroom. It was the last straw."

She was wrong. Something crashed in the kitchen. A cool draft swept the living room. A gun spoke twice, out of sight. Donny fell backwards through the doorway, a piece of brownish paper clutched in his hand. Blood gleamed on his shoulder like a red badge.

I stepped behind the cot and pulled the girl down to the floor with me. Gino came through the door, his two-colored sports shoe stepping on Donny's laboring chest. I shot the gun out of his hand. He floundered back against the wall, clutching at his wrist.

I sighted carefully for my second shot, until the black bar of his eyebrows was steady in the sights of the .38. The hole it made was invisible, Gino fell loosely forward, prone on the floor beside the man he had killed.

Ella Salanda ran across the room. She knelt, and cradled Donny's head in her lap. Incredible, he spoke, in a loud sighing voice:

"You won't go away again, Ella? I did what you told me. You promised."

"Sure I promised. I won't leave you, Donny. Crazy man. Crazy fool."

"You like me better than you used to? Now?"

"I like you, Donny. You're the most man there is."

She held the poor insignificant head in her hands. He sighed, and his life came out bright-colored at the mouth. It was Donny who went away.

His hand relaxed, and I read the lipstick note she had written him on a piece of porous tissue:

"Donny: This man will kill me unless you kill him first. His gun will be in his clothes on the chair beside the bed. Come in and get it at midnight and shoot to kill. Good luck. I'll stay and be your girl if you do this, just like you always wished. Love. Ella."

I looked at the pair on the floor. She was rocking his lifeless head against her breast. Beside them, Gino looked very small and lonely, a dummy leaking darkness from his brow.

Donny had his wish and I had mine. I wondered what Ella's was.

MARGARET MILLAR

In the classic whodunit, the focus is placed upon straight facts, surface behaviors and motive—all scrutinized by a memorable sleuth. When, in 1941, Margaret Millar (1915–1994) published her first book, *The Invisible Worm,* that was her approach, too. In that novel and two more, Millar's psychiatrist sleuth, the coyly named Dr. Paul Prye, gets to the truth in narratives that succeed as novels of manners as well as whodunits. The fact that Millar makes Prye a psychiatrist is quite significant. While, ironically, Millar worked in the classic mold in the books that feature him, she would next create a police detective, Inspector Sands, who employs psychological insight to ask not just "Whodunit?" but "Whydunit?" Exploring this preoccupation, Millar looked at a question of dual personality in her 1955 novel *The Beast in View.* Five years later, she wrote *A Stranger in My Grave,* the quintessential novel centered on a nightmare. In 1962, Millar looked at the underside of a religious cult in *How Like an Angel,* and she wrote about mental illness in the 1964 book *The Fiend.*

Introduced in the 1943 novel *Wall of Eyes,* Sands is a transitional figure in detective fiction and in Millar's work. Like so many sleuths that came before him, he is a strong figure with above normal observational skills, but his gift lies in his placing more importance on the psychological than on the physical clues. This is a man who is interested not just in motive, but in motivation.

The influence of Millar's Sands books and short stories on later writers—not just in the mystery writing field but in the broader world of mainstream fiction—cannot be underestimated. A mistress of uneasiness, Millar makes murder look predictable, once you know what Sands understands about not just the murderers but the victims he encounters. This approach makes the solution to a Millar mystery deliciously unpredictable and it gives the "Of course!" moment stunning impact for the reader. In Millar's best work, the revelation of not just what happened but *why* it did always rests on a truth that we recognize as profoundly believable. This is because that truth is anchored in human nature itself.

"The Couple Next Door" represents Millar at her best. Here, nothing is what it seems in the home of an apparently placidly married couple. Affection itself becomes the fulcrum for a grand deception and much more. Meanwhile, Millar delivers lines that rival the later work of John Updike. When, undone by his wife's sudden hysteria, Charles Rackham turns to his neighbor Sands for help, Millar writes, "The *I* had become *we,* because they were good neighbors, and along with the games and the dinners and the scent of jasmine, they shared the sound of a woman's grief." To find out why Rackham's wife was inconsolable, read on.

The Couple Next Door

IT was by accident that they lived next door to each other, but by design that they became neighbors—Mr. Sands, who had retired to California after a life of crime investigation, and the Rackhams, Charles and Alma. Rackham was a big, innocent-looking man in his fifties. Except for the accumulation of a great deal of money, nothing much had ever happened to Rackham, and he liked to listen to Sands talk, while Alma sat with her knitting, plump and contented, unimpressed by any tale that had no direct bearing on her own life. She was half Rackham's age, but the fullness of her figure, and her air of having withdrawn from life quietly and without fuss, gave her the stamp of middle-age.

Two or three times a week Sands crossed the concrete driveway, skirted the eugenia hedge, and pressed the Rackhams' door chime. He stayed for tea or for dinner, to play gin or Scrabble, or just to talk. "That reminds me of a case I had in Toronto," Sands would say, and Rackham would produce martinis and an expression of intense interest, and Alma would smile tolerantly, as if she didn't really believe a single thing Sands, or anyone else, ever said.

They made good neighbors: the Rackhams, Charles younger than his years, and Alma older than hers, and Sands who could be any age at all . . .

It was the last evening of August and through the open window of Sands' study came the scent of jasmine and the sound of a woman's harsh, wild weeping.

He thought at first that the Rackhams had a guest, a woman on a crying jag, perhaps, after a quarrel with her husband.

He went out into the front yard to listen, and Rackham came around the corner of the eugenia hedge, dressed in a bathrobe.

He said, sounding very surprised, "Alma's crying."

"I heard."

"I asked her to stop. I begged her. She won't tell me what's the matter."

"Women have cried before."

"Not Alma." Rackham stood on the damp grass, shivering, his forehead streaked with sweat. "What do you think we should do about it?"

The *I* had become *we*, because they were good neighbors, and along with the games and the dinners and the scent of jasmine, they shared the sound of a woman's grief.

"Perhaps you could talk to her," Rackham said.

"I'll try."

"I don't think there is anything physically the matter with her. We both had a check-up at the Tracy clinic last week. George Tracy is a good friend of mine—he'd have told me if there was anything wrong."

"I'm sure he would."

"If anything ever happened to Alma I'd kill myself."

Alma was crouched in a corner of the davenport in the living room, weeping rhythmically, methodically, as if she had accumulated a hoard of tears and must now spend them all in one night. Her fair skin was blotched with patches of red, like strawberry birthmarks, and her eyelids were blistered from the heat of her tears. She looked like a stranger to Sands, who had never seen her display any emotion stronger than ladylike distress over a broken teacup or an overdone roast.

Rackham went over and stroked her hair. "Alma, dear. What is the matter?"

"Nothing . . . nothing . . ."

"Mr. Sands is here, Alma. I thought he might be able—we might be able—"

But no one was able. With a long shuddering sob, Alma got up and lurched across the room, hiding her blotched face with her hands. They heard her stumble up the stairs.

Sands said, "I'd better be going."

"No, please don't. I—the fact is, I'm scared. I'm scared stiff. Alma's always been so quiet."

"I know that."

"You don't suppose—there's no chance she's losing her mind?"

If they had not been good neighbors Sands might have remarked that Alma had little mind to lose. As it was, he said cautiously, "She might have had bad news, family trouble of some kind."

"She has no family except me."

"If you're worried, perhaps you'd better call your doctor."

"I think I will."

George Tracy arrived within half an hour, a slight, fair-haired man in his early thirties, with a smooth unhurried manner that imparted confidence. He talked slowly, moved slowly, as if there was all the time in the world to minister to desperate women.

Rackham chafed with impatience while Tracy removed his coat, placed it carefully across the back of the chair, and discussed the weather with Sands.

"It's a beautiful evening," Tracy said, and Alma's moans sliding down the stairs distorted his words, altered their meaning: *a terrible evening, an awful evening.* "There's a touch of fall in the air. You live in these parts, Mr. Sands?"

"Next door."

"For heaven's sake, George," Rackham said, "will you hurry up? For all you know, Alma might be dying."

"That I doubt. People don't die as easily as you might imagine. She's in her room?"

"Yes. Now will you *please*—"

"Take it easy, old man."

Tracy picked up his medical bag and went towards the stairs, leisurely, benign.

"He's always like that." Rackham turned to Sands scowling. "Exasperating son-of-a-gun. You can bet that if he had a wife in Alma's condition he'd be taking those steps three at a time."

"Who knows?—perhaps he has."

"*I* know," Rackham said crisply. "He's not even married. Never had time for it, he told me. He doesn't look it but he's very ambitious."

"Most doctors are."

"Tracy is, anyway."

Rackham mixed a pitcher of martinis, and the two men sat in front of the unlit fire, waiting and listening. The noises from upstairs gradually ceased, and pretty soon the doctor came down again.

Rackham rushed across the room to meet him. "How is she?"

"Sleeping. I gave her a hypo."

"Did you talk to her? Did you ask her what was the matter?"

"She was in no condition to answer questions."

"Did you find anything wrong with her?"

"Not physically. She's a healthy young woman."

"Not *physically*. Does that mean—?"

"Take it easy, old man."

Rackham was too concerned with Alma to notice Tracy's choice of words, but Sands noticed, and wondered if it had been conscious or unconscious: Alma's a healthy young woman . . . Take it easy, old man.

"If she's still depressed in the morning," Tracy said, "bring her down to the clinic with you when you come in for your X-rays. We have a good neurologist on our staff." He reached for his coat and hat. "By the way, I hope you followed the instructions."

Rackham looked at him stupidly. "What instructions?"

"Before we can take specific X-rays, certain medication is necessary,"

"I don't know what you're talking about."

"I made it very clear to Alma," Tracy said, sounding annoyed. "You were to take one ounce of sodium phosphate after dinner tonight, and report to the X-ray department at 8 o'clock tomorrow morning without breakfast."

"She didn't tell me."

"Oh."

"It must have slipped her mind."

"Yes. Obviously. Well, it's too late now." He put on his coat, moving quickly for the first time, as if he were in a rush to get away. The change made Sands curious. He wondered why Tracy was suddenly so anxious to leave, and whether there was any connection between Alma's hysteria and her lapse of memory about Rackham's X-rays. He looked at Rackham and guessed, from his pallor and his worried eyes, that Rackham had already made a connection in his mind.

"I understood," Rackham said carefully, "that I was all through at the clinic. My heart, lungs, metabolism—everything fit as a fiddle."

"People," Tracy said, "are not fiddles. Their tone doesn't improve with age. I will make another appointment for you and send you specific instructions by mail. Is that all right with you?"

"I guess it will have to be."

"Well, good night, Mr. Sands, pleasant meeting you." And to Rackham, "Good night, old man."

When he had gone, Rackham leaned against the wall, breathing hard. Sweat crawled down the sides of his face like worms and hid in the collar of his bathrobe. "You'll have to forgive me, Sands. I feel—I'm not feeling very well."

"Is there anything I can do?"

"Yes," Rackham said. "Turn back the clock."

"Beyond my powers, I'm afraid."

"Yes . . . Yes, I'm afraid."

"Good night, Rackham." *Good night, old man.*

"Good night, Sands." *Good night old man to you, too.*

Sands shuffled across the concrete driveway, his head bent. It was a dark night, with no moon at all.

From his study Sands could see the lighted windows of Rackham's bedroom. Rackham's shadow moved back and forth behind the blinds as if seeking escape from the very light that gave it existence. Back and forth, in search of nirvana.

Sands read until far into the night. It was one of the solaces of growing old—if the hours were numbered, at least fewer of them need be wasted in sleep. When he went to bed, Rackham's bedroom light was still on.

They had become good neighbors by design; now, also by design, they became strangers. Whose design it was, Alma's or Rackham's, Sands didn't know.

There was no definite break, no unpleasantness. But the eugenia hedge seemed to have grown taller and thicker, and the concrete driveway a mile wide. He saw the Rackhams occasionally; they waved or smiled or said, "Lovely weather," over the backyard fence. But Rackham's smile was thin and painful, Alma waved with a leaden arm, and neither of them cared about the weather. They stayed indoors most of the time, and when they did come out they were always together, arm in arm, walking slowly and in step. It was impossible to tell whose step led, and whose followed.

At the end of the first week in September, Sands met Alma by accident in a drug store downtown. It was the first time since the night of the doctor's visit that he'd seen either of the Rackhams alone.

She was waiting at the prescription counter wearing a flowery print dress that emphasized the fullness of her figure and the bovine expression of her face. A drug-store length away, she looked like a rather dull, badly dressed young woman with a passion for starchy foods, and it was hard to understand what Rackham had seen in her. But then Rackham had never stood a drug-store length away from Alma; he saw her only in close-up, the surprising, intense blue of her eyes, and the color and texture of her skin, like whipped cream. Sands wondered whether it was her skin and eyes, or her quality of serenity which had appealed most to Rackham, who was quick and nervous and excitable.

She said, placidly, "Why, hello there."

"Hello, Alma."

"Lovely weather, isn't it?"

"Yes . . . How is Charles?"

"You must come over for dinner one of these nights."

"I'd like to."

"Next week, perhaps. I'll give you a call—I must run now, Charles is waiting for me. See you next week."

But she did not run, she walked; and Charles was not waiting for her, he was waiting for Sands. He had let himself into Sands' house and was pacing the floor of the study, smoking a cigarette. His color was bad, and he had lost weight, but he seemed to have acquired an inner calm. Sands could not tell whether it was the calm of a man who had come to an important decision, or that of a man who had reached the end of his rope and had stopped struggling.

They shook hands, firmly, pressing the past week back into shape.

Rackham said, "Nice to see you again, old man."

"I've been here all along."

"Yes. Yes, I know . . . I had things to do, a lot of thinking to do."

"Sit down. I'll make you a drink."

"No, thanks. Alma will be home shortly, I must be there."

Like a Siamese twin, Sands thought, *separated by a miracle, but returning voluntarily to the fusion—because the fusion was in a vital organ.*

"I understand," Sands said.

Rackham shook his head. "No one can understand, really, but you come very close sometimes, Sands. Very close." His cheeks flushed, like a boy's. "I'm not good at words or expressing my emotions, but I wanted to thank you before we leave, and tell you how much Alma and I have enjoyed your companionship."

"You're taking a trip?"

"Yes. Quite a long one."

"When are you leaving?"

"Today."

"You must let me see you off at the station."

"No, no," Rackham said quickly. "I couldn't think of it. I hate last minute depot farewells. That's why I came over this afternoon to say goodbye."

"Tell me something of your plans."

"I would if I had any. Everything is rather indefinite. I'm not sure where we'll end up."

"I'd like to hear from you now and then."

"Oh, you'll hear from me, of course." Rackham turned away with an impatient twitch of his shoulders as if he was anxious to leave, anxious to start the trip right now before anything happened to prevent it.

"I'll miss you both," Sands said. "We've had a lot of laughs together."

Rackham scowled out of the window. "Please, no farewell speeches. They might shake my decision. My mind is already made up, I want no second thoughts."

"Very well."

"I must go now. Alma will be wondering—"

"I saw Alma earlier this afternoon," Sands said.

"Oh?"

"She invited me for dinner next week."

Outside the open window two hummingbirds fought and fussed, darting with crazy accuracy in and out of the bougainvillaea vine.

"Alma," Rackham said carefully, "can be very forgetful sometimes."

"Not that forgetful. She doesn't know about this trip you've planned, does she? . . . Does she, Rackham?"

"I wanted it to be a surprise. She's always had a desire to see the world. She's still young enough to believe that one place is different from any other place . . . You and I know better."

"Do we?"

"Goodbye, Sands."

At the front door they shook hands again and Rackham again promised to write, and Sands promised to answer his letters. Then Rackham crossed the lawn and the concrete driveway, head bent, shoulders hunched. He didn't look back as he turned the corner of the eugenia hedge.

Sands went over to his desk, looked up a number in the telephone directory, and dialed.

A girl's voice answered, "Tracy clinic, X-ray department."

"This is Charles Rackham," Sands said.

"Yes, Mr. Rackham."

"I'm leaving town unexpectedly. If you'll tell me the amount of my bill I'll send you a check before I go."

"The bill hasn't gone through, but the standard price for a lower gastrointestinal is twenty-five dollars."

"Let's see, I had that done on the—"

"The fifth. Yesterday."

"But my original appointment was for the first, wasn't it?"

The girl gave a does-it-really-matter sigh. "Just a moment, sir, and I'll check." Half a minute later she was back on the line.

"We have no record of an appointment for you on the first, sir."

"You're sure of that?"

"Even without the record book, I'd be sure. The first was a Monday. We do only gall bladders on Monday."

"Oh. Thank you."

Sands went out and got into his car. Before he pulled away from the curb he looked over at Rackham's house and saw Rackham pacing up and down the veranda, waiting for Alma.

The Tracy clinic was less impressive than Sands had expected, a converted two-story stucco house with a red tile roof. Some of the tiles were broken and the whole building needed paint, but the furnishings inside were smart and expensive.

At the reception desk a nurse wearing a crew cut and a professional smile told Sands that Dr. Tracy was booked solid for the entire afternoon. The only chance of seeing him was to sit in the second-floor waiting room and catch him between patients.

Sands went upstairs and took a chair in a little alcove at the end of the hall, near Tracy's door. He sat with his face half hidden behind an open magazine. After a while the door of Tracy's office opened and over the top of his magazine Sands saw a woman silhouetted in the door frame—a plump, fair-haired young woman in a flowery print dress.

Tracy followed her into the hall and the two of them stood looking at each other in silence. Then Alma turned and walked away, passing Sands without seeing him because her eyes were blind with tears.

Sands stood up. "Dr. Tracy?"

Tracy turned sharply, surprised and annoyance pinching the corners of his mouth. "Well? Oh, it's Mr. Sands."

"May I see you a moment?"

"I have quite a full schedule this afternoon."

"This is an emergency."

"Very well. Come in."

They sat facing each other across Tracy's desk.

"You look pretty fit," Tracy said with a wry smile, "for an emergency case."

"The emergency is not mine. It may be yours."

"If it's mine, I'll handle it alone, without the help of a poli—I'll handle it myself."

Sands leaned forward. "Alma has told you, then, that I used to be a policeman."

"She mentioned it in passing."

"I saw Alma leave a few minutes ago. . . . She'd be quite a nice-looking woman if she learned to dress properly."

"Clothes are not important in a woman," Tracy said, with a slight flush. "Besides, I don't care to discuss my patients."

"Alma is a patient of yours?"

"Yes."

"Since the night Rackham called you when she was having hysterics?"

"Before then."

Sands got up, went to the window, and looked down at the street.

People were passing, children were playing on the sidewalk, the sun shone, the palm trees rustled with wind—everything outside seemed normal and human and real. By contrast, the shape of the idea that was forming in the back of his mind was so grotesque and ugly that he wanted to run out of the office, to join the normal people passing on the street below. But he knew he could not escape by running. The idea would follow him, pursue him until he turned around and faced it.

It moved inside his brain like a vast wheel, and in the middle of the wheel, impassive, immobile, was Alma.

Tracy's harsh voice interrupted the turning of the wheel. "Did you come here to inspect my view, Mr. Sands?"

"Let's say, instead, your viewpoint."

"I'm a busy man. You're wasting my time."

"No. I'm giving you time."

"To do what?"

"Think things over."

"If you don't leave my office immediately, I'll have you thrown out." Tracy glanced at the telephone but he didn't reach for it, and there was no conviction in his voice.

"Perhaps you shouldn't have let me in. Why did you?"

"I thought you might make a fuss if I didn't."

"Fusses aren't in my line." Sands turned from the window. "Liars are, though."

"What are you implying?"

"I've thought a great deal about that night you came to the Rackhams' house. In retrospect, the whole thing appeared too pat, too contrived: Alma had hysterics and you were called in to treat her. Natural enough, so far."

Tracy stirred but didn't speak.

"The interesting part came later. You mentioned casually to Rackham that he had an appointment for some X-rays to be taken the following day, September the first. It was assumed that Alma had forgotten to tell him. Only Alma *hadn't* forgotten. There was nothing to forget. I checked with your X-ray department half an hour ago. They have no record of any appointment for Rackham on September the first."

"Records get lost."

"This record wasn't lost. It never existed. You lied to Rackham. The lie itself wasn't important, it was the *kind* of lie. I could have understood a lie of vanity, or one to avoid punishment or to gain profit. But this seemed such a silly, senseless, little lie. It worried me. I began to wonder about Alma's part in the scene that night. Her crying was most unusual for a woman of Alma's inert nature. What if her crying was also a lie? And what was to be gained by it?"

"Nothing," Tracy said wearily. "Nothing was gained."

"But something was *intended*—and I think I know what it was. The scene was played to worry Rackham, to set him up for an even bigger scene. If that next scene has already been played, I am wasting my time here. Has it?"

"You have a vivid imagination."

"No. The plan was yours—I only figured it out."

"Very poor figuring, Mr. Sands." But Tracy's face was gray, as if mold had grown over his skin.

'I wish it were. I had become quite fond of the Rackhams."

He looked down at the street again, seeing nothing but the wheel turning inside his head. Alma was no longer in the middle of the wheel, passive and immobile; she was revolving with the others—Alma and Tracy and Rackham, turning as the wheel turned, clinging to its perimeter.

Alma, devoted wife, a little on the dull side. . . . What sudden passion of hate or love had made her capable of such consummate deceit? Sands imagined the scene the morning after Tracy's visit to the house. Rackham, worried and exhausted after a sleepless night: "*Are you feeling better now, Alma?*"

"*Yes.*"

"*What made you cry like that?*"

"*I was worried.*"

"*About me?*"

"*Yes.*"

"*Why didn't you tell me about my X-ray appointment?*"

"*I couldn't. I was frightened. I was afraid they would discover something serious the matter with you.*"

"*Did Tracy give you any reason to think that?*"

"*He mentioned something about a blockage. Oh, Charles, I'm scared! If anything ever happened to you, I'd die. I couldn't live without you!*"

For an emotional and sensitive man like Rackham, it was a perfect set-up: his devoted wife was frightened to the point of hysterics, his good friend and physician had given her reason to be frightened. Rackham was ready for the next step. . . .

"According to the records in your X-ray department," Sands said, "Rackham had a lower gastrointestinal X-ray yesterday morning. What was the result?"

"Medical ethics forbid me to—"

"You can't hide behind a wall of medical ethics that's already full of holes. What was the result?"

There was a long silence before Tracy spoke. "Nothing."

"You found nothing the matter with him?"

"That's right."

"Have you told Rackham that?"

"He came in earlier this afternoon, alone."

"Why alone?"

"I didn't want Alma to hear what I had to say."

"Very considerate of you."

"No, it was not considerate." Tracy said dully. "I had decided to back out of our—our agreement—and I didn't want her to know just yet."

"The agreement was to lie to Rackham, convince him that he had a fatal disease?"

"Yes."

"Did you?"

"No. I showed him the X-rays, I made it clear that there was nothing wrong with him. . . . I tried. I tried my best. It was no use."

"What do you mean?"

"He wouldn't believe me! He thought I was trying to keep the real truth from him." Tracy drew in his breath, sharply. "It's funny, isn't it?—after days of indecision and torment I made up my mind to do the right thing. But it was too late. Alma had played her role too well. She's the only one Rackham will believe."

The telephone on Tracy's desk began to ring but he made no move to answer it, and pretty soon the ringing stopped and the room was quiet again.

Sands said, "Have you asked Alma to tell him the truth?"

"Yes, just before you came in."

"She refused?"

Tracy didn't answer.

"She wants him to think he is fatally ill?"

"I—yes."

"In the hope that he'll kill himself, perhaps?"

Once again Tracy was silent. But no reply was necessary.

"I think Alma miscalculated," Sands said quietly. "Instead of planning suicide, Rackham is planning a trip. But before he leaves, he's going to hear the truth—from you and from Alma." Sands went towards the door. "Come on, Tracy. You have a house call to make."

"No. I can't." Tracy grasped the desk with both hands, like a child resisting the physical force of removal by a parent. "I won't go."

"You have to."

"No! Rackham will ruin me if he finds out. That's how this whole thing started. We were afraid, Alma and I, afraid of what Rackham would do if she asked him for a divorce. He's crazy in love with her, he's obsessed!"

"And so are you?"

"Not the way he is. Alma and I both want the same things—a little peace, a little quiet together. We are alike in many ways."

"That I can believe," Sands said grimly. "You wanted the same things, a little peace, a little quiet—and a little of Rackham's money?"

"The money was secondary."

"A very close second. How did you plan on getting it?"

Tracy shook his head from side to side, like an animal in pain. "You keep referring to plans, ideas, schemes. We didn't start out with plans or schemes. We just fell in love. We've been in love for nearly a year, not daring to do anything about it because I knew how Rackham would react if we told him. I have worked hard to build up this clinic; Rackham could destroy it, and me, within a month."

"That's a chance you'll have to take. Come on, Tracy."

Sands opened the door and the two men walked down the hall, slowly and in step, as if they were handcuffed together.

A nurse in uniform met them at the top of the stairs. "Dr. Tracy, are you ready for your next—?"

"Cancel all my appointments, Miss Leroy."

"But that's imposs—"

"I have a very important house call to make."

"Will it take long?"

"I don't know."

The two men went down the stairs, past the reception desk, and out into the summer afternoon. Before he got into Sands' car, Tracy looked back at the clinic, as if he never expected to see it again.

Sands turned on the ignition and the car sprang forward like an eager pup.

After a time Tracy said, "Of all the people in the world who could have been at the Rackhams' that night, it had to be an ex-policeman."

"It's lucky for you that I was there."

"Lucky." Tracy let out a harsh little laugh. "What's lucky about financial ruin?"

"It's better than some other kinds of ruin. If your plan had gone through, you could never have felt like a decent man again."

"You think I will anyway?"

"Perhaps, as the years go by."

"The years." Tracy turned, with a sigh. "What are you going to tell Rackham?"

"Nothing. You will tell him yourself."

"I can't. You don't understand, I'm quite fond of Rackham, and so is Alma. We—it's hard to explain."

"Even harder to understand." Sands thought back to all the times he had seen the Rackhams together and envied their companionship, their mutual devotion. Never, by the slightest glance or gesture of impatience or slip of the tongue, had Alma indicated that she was passionately in love with another man. He recalled the games of Scrabble, the dinners, the endless conversations with Rackham, while Alma sat with her knitting, her face reposeful, content. Rackham would ask, "Don't you want to play too, Alma?" And she would reply, "No, thank you, dear, I'm quite happy with my thoughts."

Alma, happy with her thoughts of violent delights and violent ends.

Sands said, "Alma is equally in love with you?"

"Yes." He sounded absolutely convinced. "No matter what Rackham says or does, we intend to have each other."

"I see."

"I wish you did."

The blinds of the Rackham house were closed against the sun. Sands led the way up the veranda steps and pressed the door chime, while Tracy stood, stony-faced and erect, like a bill collector or a process server.

Sands could hear the chimes pealing inside the house and feel their vibrations beating under his feet.

He said, "They may have gone already."

"Gone where?"

"Rackham wouldn't tell me. He just said he was planning the trip as a surprise for Alma."

"He can't take her away! He can't force her to leave if she doesn't want to go!"

Sands pressed the door chime again, and called out, "Rackham? Alma?" But there was no response.

He wiped the sudden moisture off his forehead with his coat sleeve. "I'm going in."

"I'm coming with you."

"No."

The door was unlocked. He stepped into the empty hall and shouted up the staircase, "Alma? Rackham? Are you there?"

The echo of his own voice teased him from the dim corners.

Tracy had come into the hall. "They've left, then?"

"Perhaps not. They might have just gone out for a drive. It's a nice day for a drive."

"Is it?"

"Go around to the back and see if their car's in the garage."

When Tracy had gone, Sands closed the door behind him and shot the bolt. He stood for a moment listening to Tracy's nervous footsteps on the concrete driveway. Then he turned and walked slowly into the living room, knowing the car would be in the garage, no matter how nice a day it was for a drive.

The drapes were pulled tight across the windows and the room was cool and dark, but alive with images and noisy with the past:

"I wanted to thank you before we leave, Sands."

"You're taking a trip?"

"Yes, quite a long one."

"When are you leaving?"

"Today."

"You must let me see you off at the station. . . ."

But no station had been necessary for Rackham's trip. He lay in front of the fireplace in a pool of blood, and beside him was his companion on the journey, her left arm curving around his waist.

Rackham had kept his promise to write. The note was on the mantel, addressed not to Sands, but to Tracy.

Dear George:

You did your best to foil me but I got the truth from Alma. She could never hide anything from me; we are too close to each other. This is the easiest way out. I am sorry that I must take Alma along, but she told me so often that she could not live without me. I cannot leave her behind to grieve.

Think of us now and then, and try not to judge me too harshly.

Charles Rackham

Sands put the note back on the mantel. He stood quietly, his heart pierced by the final splinter of irony: before Rackham had used the gun on himself, he had lain down on the floor beside Alma and placed her dead arm lovingly around his waist.

From outside came the sound of Tracy's footsteps returning along the drive-way, and then the pounding of his fists on the front door.

"Sands, I'm locked out. Open the door. Let me in! Sands, do you hear me? Open this door!"

Sands went and opened the door.

DOROTHY SALISBURY DAVIS

When Dorothy Salisbury Davis was seventeen years old, she accidentally discovered she was adopted. "The whole room tilted over on its side and then somehow fell back into place again," she recalled. "I put everything back the way I found it. Except me." The same can be said for Davis's approach to creating crime fiction. In her work, something violent occurs, disturbing the order of things. While Davis establishes order again, the world where trauma has happened is never quite the same. Nor do the characters remain unchanged.

Today's readers, who take for granted strong female characters in crime and mystery fiction, may not realize how important a groundbreaker Davis was in this regard during her early years as a writer. While so many others portrayed women as femmes fatales, helpless creatures, or other stereotypes, Davis made her women strong, complex characters. She also blazed a path that later writers would take, introducing a regional voice into crime writing.

Davis spent her childhood and youth on farms in the American Midwest, but as an adult she mostly lived in and around cities, including New York. She draws on both experiences and settings in her work, tending to use small-town environments and points of view in her short stories and the urban scene in her longer work.

Davis's short story "By the Scruff of the Soul" not only has a profoundly memorable title but also shows the author's command of regional characters, settings, and voice. Narrated by a small-town lawyer and justice of the peace, and peppered with words of wisdom that are as thought-provoking as they are offhandedly delivered, this is the poignant story of a lovelorn traveling salesman who falls for a country girl who is "a wild one from the start." With the inevitability of a Greek tragedy, the action moves toward disaster as the narrator and the reader look on aghast.

Davis said, "I had an aunt who was somewhat like the older sister in this story. She ran the roost and she didn't care where the feathers flew! At the time that I wrote this story, I was feeling pretty low," Davis added. "I had just published a novel—not a mystery—and I knew it wasn't going to prove me the Great American Novelist. I wanted to have fun, write something frivolous and especially bizarre." As for the fact that the story turned out to be heart wrenching instead of frivolous, Davis said, "I can't help the poignancy. You put heart into your work and it comes out the way it comes out."

The story is set in a fictional town in the borderland between Pennsylvania and New York. It's an area Davis got to know well when she moved from town to town, working as an advance person promoting a traveling magician just after the Great Depression. It was the loneliest time of her life. She captures this loneliness in the character of traveling paint salesman Matt Sawyer in "By the Scruff of the Soul."

By the Scruff of the Soul

1963

MOST people, when they go down from the Ragapoo Hills, never come back; or if they do, for a funeral maybe—weddings don't count for so much around here any more either—you can see them fidgeting to get away again. As for me, I'm one of those rare birds they didn't have any trouble keeping down on the farm after he'd seen Paree.

It's forty years since I've seen the bright lights, but I don't figure I've missed an awful lot. Hell, I can remember the Ku Klux Klan marching right out in the open. My first case had to do with a revenue agent—I won it, too, and we haven't had a government man up here since. And take the League of Nations—I felt awful sorry in those days for Mr. Wilson though I didn't hold with his ideas.

Maybe things have changed, but sometimes I wonder just how much. This bomb I don't understand, fallout and all, but I've seen what a plague of locusts can do to a wheat field and I don't think man's ever going to beat nature when it comes to pure, ornery destruction. I could be wrong about that. Our new parson says I am and he's a mighty knowing man. Too knowing, maybe. I figure that's why the Synod shipped him up to us in Webbtown.

As I said, I don't figure I'm missing much. There's a couple of television sets in town and sometimes of an evening I'll sit for an hour or so in front of whichever one of them's working best. One of them gets the shimmies every time the wind blows and the other don't bring in anything except by way of Canada. Same shows but different commercials. That kind of tickles me, all them companies advertising stuff you couldn't buy if you wanted to instead of stuff you wouldn't want if you could buy it.

But, as you've probably guessed by now, I'd rather talk than most anything, and since you asked about The Red Lantern, I'll tell you about the McCracken sisters who used to run it—and poor old Matt Sawyer.

I'm a lawyer, by the way. I don't get much practice up here. I'm also Justice of the Peace. I don't get much practice out of that either, but between the two I make a living. For pleasure I fish for trout and play the violin, and at this point in my life I think I can say from experience that practice ain't everything.

I did the fiddling at Clara McCracken's christening party, I remember, just after coming home from the first World War. Maudie was about my age then, so's that'd make a difference of maybe twenty years between the sisters, and neither chit nor chizzler in between, and after them, the whole family suddenly dies out. That's how it happens up here in the hills: one generation and there'll be aunts and uncles galore, and the next, you got two maiden ladies and a bobtailed cat.

The Red Lantern Inn's boarded up now, as you saw, but it was in the McCracken family since just after the American Revolution. It was burned down once—in a reprisal raid during the War of 1812, and two of the McCrackens were taken hostage. Did you know Washington, D.C. was also burned in reprisal? It was. At least that's how they tell it over in Canada—for the way our boys tore up the town they call Toronto now. You know, history's like a story in a way: it depends on who's telling it.

Anyways, Maudie ran the inn after the old folks died, and she raised Clara the best she could, but Clara was a wild one from the start. We used to call her a changeling: one minute she'd be sitting at the stove and the next she'd be off somewhere in the hills. She wasn't pretty girl—the jutting McCracken jaw spoiled that—but there were times she was mighty feminine, and many a lad got thorny feet chasing after the will-o'-the-wisp.

As Clara was coming to age, Maudie used to keep a birch stick behind the bar, and now and then I dare say she'd use it, though I never saw it happen but once myself. But that birch stick and Old Faithful, her father's shotgun, stood in the corner side by side, and I guess we made some pretty rude jokes about them in those days. Anyways, Maudie swore to tame the girl and marry her to what she called a "settled" man.

By the time Clara was of a marrying age, The Red Lantern was getting pretty well rundown. And so was Maudie. She wasn't an easy woman by any calculation. She had a tongue you'd think was sharpened on the grindstone and a store of sayings that'd shock you if you didn't know your Bible. The inn was peeling paint and wanting shutters to the northeast, which is where they're needed most. But inside, Maudie kept the rooms as clean and plain as a glass egg. And most times they were about as empty.

It was the taproom kept the sisters going. They drew the best beer this side of Cornwall, England. If they knew you, that is. If they didn't know you, they served you a labeled bottle, stuff you'd recognize by the signboard pictures. About once a month, Maudie had to buy a case of that—which gives you an idea of how many strangers stopped over in Webbtown. We had more stores then and the flour mill was working, so the farmers'd come in regular. But none of them were strangers. You see, even to go to Ragapoo City, the county seat, you've got to go twenty miles around—unless you're like Clara was, skipping over the mountain.

Matt Sawyer came through every week or two in those days and he always stopped at Prouty's Hardware Store. Matt was a paint salesman. I suppose he sold Prouty a few gallons over the years. Who bought it from Prouty, I couldn't say. But Prouty liked Matt. I did myself when I got to know him. Or maybe I just felt sorry for him.

It was during the spring storms, this particular day. The rain was popping blisters on Main Street. Most everyone in Webbtown seems to have been inside looking out that day. Half the town claimed afterwards to have seen Matt come out of Prouty's raising his black umbrella over Maudie's head and walking her home. I saw them myself, Maudie pulling herself in and Matt half in and half out. I know for a fact she'd never been under an umbrella before in her life.

Prouty told me afterwards he'd forgot she was in the store when he was talking to Matt: Maudie took a mighty long time making up her mind before buying anything. Like he always did, Prouty was joshing Matt about having enough money to find himself a nice little woman and give up the road. Maudie wasn't backward. She took a direct line: she just up and asked Matt since he had an umbrella, would he mind walking her home. Matt was more of a gentleman than anybody I ever knew. He said it would be a pleasure. Maybe it was, but that was the beginning of the doggonedest three-cornered courtship in the county history. And it's all documented today in the county court records over in Ragapoo City. But I'm getting ahead of myself.

I've got my office in my hat, you might say, and I hang that in rooms over Kincaid's Drug Store. I was standing at the window when Matt and Maudie came out of Prouty's. I remember I was trying to tune my violin. You can't keep a fiddle in tune weather like that. I played kind of ex tempore for a while, drifting from one thing to another—sad songs mostly, like "The Vacant Chair." *We shall meet but we shall miss him . . . there will be one vacant chair.* I got myself so depressed I hung up the fiddle and went down to The Red Lantern for a glass of Maudie's Own.

Well, sure enough, there was Matt Sawyer sitting at the bar advising Maudie on the costs of paint and trimming and how to estimate the amount of paint a place the size of The Red Lantern would need. Now I knew Maudie couldn't afford whitewash much less the high-class line of stuff Matt represented. But there she was, leaning on the bar, chin in hand and her rump in the air like a swaybacked mule. She drew me a beer and put a head on Matt's. Then she went back to listening to him.

I don't know how long it took me to notice what was really going on: I'm slow sometimes, but all this while Clara was standing on a stool polishing a row of fancy mugs Maudie kept on a ledge over the back mirror. The whole row of lights was on under the ledge and shining double in the mirror. Hell, Matt Sawyer wasn't actually making sense at all, what he was saying in facts and figures. He was just making up words to keep old Maudie distracted—he thought—and all the while gazing up at Clara every chance he'd get. I might as well be honest with you: it was looking at Clara myself I realized what was going on in that room. The way she was reaching up and down in front of that mirror and with a silk petticoat kind of dress on, you'd have sworn she was stark naked.

Well, sir, just think about that. Matt, being a gentleman, was blushing and yearning—I guess you'd call it that—but making conversation all the time; and Maudie was conniving a match for Clara with a man who could talk a thousand dollars' worth of paint without jumping his Adam's apple. I'll say this about Maudie: for an unmarried lady she was mighty knowing in the fundamentals. Clara was the only innocent one in the room, I got to thinking.

All of a sudden Maudie says to me, "Hank, how's your fiddle these days?"

"It's got four strings," I said.

"You bring it up after supper, hear?" It was Maudie's way never to ask for something. She told you what you were going to do and most often you did it. Clara looked round at me from that perch of hers and clapped her hands.

Maudie laid a bony finger on Matt's hand. "You'll stay to supper with us, Mr. Sawyer. Our Clara's got a leg of lamb in the oven like you never tasted. It's home hung and roasted with garden herbs."

Now I knew for a fact the only thing Clara ever put in the oven was maybe a pair of shoes to warm them of a winter's morning. And it was just about then Clara caught on, too, to what Maudie was maneuvering. Her eyes got a real wild look in them, like a fox cornered in a chicken coop. She bounded down and across that room . . .

I've often wondered what would've happened if I hadn't spoken then. It gives me a cold chill thinking about it—words said with the best intentions in the world. I called out just as she got to the door: "Clara, I'll be bringing up my fiddle."

I don't suppose there ever was a party in Webbtown like Maudie put on that night. Word got around. Even the young folks came that mightn't have if it was spooning weather. Maudie wore her best dress—the one she was saving, we used to say, for Clara's wedding and her own funeral. It was black, but on happier occasions she'd liven it up with a piece of red silk at the collar. I remember Prouty saying once that patch of red turned Maudie from a Holstein into a Guernsey. Prouty, by the way, runs the undertaking parlor as well as the hardware store.

I near split my fingers that night fiddling. Maudie tapped a special keg. Everybody paid for his first glass, but after that she put the cash box away and you might say she drew by heart.

Matt was having a grand time just watching mostly. Matt was one of those creamy-looking fellows, with cheeks as pink as winter apples. He must've been fifty but there wasn't a line or wrinkle in his face. And I never seen him without his collar and tie on. Like I said, a gentleman.

Clara took to music like a bird to wing. I always got the feeling no matter who was taking her in or out she was actually dancing alone; she could do two steps to everybody else's one. Matt never took his eyes off her, and once he danced with her when Maudie pushed him into it.

That was trouble's start—although we didn't know it at the time. Prouty said afterwards he did, but Prouty's a man who knows everything after the fact. That's being an undertaker, I dare say. Anyway, Matt was hesitating after Clara—and it was like that, her sort of skipping ahead and leading him on, when all of a sudden, young Reuben White leaped in between them and danced with Clara the way she needed to be danced with.

Now Reuben didn't have much to recommend him, especially to Maudie. He did an odd job now and then—in fact, he hauled water for Maudie from the well she had up by the brewhouse back of Maple Tree Ridge. And this you ought to know about Maudie if you don't by now—anybody she could boss around, she had no use for.

Anyways, watching that boy dance with Clara that night should've set us all to thinking, him whirling her and tossing her up in the air, them spinning round together like an August twister. My fiddle's got a devil in it at a time like that. Faster and faster I was bowing, till plunk I broke a string, but I went right on playing.

Matt fell back with the other folks, clapping and cheering, but Maudie I could see going after her stick. I bowed even faster, seeing her. It was like a race we were all in together. Then all of a sudden, like something dying high up in the sky and falling mute, my E string broke and I wasn't playing any more. In the center of the tavern floor Clara and Reuben just folded up together and slumped down into a heap.

Everybody was real still for about a half a minute. Then Maudie came charging out, slashing the air with that switch of hers. She grabbed Clara by the hair—I swear she lifted the girl to her feet that way and flung her towards the bar. Then she turned on Reuben. That boy slithered clear across the barroom floor, every time just getting out of the way of a slash from Maudie's stick. People by then were cheering in a kind of rhythm—for him or Maudie, you couldn't just be sure, and maybe they weren't for either. "Now!" they'd shout at every whistle of the switch. "Now! Now! *Now!*"

Prouty opened the door just when Reuben got there, and when the boy was out Prouty closed it against Maudie. I thought for a minute she was going to turn on him. But she just stood looking and then burst out laughing. Everybody started clouting her on the back and having a hell of a time.

I was at the bar by then and so was Matt. I heard him, leaning close to Clara, say, "Miss Clara, I never saw anything as beautiful as you in all my life."

Clara's eyes snapped back at him but she didn't say a word.

Well, it was noon the next day before Matt pulled out of town, and sure enough, he forgot his umbrella and came back that night. I went up to The Red Lantern for my five o'clock usual, and him and Maudie were tete a tete, as they say, across the bar. Maudie was spouting the praises of her Clara—how she could sew and cook and bake a cherry pie, Billy Boy. The only attention she paid me was as a collaborating witness.

I'll say this for Clara: when she did appear, she looked almost civilized, her hair in a ribbon, and her wearing a new striped skirt and a grandmother blouse clear up to her chin. That night, by glory, she went to the movie with Matt. We had movies every night except Sundays in those days. A year or so ago, they closed up the Bellevue altogether. Why did she go with him? My guess is she wanted to get away from Maudie, or maybe for Reuben to see her dressed up that way.

The next time I saw all of them together was Decoration Day. Matt was back in town, arranging his route so's he'd have to stop over the holiday in Webbtown. One of them carnival outfits had set up on the grounds back of the schoolhouse. Like I said before, we don't have any population to speak of in Webbtown, but we're central for the whole valley, and in the old days traveling entertainers could do all right if they didn't come too often.

There was all sorts of raffle booths—Indian blankets and kewpie dolls, a shooting gallery and one of those things where you throw baseballs at wooden bottles and get a cane if you knock 'em off. And there was an apparatus for testing a man's muscle: you know, you hit the target on the stand with a sledge-hammer and then a little ball runs up a track that looks like a big thermometer and registers your strength in pounds.

I knew there was a trick to it no matter what the barker said about it being fair and square. Besides, nobody cares how strong a lawyer is as long as he can whisper in the judge's ear. I could see old Maudie itching herself to have a swing at it, but she wasn't taking any chance of giving Matt the wrong impression about either of the McCracken girls.

Matt took off his coat, folded it, and gave it to Clara to hold. It was a warm day for that time of year and you could see where Matt had been sweating under the coat, but like I said, he was all gentleman. He even turned his back to the ladies before spitting on his hands. It took Matt three swings—twenty-five cents worth—but on the last one that little ball crawled the last few inches up the track and just sort of tinkled the bell at the top. The womenfolk clapped, and Matt put on his coat again, blushing and pleased with himself.

I suppose you've guessed that Reuben showed up then. He did, wearing a cotton shirt open halfway down to his belly.

"Now, my boy," the barker says, "show the ladies, show the world that you're a man! How many?"

Reuben sniggled a coin out of his watch pocket, and mighty cocky for him, he said, "Keep the change."

Well, you've guessed the next part, too: Reuben took one swing and you could hear that gong ring out clear across the valley. It brought a lot of people running and the carnival man was so pleased he took out a big cigar and gave it to Reuben. "That, young fellow, wins you a fifty-cent Havana. But I'll send you the bill if you broke the machine, ha! ha!"

Reuben grinned and took the cigar, and strutting across to Clara, he made her a present of it. Now in Matt's book, you didn't give a lady a cigar, no, sir. Not saying a word, Matt brought his fist up with everything he had dead to center under Reuben's chin. We were all of us plain stunned, but nobody more than Reuben. He lay on the ground with his eyes rolling round in his head like marbles.

You'd say that was the blow struck for romance, wouldn't you? Not if you knew our Clara. She plopped down beside Reuben like he was the dying gladiator, or maybe just something she'd come on helpless in the woods. It was Maudie who clucked and crowed over Matt. All of a sudden Clara leaped up—Reuben was coming round by then—and she gave a whisk of that fancy skirt and took off for the hills, Maudie bawling after her like a hogcaller. And at that point, Reuben scrambled to his feet and galloped after Clara. It wasn't long till all you could see of where they'd gone was a little whiff of dust at the edge of the dogwood grove. I picked up the cigar and tried to smoke it afterwards. I'd have been better off on a mixture of oak leaf and poison ivy.

Everything changed for the worse at The Red Lantern after that. Clara found her tongue and sassed her sister, giving Maudie back word for word, like a common scold. One was getting mean and the other meaner. And short of chaining her, Maudie couldn't keep Clara at home any more, not when Clara wanted to go.

Matt kept calling at The Red Lantern regularly, and Maudie kept making excuses for Clara's not being there. The only times I'd go to the inn those days was when I'd see Matt's car outside. The place would brighten up then, Maudie putting on a show for him. Otherwise, I'd have as soon sat in Prouty's cool room. It was about as cheerful. Even Maudie's beer was turning sour.

Matt was a patient man if anything, and I guess being smitten for the first time at his age he got it worse than most of us would: he'd sit all evening just waiting a sight of that girl. When we saw he wasn't going to get over it, Prouty and I undertook one day in late summer to give him some advice. What made us think we were authorities, I don't know. I've been living with my fiddle for years and I've already told you what Prouty'd been living with. Anyways, we advised Matt to get himself some hunting clothes—the season was coming round—and to put away that doggone collar and tie of his and get out in the open country where the game was.

Matt tried. Next time he came to Webbtown, as soon as he put in at The Red Lantern, he changed into a plaid wool shirt, brand-new khaki britches, and boots laced up to his knees, and with Prouty and me cheering him on, he headed for the hills. But like Cox's army, or whoever it was, he marched up the hill and marched down again.

But he kept at it. Every week-end he'd show up, change, and set out, going farther and farther every time. One day, when the wind was coming sharp from the northeast, I heard him calling out up there: "Clara . . . Clara . . ."

I'll tell you, that gave me a cold chill, and I wished to the Almighty that Prouty and I had minded our own business. Maudie would stand at the tavern door and watch him off, and I wondered how long it was going to take for her to go with him. By then, I'd lost whatever feeling I ever had for Maudie and I didn't have much left for Clara either. But what made me plain sick one day was Maudie confiding in me that she was thinking of locking Clara in her room and giving Matt the key. I said something mighty close to obscene such as I'd never said to a woman before in my life and walked out of the tavern.

It was one of those October days, you know, when the clouds keep building up like suds and then just seem to wash away. You could hear the school bell echo, and way off the hawking of the wild geese, and you'd know the only sound of birds till spring would be the lonesome cawing of the crows. I was working on a couple of things I had coming up in Quarter Sessions Court when Prouty pounded up my stairs. Prouty's a pretty dignified man who seldom runs.

"Hank," he said, "I just seen Matt Sawyer going up the hill. He's carrying old man McCracken's shotgun."

I laughed kind of, seeing the picture in my mind. "What do you think he aims to do with it?"

"If he was to fire it, Hank, he'd be likely to blow himself to eternity."

"Maybe the poor buzzard'd be as well off," I said.

"And something else, Hank—Maudie just closed up the tavern. She's stalking him into the hills."

"That's something else," I said, and reached for my pipe.

"What are we going to do?" Prouty fumbled through his pockets for some matches for me. He couldn't keep his hands still.

"Nothing," I said. "The less people in them hills right now the better."

Prouty came to see it my way, but neither one of us could do much work that afternoon. I'd go to the window every few minutes and see Prouty standing in the doorway. He'd look down toward The Red Lantern and shake his head, and I'd know Maudie hadn't come back yet.

Funny, how things go on just the same in a town at a time like that. Tom Kincaid, the druggist, came out and swept the sidewalk clean, passed the time of day with Prouty, and went inside again. The kids were coming home from school. Pretty soon they were all indoors doing their homework before chore time. Doc Sissler stopped at Kincaid's—he liked to supervise the making up of his prescriptions. It was Miss Dorman, the schoolteacher, who gave the first alarm. She always did her next day's lessons before going home, so it was maybe an hour after school let out. I heard her scream and ran to the window.

There was Matt coming down the street on Prouty's side, trailing the gun behind him. You could see he was saying something to himself or just out loud. I opened my window and shouted down to him. He came on then across the street. His step on the stair was like the drum in a death march. When he got to my doorway he just stood there, saying, "I killed her, Hank. I killed her dead."

I got him into a chair and splashed some whiskey out for him. He dropped the gun on the floor beside him and I let it lie there, stepping over it. By then Prouty had come upstairs, and by the time we got the whiskey inside Matt, Luke Weber, the constable, was there.

"He says he killed somebody," I told Weber. "I don't know who."

Matt rolled his eyes towards me like I'd betrayed him just saying what he told me. His face was hanging limp and white as a strung goose. "I know Matt Sawyer," I added then, "and if there was any killing, I'd swear before Jehovah it must've been an accident."

That put a little life back in him. "It was," he said, "it was truly." And bit by piece we got the story out of him.

"I got to say in fairness to myself, taking the gun up there wasn't my own idea," he started. "Look at me, duded up like this—I had no business from the start pretending I was something I wasn't."

"That was me and Hank's fault," Prouty said, mostly to the constable, "advising him on how to court Miss Clara."

He didn't have to explain that to Weber. Everybody in town knew it.

"I'm not blaming either one of you," Matt said. "It should've been enough for me, chasing an echo every time I thought I'd found her. And both of them once sitting up in a tree laughing at me fit to bust and pelting me with acorns . . ."

We knew he was talking about Reuben and Clara. It was pathetic listening to a man tell that kind of story on himself, and I couldn't help but think what kind of an impression it was going to make on a jury. I had to be realistic about it: there's some people up here would hang a man for making a fool of himself where they'd let him go for murder. I put the jury business straight out of my mind and kept hoping it was clear-cut accident. He hadn't said yet who was dead, but I thought I knew by then.

"Well, I found them for myself today," he made himself go on. "Clara and Reuben, that is. They were cosied in together in the sheepcote back of Maudie's well. It made me feel ashamed just being there and I was set to sneak away and give the whole thing up for good. But Maudie came up on me and took me by surprise. She held me there—by the scruff of the soul, you might say—and made me listen with her to them giggling and carrying on. I was plain sick with jealousy, I'll admit that.

"Then Maudie gave a shout: 'Come out, you two! Or else we'll blow you out!' Something like that.

"It was a minute or two: nothing happened. Then we saw Reuben going full speed the other way, off towards the woods.

" 'Shoot, Matt, now!' That's what Maudie shouted at me. 'You got him clear to sight.' But just then Clara sauntered out of the shelter towards us—just as innocent and sweet, like the first time I ever laid eyes on her."

I'm going to tell you, Prouty and me looked at each other when he said that.

The constable interrupted him and asked his question straight: "Did she have her clothes on?"

"All but her shoes. She was barefoot and I don't consider that unbecoming in a country girl."

"Go on," Weber told him.

Matt took a long drag of air and then plunged ahead. "Maudie kept hollering at the boy—insults, I guess—I know I'd have been insulted. Then he stopped running and turned around and started coming back. I forget what it was she said to me then—something about my manhood. But she kept saying, 'Shoot, Matt! Shoot, shoot!' I was getting desperate, her hounding me that way. I slammed the gun down between us, butt-end on the ground. The muzzle of it, I guess, was looking her way. And it went off.

"It was like the ground exploding underneath us. Hell smoke and brimstone—that's what went through my mind. I don't know whether it was in my imagination—my ears weren't hearing proper after all that noise—but like ringing in my head I could hear Clara laughing, just laughing like hysterics . . . And then when I could see, there was Maudie lying on the ground. I couldn't even find her face for all that was left of her head."

We stood all of us for a while after that. Listening to the tick of my alarm clock on the shelf over the washstand, I was. Weber picked up the gun then and took it over to the window where he examined the breech.

Then he said, "What did you think you were going to do with this when you took it from the tavern?"

Matt shook his head. "I don't know. When Maudie gave it to me, I thought it looked pretty good on me in the mirror."

I couldn't wait to hear the prosecutor try that one on the jury.

Weber said, "We better get on up there before dark and you show us how it happened."

We stopped by at Prouty's on the way and picked up his wicker basket. There wasn't any way of driving beyond the dogwood grove. People were following us by then. Weber sent them back to town and deputized two or three among them to be sure they kept the peace.

We hadn't got very far beyond the grove, the four of us, just walking, climbing up, and saying nothing. Hearing the crows a-screaming not far ahead gave me a crawling stomach. They're scavengers, you know.

Well, sir, down the hill fair-to-flying, her hair streaming out in the wind, came Clara to meet us. She never hesitated, throwing herself straight at Matt. It was instinct made him put his arms out to catch her and she dove into them and flung her own arms around his neck, hugging him and holding him, and saying things like, "Darling Matt . . . wonderful Matt. I love Matt." I heard her say that.

You'd have thought to see Matt, he'd turned to stone. Weber was staring at them, a mighty puzzled look on his face.

"Miss Clara," I said, "behave yourself."

She looked at me—I swear she was smiling—and said, "You hush, old Hank, or we won't let you play the fiddle at our wedding."

It was Prouty said, hoisting his basket up on his shoulder, "Let's take one thing at a time."

That got us started on our way again, Clara skipping along at Matt's side, trying to catch his hand. Luke Weber didn't say a word.

I'm not going into the details now of what we saw. It was just about like Matt had told it in my office. I was sick a couple of times. I don't think Matt had anything left in him to be sick with. When it came to telling what had happened first, Clara was called on to corroborate. And Weber asked her, "Where's Reuben now, Miss Clara?"

"Gone," she said, "and I don't care."

"Didn't care much about your sister either, did you?" Weber drawled, and I began to see how really bad a spot old Matt was in. There was no accounting Clara's change of heart about him—except he'd killed her sister. The corroborating witness we needed right then was Reuben White.

Prouty got Weber's go-ahead on the job he had to do. I couldn't help him though I tried. What I did when he asked it, was go up to Maudie's well to draw him a pail of water so's he could wash his hands when he was done. Well, sir, I'd have been better off helping him direct. I couldn't get the bucket down to where it would draw the water.

After trying a couple of times, I called out to Weber asking if he had a flash-light. He brought it and threw the beam of light down into the well. Just about the water level a pair of size-twelve shoes were staring up at us—the soles of them like Orphan Annie's eyes.

There wasn't any doubt in our minds that what was holding them up like that was Reuben White, headfirst in the well.

The constable called Clara to him and took a short-cut in his questioning. "How'd it happen, girl?"

"I guess I pushed him," Clara said, almost casual.

"It took a heap of pushing," Weber said.

"No, it didn't. I just got him to look down and then I tumbled him in."

"Why?"

"Matt," she said, and smiled like a Christmas cherub.

Matt groaned, and I did too inside.

"Leastways, it come to that," Clara explained. Then in that quick-changing way of hers, she turned deep serious. "Mr. Weber, you wouldn't believe me if I told you what Reuben White wanted me to do with him—in the sheepcote this afternoon."

"I might," Luke Weber said.

I looked at Prouty and drew my first half-easy breath. I could see he felt the same. We're both old-fashioned enough to take warmly to a girl's defending her virtue.

But Weber didn't bat an eye. "And where does Matt here come in on it?" he said.

"I figure he won't ever want me to do a thing like that," Clara said, and gazed up at old stoneface with a look of pure adoration.

"Where was Matt when you . . . tumbled Reuben in?" Weber asked, and I could tell he was well on his way to believing her.

"He'd gone down the hill to tell you what'd happened to Sister Maudie."

"And when was it Reuben made this—this proposal to you?" Weber said. I could see he was getting at the question of premeditation. Luke Weber's a pretty fair policeman.

"It was Matt proposed to me," Clara said. "That's why I'm going to marry him. Reuben just wanted . . . "

Weber interrupted. "Why, if he wasn't molesting you just then, and if you'd decided to marry Matt Sawyer, why did you have to kill him? You must've known a well's no place for diving."

Clara shrugged her pretty shoulders. "By then I was feeling kind of sorry for him. He'd have been mighty lonesome after I went to live with Matt."

Well, there isn't much more to tell. We sort of disengaged Matt, you might say. His story of how Maudie died stood up with the coroner, Prouty and I vouching for the kind of man he was. I haven't seen him since.

Clara—she'll be getting out soon, coming home to the hills, and maybe opening up The Red Lantern again. I defended her at the trial, pleading temporary insanity. Nobody was willing to say she was insane exactly. We don't like saying such things about one another up here. But the jury agreed she was a temporary sort of woman. Twenty years to life, she got, with time off for good behavior.

You come around some time next spring. I'll introduce you.

JULIAN SYMONS

Perhaps more than most mystery writers, Julian Symons (1912–1994) merits the term "man of letters." Not only did he turn out numerous mystery novels and short stories, but he won academic respect for the genre by penning a seminal literary history of crime and mystery writing. In addition, he was a respected writer of biographies, literary criticism, poetry, and military history.

Symons was born in London in 1912. The son of a severe Victorian father, whose fortunes rose and fell dramatically over the years, Symons grew up in a closely knit and unusually isolated family circle. While as a small child he wowed adults with his talent for reciting poetry, he soon developed a stammer, which caused him to be placed in a school for backward children. With encouragement from his mother and siblings, however, and thanks to his own passion for self-education, Symons overcame the speech impediment and became an accomplished writer and the valued friend of many writers and artists. His poetry was admired, and his work as editor of *Twentieth-Century Verse* is still considered to have been brilliant and influential. Symons supported that small journal by holding down a job with the slightly seedy company Victoria Lighting and Dynamo.

Eventually, Symons met and married Kathleen Clark. The couple lived for periods of years in London and in various other places, including Deal, near Dover, England, changing abodes in order to suit their differing cravings for urban and country living. As a result, Symons seems comfortable, in his fiction, in portraying people who live in a variety of situations.

Like his contemporaries, Symons was a crack hand at surprising the reader with plot twists and unexpected endings to his mystery stories and novels. However, his fiction and his own remarks about his work prove he was most preoccupied with the psychology of his characters—particularly with what he called "the violence that lurks behind respectable faces." Again and again, his work looks at small moments that cause his characters to step over the line from civilized, respectable living into that dark world of criminal behavior.

Not only did Symons's crime writing help to advance the prevalence of the "Whydunit?" over the "Whodunit?" but the publication, in 1972, of *Bloody Murder: From the Detective Story to the Crime Novel: A History,* made a convincing argument that psychologically acute crime fiction was a step forward from the classic detective story. That volume was also published, in America, under the title *Mortal Consequences.*

The short story "Flowers That Bloom in the Spring " is typical of Symons's work. Here the author gets into the head of prim Bertie Mays, a retired civil servant who has nothing better to do than attend tea parties and pry into the affairs of his neighbors. Ordinarily, the accusation "You have an overactive imagination" would be apropos regarding Mays. But that just might not be the case on the occasion Symons describes here.

Flowers that Bloom in the Spring

1971

THE outsider, Bertie Mays was fond of saying, sees most of the game. In the affair of the Purchases and the visiting cousin from South Africa he saw quite literally all of it. And the end was enigmatic and a little frightening, at least as seen through Bertie's eyes. It left him with the question whether there had been a game at all.

Bertie had retired early from his unimportant and uninteresting job in the Ministry of Welfare. He had a private income, he was unmarried, and his only extravagance was a passion for travel, so why go on working? Bertie gave up his London flat and settled down in the cottage in the Sussex countryside which he had bought years earlier as a weekend place. It was quite big enough for a bachelor, and Mrs. Last from the village came in two days a week to clean the place. Bertie himself was an excellent cook.

It was a fine day in June when he called next door to offer Sylvia Purchase a lift to the tea party at the Hall. She was certain to have been asked, and he knew she would need a lift because he had seen her husband Jimmy putting a case into the trunk of their ancient Morris. Jimmy was some sort of freelance journalist, and often went on trips, leaving Sylvia on her own. Bertie, who was flirtatious by nature, had asked if she would like him to keep her company, but she did not seem responsive to the suggestion.

Linton House, which the Purchases had rented furnished a few months earlier, was a rambling old place with oak beams and low ceilings. There was an attractive garden, some of which lay between the house and Bertie's cottage, and by jumping over the fence between them Bertie could walk across this garden. He did so that afternoon, taking a quick peek into the sitting room as he went by. He could never resist such peeks, because he always longed to know what people might be doing when they thought nobody was watching. On this occasion the sitting room was empty. He found Sylvia in the kitchen, washing dishes in a halfhearted way.

"Sylvia, you're not ready." She had on a dirty old cardigan with the buttons done up wrong. Bertie himself was, as always, dressed very suitably for the occasion in a double-breasted blue blazer with brass buttons, fawn trousers, and a neat bow tie. He always wore bow ties, which he felt gave him a touch of distinction.

"Ready for what?"

"Has the Lady of the Manor not asked you to tea?" That was his name for Lady Hussey up at the Hall.

She clapped a hand to her forehead, leaving a slight smudge. "I forgot all about it! Don't think I'll go, can't stand those bun fights."

"But I have called specially to collect you. Let me be your chauffeur. Your carriage awaits." Bertie made a sketch of a bow, and Sylvia laughed. She was a blonde in her early thirties, attractive in a slapdash sort of way.

"Bertie, you are a fool. All right, give me five minutes."

The women may call Bertie Mays a fool, Bertie thought, but how they adore him.

"Oh," Sylvia said. She was looking behind Bertie, and when he turned he saw a man standing in the shadow of the door. At first glance he thought it was Jimmy, for the man was large and square like Jimmy and had the same gingery fair coloring. But the resemblance went no further, for as the man stepped forward he saw that their features were not similar.

"This is my cousin, Alfred Wallington. He's paying us a visit from South Africa. Our next door neighbor, Bertie Mays."

"Pleased to meet you." Bertie's hand was firmly gripped. The two men went into the sitting room, and Bertie asked whether this was Mr. Wallington's first visit.

"By no means. I know England pretty well. The south, anyway."

"Ah, business doesn't take you up north?" Bertie thought of himself as a tactful but expert interrogator, and the question should have brought a response telling him Mr. Wallington's occupation. In fact, however, the other man merely said that was so.

"In the course of my work I used to correspond with several firms in Cape Town," Bertie said untruthfully. Wallington did not comment. "Is your home near there?"

"No."

The negative was so firm that it gave no room for further conversational maneuver. Bertie felt slightly cheated. If the man did not want to say where he lived in South Africa, of course he was free to say nothing, but there was a certain finesse to be observed in such matters, and a crude "no" was not at all the thing. He was able to establish at least that this was the first time Wallington had visited Linton House.

On the way up to the Hall he said to Sylvia that her cousin seemed a dour fellow.

"Alf?" Bertie winced at the abbreviation. "He's all right when you get to know him."

"He said he was often in the south. What's his particular sphere of interest?"

"I don't know. I believe he's got some sort of export business around Durban. By the way, Bertie, how did you know Jimmy was away?"

"I saw him waving good-bye to you." It would hardly do to say that he had been peeping through the curtains.

"Did you now? I was in bed when he went. You're a bit of a fibber, I'm afraid, Bertie."

"Oh, I can't remember *how* I knew." Really, it was too much to be taken up on every little point.

When they drove into the great courtyard and Sylvia got out of the car, however, he reflected that she looked very slenderly elegant, and that he was pleased to be with her. Bertie liked pretty women and they were safe with him, although he would not have thought of it that way. He might have said, rather, that he would never have compromised a lady, with the implication that all sorts of things might be said and done providing they stayed within the limits of discretion.

It occurred to him that Sylvia was hardly staying within those limits when she allowed herself to be alone at Linton House with her South African cousin. Call me old-fashioned, Bertie said to himself, but I don't like it.

The Hall was a nineteenth-century manor house and by no means, as Bertie had often said, an architectural gem, but the lawns at the back where tea was served were undoubtedly fine. Sir Reginald Hussey was a building contractor who had been knighted for some dubious service to the export drive. He was in demand for opening fêtes and fund-raising enterprises, and the Husseys entertained a selection of local people to parties of one kind or another half a dozen times a year. The parties were always done in style, and this afternoon there were maids in white caps and aprons, and a kind of majordomo who wore a frock coat and white gloves. Sir Reginald was not in evidence, but Lady Hussey presided in a regal manner.

Of course Bertie knew that it was all ridiculously vulgar and ostentatious, but still he enjoyed himself. He kissed Lady Hussey's hand and said that the scene was quite entrancing, like a Victorian period picture, and he had an interesting chat with Lucy Broadhinton, who was the widow of an Admiral. Lucy was the president and Bertie the secretary of the local historical society, and they were great friends. She told him now in the strictest secrecy about the outrageous affair Mrs. Monro was having with somebody who must be nameless, although from the details given, Bertie was quite able to guess his identity. There were other tidbits too, like the story of the scandalous misuse of the Church Fund restoration money. It was an enjoyable afternoon, and he fairly chortled about it on the way home.

"They're such snobby affairs," Sylvia said. "I don't know why I went."

"You seemed to be having a good time. I was quite jealous."

Sylvia had been at the center of a very animated circle of three or four young men. Her laughter at their jokes had positively rung out across the lawns, and Bertie had seen Lady Hussey give more than one disapproving glance in the direction of the little group. There was something undeniably attractive about Sylvia's gaiety and about the way in which she threw back her head when laughing, but her activities had a recklessness about them which was not proper for a lady.

Bertie tried to convey something of this as he drove back, but was not sure she understood what he meant. He also broached delicately the impropriety of her being alone in the house with her cousin by asking when Jimmy would be coming back. In a day or two, she said casually. He refused her invitation to come in for a drink. He had no particular wish to see Alf Wallington again.

On the following night at about midnight, when Bertie was in bed reading, he heard a car draw up next door. Doors were closed and there was the sound of voices. Just to confirm that Jimmy was back, Bertie got out of bed and lifted an edge of the curtain. A man and a woman were coming out of the garage. The woman was Sylvia. The man had his arm round her, and as Bertie watched, the man bent down and kissed her neck. Then they moved toward the front door, and the man laughed and said something. From his general build he might, seen in the dim light, have been Jimmy, but the voice had the distinctive South African accent of Wallington.

Bertie drew away from the window as though he had been scalded.

It was a feeling of moral responsibility that took him round to Linton House on the following day. To his surprise Jimmy Purchase opened the door.

"I—ah—thought you were away."

"Got back last night. What can I do for you?"

Bertie said he would like to borrow the electric hedge clippers, which he knew were in the garden shed. Jimmy led the way there and handed them over. Bertie said he had heard the car coming back at about midnight.

"Yeah." Jimmy had a deplorably Cockney voice, not at all out of the top drawer. "That was Sylvia and Alf. He took her to a dance over at Ladersham. I was too fagged out, just wanted to get my head down."

"Her cousin from South Africa?"

"Yeah, right, from the Cape. He's staying here for a bit. Plenty of room."

Was he from the Cape or from Durban? Bertie did not fail to notice the discrepancy.

Bertie's bump of curiosity was even stronger than his sense of propriety. It became important, even vital, that he should know just what was going on next door. When he returned the hedge cutters he asked them all to dinner, together with Lucy Broadhinton to make up the number. He took pains in preparing a delicious cold meal. The salmon was cooked to perfection, and the hollandaise sauce had just the right hint of something tart beneath its blandness.

The evening was not a success. Lucy had on a long dress and Bertie wore a smart velvet jacket, but Sylvia was dressed in sky-blue trousers and a vivid shirt, and the two men wore open-necked shirts and had a distinctly unkempt appearance. They had obviously been drinking before they arrived. Wallington tossed down Bertie's expensive hock as though it were water, and then said that South African wine had more flavor than that German stuff.

"You're from Durban, I believe, Mr. Wallington." Lucy fixed him with her Admiral's-lady glance. "My husband and I were there in the sixties, and thought it delightful. Do you happen to know the Morrows or the Page-Manleys? Mary Page-Manley gave such delightful parties."

Wallington looked at her from under heavy brows. "Don't know them."

"You have an export business in Durban?"

"That's right."

There was an awkward pause. Then Sylvia said, "Alf's trying to persuade us to pay him a visit out there."

"I'd like you to come out. Don't mind about him." Wallington jerked a thumb at Jimmy. "Believe me, we'd have a good time."

"I do believe you, Alf." She gave her head-back laugh, showing the fine column of her neck. "It's something we've forgotten here—how to have a good time."

Jimmy Purchase had been silent during dinner. Now he said, "People here just don't have the money. Like the song says, it's money makes the world go round."

"The trouble in Britain is that too much money has got into the wrong hands." Lucy looked round the table. Nobody seemed inclined to argue the point. "There are too many grubby little people with sticky fingers."

"I wish some of the green stuff would stick to my fingers," Jimmy said, and hiccuped. Bertie realized with horror that he was drunk. "We're broke, Sylvie, old girl."

"Oh, shut up."

"You don't believe me?" And he actually began to empty out his pockets. What appalling creatures the two men were, each as bad as the other. Bertie longed for the evening to end, and was delighted when Lucy rose to make a stately departure. He whispered an apology in the hall, but she told him not to be foolish, it had been fascinating.

When he returned, Wallington said, "What an old battleaxe. *Did you happen to know the Page-Manleys.* Didn't know they were still around, people like that."

Sylvia was looking at Bertie. "Alf, you're shocking our host."

"Sorry, man, but honest, I thought they kept her sort in museums. Stuffed."

"You mustn't say stuffed. That'll shock Bertie too."

Bertie said stiffly, "I am not in the least shocked, but I certainly regard it as the height of bad manners to criticize a guest in such a manner. Lucy is a very dear friend of mine."

Sylvia at least had some understanding of his feelings. She said sorry and smiled, so that he was at once inclined to forgive her. Then she said it was time she took her rough diamonds home.

"Thanks for the grub," Wallington said. Then he leaned across the dining table and shouted, "Wake up, man, it's tomorrow morning already." Jimmy had fallen asleep in his chair. He was hauled to his feet and supported across the garden.

Bertie called up Lucy the next morning and apologized again. She said he should think no more about it. "I didn't take to that South African feller, though. Shouldn't be surprised if he turns out to be a bad hat. And I didn't care too much for your neighbors, if you don't mind my being frank."

Bertie said of course not, although he reflected that there seemed to be a sudden spasm of frankness among his acquaintances. Mrs. Purchase, Lucy said, had a roving eye. She left it at that, and they went on to discuss the agenda for the next meeting of the historical society.

Later in the morning there was a knock on the door. Jimmy was there, hollow-eyed and slightly green. " 'Fraid we rather blotted our copybook last night. Truth is, Alf and I were fairly well loaded before we came round. Can't remember too much about it, but Syl said apologies were in order."

Bertie asked when Sylvia's cousin was leaving. Jimmy Purchase shrugged and said he didn't know. Bertie nearly said that he ought not to leave the man alone with Sylvia, but refrained. He might be inquisitive, but he was also discreet.

A couple of nights later he was doing some weeding in the garden when he heard voices raised in Linton House. One was Jimmy's, the other belonged to Sylvia. They were in the sitting room shouting at each other, not quite loudly enough for the words to be distinguishable. It was maddening not to know what was being said. Bertie moved along the fence separating the gardens, until he was as near as he could get without being seen. He was now able to hear a few phrases.

"Absolutely sick of it . . . drink because it takes my mind off . . . told you we have to wait . . . " That was Jimmy.

Then Sylvia's voice, shrill as he had never heard it, shrill and sneering. "Tell me the old, old story . . . how long do we bloody well wait then . . . you said it would be finished by now." An indistinguishable murmur from Jimmy. "None of your business," she said. More murmuring. "None of your business what I do." Murmur murmur. "You said yourself we're broke." To this there was some reply. Then she said clearly, "I shall do what I like."

"*All right*," Jimmy said, so loudly that Bertie fairly jumped. There followed a sharp crack, which sounded like hand on flesh.

Sylvia said, "You damn—that's it, then."

Nothing more. No sound, no speech. Bertie waited five minutes and then tiptoed away, fearful of being seen. Once indoors again he felt quite shaky, and had to restore himself by a nip of brandy.

What had the conversation meant? Much of it was plain enough. Sylvia saying that it was none of her husband's business if she carried on an affair. But what was it they had to wait for, what was it that should have been finished? A deal connected with the odious Alf? And where was Alf, who as Bertie had noticed went out into the village very little?

He slept badly, and was wakened in the middle of the night by a piercing, awful scream. He sat up in bed quivering, but the sound was not repeated. He decided that he must have been having a nightmare.

On the following day the car was not in the garage. Had Jimmy gone off again? He met Sylvia out shopping in the village, and she said that he had been called to an assignment on short notice.

"What sort of assignment?" He had asked before for the name of the paper Jimmy worked on, to be told that he was a freelance.

"A Canadian magazine. He's up in the Midlands, may be away a few days."

Should he say something about the row? But that would have been indiscreet, and in any case Sylvia had such a wild look in her eye that he did not care to ask further questions. It was on that morning that he read about the Small Bank Robbers.

The Small Bank Robbers had been news for some months. They specialized in fast well-organized raids on banks, and had carried out nearly 20 of these in the past year. Several men were involved in each raid. They were armed, and did not hesitate to use coshes or revolvers when necessary. In one bank a screaming woman customer had suffered a fractured skull when hit over the head, and in another a guard who resisted the robbers had been shot and killed.

The diminutive applied to them—small—referred to the banks they robbed, not to their own physical dimensions. A bank clerk who had admitted giving information to the gang had asked why they were interested in his small branch bank, and had been told that they always raided small banks because they were much more vulnerable than large ones. After the arrest of this clerk the robbers seemed to have gone underground. There had been no news of them for the last three weeks.

Bertie had heard about the Small Bank Robbers, but took no particular interest in them. He was a nervous man, and did not care to read about crime. On this morning, however, his eye was caught by the heading: "Small Bank Robbers. The South African Connection." The story was a feature by the paper's crime reporter, Derek Holmes. He said that Scotland Yard knew the identities of some of the robbers, and described his own investigations, which led to the conclusion that three or four of them were in Spain. The article continued:

"But there is another connection, and a sinister one. The men in Spain are small fry. My researches suggest that the heavy men who organized the robberies, and were very ready to use violence, came from South Africa. They provided the funds and the muscle. Several witnesses who heard the men talking to each other or giving orders during the raids have said that they used odd accents. This has been attributed to the sound distortion caused by the stocking masks they wore, but two men I spoke to, both of whom have spent time in South Africa, said that they had *no doubt the accent was South African*."

The writer suggested that these men were now probably back in South Africa. But supposing that one of them was still in England, that he knew Jimmy and Sylvia and had a hold over them? Supposing, even, that Jimmy and Sylvia were minor members of the gang themselves? The thought made Bertie shiver with fright and excitement. What should or could he do about it? And where had Jimmy Purchase gone?

Again he slept badly, and when he did fall into a doze it was a short one. He dreamed that Wallington was knocking on the door. Once inside the house the South African drew out a huge wad of notes, said that there was enough for everybody, and counted out bundles which he put on the table between them with a small decisive *thwack*. A second bundle, *thwack*, and a third, *thwack*. How many more? He tried to cry out, to protest, but the bundles went on, *thwack, thwack, thwack . . .*

He sat up in bed, crying out something inaudible. The thin gray light of early morning came through the curtains. There was a sound in the garden outside, a sound regularly repeated, the *thwack* of his dream. It took him, in his slightly dazed state, a little while to realize that if he went to the window he might see what was causing the sound. He tiptoed across the room and raised the curtain. He was trembling.

It was still almost dark, and whatever was happening was taking place at the back of Linton House, so that he could not see it. But as he listened to the regularly repeated sound, he had no doubt of its nature. Somebody was digging out there. The sound of the spade digging earth had entered his dream, and there was an occasional clink when it struck a stone. Why would somebody be digging at this time in the morning? He remembered that terrible cry on the previous night, the cry he had thought to be a dream. Supposing it had been real, who had cried out?

The digging stopped and two people spoke, although he could not hear the words or even the tones. One, light and high in pitch, was no doubt Sylvia's, but was the other voice Wallington's? And if it was, had Jimmy Purchase gone away at all?

In the half light a man and woman were briefly visible before they passed into the house. The man carried a spade, but his head was down and Bertie could not see his face, only his square bulky figure. He had little doubt that the man was Wallington.

That morning he went up to London. He had visited the city rarely since his retirement, finding that on each visit he was more worried and confused. The place seemed continually to change, so that what had been a landmark of some interest was now a kebab or hamburger restaurant. The article had appeared in the *Banner*, and their offices had moved from Fleet Street to somewhere off the Gray's Inn Road. He asked for Arnold Grayson, a deputy editor he had known slightly, to be told that Grayson had moved to another paper. He had to wait almost an hour before he was able to talk to Derek Holmes. The crime reporter remained staring at his desk while he listened to Bertie's story. During the telling of it Holmes chewed gum and said "Yup" occasionally.

"Yup," he said again at the end. "Okay, Mr. Mays. Thanks."

"What are you going to do about it?"

Holmes removed his gum and considered the question. "Know how many people been in touch about that piece, saying they've seen the robbers, their landlord's one of them, they heard two South Africans talking in a bus about how the loot should be split, et cetera? One hundred and eleven. Half of 'em are sensationalists, the other half plain crazy."

"But this is different."

"They're all different. I shouldn'ta seen you only you mentioned Arnie, and he was a good friend. But what's it amount to? Husband and wife having a shindig, husband goes off, South African cousin's digging a flowerbed—"

"At that time in the morning?"

The reporter shrugged. "People are funny."

"Have you got pictures of the South Africans you say are involved in the robberies? If I could recognize Wallington—"

Holmes put another piece of gum in his mouth, chewed on it meditatively, then produced half a dozen photographs. None of them resembled Wallington. Holmes shuffled the pictures together and put them away. "That's it then."

"But aren't you going to come down and look into it? I tell you I believe murder has been done. Wallington is her lover. Together they have killed Purchase."

"If Wallington's lying low with his share of the loot, the last thing he'd do is get involved in this sort of caper. You know your trouble, Mr. Mays? You've got an overheated imagination."

If only he knew somebody at Scotland Yard! But there was no reason to think that they would take him any more seriously than the newspaperman had. He returned feeling both chastened and frustrated. To his surprise Sylvia got out of another carriage on the train. She greeted him cheerfully.

"Hallo, Bertie. I've just been seeing Alf off."

"Seeing Alf off?" he echoed stupidly.

"Back to South Africa. He had a letter saying they needed him back there."

"Back in Durban?"

"That's right."

"Jimmy said he was from the Cape."

"Did he? Jimmy often gets things wrong."

It was not in Bertie's nature to be anything but gallant to a lady, even one he suspected of being a partner in murder. "Now that you are a grass widow again, you must come in and have a dish of tea."

"That would be lovely."

"Tomorrow?"

"It's a date."

They had reached his cottage. She pressed two fingers to her lips, touched his cheek with them. Inside the cottage the telephone was ringing. It was Holmes.

"Mr. Mays? Thought you'd like to know. Your chum Purchase is just what he said, a freelance journalist. One or two of the boys knew him. Not too successful from what I hear."

"So you did pay some attention to what I told you!"

"Always try and check a story out. Nothing to this one, far as I can see."

"Wallington has gone back to South Africa. Suddenly, just like that."

"Has he now? Good luck to him."

Triumph was succeeded by indignation. He put down the telephone without saying good-bye.

Was it all the product of an overheated imagination? He made scones for Sylvia's visit next day and served them with his home-made blackcurrant preserve. Then he put the question that still worried him. He would have liked to introduce it delicately, but somehow didn't manage that.

"What was all that digging in the garden early the other morning?"

Sylvia looked startled, and then exclaimed as a fragment of the scone she was eating dropped onto her dress. When it had been removed she said, "Sorry you were disturbed. It was Timmy."

"Timmy?"

"Our tabby. He must have eaten something poisoned and he died. Poor Timmy. Alf dug a grave and we gave him Christian burial." With hardly a pause she went on, "We're clearing out at the end of the week."

"Leaving?" For a moment he could hardly believe it.

"Right. I'm a London girl at heart, you know, always was. The idea of coming here was that Jimmy would be able to do some writing of his own, but that never seemed to work out—he was always being called away. If I'm in London I can get a job, earn some money. Very necessary at the moment. If Alf hadn't helped out, I don't know what we'd have done. It was a crazy idea coming down here, but then we're crazy people."

And at the end of that week Sylvia went. Since the house had been rented furnished, she had only suitcases to take away. She came to say good-bye. There was no sign of Jimmy, and Bertie asked about him.

"Still up on that job. But anyway he wouldn't have wanted to come down and help, he hates things like that. Good-bye, Bertie, we'll meet again I expect." A quick kiss on the cheek and she was driving off in her rented car.

She departed leaving all sorts of questions unanswered when Bertie came to think about it, mundane ones like an address if anybody should want to get in touch with her or with Jimmy, and things he would have liked to know, such as the reason for digging the cat's grave at such an extraordinary hour. He found himself more and more suspicious of the tale she had told. The row he had overheard could perhaps be explained by lack of money, but it seemed remarkable that Jimmy Purchase had not come back.

Linton House was locked up and empty, but it was easy enough to get into the garden. The area dug up was just inside the boundary fence. It was difficult to see how much had been dug because there was a patch of earth at each side, but it looked like a large area to bury a cat.

On impulse one day, a week after Sylvia had gone, Bertie took a spade into the garden and began to dig. It proved to be quite hard work, and he went down two feet before reaching the body. It was that of a cat, one he vaguely remembered seeing in the house, but Sylvia's story of its death had been untrue. Its head was mangled, shattered by one or two heavy blows.

Bertie looked at the cat with distaste—he did not care for seeing dead things—returned it, and had just finished shoveling back the earth when he was hailed from the road. He turned, and with a sinking heart saw the local constable, P.C. Harris, standing beside his bicycle.

"Ah, it's you, Mr. Mays. I was thinking it might be somebody with burglarious intent. Somebody maybe was going to dig a tunnel to get entrance into the house. But perhaps it was your *own* house you was locked out of."

P. C. Harris was well known as a local wag, and nobody laughed more loudly at his own jokes. He laughed heartily now. Bertie joined in feebly.

"But what *was* you doing digging in the next-door garden, may I ask?"

What could he say? I was digging for a man, but only found a cat? Desperately Bertie said, "I'd—ah—-lost something and thought it might have got in here. I was just turning the earth."

The constable shook his head. "You was trespassing, Mr. Mays. This is not your property."

"No, of course not. It won't happen again. I'd be glad if you could forget it." He approached the constable, a pound note in his hand.

"No need for that, sir, which might be construed as a bribe and hence an offense in itself. I shall not be reporting the matter on this occasion, nor inquiring further into the whys and wherefores, but would strongly advise you in future to keep within the bounds of your own property."

Pompous old fool, Bertie thought, but said that of course he would do just that. He scrambled back into his own garden, aware that he made a slightly ludicrous figure. P.C. Harris, in a stately manner, mounted his bicycle and rode away.

That was almost, but not quite, the end of the story.

Linton House was empty for a few weeks and then rented again, to a family called Hobson who had two noisy children. Bertie had as little to do with them as possible. He was very conscious of having been made to look a fool, and there was nothing he disliked more than that. He was also aware of a disinclination in himself to enter Linton House again.

In the late spring of the following year he went to Sardinia for a holiday, driving around on his own, looking at the curious nuraghi and the burial places made from gigantic blocks of stone which are called the tombs of the giants. He drove up the western coast in a leisurely way, spending long mornings and afternoons over lunches and dinners in the small towns, and then moving inland to bandit country. He was sitting nursing a drink in a square at Nuoro, which is the capital of the central province, when he heard his name called.

It was Sylvia, so brown that he hardly recognized her. "Bertie, what are you doing here?"

He said that he was on holiday, and returned the question.

"Just come down to shop. We have a house up in the hills—you must come and see it. Darling, look who's here."

A bronzed Jimmy Purchase approached across the square. Like Sylvia he seemed in fine spirits, and endorsed enthusiastically the suggestion that Bertie should come out to their house. It was a few miles from the city on the slopes of Mount Ortobene, a long low white modern house at the end of a rough road. They sat in a courtyard and ate grilled fish, and drank a hard dry local white wine.

Bertie felt his natural curiosity rising. How could he ask questions without appearing to be—well—nosy? Over coffee he said that he supposed Jimmy was out here on an assignment.

It was Sylvia who answered. "Oh, no, he's given all that up since the book was published."

"The book?"

"Show him, Jimmy." Jimmy went into the house. He returned with a book which said on the cover *My Tempestuous Life. As told by Anita Sorana to Jimmy Purchase.*

"You've heard of her?"

It would have been difficult not to have heard of Anita Sorana. She was a screen actress famous equally for her temperament, her five well-publicized marriages, and the variety of her love affairs.

"It was fantastic luck when she agreed that Jimmy should write her autobiography. It was all very hush-hush and we had to pretend that he was off on assignments when he was really with Anita."

Jimmy took it up. "Then she'd break appointments, say she wasn't in the mood to talk. A few days afterwards she'd ask to see me at a minute's notice. Then Sylvia started to play up—"

"I thought he was having an affair with her. She certainly fancied him. He swears he wasn't, but I don't know. Anyway, it was worth it." She yawned.

"The book was a success?"

Jimmy grinned, teeth very white in his brown face. "I'll say. Enough for me to shake off the dust of Fleet Street."

So the quarrel was explained, and Jimmy's sudden absences, and his failure to return. After a glass of some fiery local liqueur Bertie felt soporific, conscious that he had drunk a little more than usual. There was some other question he wanted to ask, but he did not remember it until they were driving him down the mountain, back to his hotel in Nuoro.

"How is your cousin?"

Jimmy was driving. "Cousin?"

"Mr. Wallington, Sylvia's cousin from South Africa."

Sylvia, from the back of the car, said, "Alf's dead."

"Dead!"

"In a car accident. Soon after he got back to South Africa. Wasn't it sad?"

Very few more words were spoken before they reached the hotel and said good-bye. The heat of the hotel room and the wine he had drunk made Bertie fall asleep at once. After a couple of hours he woke, sweating, and wondered if he believed what he had been told. Was it possible to make enough money from "ghosting" (he had heard that was the word) a life story to retire to Sardinia? It seemed unlikely. He lay on his back in the dark room, and it seemed to him that he saw with terrible clarity what had happened.

Wallington was one of the Small Bank Robbers, and he had come to the Purchases looking for a safe place to stay. He had his money, what Holmes had called the loot, with him, and they had decided to kill him for it. The quarrel had been about when Wallington would be killed, the sound that wakened him in the night had been Wallington's death cry.

Jimmy had merely pretended to go away that night, and had returned to help Sylvia dispose of the body. Jimmy dug the grave and they put Wallington in it. Then the cat had been killed and put into a shallow grave on top of the body. It was the killing of the cat, those savage blows on its head, that somehow horrified Bertie most.

He cut short his holiday and took the next plane back. At home he walked round to the place where he had dug up the cat. The Hobsons had put in bedding plants, and the wallflowers were flourishing. He had read somewhere that flowers always flourished over a grave.

"Not thinking of trespassing again, I hope, Mr. Mays?"

It was P.C. Harris, red-faced and jovial.

Bertie shook his head. What he had imagined in the hotel room might be true, but then again it might not. Supposing that he went to the police, supposing he was able to convince them that there was something in his story, supposing they dug up the flowerbed and found nothing but the cat? He would be the laughingstock of the neighborhood.

Bertie Mays knew that he would say nothing.

"I reckon you was feeling a little bit eccentric that night you was doing the digging," P.C. Harris said sagely.

"Yes, I think I must have been."

"They make a fine show, them wallflowers. Makes you more cheerful, seeing spring flowers."

"Yes," said Bertie Mays meekly. "They make a fine show."

PATRICIA HIGHSMITH

A true original, Patricia Highsmith (1921–1995) is crime writing's poet of the aberrant. In her work, she does not stop at merely getting under the skins of her disturbed characters; she seems to inhabit their psyches. She seems so fully conversant with the twisted thinking of people who live outside of the social contract that she is able to demonstrate how such characters see their own behavior as utterly normal.

Born Mary Patricia Plaughman in Fort Worth, Texas, Highsmith later used her middle name and her stepfather's last name. She lived much of her adult life in Europe, where her dark and uneasy fiction was, at first, more highly regarded than it was in her native country. Under the pseudonym Clare Morgan, Highsmith wrote an early novel, *The Price of Salt* (1952), about a lesbian relationship. It was later published as *Carol* under the Highsmith name. Chafing under categorization as a genre writer, she continued to turn out mainstream novels throughout her career, including the 1983 novel *People Who Knock on the Door*, which deals with fundamentalist religion and its impact on a family living in the American Midwest.

Highsmith's first crime novel, *Strangers on a Train*, was published in 1950 and later made into the classic Alfred Hitchcock film of the same title. That first book sets some patterns that appear in her later work, especially the intimate linking of characters in life and in death after a chance meeting. In this work, as in others—especially *The Talented Mr. Ripley* and other "Ripley" books—an enigmatic and charismatic character enters the lives of others, with deadly results. His lack of moral conscience and disregard for the bounds of normal behavior is all the more shocking for the author's straightforward depiction of his behavior, and his movement toward tragedy seems as inevitable as the progress of a Greek tragedy.

While some of Highsmith's characters exude charisma and charm, others are unattractive loners, losers, and Caspar Milquetoast types who seem bound for disaster from the minute they are introduced. Clive Wilkes is just such an oddball. In "Woodrow Wilson's Necktie," he is introduced as a courier who sneaks out of work on an average of twice a week to view the grim scenes of famous murders that are on display in a wax museum. Wilkes is an adult who still lives at home with his mother, and who seems to have no social interaction with people of his own or any other age. In this chilling story, Wilkes makes the passage from petty thievery to mass murder with hardly a blink of the eye. In fact, he sees his efforts as worthy of laughter.

Jeffery Deaver said of this story, "It's classic Highsmith, featuring her typical understated style, endearing cynicism and black humor. I don't know any other authors who use darkness to such wonderful effect."

Woodrow Wilson's Necktie

THE façade of MADAME THIBUALT'S WAXWORK HORRORS glittered and throbbed with red and yellow lights, even in the daytime. Knobs of golden balls—the yellow lights—pulsated amid the red lights, attracting the eye and holding it.

Clive Wilkes loved the place, the inside and the outside equally. Since he was a delivery boy for a grocery store, it was easy for him to say that a certain delivery had taken him longer than had been expected—he'd had to wait for Mrs. So-and-so to get home because the doorman had told him she was due back any minute, or he'd had to go five blocks to find some change because Mrs. Smith had had only a twenty-dollar bill. At these spare moments—and Clive managed one or two a week—he visited MADAME THIBAULT'S WAXWORK HORRORS.

Inside the establishment you went through a dark passage—to be put in the mood—and then you were confronted by a bloody murder scene on the left: a girl with long blond hair was sticking a knife into the neck of an old man who sat at a kitchen table eating his dinner. His dinner consisted of two wax frankfurters and wax sauerkraut. Then came the Lindbergh kidnapping scene, with Hauptmann climbing down a ladder outside a nursery window; you could see the top of the ladder out the window, and the top half of Hauptmann's figure, clutching the little boy. Also there was Marat in his bath with Charlotte nearby. And Christie with his stocking, throttling a woman.

Clive loved every tableau, and they never became stale. But he didn't look at them with the solemn, vaguely startled expression of the other people who looked at them. Clive was inclined to smile, even to laugh. They were amusing. So why not laugh?

Farther on in the museum were the torture chambers—one old, one modern, purporting to show Twentieth Century torture methods in Nazi Germany and in French Algeria. Madame Thibault—who Clive strongly suspected did not exist—kept up to date. There were the Kennedy assassination and the Tate massacre, of course, and some murder that had happened only a month ago somewhere.

Clive's first definite ambition in regard to MADAME THIBAULT'S WAXWORK HORRORS museum was to spend a night there. This he did one night, providently taking along a cheese sandwich in his pocket. It was fairly easy to accomplish. Clive knew that three people worked in the museum proper—down in the bowels, as he thought of it, though the museum was on street level—while a fourth, a plumpish middle-aged man in a nautical cap, sold tickets at a booth in front. The three who worked in the bowels were two men and a woman; the woman, also plump and with curly brown hair and glasses and about 40, took the tickets at the end of the dark corridor, where the museum proper began.

One of the inside men lectured constantly, though not more than half the people ever bothered to listen. "Here we see the fanatical expression of the true murderer, captured by the supreme wax artistry of Madame Thibault"—and so on. The other inside man had black hair and black-rimmed glasses like the woman, and he just drifted around, shooing away kids who wanted to climb into the tableaux, maybe watching for pickpockets, or maybe protecting women from unpleasant assaults in the semidarkness. Clive didn't know.

He only knew it was quite easy to slip into one of the dark corners or into a nook next to one of the Iron Molls—maybe even into one of the Iron Molls; but slender as he was, the spikes might poke into him, Clive thought, so he ruled out this idea. He had observed that people were gently urged out around 9:15 P.M., as the museum closed at 9:30 P.M. And lingering as late as possible one evening, Clive had learned that there was a sort of cloakroom for the staff behind a door in one back corner, from which direction he had also heard the sound of a toilet flushing.

So one night in November, Clive concealed himself in the shadows, which were abundant, and listened to the three people as they got ready to leave. The woman—whose name turned out to be Mildred—was lingering to take the money box from Fred, the ticket seller, and to count it and deposit it somewhere in the cloakroom. Clive was not interested in the money. He was interested only in spending a night in the place and being able to boast he had.

"Night, Mildred—see you tomorrow," called one of the men.

"Anything else to do? I'm leaving now," said Mildred. "Boy, am I tired! But I'm still going to watch Dragon Man tonight."

"Dragon Man," the other man repeated, uninterested.

Evidently the ticket seller, Fred, left from the front of the building after handing in the money box, and in fact Clive recalled seeing him close up the front once, cutting the lights from inside the entrance door, then locking the door and barring it on the outside.

Clive stood in a nook by an Iron Moll. When he heard the back door shut and the key turn in the lock, he waited for a moment in delicious silence, aloneness, and suspense, and then ventured out. He went first, on tiptoe, to the room where they kept their coats, because he had never seen it. He had brought matches—also cigarettes, though smoking was not allowed, according to several signs—and with the aid of a match he found the light switch. The room contained an old desk, four metal lockers, a tin wastebasket, an umbrella stand, and some books in a bookcase against a grimy wall that had once been white. Clive slid open a drawer and found the well-worn wooden box which he had once seen the ticket seller carrying in through the front door. The box was locked. He could walk out with the box, Clive thought, but he didn't care to, and he considered this rather decent of himself. He gave the box a wipe with the side of his hand, not forgetting the bottom where his fingertips had touched. That was funny, he thought, wiping something he wasn't going to steal.

Clive set about enjoying the night. He found the lights and put them on so that the booths with the gory tableaux were all illuminated. He was hungry, took one bite of his sandwich, then put it back in the paper napkin in his pocket. He sauntered slowly past the John F. Kennedy assassination—Mrs. Kennedy and the doctors bending anxiously over the white table on which JFK lay. This time, Hauptmann's descent of the ladder made Clive giggle. Charles Lindbergh, Jr.'s face looked so untroubled that one would think he might be sitting on the floor of his nursery, playing with blocks.

Clive swung a leg over a metal bar and climbed into the Judd-Snyder tableau. It gave him a thrill to be standing right *with* them, inches from the throttling-from-behind which the lover of the woman was administering to the husband. Clive put a hand out and touched the red-paint blood that was seeming to come from the man's throat where the cord pressed deep. Clive also touched the cool cheekbones of the victim. The popping eyes were of glass, vaguely disgusting, and Clive did not touch those.

Two hours later he was singing church hymns, *Nearer My God to Thee* and *Jesus Wants Me for a Sunbeam.* Clive didn't know all the words. And he smoked.

By two in the morning he was bored and tried to get out by both the front door and back, but couldn't—both were barred on the outside. He had thought of having a hamburger at an all-night diner between here and home. However, his enforced incarceration didn't bother him, so he finished the now-dry cheese sandwich and slept for a bit on three straight chairs which he arranged in a row. It was so uncomfortable that he knew he'd wake up in a while, which he did—at 5 A.M. He washed his face, then went for another look at the wax exhibits. This time he took a souvenir—Woodrow Wilson's necktie.

As the hour of 9:00 approached—MADAME THIBAULT'S WAXWORK HORRORS opened at 9:30 A.M.—Clive hid himself in an excellent spot, behind one of the tableaux whose backdrop was a black-and-gold Chinese screen. In front of the screen was a bed and in the bed lay a wax man with a handlebar mustache, who was supposed to have been poisoned by his wife.

The public began to trickle in shortly after 9:30 A.M., and the taller, more solemn man began to mumble his boring lecture. Clive had to wait till a few minutes past ten before he felt safe enough to mingle with the crowd and make his exit, with Woodrow Wilson's necktie rolled up in his pocket. He was a bit tired, but happy—though on second thought, who would he tell about it? Joey Vrasky, that dumb cluck who worked behind the counter at Simmons' Grocery? Hah! Why bother? Joey didn't deserve a good story. Clive was half an hour late for work.

"I'm sorry, Mr. Simmons, I overslept," Clive said hastily, but he thought quite politely, as he came into the store. There was a delivery job awaiting him. Clive took his bicycle and put the carton on a platform in front of the handlebars.

Clive lived with his mother, a thin highly strung woman who was a sales-woman in a shop that sold stockings, girdles, and underwear. Her husband had left her when Clive was nine. She had no other children. Clive had quit high school a year before graduation, to his mother's regret, and for a year he had done nothing but lie around the house or stand on street corners with his pals. But Clive had never been very chummy with any of them, for which his mother was thankful, as she considered them a worthless lot. Clive had had the delivery job at Simmons' for nearly a year now, and his mother felt that he was settling down.

When Clive came home that evening at 6:30 P.M. he had a story ready for his mother. Last night he had run into his old friend Richie, who was in the Army and home on leave, and they had sat up at Richie's house talking so late that Richie's parents had invited him to stay over, and Clive had slept on the couch. His mother accepted this explanation. She made a supper of baked beans, bacon, and eggs.

There was really no one to whom Clive felt like telling his exploit of the night. He couldn't have borne someone looking at him and saying, "Yeah? So what?" because what he had done had taken a bit of planning, even a little daring. He put Woodrow Wilson's tie among his others that hung over a string on the inside of his closet door. It was a gray silk tie, conservative and expensive-looking. Several times that day Clive imagined one of the two men in the museum, or maybe the woman named Mildred, glancing at Woodrow Wilson and exclaiming, "Hey! What happened to Woodrow Wilson's tie, I wonder?"

Each time Clive thought of this he had to duck his head to hide a smile.

After twenty-four hours, however, the exploit had begun to lose its charm and excitement. Clive's excitement only rose again—and it could rise two or three times a day—whenever he cycled past the twinkling façade of MADAME THIBAULT'S WAXWORK HORRORS. His heart would give a leap, his blood would run a little faster, and he would think of all the motionless murders going on in there, and all the stupid faces of Mr. and Mrs. Johnny Q. Public gaping at them. But Clive didn't even buy another ticket—price 65 cents—to go in and look at Woodrow Wilson and see that his tie was missing and his collar button showing—his work.

Clive did get another idea one afternoon, a hilarious idea that would make the public sit up and take notice. Clive's ribs trembled with suppressed laughter as he pedaled toward Simmons', having just delivered a bag of groceries.

When should he do it? Tonight? No, best to take a day or so to plan it. It would take brains. And silence. And sure movements—all the things Clive admired.

He spent two days thinking about it. He went to his local snack bar and drank beer and played the pinball machines with his pals. The pinball machines had pulsating lights too—*More Than One Can Play* and *It's More Fun To Compete*—but Clive thought only of MADAME THIBAULT'S as he stared at the rolling, bouncing balls that mounted a score he cared nothing about. It was the same when he looked at the rainbow-colored jukebox whose blues, reds, and yellows undulated, and when he went over to drop a coin in it. He was thinking of what he was going to do in MADAME THIBAULT'S WAXWORK HORRORS.

On the second night, after a supper with his mother, Clive went to MADAME THIBAULT'S and bought a ticket. The old guy who sold tickets barely looked at people, he was so busy making change and tearing off the stubs, which was just as well. Clive went in at 9:00 P.M.

He looked at the tableaux, though they were not so fascinating to him tonight as they had been before. Woodrow Wilson's tie was still missing, as if no one had noticed it, and Clive chuckled over this. He remembered that the solemn-faced pickpocket-watcher—the drifting snoop—had been the last to leave the night Clive had stayed, so Clive assumed he had the keys, and therefore he ought to be the last to be killed.

The woman was the first. Clive hid himself beside one of the Iron Molls again, while the crowd ambled out, and when Mildred walked by him, in her hat and coat, to leave by the back door, having just said something to one of the men in the exhibition hall, Clive stepped out and wrapped an arm around her throat from behind.

She made only a small *ur-rk* sound.

Clive squeezed her throat with his hands, stopping her voice. At last she slumped, and Clive dragged her into a dark, recessed corner to the left of the cloakroom. He knocked an empty cardboard box of some kind over, but it didn't make enough noise to attract the attention of the two men.

"Mildred's gone?" one of the men asked.

"I think she's in the office."

"No, she's not." The owner of this voice had already gone into the corridor where Clive crouched over Mildred and had looked into the empty cloakroom where the light was still on. "She's left. Well, I'm calling it a day too."

Clive stepped out then and encircled this man's neck in the same manner. The job was more difficult, because the man struggled, but Clive's arm was thin and strong; he acted with swiftness and knocked the man's head against the wooden floor.

"What's going on?" The thump had brought the second man.

This time Clive tried a punch to the man's jaw, but missed and hit his neck. However, this so stunned the man—the little solemn fellow, the snoop—that a quick second blow was easy, and then Clive was able to take him by the shirtfront and bash his head against the plaster wall which was harder than the wooden floor. Then Clive made sure that all three were dead. The two men's heads were bloody. The woman was bleeding slightly from her mouth. Clive reached for the keys in the second man's pockets. They were in his left trousers pocket and with them was a penknife. Clive also took the knife.

Then the taller man moved slightly. Alarmed, Clive opened the pearl-handled penknife and plunged it into the man's throat three times.

Close call, Clive thought, as he checked again to make sure they were all dead. They most certainly were, and that was most certainly real blood, not the red paint of MADAME THIBAULT'S WAXWORK HORRORS. Clive switched on the lights for the tableaux and went into the exhibition hall for the interesting task of choosing exactly the right places for the three corpses.

The woman belonged in Marat's bath—not much doubt about that. Clive debated removing her clothing, but decided against it, simply because she would look much funnier sitting in a bath wearing a fur-trimmed coat and hat. The figure of Marat sent him off into laughter. He'd expected sticks for legs, and nothing between the legs, because you couldn't see any more of Marat than from the middle of his torso up; but Marat had no legs at all and his wax body ended just below the waist in a fat stump which was planted on a wooden platform so that it would not topple. This crazy waxwork Clive carried into the cloakroom and placed squarely in the middle of the desk. He then carried the woman—who weighed a good deal—onto the Marat scene and put her in the bath. Her hat fell off, and he pushed it on again, a bit over one eye. Her bloody mouth hung open.

Good lord, it *was* funny!

Now for the men. Obviously, the one whose throat he had knifed would look good in the place of the old man who was eating wax franks and sauerkraut, because the girl behind him was supposed to be stabbing him in the throat. This took Clive some fifteen minutes. Since the figure of the old man was in a seated position, Clive put him on the toilet off the cloakroom. It was terribly amusing to see the old man seated on the toilet, throat apparently bleeding, a knife in one hand and a fork in the other. Clive lurched against the door jamb, laughing loudly, not even caring if someone heard him, because it was so comical it was even worth getting caught for.

Next, the little snoop. Clive looked around him and his eye fell on the Woodrow Wilson scene which depicted the signing of the armistice in 1918. A wax figure sat at a huge desk signing something, and that was the logical place for a man whose head was almost split open. With some difficulty Clive got the pen out of the wax man's fingers, laid it to one side on the desk, and carried the figure—it didn't weigh much—into the cloakroom, where Clive seated him at the desk, rigid arms in an attitude of writing. Clive stuck a ballpoint pen into his right hand. Now for the last heave. Clive saw that his jacket was now quite spotted with blood and he would have to get rid of it, but so far there was no blood on his trousers.

Clive dragged the second man to the Woodrow Wilson tableau, lifted him up, and rolled him toward the desk. He got him onto the chair, but the head toppled forward onto the green-blottered desk, onto the blank wax pages, and the pen barely stood upright in the limp hand.

But it was done. Clive stood back and smiled. Then he listened. He sat down on a straight chair and rested for a few minutes, because his heart was beating fast and he suddenly realized that every muscle in his body was tired. Ah, well, he now had the keys. He could lock up, go home, and have a good night's rest, because he wanted to be ready to enjoy tomorrow.

Clive took a sweater from one of the male figures in a log-cabin tableau of some kind. He had to pull the sweater down over the feet of the waxwork to get it off, because the arms would not bend; it stretched the neck of the sweater, but he couldn't help that. Now the wax figure had a sort of bib for a shirtfront, and naked arms and chest.

Clive wadded up his jacket and went everywhere with it, erasing finger-prints from whatever he thought he had touched. He turned the lights off, made his way carefully to the back door, locked and barred it behind him, and would have left the keys in a mailbox if there had been one; but there wasn't, so he dropped the keys on the rear doorstep. In a wire rubbish basket he found some newspapers; he wrapped up his jacket in them and walked on with it until he found another wire rubbish basket, where he forced the bundle down among candy wrappers, beer cans, and other trash.

"A new sweater?" his mother asked that night.

"Richie gave it to me—for luck."

Clive slept like the dead, too tired even to laugh again at the memory of the old man sitting on the toilet.

The next morning Clive was standing across the street when the ticket seller arrived just before 9:30 A.M. By 9:35 A.M. only four people had gone in; but Clive could not wait any longer, so he crossed the street and bought a ticket. Now the ticket seller was doubling as ticket taker, and telling people, "Just go on in. Everybody's late this morning."

The ticket man stepped inside the door to put on some lights, then walked all the way into the place to put on the display lights for the tableaux, which worked from switches in the hall that led to the cloakroom. And the funny thing, to Clive who was walking behind him, was that the ticket man didn't notice anything odd, didn't even notice Mildred in her hat and coat sitting in Marat's bathtub.

The other customers so far were a man and a woman, a boy of fourteen or so in sneakers, alone apparently, and a single man. They looked expressionlessly at Mildred in the tub as if they thought it quite "normal," which would have sent Clive into paroxysms of mirth, except that his heart was thumping madly and he could hardly breathe for the suspense. Also, the man with his face in franks and sauerkraut brought no surprise either. Clive was a bit disappointed.

Two more people came in, a man and a woman.

Then at last, in front of the Woodrow Wilson tableau, there was a reaction. One of the women, clinging to her husband's arm, asked, "Was someone shot when the armistice was signed?"

"I don't know. I don't *think* so," the man replied vaguely.

Clive's laughter pressed like an explosion in his chest; he spun on his heel to control himself, and he had the feeling he knew *all* about history, and that no one else did. By now, of course, the real blood had turned to a rust color. The green blotter was now splotched, and blood had dripped down the side of the desk.

A woman on the other side of the room, where Mildred was, let out a scream. A man laughed, but only briefly.

Suddenly everything happened. A woman shrieked, and at the same time a man yelled, "My God, it's *real!*"

Clive saw a man climbing up to investigate the corpse with his face in the frankfurters.

"The blood's *real!* It's a *dead* man!"

Another man—one of the public—slumped to the floor. He had fainted.

The ticket seller came bustling in. "What's the trouble here?"

"Coupla corpses—*real* ones!"

Now the ticket seller looked at Marat's bathtub and fairly jumped into the air with surprise. "Holy Christmas! *Holy* cripes!—it's *Mildred!*"

"And this one!"

"And the one here!"

"My God, got to—got to call the police!" said the ticket seller.

One man and woman left hurriedly. But the rest lingered, shocked, fascinated.

The ticket seller had run into the cloakroom, where the telephone was, and Clive heard him yell something. He'd seen the man at the desk, of course, the wax man, and the half body of Marat on the desk.

Clive thought it was time to drift out, so he did, sidling his way through a group of people peering in the front door, perhaps intending to come in because there was no ticket seller.

That was good, Clive thought. That was all right. Not bad. Not bad at all.

He had not intended to go to work that day, but suddenly he thought it wiser to check in and ask for the day off. Mr. Simmons was of course as sour as ever when Clive said he was not feeling well, but as Clive held his stomach and appeared weak, there was little old Simmons could do. Clive left the grocery. He had brought with him all his ready cash, about $23.

Clive wanted to take a long bus ride somewhere. He realized that suspicion might fall on him, if the ticket seller remembered his coming to MADAME THIBAULT'S often, or especially if he remembered Clive being there last night; but this really had little to do with his desire to take a bus ride. His longing for a bus ride was simply, somehow, irresistible. He bought a ticket westward for $8 and change, one way. This brought him, by about 7:00 P.M., to a good-sized town in Indiana, whose name Clive paid no attention to.

The bus spilled a few passengers, Clive included, at a terminal, where there was a cafeteria and a bar. By now Clive was curious about the newspapers, so he went to the newsstand near the street door of the cafeteria. And there were the headlines:

Triple Murder in Waxworks

Mass Murder in Museum

Mystery Killer Strikes: Three Dead in Waxworks

Clive liked the last one best. He bought the three newspapers, and stood at the bar with a beer.

"This morning at 9:30 A.M., ticket man Fred J. Carmody and several of the public who had come to see Madame Thibault's Waxwork Horrors, a noted attraction of this city, were confronted by three genuine corpses among the displays. They were the bodies of Mrs. Mildred Veery, 41; George P. Hartley, 43; and Richard K. McFadden, 37, all employed at the waxworks museum. The two men were killed by concussion and stabbing, and the woman by strangulation. Police are searching for clues on the premises. The murders are believed to have taken place shortly before 10:00 P.M. last evening, when the three employees were about to leave the museum. The murderer or murderers may have been among the last patrons of the museum before closing time at 9:30 P.M. It is thought that he or they may have concealed themselves somewhere in the museum until the rest of the patrons had left. . . ."

Clive was pleased. He smiled as he sipped his beer. He hunched over the papers, as if he did not wish the rest of the world to share his pleasure, but this was not true. After a few minutes Clive stood up and looked to the right and left to see if anyone else among the men and women at the bar was also reading the story. Two men were reading newspapers, but Clive could not tell if they were reading about him, because their newspapers were folded.

Clive lit a cigarette and went through all three newspapers to see if any clue to him was mentioned. He found nothing. One paper said specifically that Fred J. Carmody had not noticed any person or persons entering the museum last evening who looked suspicious.

". . . Because of the bizarre arrangement of the victims and of the displaced wax figures in the exhibition, in whose places the victims were put, police are looking for a psychopathic killer. Residents of the area have been warned by radio and television to take special precautions on the streets and to keep their houses locked."

Clive chuckled over that one. Psychopathic killer! He was sorry about the lack of detail, the lack of humor in the three reporters' stories. They might have said something about the old guy sitting on the toilet. Or the fellow signing the armistice with the back of his head bashed in. Those were strokes of genius. Why didn't they appreciate them?

When he had finished his beer, Clive walked out onto the sidewalk. It was now dark and the streetlights were on. He enjoyed looking around in the new town, looking into shop windows. But he was aiming for a hamburger place, and he went into the first one he came to. It was a diner made up to look like a crack railway car.

Clive ordered a hamburger and a cup of coffee. Next to him were two Western-looking men in cowboy boots and rather soiled broad-brimmed hats. Was one a sheriff, Clive wondered? But they were talking, in a drawl, about acreage somewhere. Land. They were hunched over hamburgers and coffee, one so close that his elbow kept touching Clive's. Clive was reading his newspapers all over again and he had propped one against the napkin container in front of him.

One of the men asked for a napkin and disturbed Clive, but Clive smiled and said in a friendly way, "Did you read about the murders in the waxworks?"

The man looked blank for a moment, then said, "Yep, saw the headlines."

"Someone killed the three people who worked in the place. Look." There was a photograph in one of the papers, but Clive didn't much like it because it showed the corpses lined up on the floor. He would have preferred Mildred in the bathtub.

"Yeah," said the Westerner, edging away from Clive as if he didn't like him.

"The bodies were put into a few of the exhibits. Like the wax figures. They say that, but they don't show a picture of it," said Clive.

"Yeah," said the Westerner, and went on eating.

Clive felt let down and somehow insulted. His face grew a little warm as he stared back at his newspapers. In fact, anger was growing quickly inside him, making his heart go faster, as it always did when he passed MADAME THIBAULT'S WAXWORK HORRORS, though now the sensation was not at all pleasant.

Clive put on a smile, however, and turned to the man on his left again. "I mention it, because I did it. That's my work there." He gestured toward the picture of the corpses.

"Listen, boy," said the Westerner casually, "you just keep to yourself tonight. Okay? We ain't botherin' you, so don't you go botherin' us." He laughed a little, glancing at his companion.

His friend was staring at Clive, but looked away at once when Clive stared back.

This was a double rebuff, and quite enough for Clive. He got out his money and paid for his unfinished food with a dollar bill. He left the change and walked to the sliding-door exit.

"But y'know, maybe that guy ain't kiddin'," Clive heard one of the men say.

Clive turned and said, "I *ain't* kiddin'!" Then he went out into the night.

Clive slept at a Y.M.C.A. The next day he half-expected he would be picked up by a passing cop on the beat, but he wasn't. He got a lift to another town, nearer his hometown. The day's newspapers brought no mention of his name, and no mention of clues. In another café that evening, almost the identical conversation took place between Clive and a couple of fellows his own age. They didn't believe him. It was stupid of them, Clive thought, and he wondered if they were pretending? Or lying?

Clive hitched his way home and headed for the police station. He was curious as to what *they* would say. He imagined what his mother would say after he confessed. Probably the same thing she had said to her friends sometimes, or that she'd said to a policeman when he was sixteen and had stolen a car.

"Clive hasn't been the same since his father went away. I know he needs a man around the house, a man to look up to, imitate, you know. That's what people tell me. Since he was fourteen Clive's been asking me questions like, 'Who am I, anyway?' and 'Am I a person, mom?'" Clive could see and hear her in the police station.

"I have an important confession to make," Clive said to a deskman in the front.

The man's attitude was rude and suspicious, Clive thought, but he was told to walk to an office, where he spoke with a police officer who had gray hair and a fat face. Clive told his story.

"Where do you go to school, Clive?"

"I don't. I'm eighteen." Clive told him about his job at Simmons' Grocery.

"Clive, you've got troubles, but they're not the ones you're talking about," said the officer.

Clive had to wait in a room, and nearly an hour later a psychiatrist was brought in. Then his mother. Clive became more and more impatient. They didn't believe him. They were saying his was a typical case of false confession in order to draw attention to himself. His mother's repeated statements about his asking questions like "Am I a person?" and "Who am I?" only seemed to corroborate the opinions of the psychiatrist and the police.

Clive was to report somewhere twice a week for psychiatric therapy.

He fumed. He refused to go back to Simmons' Grocery, but found another delivery job, because he liked having a little money in his pocket, and he was fast on his bicycle and honest with the change.

"You haven't *found* the murderer, have you?" Clive said to the police psychiatrist. "You're all the biggest bunch of jackasses I've ever seen in my life!"

The psychiatrist said soothingly, "You'll never get anywhere talking to people like that, boy."

Clive said, "Some perfectly ordinary strangers in Indiana said, 'Maybe that guy ain't kidding.' They had more sense than *you!*"

The psychiatrist smiled.

Clive smoldered. One thing might have helped to prove his story—Woodrow Wilson's necktie, which still hung in his closet. But these dumb clucks damned well didn't deserve to see that tie. Even as he ate his suppers with his mother, went to the movies, and delivered groceries, he was planning. He'd do something more important next time—like starting a fire in the depths of a big building or planting a bomb somewhere or taking a machine gun up to some penthouse and letting 'em have it down on the street. Kill a hundred people at least, or a thousand. They'd have to come up in the building to get him. *Then* they'd know. *Then* they'd treat him like somebody who really existed, like somebody who deserved an exhibit of himself in MADAME THIBAULT'S WAXWORK HORRORS.

RUTH RENDELL

As the author of detective fiction featuring police inspector Reginald Wexford, and as the writer of psychologically astute crime novels penned under the pseudonym Barbara Vine, Ruth Rendell is among the most respected mystery writers living today. This prolific author is more notable for the growth of her characters than for improvement in her consistently superior writing.

Her Wexford series is as admired for puzzling plots and the well-realized portrait of the fictional village of Kingsmarkham as it is for psychological development of Wexford, his associates, and his family. Over the series, Rendell brings contemporary problems, such as racism and drug abuse, to Kingsmarkham. Often Wexford's solutions to crimes are reached thanks to his realizations about various characters' psyches. Such insights may parallel new understandings he has gleaned about himself or others connected to him, thus enriching the stories.

In non-Wexford work written under her own name and as Barbara Vine, the author also takes on flawed characters who suffer from problems ranging from suicide to illiteracy to anorexia. In these books and short stories, she makes psychological understanding even more central to the tension, crime, and resolution—if and when there is a resolution. In some of her non-Wexford work, Rendell dares to eschew the tidy solution. In this, and in a preoccupation with the workings of the disturbed mind, the author follows in the footsteps of Patricia Highsmith. However, Rendell's work is more likely than Highsmith's to make the reader reflect on the social ills that spur characters' problems. While one may wonder uncomfortably about how much Highsmith identifies with her aberrant characters, there is always a sense that Rendell is observing even her most out-of-control character from a position of control.

Rendell was born in London and educated in Essex, where she worked as a journalist for four years during the 1950s. Now a widow, she was married twice—to the same man—and she is the mother of one son. Her writing has garnered many top awards around the world. Like her friend and colleague P. D. James, she is a member of the House of Lords.

In the short story "Loopy," Rendell looks at what happens when a sheepish man literally puts on wolf's clothing. With typical finesse, Rendell makes excellent use of homely details to anchor in recognizable reality this story of bizarre behavior. Like Highsmith in "Woodrow Wilson's Necktie," Rendell writes from the point of view of a momma's boy who discovers a wild way to get relief from the unwelcome challenge of leading an adult life. The result may make your skin crawl.

Loopy

A T the end of the last performance, after the curtain calls, Red Riding Hood put me on a lead and with the rest of the company we went across to the pub. No one had taken makeup off or changed, there was no time for that before the George closed. I remember prancing across the road and growling at someone on a bicycle.

They loved me in the pub—well, some of them loved me. Quite a lot were embarrassed. The funny thing was that I should have been embarrassed myself if I had been one of them. I should have ignored *me* and drunk up my drink and left. Except that it is unlikely I would have been in a pub at all. Normally, I never went near such places. But inside the wolf skin it was very different, everything was different in there.

I prowled about for a while, sometimes on all-fours—though this isn't easy for us who are accustomed to the upright stance—sometimes loping, with my forepaws held close up to my chest. I went over to tables where people were sitting and snuffled my snout at their packets of crisps. If they were smoking I growled and waved my paws in air-clearing gestures. Lots of them were forthcoming, stroking me and making jokes or pretending terror at my red jaws and wicked little eyes. There was even one lady who took hold of my head and laid it in her lap.

Bounding up to the bar to collect my small dry sherry, I heard Bill Harkness (the First Woodcutter) say to Susan Hayes (Red Riding Hood's Mother): "Old Colin's really come out of his shell tonight."

And Susan, bless her, said, "He's a real actor, isn't he?"

I was one of the few members of our company who was. I expect this is always true in amateur dramatics. There are one or two real actors, people who could have made their livings on the stage if it wasn't so overcrowded a profession, and the rest who just come for the fun of it and the social side.

Did I ever consider the stage seriously? My father had been a civil servant, both my grandfathers in the ICS. As far back as I can remember it was taken for granted I should get my degree and go into the Civil Service. I never questioned it. If you have a mother like mine, one in a million, more a friend than a parent, you never feel the need to rebel. Besides, Mother gave me all the support I could have wished for in my acting. Acting as a hobby, that is. For instance, though the company made provision for hiring all the more complicated costumes for that year's Christmas pantomime, Mother made the wolf suit for me herself. It was ten times better than anything we could have hired. The head we had to buy, but the body and the limbs she made from a long-haired grey-fur fabric such as is manufactured for ladies' coats.

157

Moira used to say I enjoyed acting so much because it enabled me to lose myself and become, for a while, someone else. She said I disliked what I was and looked for ways of escape. A strange way to talk to the man you intend to marry! But before I approach the subject of Moira or, indeed, continue with this account, I should explain what its purpose is.

The psychiatrist attached to this place or who visits it (I'm not entirely clear which), one Dr. Vernon-Peak, has asked me to write down some of my feelings and impressions. That, I said, would only be possible in the context of a narrative. Very well, he said, he had no objection. What will become of it when finished I hardly know. Will it constitute a statement to be used in court? Or will it enter Dr. Vernon-Peak's files as another case history? It's all the same to me. I can only tell the truth.

After the George closed, then, we took off our makeup and changed and went our several ways home. Mother was waiting up for me. This was not invariably her habit. If I told her I should be late and to go to bed at her usual time she always did so. But I, quite naturally, was not averse to a welcome when I got home, particularly after a triumph like that one. Besides, I had been looking forward to telling her what an amusing time I'd had in the pub.

Our house is late-Victorian, double-fronted, of grey limestone, by no means beautiful, but a comfortable, well built place. My grandfather bought it when he retired and came home from India in 1920. Mother was ten at the time, so she has spent most of her life in that house.

Grandfather was quite a famous shot and used to go big-game hunting before that kind of thing became, and rightly so, very much frowned upon. The result was that the place was full of "trophies of the chase." While Grandfather was alive, and he lived to a great age, we had no choice but to put up with the antlers and tusks that sprouted everywhere out of the walls, the elephant's-foot umbrella stand, and the snarling maws of *tigris* and *ursa*. We had to grin and bear it, as Mother, who has a fine turn of wit, used to put it.

But when Grandfather was at last gathered to his ancestors, reverently and without the least disrespect to him, we took down all those heads and horns and packed them away in trunks. The fur rugs, however, we didn't disturb. These days they are worth a fortune and I always felt that the tiger skins scattered across the hall parquet, the snow leopard draped across the back of the sofa, and the bear into whose fur one could bury one's toes before the fire gave to the place a luxurious look. I took off my shoes and snuggled my toes in it that night.

Mother, of course, had been to see the show. She had come on the first night and seen me make my onslaught on Red Riding Hood, an attack so sudden and unexpected that the whole audience had jumped to its feet and gasped. (In our version we didn't have the wolf actually devour Red Riding Hood. Unanimously, we agreed this would hardly have been the thing at Christmas.) Mother, however, wanted to see me wearing her creation once more, so I put it on and did some prancing and growling for her benefit. Again I noticed how curiously uninhibited I became once inside the wolf skin. For instance, I bounded up to the snow leopard and began snarling at it. I boxed at its great grey-white face and made playful bites at its ears. Down on all fours I went and pounced on the bear, fighting it, actually forcing its neck within the space of my jaws.

How Mother laughed! She said it was as good as anything in the pantomime and a good deal better than anything they put on television.

"Animal crackers in my soup," she said, wiping her eyes. "There used to be a song that went like that in my youth. How did it go on? Something about lions and tigers loop the loop."

"Well, *lupus* means a wolf in Latin," I said.

"And you're certainly loopy! When you put that suit on again I shall have to say you're going all loopy again!"

When I put that suit on again? Did I intend to put it on again? I had not really thought about it. Yes, perhaps if I ever went to a fancy-dress party—a remote enough contingency. Yet what a shame it seemed to waste it, to pack it away like Grandfather's tusks and antlers after all the labor Mother had put into it. That night I hung it up in my wardrobe and I remember how strange I felt when I took it off that second time, more naked than I usually felt without my clothes, almost as if I had taken off my skin.

Life kept to the "even tenor" of its way. I felt a little flat with no rehearsals to attend and no lines to learn. Christmas came. Traditionally, Mother and I were alone on the Day itself, we would not have had it any other way, but on Boxing Day Moira arrived and Mother invited a couple of neighbors of ours in as well. At some stage, I seem to recall, Susan Hayes dropped in with her husband to wish us the compliments of the season.

Moira and I had been engaged for three years. We would have got married some time before, there was no question of our not being able to afford to marry, but a difficulty had arisen over where we should live. I think I may say in all fairness that the difficulty was entirely of Moira's making. No mother could have been more welcoming to a future daughter-in-law than mine. She actually wanted us to live with her at Simla House—she said we must think of it as our home and of her simply as our housekeeper. But Moira wanted us to buy a place of our own, so we had reached a deadlock, an impasse.

It was unfortunate that on that Boxing Day, after the others had gone, Moira brought the subject up again. Her brother (an estate agent) had told her of a bungalow for sale halfway between Simla House and her parents' home that was what he called "a real snip." Fortunately, I thought, Mother managed to turn the conversation by telling us about the bungalow she and her parents had lived in India, with its great collonaded veranda, its English flower garden, and its peepul tree. But Moira interrupted her.

"This is *our* future we're talking about, not your past. I thought Colin and I were getting married."

Mother was quite alarmed. "Aren't you? Surely Colin hasn't broken things off?"

"I suppose you don't consider the possibility *I* might break things off?"

Poor Mother couldn't help smiling at that. She smiled to cover her hurt. Moira could upset her very easily. For some reason this made Moira angry.

"I'm too old and unattractive to have any choice in the matter, is that what you mean?"

"Moira," I said.

She took no notice. "You may not realize it," she said, "but marrying me will be the making of Colin. It's what he needs to make a man of him."

It must have slipped out before Mother quite knew what she was saying. She patted Moira's knee. "I can quite see it may be a tough assignment, dear."

There was no quarrel. Mother would never have allowed herself to be drawn into that. But Moira became very huffy and said she wanted to go home, so I had to get the car out and take her.

All the way to her parents' house I had to listen to a catalogue of her wrongs at my hands and my mother's. By the time we parted I felt dispirited and nervous. I even wondered if I was doing the right thing, contemplating matrimony in the "sere and yellow leaf" of forty-two.

Mother had cleared the things away and gone to bed. I went into my bedroom and began undressing. Opening the wardrobe to hang up my tweed trousers, I caught sight of the wolf suit and on some impulse I put it on.

Once inside the wolf I felt calmer and, yes, happier. I sat down in an armchair but after a while I found it more comfortable to crouch, then lie stretched out on the floor. Lying there, basking in the warmth from the gas fire on my belly and paws, I found myself remembering tales of man's affinity with wolves, Romulus and Remus suckled by a she-wolf, the ancient myth of the werewolf, abandoned children reared by wolves even in these modern times. All this seemed to deflect my mind from the discord between Moira and my mother and I was able to go to bed reasonably happily and to sleep well.

Perhaps, then, it will not seem so very strange and wonderful that the next time I felt depressed I put the suit on again. Mother was out, so I was able to have the freedom of the whole house, not just of my room. It was dusk at four, but instead of putting the lights on I prowled about the house in the twilight, sometimes catching sight of my lean grey form in the many large mirrors Mother is so fond of. Because there was so little light and our house is crammed with bulky furniture and knickknacks, the reflection I saw looked not like a man disguised but like a real wolf that has somehow escaped and strayed into a cluttered Victorian room. Or a werewolf, that animal part of man's personality that detaches itself and wanders free while leaving behind the depleted human shape.

I crept up upon the teakwood carving of the antelope and devoured the little creature before it knew what had attacked it. I resumed my battle with the bear and we struggled in front of the fireplace, locked in a desperate hairy embrace. It was then that I heard Mother let herself in at the back door. Time had passed more quickly than I had thought. I escaped and whisked my hind paws and tail round the bend in the stairs just before she came into the hall.

Dr. Vernon-Peak seems to want to know why I began this at the age of forty-two, or rather why I had not done it before. I wish I knew. Of course, there is the simple solution that I didn't have a wolf skin before, but that is not the whole answer. Was it perhaps that until then I didn't know what my needs were, though partially I had satisfied them by playing the parts I was given in dramatic productions?

There is one other thing. I have told him that I recall, as a very young child, having a close relationship with some large animal, a dog perhaps or a pony, though a search conducted into family history by this same assiduous Vernon-Peak has yielded no evidence that we ever kept a pet. But more of this anon.

Be that as it may, once I had lived inside the wolf I felt the need to do so more and more. Erect on my hind legs, drawn up to my full height, I do not think I flatter myself unduly when I say I made a fine handsome animal. And having written that, I realize that I have not yet described the wolf suit, taking for granted, I suppose, that those who see this document will also see it. Yet this may not be the case. They have refused to let *me* see it, which makes me wonder if it has been cleaned and made presentable again or if it is still—but, no, there is no point in going into unsavory details.

I have said that the body and limbs of the suit were made of long-haired grey-fur fabric. The stuff of it was coarse, hardly an attractive material for a coat, I should have thought, but very closely similar to a wolf's pelt. Mother made the paws after the fashion of fur gloves but with the padded and stiffened fingers of a pair of leather gloves for the claws. The head we bought from a jokes-and-games shop. It had tall prick ears, small yellow eyes, and a wonderful, half open mouth—red, voracious-looking, and with a double row of white fangs. The opening for me to breathe through was just beneath the lower jaw where the head joined the powerful hairy throat.

As Spring came I would sometimes drive out into the countryside, park the car, and slip into the skin. It was far from my ambition to be seen by anyone. I sought solitude. Whether I should have cared for a "beastly" companion, that is something else again. At that time I wanted merely to wander in the woods and copses or along a hedgerow in my wolf's persona. And this I did, choosing unfrequented places, avoiding anywhere that I might come in contact with the human race.

I am trying, in writing this, to explain how I felt. Principally, I felt *not human*. And to be not human is to be without human responsibilities and human cares. Inside the wolf, I laid aside my apprehensiveness about getting married, my apprehensiveness about *not* getting married, my fear of leaving Mother on her own, my justifiable resentment at not getting the leading part in our new production. All this got left behind with the depleted sleeping man I left behind to become a happy mindless wild creature.

Our wedding had once again been postponed. The purchase of the house Moira and I had finally agreed upon fell through at the last moment. I cannot say I was altogether sorry. It was near enough to my home, in the same street in fact as Simla House, but I had begun to wonder how I would feel passing our dear old house every day knowing it was not under that familiar roof I should lay my head.

Moira was very upset.

Yet, "I won't live in the same house as your mother even for three months," she said in answer to my suggestion. "That's a certain recipe for disaster."

"Mother and Daddy lived with Mother's parents for twenty years," I said.

"Yes, and look at the result!" It was then that she made that remark about my enjoying playing parts because I disliked my real self.

There was nothing more to be said except that we must keep on house-hunting,

"We can still go to Malta, I suppose," Moira said. "We don't have to cancel that."

Perhaps, but it would be no honeymoon. Anticipating the delights of matrimony was something I had not done up till then and had no intention of doing. And I was on my guard when Moira—Mother was out at her bridge evening—insisted on going up to my bedroom with me, ostensibly to check on the shade of the suit I had bought to get married in. She said she wanted to buy me a tie. Once there, she reclined on my bed, cajoling me to come and sit beside her.

I suppose it was because I was feeling depressed that I put on the wolf skin. I took off my jacket—but nothing more, of course, in front of Moira—stepped into the wolf skin, fastened it up, and adjusted the head. She watched me. She had seen me in it when she came to the pantomime.

"Why have you put that on?"

I said nothing. What could I have said? The usual contentment filled me, though, and I found myself obeying her command, loping across to the bed where she was. It seemed to come naturally to fawn on her, to rub my great prick-eared head against her breast, to enclose her hands with my paws. All kinds of fantasies filled my wolfish mind and they were of an intense piercing sweetness. If we had been on our holiday then, I do not think moral resolutions would have held me back.

But unlike the lady in the George, Moira did not take hold of my head and lay it in her lap. She jumped up and shouted at me to stop this nonsense, stop it at once, she hated it. So I did as I was told, of course I did, and got sadly out of the skin and hung it back in the cupboard. I took Moira home. On our way we called in at her brother's and looked at fresh lists of houses.

It was on one of these that we eventually settled after another month or so of picking and choosing and stalling, and we fixed our wedding for the middle of December. During the summer the company had done *Blithe Spirit* (in which I had the meager part of Dr. Bradman, Bill Harkness being Charles Condomine) and the pantomime this year was *Cinderella* with Susan Hayes in the name part and me as the Elder of the Ugly Sisters. I had calculated I should be back from my honeymoon just in time.

No doubt I would have been. No doubt I would have married and gone away on my honeymoon and come back to play my comic part had I not agreed to go shopping with Moira on her birthday. What happened that day changed everything.

It was a Thursday evening. The stores in the West End stay open late on Thursdays. We left our offices at five, met by arrangement and together walked up Bond Street. The last thing I had in view was that we should begin bickering again, though we had seemed to do little else lately. It started with my mentioning our honeymoon. We were outside Asprey's, walking along arm-in-arm. Since our house wouldn't be ready for us to move into till the middle of January, I suggested we should go back for just two weeks to Simla House. We should be going there for Christmas in any case.

"I thought we'd decided to go to a hotel," Moira said.

"Don't you think that's rather a waste of money?"

"I think," she said in a grim sort of tone, "I think it's money we daren't not spend," and she drew her arm away from mine.

I asked her what on earth she meant.

"Once get you back there with Mummy and you'll never move."

I treated that with the contempt it deserved and said nothing. We walked along in silence. Then Moira began talking in a low monotone, using expressions from paperback psychology which I'm glad to say I have never heard from Dr. Vernon-Peak. We crossed the street and entered Selfridge's. Moira was still going on about Oedipus complexes and that nonsense about making a man of me.

"Keep your voice down," I said. "Everyone can hear you."

She shouted at me to shut up, she would say what she pleased. Well, she had repeatedly told me to be a man and to assert myself, so I did just that. I went up to one of the counters, wrote her a check for, I must admit, a good deal more than I had originally meant to give her, put it into her hands, and walked off, leaving her there.

For a while I felt not displeased with myself, but on the way home in the train depression set in. I should have liked to tell Mother about it but Mother would be out, playing bridge. So I took recourse in my other source of comfort, my wolf skin. The phone rang several times while I was gamboling about the rooms but I didn't answer it, I knew it was Moira. I was on the floor with Grandfather's stuffed eagle in my paws and my teeth in its neck when Mother walked in.

Bridge had ended early. One of the ladies had been taken ill and rushed to the hospital. I had been too intent on my task to see the light come on or hear the door. She stood there in her old fur coat, looking at me. I let the eagle fall and bowed my head—I wanted to die I was so ashamed and embarrassed. How little I really knew my mother! My dear faithful companion, my only friend! Might I not say, my other self?

She smiled. I could hardly believe it but she was smiling. It was that wonderful, conspiratorial, rather naughty smile of hers. "Hallo," she said. "Are you going all loopy?"

In a moment she was down on her knees beside me, the fur coat enveloping her, and together we worried at the eagle, engaged in battle with the bear, attacked the antelope. Together we bounded into the hall to pounce upon the sleeping tigers. Mother kept laughing (and growling too) saying, "What a relief, what a relief!" I think we embraced.

Next day when I got home she was waiting for me, transformed and ready. She had made herself an animal suit. She must have worked on it all day, out of the snow-leopard skin and a length of white-fur fabric. I could see her eyes dancing through the gap in its throat.

"You don't know how I've longed to be an animal again," she said. "I used to be animals when you were a baby. I was a dog for a long time and then I was a bear, but your father found out and he didn't like it. I had to stop."

So that was what I dimly remembered. I said she looked like the Queen of the Beasts.

"Do I, Loopy?" she said.

We had a wonderful weekend, Mother and I. Wolf and leopard, we breakfasted together that morning. Then we played. We played all over the house, sometimes fighting, sometimes dancing, hunting of course, carrying off our prey to the lairs we made for ourselves among the furniture. We went out in the car, drove into the country, and there in a wood got into our skins and for many happy hours roamed wild among the trees.

There seemed no reason, during those two days, to become human again at all, but on the Tuesday I had a rehearsal and on the Monday morning I had to go off to work. It was coming down to earth, back to what we call reality, with a nasty bang. Still, it had its amusing side too. A lady in the train trod on my toe and I had growled at her before I remembered and turned it into a cough.

All through that weekend neither of us had bothered to answer the phone. In the office I had no choice and it was there that Moira caught me. Marriage had come to seem remote, something grotesque, something that others did, not me. Animals do not marry. But that was not the sort of thing I could say to Moira. I promised to ring her. I said we must meet before the week was out.

I suppose she did tell me she'd come over on the Thursday evening and show me what she'd bought with the money I had given her. She knew Mother was always out on Thursdays. I suppose Moira did tell me and I failed to take it in. Nothing was important to me but being animals with Mother—Loopy and the Queen of the Beasts.

Each night as soon as I got home we made ourselves ready for our evening's games. How harmless it all was! How innocent! Like the gentle creatures in the dawn of the world before man came. Like the Garden of Eden after Adam and Eve had been sent away.

The lady who had been taken ill at the bridge evening had since died, so this week it was cancelled. But would Mother have gone anyway? Probably not. Our animal capers meant as much to her as they did to me, almost more perhaps, for she had denied herself so long.

We were sitting at the dining table, eating our evening meal. Mother had cooked, I recall, a rack of lamb so that we might later gnaw the bones. We never ate it, of course, and I have since wondered what became of it. But we did begin on our soup. The bread was at my end of the table, with the bread board and the long sharp knife.

Moira, when she called and I was alone, was in the habit of letting herself in by the back door. We did not hear her, neither of us heard her, though I do remember Mother's noble head lifted a fraction before Moira came in, her fangs bared and her ears pricked. Moira opened the dining-room door and walked in. I can see her now, the complacent smile on her lips fading and the scream starting to come. She was wearing what must have been my present, a full-length white sheepskin coat.

And then? This is what Dr. Vernon-Peak will particularly wish to know but what I cannot clearly remember. I remember that as the door opened I was holding the bread knife in my paws. I think I remember letting out a low growling and poising myself to spring. But what came after?

The last things I can recall before they brought me here are the blood on my fur and the two wild predatory creatures crouched on the floor over the body of the lamb.

P. D. JAMES

Undoubtedly and deservedly the most celebrated of twentieth-century British crime writers, P. D. James has used the detective story form to make profound statements about human nature, life in modern society, and the contaminating effects of crime on the innocent. Early on, the quality of her work won attention from critics and scholars, the latter latching onto James's writing as proof that a genre viewed as popular but not "literary" might, at last, be viewed as literature worthy of academic study.

A secret to James's success is her dedication to writing character-driven work in a genre that has traditionally placed characterization second to plot. This is not an easy task in a form that demands that the writer keep secrets about characters' true motivations from the reader, lest the plot be given away too early in the game. Many of James's contemporaries moved away from the whodunit form in order to indulge their desires to write psychologically true portraits of individuals. James, however, mostly continued to write within the structure of the classic detective story, working effectively to pen novels of character that also succeed as puzzling murder mysteries.

James's own character was built through facing challenging life experiences. Born in Oxford, she attended Cambridge Girls' High School and became a Red Cross nurse during World War II. She married Connor Bantry White, a military doctor who returned from the war mentally ill. The couple produced two daughters, one of them born during the aerial bombardment of London known as "The Blitz." James nursed her husband until his death in 1964 while raising her girls, holding down jobs in psychiatric hospital administration, and writing her fiction in the early hours of the morning. She later worked as an administrator in the police and criminal policy departments for the Home Office, and she has served as a magistrate, a governor of the BBC, and a member of the Church of England's Liturgical Commission. She is a member of the House of Lords.

Writing "Great Aunt Allie's Fly Papers" in 1985, James proved the classic whodunit is not dead. Here we have all the elements of the country house murder: Relatives gathered at the home of the scion, a resented, lower-class interloper in attendance on her much older husband, the delivery of tainted food to the victim-to-be, a highly unusual source of poison, and everything turning on questions of timing. Or is it everything? Although Adam Dalgliesh is the consummate modern police detective, it is his consciousness of class and what it used to mean—in terms of status and the monetary kind of means—that helps him discover the truth here. That—and a keen instinct for the psychology of greed.

Great Aunt Allie's Flypapers

1985

"YOU see my dear Adam," explained the Canon gently as he walked with Chief Superintendent Dalgliesh under the Vicarage elms, "useful as the legacy would be to us, I wouldn't feel happy in accepting it if Great Aunt Allie came by her money in the first place by wrongful means."

What the Canon meant was that he and his wife wouldn't be happy to inherit Great Aunt Allie's £50,000 if, sixty-seven years earlier, she had poisoned her elderly husband with arsenic in order to get it. As Great Aunt Allie had been accused and acquitted of just that charge in a 1902 trial which, for her Hampshire neighbours, had rivalled the Coronation as a public spectacle, the Canon's scruples were not altogether irrelevant. Admittedly, thought Dalgliesh, most people faced with the prospect of £50,000 would be happy to subscribe to the commonly held convention that once an English Court has pronounced its verdict the final truth of the matter has been established once and for all. There may possibly be a higher judicature in the next world, but hardly in this. And so Hubert Boxdale might normally be happy to believe. But, faced with the prospect of an unexpected fortune, his scrupulous conscience was troubled. The gentle but obstinate voice went on:

"Apart from the moral principle of accepting tainted money, it wouldn't bring us happiness. I often think of that poor woman, driven restlessly around Europe in her search for peace, of that lonely life and unhappy death."

Dalgliesh recalled that Great Aunt Allie had moved in a predictable progress with her retinue of servants, current lover and general hangers-on from one luxury Riviera hotel to the next, with stays in Paris or Rome as the mood suited her. He was not sure that this orderly programme of comfort and entertainment could be described as being restlessly driven around Europe, or that the old lady had been primarily in search of peace. She had died, he recalled, by falling overboard from a millionaire's yacht during a rather wild party given by him to celebrate her eighty-eighth birthday. It was perhaps not an edifying death by the Canon's standards but he doubted whether she had, in fact, been unhappy at the time. Great Aunt Allie (it was impossible to think of her by any other name), if she had been capable of coherent thought, would probably have pronounced it a very good way to go. But this was hardly a point of view he could put to his companion.

Canon Hubert Boxdale was Superintendent Adam Dalgliesh's godfather. Dalgliesh's father had been his Oxford contemporary and life-long friend. He had been an admirable godfather, affectionate, uncensorious, genuinely concerned. In Dalgliesh's childhood he had been mindful of birthdays and imaginative about a small boy's preoccupations and desires. Dalgliesh was very fond of him and privately thought him one of the few really good men he had known. It was only surprising that the Canon had managed to live to seventy-one in a carnivorous world in which gentleness, humility and unworldliness are hardly conducive to survival let alone success. But his goodness had in some sense protected him. Faced with such manifest innocence, even those who exploited him, and they were not a few, extended some of the protection and compassion they might show to the slightly subnormal.

"Poor old darling", his daily woman would say, pocketing pay for six hours when she had worked five and helping herself to a couple of eggs from his refrigerator. "He's really not fit to be let out alone." It had surprised the then young and slightly priggish Detective Constable Dalgliesh to realise that the Canon knew perfectly well about the hours and the eggs but thought that Mrs Copthorne with five children and an indolent husband needed both more than he did. He also knew that if he started paying for five hours she would promptly work only four and extract another two eggs and that this small and only dishonesty was somehow necessary to her self-esteem. He was good. But he was not a fool.

He and his wife were, of course, poor. But they were not unhappy; indeed it was a word impossible to associate with the Canon. The death of his two sons in the 1939 war had saddened but not destroyed him. But he had anxieties. His wife was suffering from disseminated sclerosis and was finding it increasingly hard to manage. There were comforts and appliances which she would need. He was now, belatedly, about to retire and his pension would be small. A legacy of £50,000 would enable them both to live in comfort for the rest of their lives and would also, Dalgliesh had no doubt, give them the pleasure of doing more for their various lame dogs. Really, he thought, the Canon was an almost embarrassingly deserving candidate for a modest fortune. Why couldn't the dear silly old noodle take the cash and stop worrying? He said cunningly:

"She was found not guilty, you know, by an English jury. And it all happened nearly seventy years ago. Couldn't you bring yourself to accept their verdict?"

But the Canon's scrupulous mind was impervious to such sly innuendoes. Dalgliesh told himself that he should have remembered what, as a small boy, he had discovered about Uncle Hubert's conscience; that it operated as a warning bell and that, unlike most people, he never pretended that it hadn't sounded or that he hadn't heard it or that, having heard it, something must be wrong with the mechanism.

"Oh, I did, while she was alive. We never met, you know. I didn't wish to force myself on her. After all, she was a wealthy woman. My grandfather made a new will on his marriage and left her all he possessed. Our ways of life were very different. But I usually wrote briefly at Christmas and she sent a card in reply. I wanted to keep some contact in case, one day, she might want someone to turn to and would remember that I am a priest."

And why should she want that, thought Dalgliesh. To clear her conscience? Was that what the dear old boy had in mind? So he must have had doubts from the beginning. But of course he had! Dalgliesh knew something of the story and the general feeling of the family and friends was that Great Aunt Allie had been extremely lucky to escape the gallows. His own father's view, expressed with reticence, reluctance and compassion had not in essentials differed from that given by a local reporter at the time.

"How on earth did she expect to get away with it? Damn lucky to escape topping if you ask me."

"The news of the legacy came as a complete surprise?" asked Dalgliesh.

"Indeed yes. I only saw her once at that first and only Christmas six weeks after her marriage when my grandfather died. We always talk of her as Great Aunt Allie but in fact, as you know, she married my grandfather. But it seemed impossible to think of her as a step-grandmother. There was the usual family gathering at Colebrook Croft at the time and I was there with my parents and my twin sisters. I was barely four and the twins were just eight months old. I can remember nothing of my grandfather or of his wife. After the murder—if one has to use that dreadful word—my mother returned home with us children leaving my father to cope with the police, the solicitors and the newsmen. It was a terrible time for him. I don't think I was even told that grandfather was dead until about a year later. My old nurse, who had been given Christmas as a holiday to visit her own family, told me that soon after my return home I asked her if grandfather was now young and beautiful for always. She, poor woman, took it as a sign of infant prognostication and piety. Poor Nellie was sadly superstitious and sentimental, I'm afraid. But I knew nothing of grandfather's death at the time and certainly can recall nothing of that Christmas visit or of my new step-grandmother. Mercifully, I was little more than a baby when the murder was done."

"She was a music hall artiste, wasn't she?" asked Dalgliesh.

"Yes and a very talented one. My grandfather met her when she was working with a partner in a hall in Cannes. He had gone to the south of France with a manservant for his health. I understand that she extracted a gold watch from his chain and, when he claimed it, told him that he was English, had recently suffered from a stomach ailment, had two sons and a daughter and was about to have a wonderful surprise. It was all correct except that his only daughter had died in childbirth leaving him a granddaughter, Marguerite Goddard."

"And all easily guessable from his voice and appearance," said Dalgliesh. "I suppose the surprise was the marriage?"

"It was certainly a surprise, and a most unpleasant one for the family. It is easy to deplore the snobbishness and the conventions of another age and, indeed, there was much in Edwardian England to deplore. But it was not a propitious marriage. I think of the difference in background, education and way of life, the lack of common interest. And there was this great disparity of age. My grandfather had married a girl just three months younger than his own granddaughter. I cannot wonder that the family were concerned; that they felt that the union could not, in the end, contribute to the contentment or happiness of either party."

"And that was putting it charitably," thought Dalgliesh. The marriage certainly hadn't contributed to their happiness. From the point of view of the family it had been a disaster. He recalled hearing of an incident when the local vicar and his wife, a couple who had actually dined at Colebrook Croft on the night of the murder, first called on the bride. Apparently old Augustus Boxdale had introduced her by saying:

"Meet the prettiest little variety artiste in the business. Took a gold watch and notecase off me without any trouble. Would have had the elastic out of my pants if I hadn't watched out. Anyway she stole my heart, didn't you, sweetheart?" All this accompanied by a hearty slap on the rump and a squeal of delight from the lady who had promptly demonstrated her skill by extracting the Reverend Arthur Venables' bunch of keys from his left ear.

Dalgliesh thought it tactful not to remind the Canon of this story.

"What do you wish me to do, Sir?" he enquired.

"It's asking a great deal, I know, when you're so busy. But if I had your assurance that you believed in Aunt Allie's innocence I should feel happy about accepting the bequest. I wondered if it would be possible for you to see the records of the trial. Perhaps it would give you a clue. You're so clever at this sort of thing."

He spoke without flattery but with an innocent wonder at the strange avocations of men. Dalgliesh was, indeed, very clever at this sort of thing. A dozen or so men at present occupying security wings in H.M. prisons could testify to Chief Superintendent Dalgliesh's cleverness; as, indeed, could a handful of others walking free whose defending Counsel had been, in their own way, as clever as Chief Superintendent Dalgliesh. But to re-examine a case over sixty years old seemed to require clairvoyance rather than cleverness. The trial judge and both learned Counsel had been dead for over fifty years. Two world wars had taken their toll. Four reigns had passed. It was highly probable that, of those who had slept under the roof of Colbrook Croft on that fateful Boxing Day night of 1901, only the Canon still survived. But the old man was troubled and had sought his help and Dalgliesh, with a day or two's leave due to him, had the time to give it.

"I'll do what I can," he promised.

The transcript of a trial which had taken place sixty-seven years ago took time and trouble to obtain, even for a Chief Superintendent of the Metropolitan Police. It provided little potential comfort for the Canon. Mr Justice Bellow had summed up with that avuncular simplicity with which he was wont to address juries, regarding them apparently as a panel of well-intentioned but cretinous children. And the facts could have been comprehended by any intelligent child. Part of the summing up set them out with admirable lucidity:

"And so, gentlemen of the jury, we come to the night of December 26th. Mr Augustus Boxdale, who had perhaps indulged a little unwisely on Christmas Day, had retired to bed in his dressing-room after luncheon suffering from a recurrence of the slight indigestive trouble which had afflicted him for most of his life. You have heard that he had taken luncheon with the members of his family and ate nothing which they too did not eat. You may feel you can acquit luncheon of anything worse than overrichness.

"Dinner was served at eight P.M. promptly, as was the custom at Colebrook Croft. There were present at that meal, Mrs Augustus Boxdale the deceased's bride; his elder son Captain Maurice Boxdale with his wife; his younger son the Reverend Henry Boxdale with his wife; his granddaughter Miss Marguerite Goddard; and two neighbours, the Reverend and Mrs Arthur Venables.

"You have heard how the accused took only the first course at dinner which was ragoût of beef and then, at about eight-twenty, left the dining-room to sit with her husband. Shortly after nine o'clock she rang for the parlour-maid, Mary Huddy, and ordered a basin of gruel to be brought up to Mr Boxdale. You have heard that the deceased was fond of gruel, and, indeed, as prepared by Mrs Muncie the cook, it sounds a most nourishing and comforting dish for an elderly gentleman of weak digestion.

"You have heard Mrs Muncie describe how she prepared the gruel according to Mrs Beaton's admirable recipe and in the presence of Mary Huddy in case, as she said, 'the master should take a fancy to it when I'm not at hand and you have to make it'. After the gruel had been prepared, Mrs Muncie tasted it with a spoon and Mary Huddy carried it upstairs to the main bedroom, together with a jug of water to thin the gruel if it were too strong. As she reached the door, Mrs Boxdale came out, her hands full of stockings and underclothes. She has told you that she was on her way to the bathroom to wash them through. She asked the girl to put the basin of gruel on the washstand by the window and Mary Huddy did so in her presence. Miss Huddy has told you that, at the time, she noticed the bowl of flypapers soaking in water and she knew that this solution was one used by Mrs Boxdale as a cosmetic wash. Indeed, all the women who spent that evening in the house, with the exception of Mrs Venables, have told you that they knew it was Mrs Boxdale's practice to prepare this solution of flypapers.

"Mary Huddy and the accused left the bedroom together and you have heard the evidence of Mrs Muncie that Miss Huddy returned to the kitchen after an absence of only a few minutes. Shortly after nine o'clock the ladies left the dining-room and entered the drawing-room to take coffee. At nine-fifteen p.m. Miss Goddard excused herself to the company and said that she would go to see if her grandfather needed anything. The time is established precisely because the clock struck the quarter-hour as she left and Mrs Venables commented on the sweetness of its chime. You have also heard Mrs Venables' evidence and the evidence of Mrs Maurice Boxdale and Mrs Henry Boxdale that none of the ladies left the drawing-room during the evening; and Mr Venables has testified that the three gentlemen remained together until Miss Goddard appeared about three-quarters of an hour later to inform them that her grandfather had become very ill and to request that the doctor be sent for immediately.

"Miss Goddard has told you that, when she entered her grandfather's room, he was just finishing his gruel and was grumbling about its taste. She got the impression that this was merely a protest at being deprived of his dinner rather than that he genuinely considered that there was something wrong with the gruel. At any rate, he finished most of it and appeared to enjoy it despite his grumbles.

"You have heard Miss Goddard describe how, after her grandfather had had as much as he wanted of the gruel, she took the bowl next door and left it on the washstand. She then returned to her grandfather's bedroom and Mr Boxdale, his wife and his granddaughter played three-handed whist for about three-quarters of an hour.

"At ten o'clock Mr Augustus Boxdale complained of feeling very ill. He suffered from griping pains in the stomach, from sickness, and from looseness of the bowel. As soon as the symptoms began Miss Goddard went downstairs to let her uncles know that her grandfather was worse and to ask that Doctor Eversley should be sent for urgently. Doctor Eversley has given you his evidence. He arrived at Colebrook Croft at ten-thirty P.M. when he found his patient very distressed and weak. He treated the symptoms and gave what relief he could, but Mr Augustus Boxdale died shortly before midnight.

"Gentlemen of the jury, you have heard Marguerite Goddard describe how, as her grandfather's paroxysms increased in intensity, she remembered the gruel and wondered whether it could have disagreed with him in some way. She mentioned this possibility to her elder uncle, Captain Maurice Boxdale. Captain Boxdale has told you how he at once handed the bowl, with its residue of gruel, to Doctor Eversley with the request that the Doctor should lock it in a cupboard in the library, seal the lock, and himself keep the key. You have heard how the contents of the bowl were later analysed and with what result."

An extraordinary precaution for the gallant Captain to have taken, thought Dalgliesh, and a most perspicacious young woman. Was it by chance or by design that the bowl hadn't been taken down to be washed up as soon as the old man had finished with it? Why was it, he wondered, that Marguerite Goddard hadn't rung for the parlour-maid and requested her to remove it? Miss Goddard appeared the only other suspect. He wished he knew more about her.

But, except for the main protagonists, the characters in the drama did not emerge very clearly from the trial report. Why, indeed, should they? The British accusatorial system of trial is designed to answer one question: is the accused guilty, beyond reasonable doubt, of the crime charged? Exploration of the nuances of personality, speculation and gossip have no place in the witness-box. The two Boxdale brothers came out as very dull fellows indeed. They and their estimable, respectable, sloping-bosomed wives had sat at dinner in full view of each other from eight until after nine o'clock (a substantial meal that dinner) and had said so in the witness-box more or less in identical words. The ladies' bosoms might have been heaving with far from estimable emotions of dislike, envy, embarrassment, or resentment of the interloper. If so, they didn't tell the Court.

But the two brothers and their wives were clearly innocent, even if a detective of that time could have conceived of the guilt of gentlefolk so well respected, so eminently respectable. Even their impeccable alibis had a nice touch of social and sexual distinction. The Reverend Arthur Venables had vouched for the gentlemen, his good wife for the ladies. Besides, what motive had they? They could no longer gain financially by the old man's death. If anything, it was in their interests to keep him alive in the hope that disillusion with his marriage, or a return to sanity, might occur to cause him to change his will. So far Dalgliesh had learned nothing that could cause him to give the Canon the assurance for which he hoped.

It was then that he remembered Aubrey Glatt. Glatt was a wealthy amateur criminologist who had made a study of all the notable Victorian and Edwardian poison cases. He was not interested in anything earlier or later, being as obsessively wedded to his period as any serious historian, which, indeed, he had some claim to call himself. He lived in a Georgian house in Winchester—his affection for the Victorian and Edwardian age did not extend to its architecture—and was only three miles from Colebrook Croft. A visit to the London Library disclosed that he hadn't written a book on the case, but it was improbable that he had totally neglected a crime so close at hand and so in period. Dalgliesh had occasionally helped him with technical details of police procedure. Glatt, in response to a telephone call, was happy to return the favour with the offer of afternoon tea and information.

Tea was served in his elegant drawing-room by a parlour-maid in goffered cap with streamers. Dalgliesh wondered what wage Glatt paid her to persuade her to wear it. She looked as if she could have played a role in any of his favourite Victorian dramas, and Dalgliesh had an uncomfortable thought that arsenic might be dispensed with the cucumber sandwiches.

Glatt nibbled away and was expansive.

"It's interesting that you should have taken this sudden and, if I may say so, somewhat inexplicable interest in the Boxdale murder. I got out my notebook on the case only yesterday. Colebrook Croft is being demolished to make way for a new housing estate and I thought I would visit it for the last time. The family, of course, haven't lived there since the 1914–18 war. Architecturally it's completely undistinguished but one grieves to see it go. We might drive over after tea if you are agreeable.

"I never wrote my book on the case, you know. I planned a work entitled 'The Colebrook Croft Mystery' or 'Who Killed Augustus Boxdale?' But the answer was all too obvious."

"No real mystery?" suggested Dalgliesh.

"Who else could it have been but Allegra Boxdale? She was born Allegra Porter, you know. Do you think her mother could have been thinking of Byron? I imagine not. There's a picture of her on page two of the notebook, by the way, taken by a photographer in Cannes on her wedding day. I call it beauty and the beast."

The photograph had scarcely faded and Great Aunt Allie smiled clearly at Dalgliesh across nearly seventy years. Her broad face, with its wide mouth and rather snub nose, was framed by two wings of dark hair swept high and topped in the fashion of the day by an immense flowered hat. The features were too coarse for real beauty, but the eyes were magnificent, deep-set and well-spaced, and the chin round and determined. Beside this vital young Amazon, poor Augustus Boxdale, smiling fatuously at the camera and clutching his bride as if for support, was but a frail and undersized beast. Their pose was unfortunate. She looked as if she were about to fling him over her shoulder.

Glatt shrugged. "The face of a murderess? I've known less likely ones. Her Counsel suggested, of course, that the old man had poisoned his own gruel during the short time she left it on the washstand to cool while she visited the bathroom. But why should he? All the evidence suggests that he was in a state of post-nuptial euphoria, poor senile old booby. Our Augustus was in no hurry to leave this world, particularly by such an agonizing means. Besides, I doubt whether he even knew the gruel was there. He was in bed next door in his dressing-room, remember."

Dalgliesh asked:

"What about Marguerite Goddard? There's no evidence about the exact time when she entered the bedroom."

"I thought you'd get on to that. She could have arrived while her step-grandmother was in the bathroom, poisoned the gruel, hidden herself either in the main bedroom or elsewhere until it had been taken in to Augustus, then joined her grandfather and his bride as if she had just come upstairs. It's possible, I admit. But is it likely? She was less inconvenienced than any of the family by her grandfather's second marriage. Her mother was Augustus Boxdale's eldest child and married, very young, a wealthy patent-medicine manufacturer. She died in childbirth and the husband only survived her by a year. Marguerite Goddard was an heiress. She was also most advantageously engaged to Captain the Honourable John Brize-Lacey. It was quite a catch for a Boxdale—or a Goddard. Marguerite Goddard, young, beautiful, secure in her possession of the Goddard fortune, not to mention the Goddard emeralds and the eldest son of a Lord, was hardly a serious suspect. In my view, Defence Counsel, that was Roland Gort Lloyd remember, was wise to leave her strictly alone."

"It was a memorable defence, I believe."

"Magnificent. There's no doubt Allegra Boxdale owed her life to Gort Lloyd. I know that concluding speech by heart.

"'Gentlemen of the jury, I beseech you, in the sacred name of Justice, to consider what you are at. It is your responsibility, and yours alone, to decide the fate of this young woman. She stands before you now, young, vibrant, glowing with health, the years stretching before her with their promise and their hopes. It is in your power to cut off all this as you might top a nettle with one swish of your cane. To condemn her to the slow torture of those last waiting weeks; to that last dreadful walk; to heap calumny on her name; to desecrate those few happy weeks of marriage with the man who loved her so greatly; to cast her into the final darkness of an ignominious grave.'

"Pause for dramatic effect. Then the crescendo in that magnificent voice. 'And on what evidence, gentlemen? I ask you.' Another pause. Then the thunder. 'On what evidence?'"

"A powerful defence," said Dalgliesh. "But I wonder how it would go down with a modern judge and jury."

"Well, it went down very effectively with that 1902 jury. Of course the abolition of capital punishment has rather cramped the more histrionic style. I'm not sure that the reference to topping nettles was in the best of taste. But the jury got the message. They decided that, on the whole, they preferred not to have the responsibility of sending the accused to the gallows. They were out six hours reaching their verdict and it was greeted with some applause. If any of those worthy citizens had been asked to wager five pounds of their own good money on her innocence, I suspect that it would have been a different matter. Allegra Boxdale had helped him, of course. The Criminal Evidence Act, passed three years earlier, enabled him to put her in the witness-box. She wasn't an actress of a kind for nothing. Somehow she managed to persuade the jury that she had genuinely loved the old man."

"Perhaps she had," suggested Dalgliesh. "I don't suppose there had been much kindness in her life. And he was kind."

"No doubt. No doubt. But love!" Glatt was impatient. "My dear Dalgliesh! He was a singularly ugly old man of sixty-nine. She was an attractive girl of twenty-one!"

Dalgliesh doubted whether love, that iconoclastic passion, was susceptible to this kind of simple arithmetic but he didn't argue. Glatt went on:

"And the prosecution couldn't suggest any other romantic attachment. The police got in touch with her previous partner, of course. He was discovered to be a bald, uxorious little man sharp as a weasel, with a buxom wife and five children. He had moved down the coast after the partnership broke up and was now working with a new girl. He said, regretfully, that she was coming along nicely, thank you, gentlemen, but would never be a patch on Allie and that, if Allie got her neck out of the noose and ever wanted a job, she knew where to come. It was obvious even to the most suspicious policeman that his interest was purely professional. As he said: 'What was a grain or two of arsenic between friends?'

"The Boxdales had no luck after the trial. Captain Maurice Boxdale was killed in 1916, leaving no children, and the Reverend Henry lost his wife and their twin daughters in the 1918 influenza epidemic. He survived until 1932. The boy Hubert may still be alive, but I doubt it. That family were a sickly lot.

"My greatest achievement, incidentally, was in tracing Marguerite Goddard. I hadn't realised that she was still alive. She never married Brize-Lacey or, indeed, anyone else. He distinguished himself in the 1914–18 war, came successfully through, and eventually married an eminently suitable young woman, the sister of a brother officer. He inherited the title in 1925 and died in 1953. But Marguerite Goddard may be alive now for all I know. She may even be living in the same modest Bournemouth hotel where I found her. Not that my efforts in tracing her were rewarded. She absolutely refused to see me. That's the note that she sent out to me by the way."

It was meticulously pasted into the notebook in its chronological order and carefully annotated. Aubrey Glatt was a natural researcher; Dalgliesh couldn't help wondering whether this passion for accuracy might not have been more rewardingly spent than in the careful documentation of murder.

The note was written in an elegant upright hand, the strokes black and very thin but unwavering.

"Miss Goddard presents her compliments to Mr Aubrey Glatt. She did not murder her grandfather and has neither the time nor inclination to gratify his curiosity by discussing the person who did."

Aubrey Glatt said: "After that extremely disobliging note, I felt there was really no point in going on with the book."

Glatt's passion for Edwardian England extended to more than its murders and they drove to Colebrook Croft through the green Hampshire lanes, perched high in an elegant 1910 Daimler. Aubrey wore a thin tweed coat and deerstalker hat and looked, Dalgliesh thought, rather like a Sherlock Holmes with himself as attendant Watson.

"We are only just in time, my dear Dalgliesh," he said when they arrived. "The engines of destruction are assembled. That ball on a chain looks like the eyeball of God, ready to strike. Let us make our number with the attendant artisans. You, as a guardian of the law, will have no wish to trespass."

The work of demolition had not yet begun, but the inside of the house had been stripped and plundered, and the great rooms echoed to their footsteps like gaunt and deserted barracks after the final retreat. They moved from room to room, Glatt mourning the forgotten glories of an age he had been born thirty years too late to enjoy, Dalgliesh with his mind on more immediate and practical concerns.

The design of the house was simple and formalized. The first floor, on which were most of the main bedrooms, had a long corridor running the whole length of the façade. The master bedroom was at the southern end with two large windows giving a distant view of Winchester Cathedral tower. A communicating door led to a small dressing-room.

The main corridor had a row of four identical large windows. The brass curtain-rods and wooden rings had been removed (they were collectors' items now) but the ornate carved pelmets were still in place. Here must have hung pairs of heavy curtains giving cover to anyone who wished to slip out of view. And Dalgliesh noted with interest that one of the windows was exactly opposite the door of the main bedroom. By the time they had left Colebrook Croft and Glatt had dropped him at Winchester Station, Dalgliesh was beginning to formulate a theory.

His next move was to trace Marguerite Goddard, if she were still alive. It took him nearly a week of weary searching, a frustrating trail along the south coast from hotel to hotel. Almost everywhere, his enquiries were met with defensive hostility. It was the usual story of a very old lady who had become more demanding, arrogant and eccentric as her health and fortune waned; an unwelcome embarrassment to manager and fellow guests alike. The hotels were all modest, a few almost sordid. What, he wondered, had become of the Goddard fortune?

From the last landlady he learned that Miss Goddard had become ill, really very sick indeed, and had been removed six months previously to the local district general hospital. And it was there that he found her.

The Ward Sister was surprisingly young, a petite, dark-haired girl with a tired face and challenging eyes.

"Miss Goddard is very ill. We've put her in one of the side wards. Are you a relative? If so, you're the first one who has bothered to call and you're lucky to be in time. When she is delirious she seems to expect a Captain Brize-Lacey to call. You're not he by any chance?"

"Captain Brize-Lacey will not be calling. No, I'm not a relative. She doesn't even know me. But I would like to visit her if she's well enough and is willing to see me. Could you please give her this note?"

He couldn't force himself on a defenceless and dying woman. She still had the right to say no. He was afraid she would refuse him. And if she did, he might never learn the truth. He thought for a second and then wrote four words on the back page of his diary, signed them, tore out the page, folded it and handed it to the Sister.

She was back very shortly.

"She'll see you. She's weak, of course, and very old, but she's perfectly lucid now. Only please don't tire her."

"I'll try not to stay too long."

The girl laughed:

"Don't worry. She'll throw you out soon enough if she gets bored. The Chaplain and the Red Cross librarian have a terrible time with her. Third door on the left. There's a stool to sit on under the bed. We ring a bell at the end of visiting time."

She bustled off, leaving him to find his own way. The corridor was very quiet. At the far end he could glimpse through the open door of the main ward the regimented rows of beds, each with its pale blue coverlet; the bright flow of flowers on the over-bed tables and the laden visitors making their way in pairs to each bedside. There was a faint buzz of welcome, a hum of conversation. But no one was visiting the side wards. Here in the silence of the aseptic corridor Dalgliesh could smell death.

The woman propped high against the pillows in the third room on the left no longer looked human. She lay rigidly, her long arms disposed like sticks on the coverlet. This was a skeleton, clothed with a thin membrane of flesh, beneath whose yellow transparency the tendons and veins were plainly visible as if in an anatomist's model. She was nearly bald, and the high-domed skull under its spare down of hair was as brittle and vulnerable as a child's. Only the eyes still held life, burning in their deep sockets with an animal vitality. But when she spoke, her voice was distinctive and unwavering, evoking, as her appearance never could, the memory of imperious youth.

She took up his note and read aloud four words:

" 'It was the child'. You are right, of course. The four-year-old Hubert Boxdale killed his grandfather. You signed this note Adam Dalgliesh. There was no Dalgliesh connected with the case."

"I am a detective of the Metropolitan Police. But I'm not here in any official capacity. I have known about this case for a number of years from a dear friend. I have a natural curiosity to learn the truth. And I have formed a theory."

"And now, like that poseur Aubrey Glatt, you want to write a book?"

"No. I shall tell no one. You have my promise."

Her voice was ironic.

"Thank you. I am a dying woman, Mr Dalgliesh. I tell you that not to invite your sympathy, which it would be an impertinence for you to offer and which I neither want nor require, but to explain why it no longer matters to me what you say or do. But I too have a natural curiosity. Your note, cleverly, was intended to provoke it. I should like to know how you discovered the truth."

Dalgliesh drew the visitors' stool from under the bed and sat down beside her. She did not look at him. The skeleton hands still holding his note did not move.

"Everyone in Colebrook Croft who could have killed Augustus Boxdale was accounted for, except the one person whom nobody considered, the small boy. He was an intelligent, articulate and lonely child. He was almost certainly left to his own devices. His nurse did not accompany the family to Colebrook Croft, and the servants who were there had the extra work of Christmas and the care of the delicate twin girls. The boy probably spent much time with his grandfather and the new bride. She too was lonely and disregarded. He could have trotted around with her as she went about her various activities. He could have watched her making her arsenical face wash and when he asked, as a child will, what it was for, could have been told 'to make me young and beautiful'. He loved his grandfather, but he must have known that the old man was neither young nor beautiful. Suppose he woke up on that Boxing Day night, overfed and excited after the Christmas festivities. Suppose he went to Allegra Boxdale's room in search of comfort and companionship, and saw the basin of gruel and the arsenical mixture together on the washstand. Suppose he decided that here was something he could do for his grandfather."

The voice from the bed said quietly:

"And suppose someone stood unnoticed in the doorway and watched him."

"So you were behind the window curtains on the landing looking through the open door?"

"Of course. He knelt on the chair, two chubby hands clasping the bowl of poison, pouring it with infinite care into his grandfather's gruel. I watched while he replaced the linen cloth over the basin, got down from his chair, replaced it with careful art against the wall and trotted out into the corridor and back to the nursery. About three seconds later Allegra came out of the bathroom, and I watched while she carried the gruel into my grandfather. A second later I went into the main bedroom. The bowl of poison had been a little heavy for Hubert's small hands to manage, and I saw that a small pool had been spilt on the polished top of the washstand. I mopped it up with my handkerchief. Then I poured some of the water from the jug into the poison bowl to bring up the level. It only took a couple of seconds, and I was ready to join Allegra and my grandfather in the bedroom and sit with him while he ate his gruel. I watched him die without pity and without remorse. I think I hated them both equally. The grandfather who had adored, petted and indulged me all through my childhood had deteriorated into this disgusting old lecher, unable to keep his hands off his woman even when I was in the room. He had rejected me and his family, jeopardised my engagement, made our name a laughing-stock in the County—and for a woman my grandmother wouldn't have employed as a kitchen-maid. I wanted them both dead. And they were both going to die. But it would be by other hands than mine. I could deceive myself that it wasn't my doing."

Dalgliesh asked: "When did she find out?"

"She knew that evening. When my grandfather's agony began, she went outside for the jug of water. She wanted a cool cloth for his head. It was then that she noticed that the level of water in the jug had fallen and that a small pool of liquid on the washstand had been mopped up. I should have realised that she would have seen that pool. She had been trained to register every detail; it was almost subconscious with her. She thought at the time that Mary Huddy had spilt some of the water when she set down the tray and the gruel. But who but I could have mopped it up? And why?"

"And when did she face you with the truth?"

"Not until after the trial. Allegra had magnificent courage. She knew what was at stake. But she also knew what she stood to gain. She gambled with her life for a fortune."

And then Dalgliesh understood what had happened to the Goddard inheritance.

"So she made you pay?"

"Of course. Every penny. The Goddard fortune, the Goddard emeralds. She lived in luxury for sixty-seven years on my money. She ate and dressed on my money. When she moved with her lovers from hotel to hotel, it was on my money. She paid them with my money. And if she has left anything, which I doubt, it is my money. My grandfather left very little. He had been senile and had let money run through his fingers like sand."

"And your engagement?"

"It was broken, you could say by mutual consent. A marriage, Mr Dalgliesh, is like any other legal contract. It is most successful when both parties are convinced they have a bargain. Captain Brize-Lacey was sufficiently discouraged by the scandal of a murder in the family. He was a proud and highly conventional man. But that alone might have been accepted with the Goddard fortune and the Goddard emeralds to deodorize the bad smell. But the marriage couldn't have succeeded if he had discovered that he had married socially beneath him, into a family with a major scandal and no compensating fortune."

Dalgliesh said: "Once you had begun to pay you had no choice but to go on. I see that. But why did you pay? She could hardly have told her story. It would have meant involving the child."

"Oh no! That wasn't her plan at all. She never meant to involve the child. She was a sentimental woman and she was fond of Hubert. No, she intended to accuse me of murder outright. Then, if I decided to tell the truth, how would it help me? How could I admit that I had watched Hubert, actually watched a child barely four years old preparing an agonizing death for his grandfather without speaking a word to stop him? I could hardly claim that I hadn't understood the implication of what I had seen. After all, I wiped up the spilled liquid, I topped up the bowl. She had nothing to lose, remember, neither life nor reputation. They couldn't try her twice. That's why she waited until after the trial. It made her secure for ever. But what of me? In the circles in which I moved reputation was everything. She needed only to breathe the story in the ears of a few servants and I was finished. The truth can be remarkably tenacious. But it wasn't only reputation. I paid in the shadow of the gallows."

Dalgliesh asked, "But could she ever prove it?"

Suddenly she looked at him and gave an eerie screech of laughter. It tore at her throat until he thought the taut tendons would snap.

"Of course she could! You fool! Don't you understand? She took my handkerchief, the one I used to mop up the arsenic mixture. That was her profession, remember. Some time during that evening, perhaps when we were all crowding around the bed, two soft plump fingers insinuated themselves between the satin of my evening dress and my flesh and extracted that stained and damning piece of linen."

She stretched out feebly towards the bedside locker. Dalgliesh saw what she wanted and pulled open the drawer. There on the top was a small square of very fine linen with a border of hand-stitched lace. He took it up. In the corner was her monogram delicately embroidered. And half of the handkerchief was still stiff and stained with brown.

She said: "She left instructions with her solicitors that this was to be returned to me after her death. She always knew where I was. She made it her business to know. You see, it could be said that she had a life interest in me. But now she's dead. And I shall soon follow. You may have the handkerchief, Mr Dalgliesh. It can be of no further use to either of us now."

Dalgliesh put it in his pocket without speaking. As soon as possible, he would see that it was burnt. But there was something else he had to say. "Is there anything you would wish me to do? Is there anyone you want told, or to tell? Would you care to see a priest?"

Again there was that uncanny screech of laughter, but it was softer now:

"There's nothing I can say to a priest. I only regret what I did because it wasn't successful. That is hardly the proper frame of mind for a good confession. But I bear her no ill will. No envy, malice or uncharitableness. She won; I lost. One should be a good loser. But I don't want any priest telling me about penance. I've paid, Mr Dalgliesh. For sixty-seven years I've paid. And in this world, young man, the rich only pay once."

She lay back as if suddenly exhausted. There was silence for a moment. Then she said with sudden vigour:

"I believe your visit has done me good. I would be obliged if you would make it convenient to return each afternoon for the next three days. I shan't trouble you after that."

Dalgliesh extended his leave with some difficulty and stayed at a local inn. He saw her each afternoon. They never spoke again of the murder. And when he came punctually at 2 P.M. on the fourth day it was to be told that Miss Goddard had died peacefully in the night with apparently no trouble to anyone. She was, as she had said, a good loser.

A week later Dalgliesh reported to the Canon.

"I was able to see a man who has made a detailed study of the case. He had already done most of the work for me. I have read the transcript of the trial and visited Colebrook Croft. And I have seen one other person, closely connected with the case but who is now dead. I know you will want me to respect confidences and to say no more than I need."

It sounded pompous and minatory but he couldn't help that. The Canon murmured his quiet assurance. Thank God he wasn't a man to question. Where he trusted, he trusted absolutely. If Dalgliesh gave his word there would be no more questioning. But he was anxious. Suspense hung around them. Dalgliesh went on quickly:

"As a result I can give you my word that the verdict was a just verdict and that not one penny of your grandfather's fortune is coming to you through anyone's wrong-doing."

He turned his face away and gazed out of the vicarage window at the sweet green coolness of the summer's day, so that he did not have to watch the Canon's happiness and relief. There was a silence. The old man was probably giving thanks in his own way. Then he was aware that his godfather was speaking. Something was being said about gratitude, about the time he had given up to the investigation.

"Please don't misunderstand me, Adam. But when the formalities have been completed, I should like to denote something to a charity named by you, one close to your heart."

Dalgliesh smiled. His contributions to charity were impersonal; a quarterly obligation discharged by banker's order. The Canon obviously regarded charities as so many old clothes; all were friends, but some fitted better and were more affectionately regarded than others.

But inspiration came:

"It's good of you to think of it, Sir. I rather liked what I learned about Great Aunt Allie. It would be pleasant to give something in her name. Isn't there a society for the assistance of retired and indigent variety artists, conjurers and so on?"

The Canon, predictably, knew that there was and could name it.

Dalgliesh said: "Then I think, Canon, that Great Aunt Allie would agree that a donation in her name would be entirely appropriate."

TONY HILLERMAN

It's no wonder the Navajo honored Tony Hillerman as a "A friend of the Dineh"—a friend of the People. Ever since his boyhood in Sacred Heart, Oklahoma, where his pals were Potawatomie and Seminole Indians, he has been at ease in the intersection of Anglo- and Native American worlds. In his many mystery novels, tribal police officers Joe Leaphorn and Jim Chee must straddle the rift between both worlds in order to get to the truth of violent crimes.

The son of a farmer and jack-of-all-trades father and of a mom who had worked as a nurse, Hillerman spent his boyhood in a household without telephone or electricity. But it was a home where storytelling was valued and books were acquired through a library system that would mail them to patrons. In one of those book parcels, Hillerman discovered the work of Arthur Upfield, who wrote about detectives of mixed racial heritage who solved crimes in the Australian outback.

Hillerman attended Oklahoma State University but interrupted his studies to serve in the U.S. Army during World War II. Wounded in action in France, he returned home and worked as a truck driver. Meanwhile, a reporter who had read his letters home urged him to try his hand at writing. Then, while driving a truck on the Navajo reservation, he came upon tribesmen en route to attend a curing ceremony. Fascinated, he accepted their invitation to join them. His first novel, *The Blessing Way* (1970), was inspired by the experience.

Before he became a full-time writer, Tony married and supported a large family, including five adopted children, by working as a journalist and then as a professor of journalism.

We have decided to publish two of Hillerman's stories in this volume, because they show two directions that crime writing has taken since Dorothy L. Sayers's day. The first of the Hillerman stories, "First Lead Gasser," draws on the author's experience as a UPI reporter. Following are the author's comments about the story's genesis.

—*Rosemary Herbert*

This plotless short story of mine is an extreme departure from the whodunit form. The culprit is in death row awaiting execution. The mystery lies in what led him to the crime and then leads the reader to ponder just where the real guilt lies. As one whose career led him to cover the "crime and violence" beat on newspapers in Texas, Oklahoma, and New Mexico, I often found myself pondering exactly that. In fact, I wrote "Gasser" after covering the execution of the last man to die in the New Mexico gas chamber, because I wanted to see if I could tell the sad story of that crime more truthfully in fiction than within the "just the facts" rules of newspaper journalism.

—*Tony Hillerman*

First Lead Gasser

1993

JOHN Hardin walked into the bureau, glanced at the wall clock (which told him it was 12:22 A.M.), laid his overcoat over a chair, flicked the switch on the teletype to ON, tapped on the button marked BELL, and then punched on the keys with a stiff forefinger:

ALBUQUERQUE ... YOU TURNED ON? ... SANTA FE

He leaned heavily on the casing of the machine, waiting, feeling the coolness under his palms, noticing the glass panel was dusty, and hearing the words again and that high, soft voice. Then the teletype bumped tentatively and said:

SANTA FE ... AYE AYE GO WITH IT ... ALBUQUERQUE

And John Hardin punched:

ALBUQUERQUE ... WILL FILE LEAD SUBBING OUT GASSER ITEM IN MINUTE. PLEASE SEND SCHEDULE FOR 300 WORDS TO DENVER ... SANTA FE

The teletype was silent as Hardin removed the cover from the typewriter (dropping it to the floor). Then the teletype carriage bumped twice and said:

SANTA FE ... NO RUSH DENVER UNTHINKS GASSER WORTH FILING ON NATIONAL TRUNK DIXIE TORNADOES JAMMING WIRE AND HAVE DANDY HOTEL FIRE AT CHICAGO FOLKS OUTJUMPING WINDOWS ETC HOWEVER STATE OVERNIGHT FILE LUKS LIKE HOTBED OF TRANQUILITY CAN USE LOTS OF GORY DETAILS THERE ... ALBUQUERQUE

Their footsteps had echoed down the long concrete tube, passed the dark barred mouths of cell blocks, and Thompson had said, "Is it always this goddam quiet?" and the warden said, "The cons are always quiet on one of these nights."
Hardin sighed and said something under his breath and punched:

ALBUQUERQUE ... REMIND DENVER NITESIDE THAT DENVER DAYSIDE HAS REQUEST FOR 300 WORDS TO BE FILED FOR OHIO PM POINTS ... S F

He turned his back on the machine, put a carbon book in the typewriter, hit the carriage return twice, and stared at the clock, which now reported the time to be 12:26. While he stared, the second hand made the laborious climb toward 12 and something clicked and the clock said it was 12:27.

Hardin started typing, rapidly:

First Lead Gasser
   Santa Fe, N.M., March 28—(UPI)—George Tobias Small, 38, slayer of a young Ohio couple who sought to befriend him, died a minute after midnight today in the gas chamber at the New Mexico State Penitentiary.

He examined the paragraph, pulled the paper from the typewriter, and dropped it. It slid from the top of the desk and planed to the floor, spilling its carbon insert. On a fresh carbon book Hardin typed:

First Lead Gasser
   Santa Fe, N.M., March 28—(UPI)—George Tobias Small, 38, who clubbed to death two young Ohio newlyweds last July 4, paid for his crime with his life early today in the New Mexico State Penitentiary gas chamber.
   The hulking killer smiled nervously at execution witnesses as three guards pushed three unmarked buttons, one of which dropped cyanide pills into a container of acid under the chair in which he was strapped.

Hulking? Maybe tall, stooped killer: maybe gangling. Not really nervously. Better timidly: smiled timidly. But actually it was an embarrassed smile. Shy. Stepping from the elevator into that too-bright basement room, Small had blinked against the glare and squinted at them lined by the railing—the press corps and the official creeps in the role of "official witnesses." He looked surprised and then embarrassed and looked away, then down at his feet. The warden had one hand on his arm: the two of them walking fast toward the front of the chamber, hurrying, while a guard held the steel door open. Above their heads, cell block eight was utterly silent.

Hardin hit the carriage return.

   The end came quickly for Small. He appeared to hold his breath for a moment and then breathed deeply of the deadly fumes. His head fell forward and his body slumped in death.

The room had been hot. Stuffy. Smelling of cleaning fluid. But under his hand, the steel railing was cold. "Looks like a big incinerator," Thompson said. "Or like one of those old wood stoves with the chimney out the top." And the man from the *Albuquerque Journal* said, "The cons call it the space capsule. Wonder why they put windows in it. There's not much to see," And Thompson said, with a sort of laugh, that it was the world's longest view. Then it was quiet. Father McKibbon had looked at them a long time when they came in,

unsmiling, studying them. Then he had stood stiffly by the open hatch, looking at the floor.

Small, who said he had come to New Mexico from Colorado in search of work,
was sentenced to death last November after a district court jury at Raton found
him guilty of murder in the deaths of Mr. and Mrs. Robert M. Martin of
Cleveland. The couple had been married only two days earlier and was en route to
California on a honeymoon trip.

You could see Father McKibbon saying something to Small—talking rapidly—and Small nodded and then nodded again, and then the warden said
something and Small looked up and licked his lips. Then he stepped through
the hatch. He tripped on the sill, but McKibbon caught his arm and helped
him sit in the little chair, and Small looked up at the priest. And smiled. How
would you describe it? Shy, maybe, or grateful. Or maybe sick. Then the guard
was reaching in, doing something out of sight. Buckling the straps probably,
buckling leather around a warm ankle and a warm forearm which had
MOTHER tattooed on it, inside a heart.

Small had served two previous prison terms. He had compiled a police record
beginning with a Utah car theft when he was fifteen. Arresting officers testified that
he confessed killing the two with a jack handle after Martin resisted Small's attempt
at robbery. They said Small admitted flagging down the couple's car after raising the
hood on his old-model truck to give the impression he was having trouble.

Should it be flagging down or just flagging? The wall clock inhaled electricity
above Hardin's head with a brief buzzing sigh and said 12:32. How long had
Small been dead now? Thirty minutes, probably, if cyanide worked as fast as they
said. And how long had it been since yesterday, when he had stood outside Small's
cell in death row? It was late afternoon, then. You could see the sunlight far down
the corridor, slanting in and striped by the bars. Small had said, "How much time
have I got left?" and Thompson looked at his watch and said, "Four-fifteen from
midnight leaves seven hours and forty-five minutes," and Small's bony hands
clenched and unclenched on the bars. Then he said, "Seven hours and forty-five
minutes now," and Thompson said, "Well, my watch might be off a little."

Behind Hardin the teletype said *ding, ding, ding, dingding.*

SANTA FE . . . DENVER NOW SEZ WILL CALL IN 300 FOR OHIO PM
WIRE SHORTLY. HOW BOUT LEADING SAD SLAYER SAMMY
SMALL TODAY GRIMLY GULPED GAS. OR SOME SUCH????? . . .
ALBUQUERQUE

The teletype lapsed into expectant silence, its electric motor purring.
Outside, a car drove by with a rush of sound.

Hardin typed:

Small refuted the confession at his trial. He claimed that after Martin stopped to assist him the two men argued and that Martin struck him. He said he then "blacked out" and could remember nothing more of the incident. Small was arrested when two state policemen who happened by stopped to investigate the parked vehicles.

"The warden told me you was the two that work for the outfits that put things in the papers all over, and I thought maybe you could put something in about finding . . . about maybe . . . something about needing to know where my mother is. You know, so they can get the word to her." He walked back to his bunk, back into the darkness, and sat down and then got up again and walked back to the barred door, three steps. "It's about getting buried. I need someplace for that." And Thompson said, "What's her name?" and Small looked down at the floor. "That's part of the trouble. You see, this man she was living with when we were there in Salt Lake, well, she and him . . ."

Arresting officers and other witnesses testified there was nothing mechanically wrong with Small's truck, that there was no mark on Small to indicate he had been struck by Martin, and that Martin had been slain by repeated blows on the back of his head.

Small was standing by the bars now, gripping them so that the stub showed where the end of his ring finger had been cut off. Flexing his hands, talking fast. "The warden, well, he told me they'd send me wherever I said after it's over, back home, he said. They'd pay for it. But I won't know where to tell them unless somebody can find Mama. There was a place we stayed for a long time before we went to San Diego, and I went to school there some but I don't remember the name of it, and then we moved someplace up the coast where they grow figs and like that, and then I think it was Oregon next, and then I believe it was we moved on out to Salt Lake." Small stopped talking then, and let his hands rest while he looked at them, at Thompson and him, and said, "But I bet Mama would remember where I'm supposed to go."

Mrs. Martin's body was found in a field about forty yards from the highway. Officers said the pretty bride had apparently attempted to flee, had tripped and injured an ankle, and had then been beaten to death by Small.

Subject: George Tobias Small, alias Toby Small, alias G. T. Small. White male, about 38 (birth date, place unknown); weight, 188, height, 6´4´´; eyes, brown; complexion, ruddy; distinguishing characteristics: noticeable stoop, carries right shoulder higher than left. Last two joints missing from left ring finger, deep scar on left upper lip, tattoo of heart with word MOTHER on inner right forearm. Charge: Violation Section 12-2 (3) Criminal Code.
Disposition: Guilty of Murder, Colfax County District Court.
Sentence: Death.

Previous Record: July 28, 1941, sentenced Utah State Reformatory, car theft.
April 7, 1943, returned Utah State Reformatory, B&E and parole violation.
February 14, 1945, B&E, resisting arrest. Classified juvenile incorrigible.
August 3, 1949, armed robbery, 5–7 years at . . .

Small had been in trouble with the law since boyhood, starting his career with a
car theft at twelve and then violating reformatory parole with a burglary. Before
his twenty-first birthday he was serving the first of three prison terms.

Small had rested his hands on the brace between the bars, but they
wouldn't rest. The fingers twisted tirelessly among themselves. Blind snakes,
even the stub of the missing finger moving restlessly. "Rock fell on it when I
was little. Think it was that. The warden said he sent the word around about
Mama, but I guess nobody found her yet. Put it down that she might be living in Los Angeles. That man with us there in Salt Lake, he wanted to go out
to the coast and maybe that's where they went."

It was then Thompson stopped him. "Wait a minute," Thompson said.
"Where was she from, your mother? Why not . . ."

"I don't remember that," Small said. He was looking down at the floor.

And Thompson asked, "Didn't she tell you?" and Small said, still not looking at us, "Sure, but I was little."

"You don't remember the town or anything? How little were you?" And
Small sort of laughed and said, "Just exactly twelve," and laughed again, and
said, "That's why I thought maybe I could come home, it was my birthday. We
was living in a house trailer then, and Mama's man had been drinking. Her
too. When he did that, he'd whip me and run me off. So I'd been staying with
a boy I knew there at school, in the garage but his folks said I couldn't stay anymore and it was my birthday, so I thought I'd go by, maybe it would be all
right."

Small had taken his hands off the bars then. He walked back to the bunk and
sat down. And when he started talking again it was almost too low to hear it all.

"They was gone. The trailer was gone. The man at the office said they'd just
took off in the night. Owed him rent, I guess," Small said. He was quiet again.

Thompson said, "Well," and then he cleared his throat, said, "Leave you a
note or anything?"

And Small said, "No, sir. No note."

"That's when you stole the car, I guess," Thompson said. "The car theft you
went to the reformatory for."

"Yes, sir," Small said. "I thought I'd go to California and find her. I thought
she was going to Los Angeles, but I never knowed no place to write. You could
write all the letters you wanted there at the reformatory, but I never knowed
the place to send it to."

Thompson said, "Oh," and Small got up and came up to the bars and
grabbed them.

"How much time have I got now?"

Small stepped through the oval hatch in the front of the gas chamber at two minutes before midnight, and the steel door was sealed behind him to prevent seepage of the deadly gas. The prison doctor said the first whiff of the cyanide fumes would render a human unconscious almost instantly.

"We believe Mr. Small's death will be almost painless," he said.

"The warden said they can keep my body a couple days but then they'll just have to go on ahead and bury me here at the pen unless somebody claims it. They don't have no place cold to keep it from spoiling on 'em. Anyway, I think a man oughta be put down around his kin if he has any. That's the way I feel about it."

And Thompson started to say something and cleared his throat and said, "How does it feel to—I mean, about tonight?" and Small's hands tightened on the bars. "Oh, I won't say I'm not scared. I never said that but they say it don't hurt but I been hurt before, cut and all, and I never been scared of that so much."

Small's words stopped coming and then they came loud, and the guard reading at the door in the corridor looked around and then back at his book. "It's the not knowing," he said, and his hands disappeared from the bars and he walked back to the dark end of the cell and sat on the bunk and got up again and walked and said, "Oh, God, it's not knowing."

Small cooperated with his executioners. While the eight witnesses required by law watched, the slayer appeared to be helping a guard attach the straps which held his legs in place in the gas chamber. He leaned back while his forearms were strapped to the chair.

The clock clicked and sighed and the minute hand pointed at the eight partly hidden behind a tear-shaped dribble of paint on the glass, and the teletype, stirred by this, said *ding, ding, ding*.

SANTA FE . . . DENVER WILL INCALL GASSER AFTER SPORTS ROUNDUP NOW MOVING. YOU BOUT GOT SMALL WRAPPED UP? . . . ALBUQUERQUE

Hardin pulled the carbon book from the typewriter and marked out "down" after the verb "flagging." He penciled a line through "give the impression he was" and wrote in "simulate." He clipped the copy to the holder above the teletype keyboard, folding it to prevent obscuring the glass panel, switched the key from KEYBOARD to TAPE, and began punching. The thin yellow strip, lacy with perforations, looped downward toward the floor and built rapidly there into a loopy pile.

He had seen Small wiping the back of his hand across his face. When he came back to the bars he had looked away.

"The padre's been talking to me about it every morning," Small had said. "That's Father McKibbon. He told me a lot I never knew before, mostly about Jesus, and I'd heard about that, of course. It was back when I was in that place at Logan, that chaplain there, he talked about Jesus some, and I remembered some of it. But that one there at Logan, he talked mostly about sin and about hell and things like that, and this McKibbon, the padre here, well, he talked different." Small's hands had been busy on the bars again and then Small had looked directly at him, directly into his face, and then at Thompson. He remembered the tense heavy face, sweaty, and the words and the voice too soft and high for the size of the man.

"I wanted to ask you to do what you could about finding my mama. I looked for her all the time. When they'd turn me loose, I'd hunt for her. But maybe you could find her. With the newspapers and all. And I want to hear what you think about it all," Small said. "About what happens to me after they take me out of that gas chamber. I wanted to see what you say about that." And then Small said into the long silence, "Well, whatever it's going to be, it won't be any worse than it's been." And he paused again, and looked back into the cell as if he expected to see someone there, and then back at us.

"But when I walk around in here and my foot hits the floor I feel it, you know, and I think that's Toby Small I'm feeling there with his foot on the cement. It's *me*. And I guess that don't sound like much, but after tonight I guess there won't be that for one thing. And I hope there's somebody there waiting for me. I hope there's not just me." And he sat down on the bunk.

"I was wondering what you thought about this Jesus and what McKibbon has been telling me." He had his head between his hands now, looking at the floor, and it made his voice muffled. "You reckon he was lying about it? I don't see any cause for it, but how can a man know all that and be sure about it?"

The clatter of the transmission box joined the chatter of the perforator. Hardin marked his place in the copy and leaned over to fish a cigarette out of his overcoat. He lit it, took it out of his mouth, and turned back to the keyboard. Above him, above the duet chatter of tape and keyboard, he heard the clock strike again, and click, and when he looked up it was 12:46.

McKibbon had his hand on Small's elbow, crushing the pressed prison jacket, talking to him, his face fierce and intent. And Small was listening, intent. Then he nodded and nodded again and when he stepped through the hatch he bumped his head on the steel hard enough so you could hear it back at the railing, and then Hardin could see his face through the round glass and it looked numb and pained.

McKibbon had stepped back, and while the guard was working with the straps, he began reading from a book. Loud, wanting Small to hear. Maybe wanting all of them to hear.

"Have mercy on me, O Lord; for unto thee have I cried all the day, for thou, O Lord, art sweet and mild: and plenteous in mercy unto all that call upon thee. Incline thine ear, O Lord, and hear me: for I am needy and poor. Preserve my soul; for I am holy: O thou my God, save they servant that trusteth in thee."

The pile of tape on the floor diminished and the final single loop climbed toward the stop bar and the machine was silent. Hardin looked through the dusty glass, reading the last paragraph for errors.

There was his face, there through the round window, and his brown eyes unnaturally wide, looking at something or looking for something. And then the pump made a sucking noise and the warden came over and said, "Well, I guess we can all go home now."

He switched the machine back from TAPE to KEYBOARD and punched:

SMALL'S BODY WILL BE HELD UNTIL THURSDAY, THE WARDEN SAID, IN THE EVENT THE SLAYER'S MOTHER CAN BE LOCATED TO CLAIM IT. IF NOT, IT WILL BE BURIED IN THE PRISON LOT.

He switched off the machine. And in the room the only sound was the clock, which was buzzing again and saying it was 12:49.

TONY HILLERMAN

Typical of several trends in more recent crime fiction, my story "Chee's Witch" uses regional landscape, regional beliefs, and some of the elements of the "realism" of the police procedural to tell the story. It seems to concern the investigation of the murder of a Navajo, but the reader learns—through the eyes of Navajo Tribal Policeman Jim Chee—that the cause of death is the invincible ignorance of local agents regarding local culture.

—*Tony Hillerman*

Chee's Witch

1986

SNOW is so important to the Eskimos they have nine nouns to describe its variations. Corporal Jimmy Chee of the Navajo Tribal Police had heard that as an anthropology student at the University of New Mexico. He remembered it now because he was thinking of all the words you need in Navajo to account for the many forms of witchcraft. The word Old Woman Tso had used was "anti'l," which is the ultimate sort, the absolute worst. And so, in fact, was the deed which seemed to have been done. Murder, apparently. Mutilation, certainly, if Old Woman Tso had her facts right. And then, if one believed all the mythology of witchery told among the fifty clans who comprised The People, there must also be cannibalism, incest, even necrophilia.

On the radio in Chee's pickup truck, the voice of the young Navajo reading a Gallup used-car commercial was replaced by Willie Nelson singing of trouble and a worried mind. The ballad fit Chee's mood. He was tired. He was thirsty. He was sticky with sweat. He was worried. His pickup jolted along the ruts in a windless heat, leaving a white fog of dust to mark its winding passage across the Rainbow Plateau. The truck was gray with it. So was Jimmy Chee. Since sunrise he had covered maybe two hundred miles of half-graded gravel and unmarked wagon tracks of the Arizona–Utah–New Mexico border country. Routine at first—a check into a witch story at the Tsossie hogan north of Teec Nos Pos to stop trouble before it started. Routine and logical. A bitter winter, a sand storm spring, a summer of rainless, desiccating heat. Hopes dying, things going wrong, anger growing, and then the witch gossip. The logical. A bitter winter, a sand storm spring, a summer awry. The trouble at the summer hogan of the Tsossies was a sick child and a water well that had turned alkaline—nothing unexpected. But you didn't expect such a specific witch. The skinwalker, the Tsossies agreed, was the City Navajo, the man who had come to live in one of the government houses at Kayenta. Why the City Navajo? Because everybody knew he was a witch. Where had they heard that, the first time? The People who came to the trading post at Mexican Water said it. And so Chee had driven westward over Tohache Wash, past Red Mesa and Rabbit Ears to Mexican Water. He had spent hours on the shady porch giving those who came to buy, and to fill their water barrels, and to visit, a chance to know who he was until finally they might risk talking about witchcraft to a stranger. They were Mud Clan, and Many Goats People, and Standing Rock Clan—foreign to Chee's own Slow Talking People—but finally some of them talked a little.

A witch was at work on the Rainbow Plateau. Adeline Etcitty's mare had foaled a two-headed colt. Hosteen Musket had seen the witch. He'd seen a man walk into a grove of cottonwoods, but when he got there an owl flew away.

Rudolph Bisti's boys lost three rams while driving their flocks up into the Chuska high pastures, and when they found the bodies, the huge tracks of a werewolf were all around them. The daughter of Rosemary Nashibitti had seen a big dog bothering her horses and had shot at it with her .22 and the dog had turned into a man wearing a wolfskin and had fled, half running, half flying. The old man they called Afraid of His Horses had heard the sound of the witch on the roof of his winter hogan, and saw the dirt falling through the smoke hole as the skinwalker tried to throw in his corpse powder. The next morning the old man had followed the tracks of the Navajo Wolf for a mile, hoping to kill him. But the tracks had faded away. There was nothing very unusual in the stories, except their number and the recurring hints that the City Navajo was the witch. But then came what Chee hadn't expected. The witch had killed a man.

The police dispatcher at Window Rock had been interrupting Willie Nelson with an occasional blurted message. Now she spoke directly to Chee. He acknowledged. She asked his location.

"About fifteen miles south of Dennehotso," Chee said. "Homeward bound for Tuba City. Dirty, thirsty, hungry, and tired."

"I have a message."

"Tuba City," Chee repeated, "which I hope to reach in about two hours, just in time to avoid running up a lot of overtime for which I never get paid."

"The message is FBI Agent Wells needs to contact you. Can you make a meeting at Kayenta Holiday Inn at eight P.M.?"

"What's it about?" Chee asked. The dispatcher's name was Virgie Endecheenie, and she had a very pretty voice and the first time Chee had met her at the Window Rock headquarters of the Navajo Tribal Police he had been instantly smitten. Unfortunately, Virgie was a born-into Salt Cedar Clan, which was the clan of Chee's father, which put an instant end to that. Even thinking about it would violate the complex incest taboo of the Navajos.

"Nothing on what it's about," Virgie said, her voice strictly business. "It just says confirm meeting time and place with Chee or obtain alternate time."

"Any first name on Wells?" Chee asked. The only FBI Wells he knew was Jake Wells. He hoped it wouldn't be Jake.

"Negative on the first name," Virgie said.

"All right," Chee said. "I'll be there."

The road tilted downward now into the vast barrens of erosion which the Navajos call Beautiful Valley. Far to the west, the edge of the sun dipped behind a cloud—one of the line of thunderheads forming in the evening heat over the San Francisco Peaks and the Cococino Rim. The Hopis had been holding their Niman Kachina dances, calling the clouds to come and bless them.

Chee reached Kayenta just a little late. It was early twilight and the clouds had risen black against the sunset. The breeze brought the faint smells that rising humidity carries across desert country—the perfume of sage, creosote brush, and dust. The desk clerk said that Wells was in room 284 and the first name was Jake. Chee no longer cared. Jake Wells was abrasive but he was also smart. He had the best record in the special FBI Academy class Chee had attended, a quick, tough intelligence. Chee could tolerate the man's personality for a while to learn what Wells could make of his witchcraft puzzle.

"It's unlocked," Wells said. "Come on in." He was propped against the padded headboard of the bed, shirt off, shoes on, glass in hand. He glanced at Chee and then back at the television set. He was as tall as Chee remembered, and the eyes were just as blue. He waved the glass at Chee without looking away from the set. "Mix yourself one," he said, nodding toward a bottle beside the sink in the dressing alcove.

"How you doing, Jake?" Chee asked.

Now the blue eyes reexamined Chee. The question in them abruptly went away. "Yeah," Wells said. "You were the one at the Academy." He eased himself on his left elbow and extended a hand. "Jake Wells," he said.

Chee shook the hand. "Chee," he said.

Wells shifted his weight again and handed Chee his glass. "Pour me a little more while you're at it," he said, "and turn down the sound."

Chee turned down the sound.

"About thirty percent booze," Wells demonstrated the proportion with his hands. "This is your district then. You're in charge around Kayenta? Window Rock said I should talk to you. They said you were out chasing around in the desert today. What are you working on?"

"Nothing much," Chee said. He ran a glass of water, drinking it thirstily. His face in the mirror was dirty—the lines around mouth and eyes whitish with dust. The sticker on the glass reminded guests that the laws of the Navajo Tribal Council prohibited possession of alcoholic beverages on the reservation. He refilled his own glass with water and mixed Wells's drink. "As a matter of fact, I'm working on a witchcraft case."

"Witchcraft?" Wells laughed. "Really?" He took the drink from Chee and examined it. "How does it work? Spells and like that?"

"Not exactly," Chee said. "It depends. A few years ago a little girl got sick down near Burnt Water. Her dad killed three people with a shotgun. He said they blew corpse powder on his daughter and made her sick."

Wells was watching him. "The kind of crime where you have the insanity plea."

"Sometimes," Chee said. "Whatever you have, witch talk makes you nervous. It happens more when you have a bad year like this. You hear it and you try to find out what's starting it before things get worse."

"So you're not really expecting to find a witch?"

"Usually not," Chee said.

"Usually?"

"Judge for yourself," Chee said. "I'll tell you what I've picked up today. You tell me what to make of it. Have time?"

Wells shrugged. "What I really want to talk about is a guy named Simon Begay." He looked quizzically at Chee. "You heard the name?"

"Yes," Chee said.

"Well, shit," Wells said. "You shouldn't have. What do you know about him?"

"Showed up maybe three months ago. Moved into one of those U.S. Public Health Service houses over by the Kayenta clinic. Stranger. Keeps to himself. From off the reservation somewhere. I figured you federals put him here to keep him out of sight."

Wells frowned. "How long you known about him?"

"Quite a while," Chee said. He'd known about Begay within a week after his arrival.

"He's a witness," Wells said. "They broke a car-theft operation in Los Angeles. Big deal. National connections. One of those where they have hired hands picking up expensive models and they drive 'em right on the ship and off-load in South America. This Begay is one of the hired hands. Nobody much. Criminal record going all the way back to juvenile, but all nickel-and-dime stuff. I gather he saw some things that help tie some big boys into the crime, so Justice made a deal with him."

"And they hide him out here until the trial?"

Something apparently showed in the tone of the question. "If you want to hide an apple, you drop it in with the other apples," Wells said. "What better place?"

Chee had been looking at Wells's shoes, which were glossy with polish. Now he examined his own boots, which were not. But he was thinking of Justice Department stupidity. The appearance of any new human in a country as empty as the Navajo Reservation provoked instant interest. If the stranger was a Navajo, there were instant questions. What was his clan? Who was his mother? What was his father's clan? Who were his relatives? The City Navajo had no answers to any of these crucial questions. He was (as Chee had been repeatedly told) unfriendly. It was quickly guessed that he was a "relocation Navajo," born to one of those hundreds of Navajo families which the federal government had tried to reestablish forty years ago in Chicago, Los Angeles, and other urban centers. He was a stranger. In a year of witches, he would certainly be suspected. Chee sat looking at his boots, wondering if that was the only basis for the charge that City Navajo was a skinwalker. Or had someone seen something? Had someone seen the murder?

"The thing about apples is they don't gossip," Chee said.

"You hear gossip about Begay?" Wells was sitting up now, his feet on the floor.

"Sure," Chee said. "I hear he's a witch."

Wells produced a pro-forma chuckle. "Tell me about it," he said.

Chee knew exactly how he wanted to tell it. Wells would have to wait awhile before he came to the part about Begay. "The Eskimos have nine nouns for snow," Chee began. He told Wells about the variety of witchcraft on the reservations and its environs: about frenzy witchcraft, used for sexual conquests, of witchery distortions, of curing ceremonials, of the exotic two-heart witchcraft of the Hopi Fog Clan, of the Zuni Sorcery Fraternity, of the Navajo "chindi," which is more like a ghost than a witch, and finally of the Navajo Wolf, the anti'l witchcraft, the werewolves who pervert every taboo of the Navajo Way and use corpse powder to kill their victims.

Wells rattled the ice in his glass and glanced at his watch.

"To get to the part about your Begay," Chee said, "about two months ago we started picking up witch gossip. Nothing much, and you expect it during a drought. Lately it got to be more than usual." He described some of the tales and how uneasiness and dread had spread across the plateau. He described what he had learned today, the Tsossies's naming City Navajo as the witch, his trip to Mexican Water, of learning there that the witch had killed a man.

"They said it happened in the spring—couple of months ago. They told me the ones who knew about it were the Tso outfit." The talk of murder, Chee noticed, had revived Wells's interest. "I went up there," he continued, "and found the old woman who runs the outfit. Emma Tso. She told me her son-in-law had been out looking for some sheep, and smelled something, and found the body under some chamiso brush in a dry wash. A witch had killed him."

"How—"

Chee cut off the question. "I asked her how he knew it was a witch killing. She said the hands were stretched out like this." Chee extended his hands, palms up. "They were flayed. The skin was cut off the palms and fingers."

Wells raised his eyebrows.

"That's what the witch uses to make corpse powder," Chee explained. "They take the skin that has the whorls and ridges of the individual personality—the skin from the palms and the finger pads, and the soles of the feet. They take that, and the skin from the glans of the penis, and the small bones where the neck joins the skull, and they dry it, and pulverize it, and use it as poison."

"You're going to get to Begay any minute now," Wells said. "That right?"

"We got to him," Chee said. "He's the one they think is the witch. He's the City Navajo."

"I thought you were going to say that," Wells said. He rubbed the back of his hand across one blue eye. "City Navajo. Is it that obvious?"

"Yes," Chee said. "And then he's a stranger. People suspect strangers."

"Were they coming around him? Accusing him? Any threats? Anything like that, you think?"

"It wouldn't work that way—not unless somebody had someone in their family killed. The way you deal with a witch is hire a singer and hold a special kind of curing ceremony. That turns the witchcraft around and kills the witch."

Wells made an impatient gesture. "Whatever," he said. "I think something has made this Begay spooky." He stared into his glass, communing with the bourbon. "I don't know."

"Something unusual about the way he's acting?"

"Hell of it is I don't know how he usually acts. This wasn't my case. The agent who worked him retired or some damn thing, so I got stuck with being the delivery man." He shifted his eyes from glass to Chee. "But if it was me, and

I was holed up here waiting, and the guy came along who was going to take me home again, then I'd be glad to see him. Happy to have it over with. All that."

"He wasn't?"

Wells shook his head. "Seemed edgy. Maybe that's natural, though. He's going to make trouble for some hard people."

"I'd be nervous," Chee said.

"I guess it doesn't matter much anyway." Wells said. "He's small potatoes. The guy who's handling it now in the U.S. Attorney's Office said it must have been a toss-up whether to fool with him at all. He said the assistant who handled it decided to hide him out just to be on the safe side." '

"Begay doesn't know much?"

"I guess not. That, and they've got better witnesses."

"So why worry?"

Wells laughed. "I bring this sucker back and they put him on the witness stand and he answers all the questions with I don't know and it makes the USDA look like a horse's ass. When a U.S. Attorney looks like that, he finds an FBI agent to blame it on." He yawned. "Therefore," he said through the yawn, "I want to ask you what you think. This is your territory. You are the officer in charge. Is it your opinion that someone got to my witness?"

Chee let the question hang. He spent a fraction of a second reaching the answer, which was they could have if they wanted to try. Then he thought about the real reason Wells had kept him working late without a meal or a shower. Two sentences in Wells's report. One would note that the possibility the witness had been approached had been checked with local Navajo Police. The next would report whatever Chee said next. Wells would have followed Federal Rule One—Protect Your Ass.

Chee shrugged. "You want to hear the rest of my witchcraft business?"

Wells put his drink on the lamp table and untied his shoe. "Does it bear on this?"

"Who knows? Anyway there's not much left. I'll let you decide. The point is we had already picked up this corpse Emma Tso's son-in-law found. Somebody had reported it weeks ago. It had been collected, and taken in for an autopsy. The word we got on the body was Navajo male in his thirties probably. No identification on him."

"How was this bird killed?"

"No sign of foul play," Chee said. "By the time the body was brought in, decay and the scavengers hadn't left a lot. Mostly bone and gristle, I guess. This was a long time after Emma Tso's son-in-law saw him."

"So why do they think Begay killed him?" Wells removed his second shoe and headed for the bathroom.

Chee picked up the telephone and dialed the Kayenta clinic. He got the night supervisor and waited while the supervisor dug out the file. Wells came out of the bathroom with his toothbrush. Chee covered the mouthpiece. "I'm having them read me the autopsy report," Chee explained. Wilson began brushing his teeth at the sink in the dressing alcove. The voice of the night supervisor droned into Chee's ear.

"That all?" Chee asked. "Nothing added on? No identity yet? Still no cause?"

"That's him," the voice said.

"How about shoes?" Chee asked. "He have shoes on?"

"Just a sec," the voice said. "Yep. Size ten D. And a hat, and . . ."

"No mention of the neck or skull, right? I didn't miss that? No bones missing?" Silence. "Nothing about neck or skull bones."

"Ah," Chee said. "Fine. I thank you." He felt great. He felt wonderful. Finally things had clicked into place. The witch was exorcised. "Jake," he said. "Let me tell you a little more about my witch case."

Wells was rinsing his mouth. He spit out the water and looked at Chee, amused. "I didn't think of this before," Wells said, "but you really don't have a witch problem. If you leave that corpse a death by natural causes, there's no case to work. If you decide it's a homicide, you don't have jurisdiction anyway. Homicide on an Indian reservation, FBI has jurisdiction." Wells grinned. "We'll come in and find your witch for you."

Chee looked at his boots, which were still dusty. His appetite had left him, as it usually did an hour or so after he missed a meal. He still hungered for a bath. He picked up his hat and pushed himself to his feet.

"I'll go home now," he said. "The only thing you don't know about the witch case is what I just got from the autopsy report. The corpse had his shoes on and no bones were missing from the base of the skull."

Chee opened the door and stood in it, looking back. Wells was taking his pajamas out of his suitcase. "So what advice do you have for me? What can you tell me about my witch case?"

"To tell the absolute truth, Chee, I'm not into witches," Wells said. "Haven't been since I was a boy."

"But we don't really have a witch case now," Chee said. He spoke earnestly. "The shoes were still on, so the skin wasn't taken from the soles of his feet. No bones missing from the neck. You need those to make corpse powder."

Wells was pulling his undershirt over his head. Chee hurried.

"What we have now is another little puzzle," Chee said. "If you're not collecting stuff for corpse powder, why cut the skin off this guy's hands?"

"I'm going to take a shower," Wells said. "Got to get my Begay back to L.A. tomorrow."

Outside the temperature had dropped. The air moved softly from the west, carrying the smell of rain. Over the Utah border, over the Cococino Rim, over the Rainbow Plateau, lightning flickered and glowed. The storm had formed. The storm was moving. The sky was black with it. Chee stood in the darkness, listening to the mutter of thunder, inhaling the perfume, exulting in it.

He climbed into the truck and started it. How had they set it up, and why? Perhaps the FBI agent who knew Begay had been ready to retire. Perhaps an accident had been arranged. Getting rid of the assistant prosecutor who knew the witness would have been even simpler—a matter of hiring him away from the government job. That left no one who knew this minor witness was not Simon Begay. And who was he? Probably they had other Navajos from the Los Angeles community stealing cars for them. Perhaps that's what had suggested the scheme. To most white men all Navajos looked pretty much alike, just as in his first years at college all Chee had seen in white men was pink skin, freckles, and light-colored eyes. And what would the imposter say? Chee grinned. He'd say whatever was necessary to cast doubt on the prosecution, to cast the fatal "reasonable doubt," to make—as Wells had put it—the U.S. District Attorney look like a horse's ass.

Chee drove into the rain twenty miles west of Kayenta. Huge, cold drops drummed on the pickup roof and turned the highway into a ribbon of water. Tomorrow the backcountry roads would be impassable. As soon as they dried and the washouts had been repaired, he'd go back to the Tsossie hogan, and the Tso place, and to all the other places from which the word would quickly spread. He'd tell the people that the witch was in custody of the FBI and was gone forever from the Rainbow Plateau.

DONALD E. WESTLAKE

Prolific and versatile, Donald E. Westlake has written everything from sexy adventure novels, political thrillers, and science fiction to comic crime capers, thoughtful crime thrillers, and screenplays. Probably he is best known for two mystery series. The more humorous one centers on capers featuring John Dortmunder, a hapless character who is often in a fix. Dortmunder is introduced in the 1972 novel *Bank Shot,* which established Westlake's forte in coming up with situations that invite criminal activity. Westlake got the idea for this plot during a boring commute, when he saw a bank doing business in a trailer while the building was being repaired. It occurred to the author then that the entire bank might be stolen, if a thief literally hauled it away. Another well-known Westlake series features the thief Parker, who is introduced in the 1962 novel *The Hunter.* In these books, written under the pseudonym Richard Stark, the reader is most interested in finding out how Parker will get away with thievery again and again.

Additional Westlake characters include the ex-cop Mitch Tobin, who appears in a series of books the author wrote under the pseudonym Tucker Coe; actor-thief Alan Grofield; and ex-policeman-turned-television-personality Samuel Holt. Westlake has also written numerous nonseries books, including *The Hook*, a novel published in 2000 that comments not only on the life of a writer but on a publishing industry that values big names and money more than literary quality. Westlake's screenplays include *Cops and Robbers* (1972) and *The Grifters* (1990).

Over his long career, Westlake has become a master of many things: manipulating mood to match his plots, establishing character and setting using an economy of words, and grabbing the reader by the funny bone or the heartstrings, as he wishes. No doubt his screenwriting experience has led him to know exactly when to cut the scene.

Westlake's short story "Breathe Deep" may not feature any of his series characters, but it still represents the author at his best, in a mere three pages. The story stemmed from a situation Westlake observed in Las Vegas decades ago. We want you to hold your breath until the end of this story. Then we'll let Westlake tell you what he saw at the Vegas casino.

Breathe Deep

1985

BLACK stitching over the left pocket of his white-silk shirt read CHUCK in cursive script. His pale, wiry arms were crossed below the name; his large Adam's apple moved arrhythmically above. Before him on the small lima-bean-shaped green table the 200 playing cards were fanned out, awaiting fresh players.

It was 3:30 in the morning and fewer than half the tables in the main casino were staffed. A noisy crowd at one crap table gave an illusion of liveliness, but only four of the seven blackjack dealers on duty had any action. Chuck had stood here at the ten-dollar-limit table for nearly an hour; it was looking as though he wouldn't deal a single round before his break.

"Hey, Chuck."

At the left extreme of the table stood a small old man in a COORS cap, smiling, hands in raincoat pockets. The raincoat hung open, showing a white shirt, a sloppily knotted, dark, thin tie and a bit of dark jacket. The old man had shaved recently but not well, and his gray eyes were red-rimmed and merry. The dealer saw not much hope here, but he said, "A game, sir?"

"Maybe in a while, Chuck," the old man said, and grinned as though he were thinking of some joke. "Did you know I came out of the hosptial just this morning?"

The dealer, his foot near the button that calls security, looked at the old man. He said, "Is that right, sir?"

"Sun City Hospital, right here in Las Vegas, Nevada. Fixed me up just fine. No more broken bones." That I-know-a-joke grin appeared again.

"Sir, if you're not interested in playing—"

"Oh, I *could* be, Chuck," the old man said, "I *might* be."

The night was slow, and the dealer's break was due in just a few minutes. So he didn't touch his foot to the button that calls security. "Take your time, sir," he said.

"That's all I've got," the old man said, but then he grinned again. "I love the big Strip hotels at night."

"You do, sir?"

"Oh, yeah. Oh, yeah. I hate Vegas, you know, but I love the hotels at night. I come in, I breathe deep, I'm a young man again. All the old words come back, run around inside my mind like squirrels. You know what I mean, Chuck?"

"Excitement," suggested the dealer, flat-voiced.

"Oh, sure. Oh, yes. By day, you know, I hang around downtown. You know those places. Big sign out front: PENNY SLOTS. FREE BREAKFAST. Penny slots." The old man made a laugh sound in his throat—heh heh—that turned into something like a cough.

"Sir," said the dealer, "I want to give you some friendly advice." He'd seen past the imperfectly shaved cheeks now, the frayed raincoat, the charity-service necktie. This was an old bum, a derelict, one of the many ancient, alcoholic, homeless, friendless, familyless husks the dry wind blows across the desert into the stone-and-neon baffle of Las Vegas. "You don't belong here, sir," he explained. "I'm doing you a favor. Security can get kind of rough, to discourage you from coming back."

"Oh, I know about that, Chuck!" the old man said, and this time he laughed outright. "I *belong* downtown, with those penny slots. Start all over again, Chuck! Build a stake on those slot machines down there, penny by penny, *penny by penny*, come back!"

"Sir, I'm telling you for your own good."

"Chuck, listen." Hands in raincoat pockets, the old man leaned closer over the table. "I want to tell you a quick story," he said, "and then I'll go. Then *we'll* go. OK?"

The dealer's eyes moved left and right. His shift boss was down by the active tables. His relief dealer was almost due. "Keep it short," he said.

"Oh, I will!" His hands almost came out of the raincoat pockets, then didn't. "Chuck," he said, "I *know* where I belong, but I just keep coming out to the Strip, late at night. It's a fatal attraction. You know what that is, Chuck?"

"I think so," the dealer said. He thought about showgirls.

"But what makes it, Chuck? Look around. No windows, no clocks, no day or night in here. But it's only at night. I *like* these places. That's when they make me feel . . . good. Now, why's that?"

"I wouldn't know, sir."

The old man said, "Well, I was in here one time, and a couple of security fellows took me out back by the loading dock to *discourage* me a little. There were all these tall green-metal cans there, like if you have bottled gas delivered to your house out in the country, and I bumped into them and fell off the loading dock and all these big green-metal cans rolled off and landed on me. And that's why I was in the hospital."

The dealer looked at him. "But here you are back again."

"It's the old fatal attraction, Chuck."

"You'd better get over it,"

"Oh, I'm going to." Once again, the old man's hands almost came out of his raincoat pockets but didn't. "But I thought I'd tell somebody first about those green cans. Because, Chuck, here's the funny part. They had them in the hospital, too."

"Is that right?"

"That's right. 'What's that?' I asked the nurse. 'Oxygen', she said. 'Any time you see a tall can like that, if it's green, you know it's oxygen. That's a safety measure on account of oxygen's so dangerous. You get that stuff near any kind of fire and the whole thing'll burn like fury.' Did you know that, Chuck? About green meaning oxygen?"

"No, I didn't."

"Well, what I kept thinking was: Why does a big Strip hotel need about fifty cans of oxygen? And then I remembered the big hotel fire on the Strip a couple years ago. Remember that one?"

"I do," the dealer said.

"It said in the papers there was a fireball crossed six hundred feet of main casino in seventeen seconds. That's *fast*, Chuck."

"I suppose it is."

"In there, in the hospital," the old man said, "I had this thought: What if, late at night, here in the casino, with no windows and no clocks, air-conditioning out of vents all over, what if . . . Chuck, what if they add oxygen to the *air*? The very air we breathe, Chuck, this air all around us." The old man looked around. "Here in this spider's parlor."

"I wouldn't know anything about that," the dealer said, which was the absolute truth.

"Well, I wouldn't *know*, either, Chuck. But what if it's true? Spice up the air at night with extra oxygen, make the gamblers feel a little happier, a little more awake?"

"I'm going to have to call security now," the dealer said.

"Oh, I'm almost done, Chuck. You see, those penny slots downtown, they won't lead me back anywhere. I threw myself away, and I'm not coming back at all. I would have checked out of this rotten life two or three years ago, Chuck, if it hadn't been for this *fatal attraction*. Come out to the Strip late at night. Breathe deep. Get a little high on that extra oxygen, begin to *hope* again, get roughed up by security.'

"They don't do that with the oxygen."

"They don't? Well, Chuck, you may be right." The old man took his hands from his raincoat pockets. In his right hand, he held a can of lighter fluid; in his left, a kitchen match. "Let's see," he said and squirted a trail of lighter fluid onto the green felt of the table.

The dealer, wide-eyed, stomped down hard on the button. "Stop that!" he said.

The old man kept squirting lighter fluid, making dark puddles in the felt. "Security coming, Chuck?" he asked.

"Yes!"

"Good. I'd like them to travel with us," the old man said, and scraped the match along the edge of the table.

Westlake recalls: "In the late 1970s, I spent some time in Las Vegas writing a screenplay with a famous comedian for a movie that never got made. At the one hotel, to get to the dressing rooms, one not only had to go through the kitchen in the usual fashion, but also out along the loading dock. I was doing that one night and saw a whole lot of tall green canisters and said to the person I was with, 'That's oxygen. What do they need all that oxygen for?' He told me about the air sweetening. A couple of years later, when that place caught fire, shortly before eight A.M., witnesses described the fireball crossing the entire casino in something like six seconds, not possible with your civilian air."

JOHN MORTIMER

With wit and wisdom won through years of work as a barrister, playwright, mainstream novelist, screenwriter, and literary critic, John Mortimer has created a body of fiction centered on the Old Bailey hack Horace Rumpole. That work seems destined to stand, like Sir Arthur Conan Doyle's Sherlock Holmes stories, as a kind of canon. In these stories, Mortimer not only amuses by showing the interaction of a comical cast of characters, but he manages to make points about morality, social conscience, social climbing, marriage, and the law—all without ever seeming to moralize.

Mortimer grew up as an only child in an eccentric household in England's Cotswold Hills. His father, who was blinded in a garden accident but never mentioned aloud his loss of sight, was a divorce barrister who depended upon his wife to accompany him to court. Fond of spouting poetry and memorized lines from literature, he took his son on long country walks, during which he retold the Sherlock Holmes stories aloud, from memory. Mortimer became a divorce lawyer, too, but he wrote novels, radio plays and more, even while pursuing a life in the law. Equally comfortable with writing scripts and narrative prose, Mortimer wrote about coming of age in the shadow of his father in the play *A Voyage Round My Father* (1971) and in the narrative memoir *Clinging to the Wreckage* (1982). Mortimer later wrote two versions of many of his Rumpole stories—for publication and for televised broadcast. He did the same for some of his novels and also wrote screenplays of other writers' work, notably Evelyn Waugh's *Brideshead Revisited*.

"Rumpole and the Bubble Reputation" is a sterling example of Mortimer's work. In this short story, he uses Rumpole's interior monologue to deliver comments upon everything from human foibles to the role of the defense lawyer and the nature of justice, as Rumpole takes on the case of a tabloid newspaper editor who has been sued for libel by a writer of sugary romance novels. Along the way, Rumpole quietly demonstrates his friendship for—if not his patience with—his pretentious but hapless opera-loving colleague, Claude Erskine-Brown. He also shows unswerving dedication to getting to the truth of the matter, even if it costs him the loss of handsome legal fees. Most of all, Mortimer makes us realize Rumpole is no fool. Even as he moves out of the criminal court to take on a civil suit, and as others try to use him, he masters the challenges by means of his honest pursuit of the truth and a keen eye for others' ruses. The experience leads him to long for a straightforward crime, one that "shows human nature in a better light than civil law."

Rumpole and the Bubble Reputation

1988

IT is now getting on for half a century since I took to crime, and I can honestly say I haven't regretted a single moment of it.

Crime is about life, death and the liberty of the subject; civil law is entirely concerned with that most tedious of all topics, money. Criminal law requires an expert knowledge of bloodstains, policemen's notebooks and the dark flow of human passion, as well as the argot currently in use round the Elephant and Castle. Civil law calls for a close study of such yawn-producing matters as bills of exchange, negotiable instruments and charter parties. It is true, of course, that the most enthralling murder produces only a small and long-delayed Legal Aid cheque, sufficient to buy a couple of dinners at some Sunday supplement eaterie for the learned friends who practise daily in the commercial courts. Give me, however, a sympathetic jury, a blurred thumbprint and a dodgy confession, and you can keep *Mega-Chemicals Ltd* v. *The Sunshine Bank of Florida* with all its fifty days of mammoth refreshers for the well-heeled barristers involved.

There is one drawback, however, to being a criminal hack; the Judges and the learned friends are apt to regard you as though you were the proud possessor of a long line of convictions. How many times have I stood up to address the tribunal on such matters as the importance of intent or the presumption of innocence only to be stared at by the old darling on the Bench as though I were sporting a black mask or carrying a large sack labelled SWAG? Often, as I walk through the Temple on my way down to the Bailey, my place of work, I have seen bowler-hatted commercial or revenue men pass by on the other side and heard them mutter, 'There goes old Rumpole. I wonder if he's doing a murder or a rape this morning?' The sad truth of the matter is that civil law is regarded as the Harrods and crime the Tesco's of the legal profession. And of all the varieties of civil action the most elegant, the smartest, the one which attracts the best barristers like bees to the honey-pot, is undoubtedly the libel action. Star in a libel case on the civilized stage of the High Court of Justice and fame and fortune will be yours, if you haven't got them already.

It's odd, isn't it? Kill a person or beat him over the head and remove his wallet, and all you'll get is an Old Bailey judge and an Old Bailey hack. Cast a well-deserved slur on his moral character, ridicule his nose or belittle his bank balance and you will get a High Court judge and some of the smoothest silks in the business. I can only remember doing one libel action, and after it I asked my clerk, Henry, to find me a nice clean assault or an honest break and entering. Exactly why I did so will become clear to you when I have revealed the full and hitherto unpublished details of *Amelia Nettleship* v. *The Daily*

Beacon and Maurice Machin. If, after reading what went on in that particular defamation case, you don't agree that crime presents a fellow with a more honourable alternative, I shall have to think seriously about issuing a writ for libel.

You may be fortunate enough never to have read an allegedly 'historical' novel by that much-publicized authoress Miss Amelia Nettleship. Her books contain virginal heroines and gallant and gentlemanly heroes and thus present an extremely misleading account of our rough island story. She is frequently photographed wearing cotton print dresses, with large spectacles on her still pretty nose, dictating to a secretary and a couple of long-suffering cats in a wistaria-clad Tudor cottage somewhere outside Godalming. In the interviews she gives, Miss Nettleship invariably refers to the evils of the permissive society and the consequences of sex before marriage. I have never, speaking for myself, felt the slightest urge to join the permissive society; the only thing which would tempt me to such a course is hearing Amelia Nettleship denounce it.

Why, you may well ask, should I, whose bedtime reading is usually confined to *The Oxford Book of English Verse* (the Quiller-Couch edition), Archbold's *Criminal Law* and Professor Ackerman's *Causes of Death*, become so intimately acquainted with Amelia Nettleship? Alas, she shares my bed, not in person but in book form, propped up on the bosom of She Who Must Be Obeyed, alias my wife, Hilda, who insists on reading her far into the night. While engrossed in *Lord Stingo's Fancy*, I distinctly heard her sniff, and asked if she had a cold coming on. 'No, Rumpole,' she told me. 'Touching!'

'Oh, I'm sorry.' I moved further down the bed.

'Don't be silly. The book's touching. Very touching. We all thought Lord Stingo was a bit of a rake but he's turned out quite differently.'

'Sounds a sad disappointment.'

'Nonsense! It's ending happily. He swore he'd never marry, but Lady Sophia has made him swallow his words.'

'And if they were written by Amelia Nettleship I'm sure he found them extremely indigestible. Any chance of turning out the light?'

'Not yet. I've got another three chapters to go.'

'Oh, for God's sake! Can't Lord Stingo get on with it?' As I rolled over, I had no idea that I was soon to become legally involved with the authoress who was robbing me of my sleep.

My story starts in Pommeroy's Wine Bar to which I had hurried for medical treatment (my alcohol content had fallen to a dangerous low) at the end of a day's work. As I sipped my large dose of Château Thames Embankment, I saw my learned friend Erskine-Brown, member of our Chambers at Equity Court, alone and palely loitering. 'What can ail you, Claude?' I asked, and he told me it was his practice.

'Still practising?' I raised an eyebrow. 'I thought you might have got the hang of it by now.'

'I used to do a decent class of work,' he told me sadly. 'I once had a brief in a libel action. You were never in a libel, Rumpole?'

'Who cares about the bubble reputation? Give me a decent murder and a few well-placed bloodstains.'

'Now, guess what I've got coming up?' The man was wan with care.

'Another large claret for me, I sincerely hope.'

'Actual bodily harm and affray in the Kitten-A-Go-Go Club, Soho.' Claude is married to the Portia of our Chambers, the handsome Phillida Erskine-Brown, Q.C., and they are blessed with issue rejoicing in the names of Tristan and Isolde. He is, you understand, far more at home in the Royal Opera House than in any Soho Striperama. 'Two unsavoury characters in leather jackets were duelling with broken Coca-Cola bottles.'

'Sounds like my line of country,' I told him.

'Exactly! I'm scraping the bottom of your barrel, Rumpole. I mean, you've got a reputation for sordid cases. I'll have to ask you for a few tips.'

'Visit the *locus in quo*' was my expert advice. 'Go to the scene of the crime. Inspect the geography of the place.'

'The geography of the Kitten-A-Go-Go? Do I have to?'

'Of course. Then you can suggest it was too dark to identify anyone, or the witness couldn't see round a pillar, or . . .'

But at that point we were interrupted by an eager, bespectacled fellow of about Erskine-Brown's age who introduced himself as Ted Spratling from the *Daily Beacon*. 'I was just having an argument with my editor over there, Mr Rumpole,' he said. 'You do libel cases, don't you?'

'Good heavens, yes!' I lied with instant enthusiasm, sniffing a brief. 'The law of defamation is mother's milk to me. I cut my teeth on hatred, ridicule and contempt.' As I was speaking, I saw Claude Erskine-Brown eyeing the journalist like a long-lost brother. 'Slimey Spratling!' he hallooed at last.

'Collywobbles Erskine-Brown!' The hack seemed equally amazed. There was no need to tell me that they were at school together.

'Look, would you join my editor for a glass of Bolly?' Spratling invited me. 'What?'

'Bollinger.'

'I'd love to!' Erskine-Brown was visibly cheered.

'Oh, you too, Colly. Come on, then.'

'Golly, Colly!' I said as we crossed the bar towards a table in the corner. 'Bolly!'

So I was introduced to Mr Maurice—known as 'Morry'—Machin, a large silver-haired person with distant traces of a Scots accent, a blue silk suit and a thick gold ring in which a single diamond winked sullenly. He was surrounded with empty Bolly bottles and a masterful-looking woman whom he introduced as Connie Coughlin, the features editor. Morry himself had, I knew, been for many years at the helm of the tabloid *Daily Beacon*, and had blasted many precious reputations with well-aimed scandal stories and reverberating 'revelations'. 'They say you're a fighter, Mr Rumpole, that you're a terrier, sir, after a legal rabbit,' he started, as Ted Spratling performed the deputy editor's duty of pouring the bubbly.

'I do my best. This is my learned friend, Claude Erskine-Brown, who specializes in affray.'

'I'll remember you, sir, if I get into a scrap.' But the Editor's real business was with me. 'Mr Rumpole, we are thinking of briefing you. We're in a spot of bother over a libel.'

'Tell him,' Claude muttered to me, 'you can't do libel.'

'I never turn down a brief in a libel action.' I spoke with confidence, although Claude continued to mutter, 'You've never been offered a brief in a libel action.'

'I don't care,' I said, 'for little scraps in Soho. Sordid stuff. Give me a libel action, when a reputation is at stake.'

'You think that's important?' Morry looked at me seriously, so I treated him to a taste of *Othello*. 'Good name in man or woman, dear my lord' (I was at my most impressive),

> 'Is the immediate jewel of their souls;
> Who steals my purse steals trash; 'tis something, nothing.
> 'Twas mine, 'tis his, and has been slave to thousands;
> But he that filches from me my good name
> Robs me of that which not enriches him,
> And makes me poor indeed.'

Everyone, except Erskine-Brown, was listening reverently. After I had finished there was a solemn pause. Then Morry clapped three times.

'Is that one of your speeches, Mr Rumpole?'

'Shakespeare's.'

'Ah, yes . . .'

'Your good name, Mr Machin, is something I shall be prepared to defend to the death,' I said.

'Our paper goes in for a certain amount of fearless exposure,' the *Beacon* Editor explained.

'The "*Beacon* Beauties".' Erskine-Brown was smiling. 'I catch sight of it occasionally in the clerk's room.'

'Not that sort of exposure, Collywobbles!' Spratling rebuked his old school-friend. 'We tell the truth about people in the public eye.'

'Who's bonking who and who pays,' Connie from Features explained. 'Our readers love it.'

'I take exception to that, Connie. I really do,' Morry said piously. 'I don't want Mr Rumpole to get the idea that we're running any sort of a cheap scandal-sheet.'

'Scandal-sheet? Perish the thought!' I was working hard for my brief.

'You wouldn't have any hesitation in acting for the *Beacon*, would you?' the Editor asked me.

'A barrister is an old taxi plying for hire. That's the fine tradition of our trade,' I explained carefully. 'So it's my sacred duty, Mr Morry Machin, to take on anyone in trouble. However repellent I may happen to find them.'

'Thank you, Mr Rumpole.' Morry was genuinely grateful.

'Think nothing of it.'

'We are dedicated to exposing hypocrisy in our society. Wherever it exists. High or low.' The Editor was looking noble. 'So when we find this female pretending to be such a force for purity and parading her morality before the Great British Public . . . '

'Being all for saving your cherry till the honeymoon,' Connie Coughlin translated gruffly.

'Thank you, Connie. Or, as I would put it, denouncing premarital sex,' Morry said.

'She's even against the *normal* stuff!' Spratling was bewildered.

'Whereas her own private life is extremely steamy. We feel it our duty to tell our public. Show Mr Rumpole the article in question, Ted.'

I don't know if they had expected to meet me in Pommeroy's but the top brass of the *Daily Beacon* had a cutting of the alleged libel at the ready. THE PRIVATE LIFE OF AMELIA NETTLESHIP BY BEACON GIRL ON THE SPOT, STELLA JANUARY I read, and then glanced at the story that followed. 'This wouldn't be *the* Amelia Nettleship?' I was beginning to warm to my first libel action. 'The expert bottler of pure historical bilge-water?'

'The lady novelist and hypocrite,' Morry told me. 'Of course I've never met the woman.'

'She robs me of my sleep. I know nothing of her morality, but her prose style depraves and corrupts the English language. We shall need a statement from this Stella January.' I got down to business.

'Oh, Stella left us a couple of months ago,' the Editor told me.

'And went where?'

'God knows. Overseas, perhaps. You know what these girls are.'

'We've got to find her,' I insisted and then cheered him up with 'We shall fight, Mr Machin—Morry. And we shall conquer! Remember, I never plead guilty.'

'There speaks a man who knows damn all about libel.' Claude Erskine-Brown had a final mutter.

It might be as well if I quoted here the words in Miss Stella January's article which were the subject of legal proceedings. They ran as follows: *Miss Amelia Nettleship is a bit of a puzzle. The girls in her historical novels always keep their legs crossed until they've got a ring on their fingers. But her private life is rather different. Whatever lucky young man leads the 43-year-old Amelia to the altar will inherit a torrid past which makes Mae West sound like Florence Nightingale. Her home, Hollyhock Cottage, near Godalming, has been the scene of one-night stands and longer liaisons so numerous that the neighbours have given up counting. There is considerably more in her jacuzzi than bath salts. Her latest Casanova, so far unnamed, is said to be a married man who's been seen leaving in the wee small hours.* From the style of this piece of prose you may come to the conclusion that Stella January and Amelia Nettleship deserved each other.

One thing you can say for my learned friend Claude Erskine-Brown is that he takes advice. Having been pointed in the direction of the Kitten-A-Go-Go, he set off obediently to find a cul-de-sac off Wardour Street with his instructing solicitor. He wasn't to know, and it was entirely his bad luck, that Connie Coughlin had dreamt up a feature on London's Square Mile of Sin for the *Daily Beacon* and ordered an ace photographer to comb the sinful purlieus between Oxford Street and Shaftesbury Avenue in search of nefarious goings-on.

Erskine-Brown and a Mr Thrower, his sedate solicitor, found the Kitten-A-Go-Go, paid a sinister-looking myrmidon at the door ten quid each by way of membership and descended to a damp and darkened basement where two young ladies were chewing gum and removing their clothes with as much enthusiasm as they might bring to the task of licking envelopes. Claude took a seat in the front row and tried to commit the geography of the place to memory. It must be said, however, that his eyes were fixed on the plumpest of the disrobing performers when a sudden and unexpected flash preserved his face and more of the stripper for the five million readers of the *Daily Beacon* to enjoy with their breakfast. Not being a particularly observant barrister, Claude left the strip joint with no idea of the ill luck that had befallen him.

Whilst Erskine-Brown was thus exploring the underworld, I was closeted in the Chambers of that elegant Old Etonian civil lawyer Robin Peppiatt, Q.C., who, assisted by his Junior, Dick Garsington, represented the proprietor of the *Beacon*. I was entering the lists in the defence of Morry Machin, and our joint solicitor was an anxious little man called Cuxham, who seemed ready to pay almost any amount of someone else's money to be shot of the whole business. Quite early in our meeting, almost as soon, in fact, as Peppiatt had poured Earl Grey into thin china cups and handed round the *petit' beurres*, it became clear that everyone wanted to do a deal with the other side except my good self and my client, the Editor.

'We should work as a team,' Peppiatt started. 'Of which, as leading Counsel, I am, I suppose, the Captain.'

'Are we playing cricket, old chap?' I ventured to ask him.

'If we were it would be an extremely expensive game for the *Beacon*.' The Q.C. gave me a tolerant smile. 'The proprietors have contracted to indemnify the Editor against any libel damages.'

'I insisted on that when I took the job,' Morry told us with considerable satisfaction.

'Very sensible of your client, no doubt, Rumpole. Now, you may not be used to this type of case as you're one of the criminal boys . . . '

'Oh, I know'—I admitted the charge—'I'm just a juvenile delinquent.'

'But it's obvious to me that we mustn't attempt to justify these serious charges against Miss Nettleship's honour.' The Captain of the team gave his orders and I made bold to ask, 'Wouldn't that be cricket?'

'If we try to prove she's a sort of amateur tart the Jury might bump the damages up to two or three hundred grand,' Peppiatt explained as patiently as he could.

'Or four.' Dick Garsington shook his head sadly. 'Or perhaps half a million.' Mr Cuxham's mind boggled.

'But you've filed a defence alleging that the article's a true bill.' I failed to follow the drift of these faint-hearts.

'That's our bargaining counter.' Peppiatt spoke to me very slowly, as though to a child of limited intelligence.

'Our what?'

'Something to give away. As part of the deal.'

'When we agree terms with the other side we'll abandon all our allegations. Gracefully,' Garsington added.

'We put up our hands?' I contemptuously tipped ash from my small cigar on to Peppiatt's Axminster. Dick Garsington was sent off to get 'an ashtray for Rumpole'.

'Peregrine Landseer's agin us.' Peppiatt seemed to be bringing glad tidings of great joy to all of us. 'I'm lunching with Perry at the Sheridan Club to discuss another matter. I'll just whisper the thought of a quiet little settlement into his ear.'

'Whisper sweet nothings!' I told him. 'I'll not be party to any settlement. I'm determined to defend the good name of my client Mr Maurice Machin as a responsible editor.'

'At our expense?' Peppiatt looked displeased.

'If neccessary, Yes! He wouldn't have published that story unless there was some truth in it. Would you?' I asked Morry, assailed by some doubt.

'Certainly not'—my client assured me—'as a fair and responsible journalist.'

'The trouble is that there's no evidence that Miss Nettleship has done any of these things.' Clearly Mr Cuxham had long since thrown in the towel.

'Then we must find some! Isn't that what solicitors are for?' I asked, but didn't expect an answer. 'I'm quite unable to believe that anyone who writes so badly hasn't got *some* other vices.'

A few days later I entered the clerk's room of our Chambers in Equity Court to see our clerk, Henry, seated at his desk looking at the centre pages of the *Daily Beacon*, which Dianne, our fearless but somewhat hit-and-miss typist, was showing him. As I approached, Dianne folded the paper, retreated to her desk and began to type furiously. They both straightened their faces and the smiles of astonishment I had noticed when I came in were replaced by looks of legal seriousness. In fact Henry spoke with almost religious awe when he handed me my brief in *Nettleship* v. *The Daily Beacon and anor*. Not only was a highly satisfactory fee marked on the front but refreshers, that is the sum required to keep a barrister on his feet and talking, had been agreed at no less than five hundred pounds a day.

'You *can* make the case last, can't you, Mr Rumpole?' Henry asked with understandable concern.

'Make it last?' I reassured him. 'I can make it stretch on till the trump of doom! We have serious and lengthy allegations, Henry. Allegations that will take days and days, with any luck. For the first time in a long career at the Bar I begin to see . . . '

'See what, Mr Rumpole?'

'A way of providing for my old age.'

The door then opened to admit Claude Erskine-Brown. Dianne and Henry regarded him with solemn pity, as though he'd had a death in his family.

'Here comes the poor old criminal lawyer,' I greeted him. 'Any more problems with your affray, Claude?'

'All under control, Rumpole. Thank you very much. Morning, Dianne. Morning, Henry.' Our clerk and secretary returned his greeting in mournful voices. At that point, Erskine-Brown noticed Dianne's copy of the *Beacon*, wondered who the 'Beauty' of that day might be, and picked it up before she could stop him.

'What've you got there? The *Beacon*! A fine crusading paper. Tells the truth without fear or favour.' My refreshers had put me in a remarkably good mood. 'Are you feeling quite well, Claude?'

Erskine-Brown was holding the paper in trembling hands and had gone extremely pale. He looked at me with accusing eyes and managed to say in strangled tones, '*You* told me to go there!'

'For God's sake, Claude! Told you to go where?'

'The *locus in quo*!'

I took the *Beacon* from him and saw the cause of his immediate concern. The *locus in quo* was the Kitten-A-Go-Go, and the blown-up snap on the centre page showed Claude closely inspecting a young lady who was waving her underclothes triumphantly over her head. At that moment, Henry's telephone rang and he announced that Soapy Sam Ballard, our puritanical Head of Chambers, founder member of the Lawyers As Christians Society (L.A.C.) and the Savonarola of Equity Court, wished to see Mr Erskine-Brown in his room without delay. Claude left us with the air of a man climbing up into the dock to receive a stiff but inevitable sentence.

I wasn't, of course, present in the Head of Chambers' room where Claude was hauled up. It was not until months later, when he had recovered a certain calm, that he was able to tell me how the embarrassing meeting went and I reconstruct the occasion for the purpose of this narrative.

'You wanted to see me, Ballard?' Claude started to babble. 'You're looking well. In wonderful form. I don't remember when I've seen you looking so fit.' At that early stage he tried to make his escape from the room. 'Well, nice to chat. I've got a summons, across the road.'

'Just a minute!' Ballard called him back. 'I don't read the *Daily Beacon*.'

'Oh, don't you? Very wise,' Claude congratulated him. 'Neither do I. Terrible rag. Half-clad beauties on page four and no law reports. So they tell me. Absolutely no reason to bother with the thing!'

'But, coming out of the Temple tube station, Mr Justice Fishwick pushed this in my face.' Soapy Sam lifted the fatal newspaper from his desk. 'It seems he's just remarried and his new wife takes in the *Daily Beacon*.'

'How odd!'

'What's odd?'

'A judge's wife. Reading the *Beacon*.'

'Hugh Fishwick married his cook,' Ballard told him in solemn tones.

'Really? I didn't know. Well, that explains it. But I don't see why he should push it in your face, Ballard.'

'Because he thought I ought to see it.'

'Nothing in that rag that could be of the slightest interest to you, surely?'

'Something is.'

'What?'

'You.'

Ballard held out the paper to Erskine-Brown who approached it gingerly and took a quick look.

'Oh, really? Good heavens! Is that me?'

'Unless you have a twin brother masquerading as yourself. You feature in an article on London's Square Mile of Sin.'

'It's all a complete misunderstanding!' Claude assured our leader.

'I'm glad to hear it.'

'I can explain everything.'

'I hope so.'

'You see, I got into this affray.'

'You got into what?' Ballard saw even more cause for concern.

'This fight'—Claude wasn't improving his case—'in the Kitten-A-Go-Go.'

'Perhaps I ought to warn you, Erskine-Brown.' Ballard was being judicial. 'You needn't answer incriminating questions.'

'No, *I* didn't get into a fight.' Claude was clearly rattled. 'Good heavens, no. I'm doing a case, about a fight. An affray. With Coca-Cola bottles. And Rumpole advised me to go to this club.'

'Horace Rumpole is an habitué of this house of ill-repute? At *his* age?' Ballard didn't seem to be in the least surprised to hear it.

'No, not at all. But he said I ought to take a view. Of the scene of the crime. This wretched scandal-sheet puts the whole matter in the wrong light. Entirely.'

There was a long and not entirely friendly pause before Ballard proceeded to judgment. 'If that is so, Erskine-Brown,' he said, 'and I make no further comment while the matter is *sub judice*, you will no doubt be suing the *Daily Beacon* for libel?'

'You think I should?' Claude began to count the cost of such an action.

'It is quite clearly your duty. To protect your own reputation and the reputation of this Chambers.'

'Wouldn't it be rather expensive?' I can imagine Claude gulping, but Ballard was merciless.

'What is money' he said, 'compared to the hitherto unsullied name of number three, Equity Court?'

Claude's next move was to seek out the friend of his boyhood, 'Slimey' Spratling, whom he finally found jogging across Hyde Park. When he told the *Beacon* deputy editor that he had been advised to issue a writ, the man didn't even stop and Erskine-Brown had to trot along beside him. 'Good news!' Spratling said. 'My editor seems to enjoy libel actions. Glad you liked your pic.'

'Of course I didn't like it. It'll ruin my career.'

'Nonsense, Collywobbles.' Spratling was cheerful. 'You'll get briefed by all the clubs. You'll be the strippers' Q.C.'

'However did they get my name?' Claude wondered.

'Oh, I recognized you at once,' Slimey assured him. 'Bit of luck, wasn't it?' Then he ran on, leaving Claude outraged. They had, after all, been to Winchester together.

When I told the helpless Cuxham that the purpose of solicitors was to gather evidence, I did so without much hope of my words stinging him into any form of activity. If evidence against Miss Nettleship were needed, I would have to look elsewhere, so I rang up that great source of knowledge 'Fig' Newton and invited him for a drink at Pommeroy's.

Ferdinand Isaac Gerald, known to his many admirers as 'Fig' Newton, is undoubtedly the best in the somewhat unreliable band of professional private eyes. I know that Fig is now knocking seventy; that, with his filthy old mackintosh and collapsing hat, he looks like a scarecrow after a bad night; that his lantern jaw, watery eye and the frequently appearing drip on the end of the nose don't make him an immediately attractive figure. Fig may look like a scarecrow but he's a very bloodhound after a clue.

'I'm doing civil work now, Fig,' I told him when we met in Pommeroy's. 'Just got a big brief in a libel action which should provide a bit of comfort for my old age. But my instructing solicitor is someone we would describe, in legal terms, as a bit of a wally. I'd be obliged if you'd do his job for him and send him the bill when we win.'

'What is it that I am required to do, Mr Rumpole?' the great detective asked patiently.

'Keep your eye on a lady.'

'I usually am, Mr Rumpole. Keeping my eye on one lady or another.'

'This one's a novelist. A certain Miss Amelia Nettleship. Do you know her works?'

'Can't say I do, sir.' Fig had once confessed to a secret passion for Jane Austen. 'Are you on to a winner?'

'With a bit of help from you, Fig. Only one drawback here, as in most cases.'

'What's that, sir?'

'The client.' Looking across the bar I had seen the little group from the *Beacon* round the Bollinger. Having business with the Editor, I left Fig Newton to his work and crossed the room. Sitting myself beside my client I refused champagne and told him that I wanted him to do something about my learned friend Claude Erskine-Brown.

'You mean the barrister who goes to funny places in the afternoon? What're you asking me to do, Mr Rumpole?'

'Apologize, of course. Print the facts. Claude Erskine-Brown was in the Kitten-A-Go-Go purely in pursuit of his legal business.'

'I love it!' Morry's smile was wider than ever. 'There speaks the great defender. You'd put up any story, wouldn't you, however improbable, to get your client off.'

'It happens to be true.'

'So far as we are concerned'—Morry smiled at me patiently—'we printed a pic of a gentleman in a pin-striped suit examining the goods on display. No reason to apologize for that, is there, Connie? What's your view, Ted?'

'No reason at all, Morry.' Connie supported him and Spratling agreed.

'So you're going to do nothing about it?' I asked with some anger.

'Nothing we *can* do.'

'Mr Machin.' I examined the man with distaste. 'I told you it was a legal rule that a British barrister is duty-bound to take on any client however repellent.'

'I remember you saying something of the sort.'

'You are stretching my duty to the furthest limits of human endurance.'

'Never mind, Mr Rumpole. I'm sure you'll uphold the best traditions of the Bar!'

When Morry said that I left him. However, as I was wandering away from Pommeroy's towards the Temple station, Gloucester Road, home and beauty, a somewhat breathless Ted Spratling caught up with me and asked me to do my best for Morry. 'He's going through a tough time.' I didn't think the man was entirely displeased by the news he had to impart. 'The Proprietor's going to sack him.'

'Because of this case?'

'Because the circulation's dropping. Tits and bums are going out of fashion. The wives don't like it.'

'Who'll be the next editor?'

'Well, I'm the deputy now . . . ' He did his best to sound modest.

'I see. Look'—I decided to enlist an ally—'would you help me with the case? In strict confidence, I want some sort of a lead to this Stella January. Can you find how her article came in? Get hold of the original. It might have an address. Some sort of clue . . . '

'I'll have a try, Mr Rumpole. Anything I can do to help old Morry.' Never had I heard a man speak with such deep insincerity.

The weather turned nasty, but, in spite of heavy rain, Fig Newton kept close observation for several nights on Hollyhock Cottage, home of Amelia Nettleship, without any particular result. One morning I entered our Chambers early and on my way to my room I heard a curious buzzing sound, as though an angry bee were trapped in the lavatory. Pulling open the door, I detected Erskine-Brown plying a cordless electric razor.

'Claude,' I said, 'you're shaving!'

'Wonderful to see the workings of a keen legal mind.' The man sounded somewhat bitter.

'I'm sorry about all this. But I'm doing my best to help you.'

'Oh, please!' He held up a defensive hand. 'Don't try and do anything else to help me. "Visit the scene of the crime," you said. "Inspect the *locus in quo*!" So where has your kind assistance landed me? My name's mud. Ballard's as good as threatened to kick me out of Chambers. I've got to spend my life's savings on a speculative libel action. And my marriage is on the rocks. Wonderful what you can do, Rumpole, with a few words of advice. Your clients must be everlastingly grateful.'

'Your marriage, on the rocks, did you say?'

'Oh, yes. Philly was frightfully reasonable about it. As far as she was concerned, she said, she didn't care what I did in the afternoons. But we'd better live apart for a while, for the sake of the children. She didn't want Tristan and Isolde to associate with a father dedicated to the exploitation of women.'

'Oh, Portia!' I felt for the fellow. 'What's happened to the quality of mercy?'

'So, thank you very much, Rumpole. I'm enormously grateful. The next time you've got a few helpful tips to hand out, for God's sake keep them to yourself!'

He switched on the razor again. I looked at it and made an instant deduction. 'You've been sleeping in Chambers. You want to watch that, Claude. Ballard nearly got rid of me for a similar offence."

'Where do you expect me to go? Phillida's having the locks changed in Islington.'

'Have you no friends?'

'Philly and I have reached the end of the line. I don't exactly want to advertise the fact among my immediate circle. I seem to remember, Rumpole, when you fell out with Hilda you planted yourself on us!' As he said this I scented danger and tried to avoid what I knew was coming.

'Oh. Now. Erskine-Brown. Claude. I was enormously grateful for your hospitality on that occasion.'

'Quite an easy run in on the Underground, is it, from Gloucester Road?' He spoke in a meaningful way.

'Of course. My door is always open. I'd be delighted to put you up, just until this mess is straightened out. But . . .'

---

* See 'Rumpole and the Old, Old Story' in *Rumpole's Last Case*, Penguin Books, 1987.

'The least you could do, I should have thought, Rumpole.'

'It's not a sacrifice I could ask, old darling, even of my dearest friend. I couldn't ask you to shoulder the burden of daily life with She Who Must Be Obeyed. Now I'm sure you can find a very comfortable little hotel, somewhere cheap and cosy, around the British Museum. I promise you, life is by no means a picnic, in the Gloucester Road.'

Well, that was enough, I thought, to dissuade the most determined visitor from seeking hospitality under the Rumpole roof. I went about my daily business and, when my work was done, I thought I should share some of the good fortune brought with my brief in the libel action with She Who Must Be Obeyed. I lashed out on two bottles of Pommeroy's bubbly, some of the least exhausted flowers to be found outside the tube station and even, such was my reckless mood, lavender water for Hilda.

'All the fruits of the earth,' I told her. 'Or, let's say, the fruits of the first cheque in *Nettleship* v. *The Beacon*, paid in advance. The first of many, if we can spin out the proceedings.'

'You're doing that awful case!' She didn't sound approving.

'That awful case will bring us in five hundred smackers a day in refreshers.'

'Helping that squalid newspaper insult Amelia Nettleship.' She looked at me with contempt.

'A barrister's duty, Hilda, is to take on all comers. However squalid.'

'Nonsense!'

'What?'

'Nonsense. You're only using that as an excuse.'

'Am I?'

'Of course you are. You're doing it because you're jealous of Amelia Nettleship!'

'Oh, I don't think so,' I protested mildly. 'My life has been full of longings, but I've never had the slightest desire to become a lady novelist.'

'You're jealous of her because she's got high principles.' Hilda was sure of it. 'You haven't got high principles, have you, Rumpole?'

'I told you. I will accept any client, however repulsive.'

'That's not a principle, that's just a way of making money from the most terrible people. Like the editor of the *Daily Beacon*. My mind is quite made up, Rumpole. I shall not use a single drop of that corrupt lavender water.'

It was then that I heard a sound from the hallway which made my heart sink. An all-too-familiar voice was singing '*La donna e mobile*' in a light tenor. Then the door opened to admit Erskine-Brown wearing my dressing-gown and very little else. 'Claude telephoned and told me all his troubles.' Hilda looked at the man with sickening sympathy. 'Of course I invited him to stay.'

'You're wearing my dressing-gown!' I put the charge to him at once.

'I had to pack in a hurry.' He looked calmly at the sideboard. 'Thoughtful of you to get in champagne to welcome me, Rumpole.'

'Was the bath all right, Claude?' Hilda sounded deeply concerned.

'Absolutely delightful, thank you, Hilda.'

'What a relief! That geyser can be quite temperamental.'

'Which is your chair, Horace?' Claude had the courtesy to ask.

'I usually sit by the gas fire. Why?'

'Oh, do sit there, Claude,' Hilda urged him and he gracefully agreed to pinch my seat. 'We mustn't let you get cold, must we. After your bath.'

So they sat together by the gas fire and I was allowed to open champagne for both of them. As I listened to the rain outside the window my spirits, I had to admit, had sunk to the lowest of ebbs. And around five o'clock the following morning, Fig Newton, the rain falling from the brim of his hat and the drop falling off his nose, stood watching Hollyhock Cottage. He saw someone—he was too far away to make an identification—come out of the front door and get into a parked car. Then he saw the figure of a woman in a nightdress, no doubt Amelia Nettleship, standing in the lit doorway waving goodbye. The headlights of the car were switched on and it drove away.

When the visitor had gone, and the front door was shut, Fig moved nearer to the cottage. He looked down at the muddy track on which the car had been parked and saw something white. He stooped to pick it up, folded it carefully and put it in his pocket.

On the day that *Nettleship* v. *The Beacon* began its sensational course, I breakfasted with Claude in the kitchen of our so-called 'mansion' flat in the Gloucester Road. I say breakfasted, but Hilda told me that bacon and eggs were off as our self-invited guest preferred a substance, apparently made up of sawdust and bird droppings, which he called muesli. I was a little exhausted, having been kept awake by the amplified sound of grand opera from the spare bedroom, but Claude explained that he always found that a little Wagner settled him down for the night. He then asked for some of the goat's milk that Hilda had got in for him specially. As I coated a bit of toast with Oxford marmalade, the man only had to ask for organic honey to have it instantly supplied by She Who Seemed Anxious to Oblige.

'And what the hell,' I took the liberty of asking, 'is organic honey?'

'The bees only sip from flowers grown without chemical fertilizers,' Claude explained patiently.

'How does the bee know?'

'What?'

'I suppose the other bees tell it, "Don't sip from that, old chap. It's been grown with chemical fertilizers."'

So, ill-fed and feeling like a cuckoo in my own nest, I set off to the Royal Courts of Justice, in the Strand, that imposing turreted château which is the Ritz Hotel of the legal profession, the place where a gentleman is remunerated to the tune of five hundred smackers a day. It is also the place where gentlemen prefer an amicable settlement to the brutal business of fighting their cases.

I finally pitched up, wigged and robed, in front of the Court which would provide the battle-ground for our libel action. I saw the combatants, Morry Machin and the fair Nettleship, standing a considerable distance apart. Peregrine Landseer, Q.C., Counsel for the Plaintiff, and Robin Peppiatt, Q.C., for the Proprietor of the *Beacon*, were meeting on the central ground for a peace conference, attended by assorted juniors and instructing solicitors.

'After all the publicity, my lady couldn't take less than fifty thousand.' Landseer, Chairman of the Bar Council and on the brink of becoming a judge, was nevertheless driving as hard a bargain as any second-hand car dealer.

'Forty and a full and grovelling apology.' And Peppiatt added the bonus. 'We could wrap it up and lunch together at the Sheridan.'

'It's steak and kidney pud day at the Sheridan,' Dick Garsington remembered wistfully.

'Forty-five.' Landseer was not so easily tempted. 'And that's my last word on the subject.'

'Oh, all right,' Peppiatt conceded. 'Forty-five and a full apology. You happy with that, Mr Cuxham?'

'Well, sir. If you advise it.' Cuxham clearly had no stomach for the fight.

'We'll chat to the Editor. I'm sure we're all going to agree'—Peppiatt gave me a meaningful look—'in the end.'

While Landseer went off to sell the deal to his client, Peppiatt approached my man with 'You only have to join in the apology, Mr Machin, and the *Beacon* will pay the costs and the forty-five grand.'

'"Who steals my purse steals trash,"' I quoted thoughtfully. ' "But he that filches from me my good name . . . " You're asking my client to sign a statement admitting he printed lies.'

'Oh, for heaven's sake, Rumpole!' Peppiatt was impatient. 'They gave up quoting that in libel actions fifty years ago.'

'Mr Rumpole's right.' Morry nodded wisely. 'My good name—I looked up the quotation—it's the immediate jewel of my soul.'

'Steady on, old darling,' I murmured. 'Let's not go *too* far.' At which moment Peregrine Landseer returned from a somewhat heated discussion with his client to say that there was no shifting her and she was determined to fight for every penny she could get.

'But Perry . . . ' Robin Peppiatt lamented, 'the case is going to take two weeks!' At five hundred smackers a day I could only thank God for the stubbornness of Amelia Nettleship.

So we went into Court to fight the case before a jury and Mr Justice Teasdale, a small, highly opinionated and bumptious little person who is unmarried, lives in Surbiton with a Persian cat, and was once an unsuccessful Tory candidate for Weston-super-Mare North. It takes a good deal of talent for a Tory to lose Weston-super-Mare North. Worst of all, he turned out to be a devoted fan of the works of Miss Amelia Nettleship.

'Members of the Jury,' Landseer said in opening the Plaintiff's case, 'Miss Nettleship is the authoress of a number of historical works.'

'Rattling good yarns, Members of the Jury,' Mr Justice Teasdale chirped up.

'I beg your Lordship's pardon.' Landseer looked startled.

'I said 'rattling good yarns', Mr Peregrine Landseer. The sort your wife might pick up without the slightest embarrassment. Unlike so much of the distasteful material one finds between hard covers today.'

'My Lord.' I rose to protest with what courtesy I could muster.

'Yes, Mr Rumbold?'

'Rum*pole*, my Lord.'

'I'm so sorry.' The Judge didn't look in the least apologetic. 'I understand you are something of a stranger to these Courts.'

'Would it not be better to allow the Jury to come to their own conclusions about Miss Amelia Nettleship?' I suggested, ignoring the Teasdale manners.

'Well. Yes. Of course. I quite agree.' The Judge looked serious and then cheered up. 'And when they do they'll find she can put together a rattling good yarn.'

There was a sycophantic murmur of laughter from the Jury, and all I could do was subside and look balefully at the Judge. I felt a pang of nostalgia for the Old Bailey and the wild stampede of the mad Judge Bullingham.

As Peregrine Landseer bored on, telling the Jury what terrible harm the *Beacon* had done to his client's hitherto unblemished reputation, Ted Spratling, the deputy editor, leant forward in the seat behind me and whispered in my ear. 'About that Stella January article,' he said. 'I bought a drink for the systems manager. The copy's still in the system. One rather odd thing.'

'Tell me . . . '

'The logon—that's the identification of the word processor. It came from the Editor's office.'

'You mean it was written there?'

'No one writes things any more.'

'Of course not. How stupid of me.'

'It looks as if it had been put in from his word processor.'

'That is extremely interesting.'

'If Mr Rum*pole* has quite finished his conversation!' Peregrine Landseer was rebuking me for chattering during his opening speech.

I rose to apologize as humbly as I could. 'My Lord, I can assure my learned friend I was listening to every word of his speech. It's such a rattling good yarn.'

So the morning wore on, being mainly occupied by Landseer's opening. The luncheon adjournment saw me pacing the marble corridors of the Royal Courts of Justice with that great source of information, Fig Newton. He gave me a lengthy account of his observation on Hollyhock Cottage, and when he finally got to the departure of Miss Nettleship's nocturnal visitor, I asked impatiently, 'You got the car number?'

'Alas. No. Visibility was poor and weather conditions appalling.' The sleuth's evidence was here interrupted by a fit of sneezing.

'Oh, Fig!' I was, I confess, disappointed. 'And you didn't see the driver?'

'Alas. No, again.' Fig sneezed apologetically. 'However, when Miss Nettleship had closed the door and extinguished the lights, presumably in order to return to bed, I proceeded to the track in front of the house where the vehicle had been standing. There I retrieved an article which I thought might just possibly have been dropped by the driver in getting in or out of the vehicle.'

'For God's sake, show me!'

The detective gave me his treasure trove, which I stuffed into a pocket just as the Usher came out of Court to tell me that the Judge was back from lunch, Miss Nettleship was entering the witness-box, and the world of libel awaited my attention.

If ever I saw a composed and confident witness, that witness was Amelia Nettleship. Her hair was perfectly done, her black suit was perfectly discreet, her white blouse shone, as did her spectacles. Her features, delicately cut as an intaglio, were attractive, but her beauty was by no means louche or abundant. So spotless did she seem that she might well have preserved her virginity until what must have been, in spite of appearances to the contrary, middle age. When she had finished her evidence-in-chief the Judge thanked her and urged her to go on writing her 'rattling good yarns'. Peppiatt then rose to his feet to ask her a few questions designed to show that her books were still selling in spite of the *Beacon* article. This she denied, saying that sales had dropped off. The thankless task of attacking the fair name of Amelia was left to Rumpole.

'Miss Nettleship,' I started off with my guns blazing, 'are you a truthful woman?'

'I try to be.' She smiled at his Lordship, who nodded encouragement.

'And you call yourself an historical novelist?'

'I try to write books which uphold certain standards of morality.'

'Forget the morality for a moment. Let's concentrate on the history.'

'Very well.'

One of the hardest tasks in preparing for my first libel action was reading through the works of Amelia Nettleship. Now I had to quote from Hilda's favourite. 'May I read you a short passage from an alleged historical novel of yours entitled *Lord Stingo's Fancy*?' I asked as I picked up the book.

'Ah, yes.' The Judge looked as though he were about to enjoy a treat. 'Isn't that the one which ends happily?'

'Happily, all Miss Nettleship's books end, my Lord,' I told him. 'Eventually.' There was a little laughter in Court, and I heard Landseer whisper to his Junior, 'This criminal chap's going to bump up the damages enormously.'

Meanwhile I started quoting from *Lord Stingo's Fancy*. '"Sophia had first set eyes on Lord Stingo when she was a dewy eighteen-year-old and he had clattered up to her father's castle, exhausted from the Battle of Nazeby,"' I read. '"Now at the ball to triumphantly celebrate the gorgeous, enthroning coronation of the Merry Monarch King Charles II they were to meet again. Sophia was now in her twenties but, in ways too numerous to completely describe, still an unspoilt girl at heart." You call that a *historical* novel?'

'Certainly,' the witness answered unashamed.

'Haven't you forgotten something?' I put it to her.

'I don't think so. What?'

'Oliver Cromwell.'

'I really don't know what you mean.'

'Clearly, if this Sophia . . . this girl . . . How do you describe her?'

'"Dewy", Mr Rumpole.' The Judge repeated the word with relish.

'Ah, yes. "Dewy". I'm grateful to your Lordship. I had forgotten the full horror of the passage. If this dew-bespattered Sophia had been eighteen at the time of the Battle of Naseby in the reign of Charles I, she would have been thirty-three in the year of Charles II's coronation. Oliver Cromwell came in between.'

'I am an artist, Mr Rumpole.' Miss Nettleship smiled at my pettifogging objections.

'What kind of an artist?' I ventured to ask.

'I think Miss Nettleship means an artist in words,' was how the Judge explained it.

'Are you, Miss Nettleship?' I asked. 'Then you must have noticed that the short passage I have read to the Jury contains two split infinitives and a tautology.'

'A what, Mr Rumpole?' The Judge looked displeased.

'Using two words that mean the same thing, as in "the enthroning coronation". My Lord, t – a – u . . . " I tried to be helpful.

'I can *spell*, Mr Rumpole.' Teasdale was now testy.

"Then your Lordship has the advantage of the witness. I notice she spells Naseby with a "z".'

'My Lord. I hesitate to interrupt.' At least I was doing well enough to bring Landseer languidly to his feet. 'Perhaps this sort of cross-examination is common enough in the criminal courts, but I cannot see how it can possibly be relevant in an action for libel.'

'Neither can I, Mr Landseer, I must confess.' Of course the Judge agreed.

I did my best to put him right. 'These questions, my Lord, go to the heart of this lady's credibility.' I turned to give the witness my full attention. 'I have to suggest, Miss Nettleship, that as an historical novelist you are a complete fake.'

'My Lord. I have made my point.' Landseer sat down then, looking well pleased, and immediately whispered to his Junior, 'We'll let him go on with that line and they'll give us four hundred thousand.'

'You have no respect for history and very little for the English language.' I continued to chip away at the spotless novelist.

'I try to tell a story, Mr Rumpole.'

'And your evidence to this Court has been, to use my Lord's vivid expression, "a rattling good yarn"?' Teasdale looked displeased at my question.

'I have sworn to tell the truth.'

'Remember that. Now let us see how much of this article is correct.' I picked up Stella January's offending contribution. 'You do live at Hollyhock Cottage, near Godalming, in the county of Surrey?'

'That is so.'

'You have a jacuzzi?'

'She has *what*, Mr Rumpole?' I had entered a world unknown to a judge addicted to cold showers.

'A sort of bath, my Lord, with a whirlpool attached.'

'I installed one in my converted barn,' Miss Nettleship admitted. 'I find it relaxes me, after a long day's work.'

'You don't twiddle round in there with a close personal friend occasionally?'

'That's worth another ten thousand to us,' Landseer told his Junior, growing happier by the minute. In fact the Jury members were looking at me with some disapproval.

'Certainly not. I do not believe in sex before marriage.'

'And have no experience of it?'

'I was engaged once, Mr Rumpole.'

'Just once?'

'Oh, yes. My fiancé was killed in an air crash ten years ago. I think about him every day, and every day I'm thankful we didn't—' she looked down modestly—'do anything before we were married. We were tempted, I'm afraid, the night before he died. But we resisted the temptation.'

'Some people would say that's a very moving story,' Judge Teasdale told the Jury after a reverent hush.

'Others might say it's the story of *Sally on the Somme*, only there the fiancé was killed in the war.' I picked up another example of the Nettleship *œuvre*.

'That, Mr Rumpole,' Amelia looked pained, 'is a book that's particularly close to my heart. At least I don't do anything my heroines wouldn't do.'

'He's getting worse all the time,' Robin Peppiatt, the *Beacon* barrister, whispered despairingly to his Junior, Dick Garsington, who came back with 'The damages are going to hit the roof!'

'Miss Nettleship, may I come to the last matter raised in the article?'

'I'm sure the Jury will be grateful that you're reaching the end, Mr Rumpole,' the Judge couldn't resist saying, so I smiled charmingly and told him that I should finish a great deal sooner if I were allowed to proceed without further interruption. Then I began to read Stella January's words aloud to the witness. ' "Her latest Casanova, so far unnamed, is said to be a married man who's been seen leaving in the wee small hours." '

'I read that,' Miss Nettleship remembered.

'You had company last night, didn't you? Until what I suppose might be revoltingly referred to as "the wee small hours"?'

'What are you suggesting?'

'That someone was with you. And when he left at about five thirty in the morning you stood in your nightdress waving goodbye and blowing kisses. Who was it, Miss Nettleship?'

'That is an absolutely uncalled-for suggestion.'

'You called for it when you issued a writ for libel.'

'Do I have to answer?' She turned to the Judge for help. He gave her his most encouraging smile and said that it might save time in the end if she were to answer Mr Rumpole's question.

'That is absolutely untrue!' For the first time Amelia's look of serenity vanished and I got, from the witness-box, a cold stare of hatred. 'Absolutely untrue.' The Judge made a grateful note of her answer. 'Thank you, Miss Nettleship. I think we might continue with this tomorrow morning, if you have any further questions, Mr Rumpole?'

'I have indeed, my Lord.' Of course I had more questions and by the morning I hoped also to have some evidence to back them up.

I was in no hurry to return to the alleged 'mansion' flat that night. I rightly suspected that our self-invited guest, Claude Erskine-Brown, would be playing his way through *Die Meistersinger* and giving Hilda a synopsis of the plot as it unfolded. As I reach the last of a man's Seven Ages I am more than ever persuaded that life is too short for Wagner, a man who was never in a hurry when it came to composing an opera. I paid a solitary visit to Pommeroy's well-known watering-hole after Court in the hope of finding the representatives of the *Beacon*; but the only one I found was Connie Coughlin, the features editor, moodily surveying a large gin and tonic. 'No champagne tonight?' I asked as I wandered over to her table, glass in hand.

'I don't think we've got much to celebrate.'

'I wanted to ask you'—I took a seat beside the redoubtable Connie—'about Miss Stella January. Our girl on the spot. Bright, attractive kind of reporter, was she?'

'I don't know,' Connie confessed.

'But surely you're the features editor?'

'I never met her.' She said it with the resentment of a woman whose editor had been interfering with her page.

'Any idea how old she was, for instance?'

'Oh, young, I should think.' It was the voice of middle age speaking. 'Morry said she was young. Just starting in the business.'

'And I was going to ask you . . . '

'You're very inquisitive.'

'It's my trade.' I downed what was left of my claret. '. . . About the love life of Mr Morry Machin.'

'Good God. Whose side are you on, Mr Rumpole?'

'At the moment, on the side of the truth. Did Morry have some sort of a romantic interest in Miss Stella January?'

'Short-lived, I'd say.' Connie clearly had no pity for the girl if she'd been enjoyed and then sacked.

'He's married?'

'Oh, two or three times.' It occurred to me that at some time, during one or other of these marriages, Morry and La Coughlin might have been more than fellow hacks on the *Beacon*. 'Now he seems to have got some sort of steady girl-friend.' She said it with some resentment.

'You know her?'

'Not at all. He keeps her under wraps.'

I looked at her for a moment. A woman, I thought, with a lonely evening in an empty flat before her. Then I thanked her for her help and stood up.

'Who are you going to grill next?' she asked me over the rim of her gin and tonic.

'As a matter of fact,' I told her, 'I've got a date with Miss Stella January.'

Quarter of an hour later I was walking across the huge floor, filled with desks, telephones and word processors, where the *Beacon* was produced, towards the glass-walled office in the corner, where Morry sat with his deputy Ted Spratling, seeing that all the scandal that was fit to print, and a good deal of it that wasn't, got safely between the covers of the *Beacon*. I arrived at his office, pulled open the door and was greeted by Morry, in his shirtsleeves, his feet up on the desk. 'Working late, Mr Rumpole? I hope you can do better for us tomorrow,' he greeted me with amused disapproval.

'I hope so too. I'm looking for Miss Stella January.'

'I told you, she's not here any more. I think she went overseas.'

'I think she's here,' I assured him. He was silent for a moment and then he looked at his deputy. 'Ted, perhaps you'd better leave me to have a word with my learned Counsel.'

'I'll be on the back bench.' Spratling left for the desk on the floor which the editors occupied.

When he had gone, Morry looked up at me and said quietly, 'Now then, Mr Rumpole, sir. How can I help you?'

'Stella certainly wasn't a young woman, was she?' I was sure about that.

'She was only with us a short time. But she was young, yes,' he said vaguely.

'A quotation from her article that Amelia Nettleship "makes Mae West sound like Florence Nightingale". No young woman today's going to have heard of Mae West. Mae West's as remote in history as Messalina and Helen of Troy. That article, I would hazard a guess, was written by a man well into his middle age.'

'Who?'

'You.'

There was another long silence and the Editor did his best to smile. 'Have you been drinking at all this evening?'

I took a seat then on the edge of his desk and lit a small cigar. 'Of course I've been drinking *at all*. You don't imagine I have these brilliant flashes of deduction when I'm perfectly sober, do you?'

'Then hadn't you better go home to bed?'

'So you wrote the article. No argument about that. It's been found in the system with your word processor number on it. Careless, Mr Machin. You clearly have very little talent for crime. The puzzling thing is, why you should attack Miss Nettleship when she's such a good friend of yours.'

'Good friend?' He did his best to laugh. 'I told you. I've never even met the woman.'

'It was a lie, like the rest of this pantomime lawsuit. Last night you were with her until past five in the morning. And she said goodbye to you with every sign of affection.'

'What makes you say that?'

'Were you in a hurry? Anyway, this was dropped by the side of your car.' Then I pulled out the present Fig Newton had given me outside Court that day and put it on the desk.

'Anyone can buy the *Beacon*.' Morry glanced at the mud-stained exhibit.

'Not everyone gets the first edition, the one that fell on the Editor's desk at ten o'clock that evening. I would say that's a bit of a rarity around Godalming.'

'Is that all?'

'No. You were watched.'

'Who by?'

'Someone I asked to find out the truth about Miss Nettleship. Now he's turned up the truth about both of you.'

Morry got up then and walked to the door which Ted Spratling had left half open. He shut it carefully and then turned to me. 'I went down to ask her to drop the case.'

'To use a legal expression, pull the other one, it's got bells on it.'

'I don't know what you're suggesting.'

And then, as he stood looking at me, I moved round and sat in the Editor's chair, 'Let me enlighten you.' I was as patient as I could manage. 'I'm suggesting a conspiracy to pervert the course of justice.'

'What's that mean?'

'I told you I'm an old taxi, waiting on the rank, but I'm not prepared to be the get-away driver for a criminal conspiracy.'

'You haven't said anything? To anyone?' He looked older and very frightened.

'Not yet.'

'And you won't.' He tried to sound confident. 'You're my lawyer.'

'Not any longer, Mr Machin. I don't belong to you any more. I'm an ordinary citizen, about to report an attempted crime.' It was then I reached for the telephone. 'I don't think there's any limit on the sentence for conspiracy.'

'What do you mean, "conspiracy"?'

'You're getting sacked by the *Beacon*; perhaps your handshake is a bit less than golden. Sales are down on historical virgins. So your steady girl-friend and you get together to make half a tax-free million.'

'I wish I knew how.' He was doing his best to smile.

'Perfectly simple. You turn yourself into Stella January, the unknown girl reporter, for half an hour and libel Amelia. She sues the paper and collects. Then you both sail into the sunset and share the proceeds. There's one thing I shan't forgive you for.'

'What's that?'

'The plan called for an Old Bailey hack, a stranger to the civilized world of libel who wouldn't settle, an old war-horse who'd attack La Nettleship and inflame the damages. So you used me, Mr Morry Machin!'

'I thought you'd be accustomed to that.' He stood over me, suddenly looking older. 'Anyway, they told me in Pommeroy's that you never prosecute.'

'No, I don't, do I? But on this occasion, I must say, I'm sorely tempted.' I thought about it and finally pushed away the telephone. 'Since it's a libel action I'll offer you terms of settlement.'

'What sort of terms?'

'The fair Amelia to drop her case. You pay the costs, including the fees of Fig Newton, who's caught a bad cold in the course of these proceedings. Oh, and in the matter of my learned friend Claude Erskine-Brown . . .'

'What's he got to do with it?'

' . . . Print a full and grovelling apology on the front page of the *Beacon*. And get them to pay him a substantial sum by way of damages. And that's my last word on the subject.' I stood up then and moved to the door.

'What's it going to cost me?' was all he could think of saying.

'I have no idea, but I know what it's going to cost me. Two weeks at five hundred a day. A provision for my old age.' I opened the glass door and let in the hum and clatter which were the birth-pangs of the *Daily Beacon*. 'Goodnight, Stella,' I said to Mr Morry Machin. And then I left him.

So it came about that next morning's *Beacon* printed a grovelling apology to 'the distinguished barrister Mr Claude Erskine-Brown' which accepted that he went to the Kitten-A-Go-Go Club purely in the interests of legal research and announced that my learned friend's hurt feelings would be soothed by the application of substantial, and tax-free, damages. As a consequence of this, Mrs Phillida Erskine-Brown rang Chambers, spoke words of forgiveness and love to her husband, and he arranged, in his new-found wealth, to take her to dinner at Le Gavroche. The cuckoo flew from our nest, Hilda and I were left alone in the Gloucester Road, and we never found out how *Die Meistersinger* ended.

In Court my one and only libel action ended in a sudden outburst of peace and goodwill, much to the frustration of Mr Justice Teasdale, who had clearly been preparing a summing-up which would encourage the Jury to make Miss Nettleship rich beyond the dreams of avarice. All the allegations against her were dropped; she had no doubt been persuaded by her lover to ask for no damages at all and the *Beacon*'s Editor accepted the bill for costs with extremely bad grace. This old legal taxi moved off to ply for hire elsewhere, glad to be shot of Mr Morry Machin. 'Is there a little bit of burglary around, Henry?' I asked our clerk, as I have recorded. 'Couldn't you get me a nice little gentle robbery? Something which shows human nature in a better light than civil law?'

'Good heavens!' Hilda exclaimed as we lay reading in the matrimonial bed in Froxbury Mansions. I noticed that there had been a change in her reading matter and she was already well into *On the Make* by Suzy Hutchins. 'This girl's about to go to Paris with a man old enough to be her father.'

'That must happen quite often.'

'But it seems he *is* her father.'

'Well, at least you've gone off the works of Amelia Nettleship.'

'The way she dropped that libel action. The woman's no better than she should be.'

'Which of us is? Any chance of turning out the light?' I asked She Who Must Be Obeyed, but she was too engrossed in the doings of her delinquent heroine to reply.

SUE GRAFTON

When Sue Grafton published her first Kinsey Millhone novel, *A Is for Alibi*, in 1982, she was among the vanguard of women writers creating strong female private eye characters. Since then, Grafton's spunky sleuth has made her way through eighteen cases, all "Respectfully submitted" in novels titled after the letters in the alphabet and narrated by Millhone. Her latest adventure, *R Is for Richochet*, was published in 2004.

Like her sleuth, Grafton takes on challenges with a "can do" attitude and a certain amount of spunk. The daughter of a teacher and of the mystery writer and lawyer C. W. Grafton, she grew up in a home where reading was revered. But, as Grafton has said, the household was also "classically dysfunctional," thanks to her parents' alcoholism. Instead of wallowing in these troubles, she used them to advantage, honing sensitivity to behavioral cues and enjoying lots of unsupervised time playing imaginative adventure games outdoors with her friends.

Grafton married early, at age eighteen, and graduated from Western Kentucky State College with an English degree. The mother of three children, she was a homemaker, consciousness-raising group leader, and writer of mainstream novels and teleplays before she turned her hand to mystery writing. She created the capable Millhone as an answer to the helplessness she felt over a difficult custody battle for her children.

Millhone looks at motherhood and more in the short story "A Poison That Leaves No Trace." The story's title refers to the substance every would-be murderer must long to possess. Of course, if such a thing existed, it would be the end of crime solving—in fact and in fiction. To retain the story's surprise ending, we'll add Grafton's comment about the genesis of it at the story's close.

A Poison That Leaves No Trace

1990

THE woman was waiting outside my office when I arrived that morning. She was short and quite plump, wearing jeans in a size I've never seen on the rack. Her blouse was tunic-length, ostensibly to disguise her considerable rear end. Someone must have told her never to wear horizontal stripes, so the bold red-and-blue bands ran diagonally across her torso with a dizzying effect. Big red canvas tote, matching canvas wedgies. Her face was round, seamless, and smooth, her hair a uniformly dark shade that suggested a rinse. She might have been any age between forty and sixty. "You're not Kinsey Millhone," she said as I approached.

"Actually, I am. Would you like to come in?" I unlocked the door and stepped back so she could pass in front of me. She was giving me the once-over, as if my appearance was as remarkable to her as hers was to me.

She took a seat, keeping her tote squarely on her lap. I went around to my side of the desk, pausing to open the French doors before I sat down. "What can I help you with?"

She stared at me openly. "Well, I don't know. I thought you'd be a man. What kind of name is Kinsey? I never heard such a thing."

"My mother's maiden name. I take it you're in the market for a private investigator."

"I guess you could say that. I'm Shirese Dunaway, but everybody calls me Sis. Exactly how long have you been doing this?" Her tone was a perfect mating of skepticism and distrust.

"Six years in May. I was with the police department for two years before that. If my being a woman bothers you, I can recommend another agency. It won't offend me in the least."

"Well, I might as well talk to you as long as I'm here. I drove all the way up from Orange County. You don't charge for a consultation, I hope."

"Not at all. My regular fee is thirty dollars an hour plus expenses, but only if I believe I can be of help. What sort of problem are you dealing with?"

"Thirty dollars an hour! My stars. I had no idea it would cost so *much*."

"Lawyers charge a hundred and twenty," I said with a shrug.

"I know, but that's in case of a lawsuit. Contingency, or whatever they call that. Thirty dollars an *hour*. . . ."

I closed my mouth and let her work it out for herself. I didn't want to get into an argument with the woman in the first five minutes of our relationship. I tuned her out, watching her lips move while she decided what to do.

"The problem is my sister," she said at long last. "Here, look at this." She handed me a little clipping from the Santa Teresa newspaper. The death notice

233

read: "Crispin, Margery, beloved mother of Justine, passed away on December 10. Private arrangements. Wynington-Blake Mortuary."

"Nearly two months ago," I remarked.

"Nobody even told me she was sick! That's the point," Sis Dunaway snapped. "I wouldn't know to this day if a former neighbor hadn't spotted this and cut it out." She tended to speak in an indignant tone regardless of the subject.

"You just received this?"

"Well, no. It came back in January, but of course I couldn't drop everything and rush right up. This is the first chance I've had. You can probably appreciate that, upset as I was."

"Absolutely," I said. "When did you last talk to Margery?"

"I don't remember the exact date. It had to be eight or ten years back. You can imagine my shock! To get something like this out of a clear blue sky."

I shook my head. "Terrible," I murmured, "Have you talked to your niece?"

She gestured dismissively. "That Justine's a mess. Marge had her hands full with that one," she said. "I stopped over to her place and you should have seen the look I got. I said, 'Justine, whatever in the world did Margery die of?' And you know what she said? Said, 'Aunt Sis, her heart gave out.' Well, I knew that was bull the minute she said it. We have never had heart trouble in our family. . . . "

She went on for a while about what everybody'd died of; Mom, Dad, Uncle Buster, Rita Sue. We're talking cancer, lung disorders, an aneurysm or two. Sure enough, no heart trouble. I was making sympathetic noises, just to keep the tale afloat until she got to the point. I jotted down a few notes, though I never did quite understand how Rita Sue was related. Finally, I said, "Is it your feeling there was something unusual in your sister's death?"

She pursed her lips and lowered her gaze. "Let's put it this way. I can smell a rat. I'd be willing to *bet* Justine had a hand in it."

"Why would she do that?"

"Well, Marge had that big insurance policy. The one Harley took out in 1966. If that's not a motive for murder, I don't know what is." She sat back in her chair, content that she'd made her case.

"Harley?"

"Her husband . . . until he passed on, of course. They took out policies on each other and after he went, she kept up the premiums on hers. Justine was made the beneficiary. Marge never remarried and with Justine on the policy, I guess she'll get all the money and do I don't know what. It just doesn't seem right. She's been a sneak all her natural life. A regular con artist. She's been in jail four times! My sister talked till she was blue in the face, but she never could get Justine to straighten up her act."

"How much money are we talking about?"

"A hundred thousand dollars," she said. "Furthermore, them two never did get along. Fought like cats and dogs since the day Justine was born. Competitive? My God. Always trying to get the better of each other. Justine as good as told me they had a failing-out not two months before her mother died! The two had not exchanged a word since the day Marge got mad and stomped off."

"They lived together?"

"Well, yes, until this big fight. Next thing you know, Marge is dead. You tell me there's not something funny going on."

"Have you talked to the police?"

"How can I do that? I don't have any *proof*."

"What about the insurance company? Surely, if there were something irregular about Marge's death, the claims investigator would have picked up on it."

"Oh, honey, you'd think so, but you know how it is. Once a claim's been paid, the insurance company doesn't want to hear. Admit they made a mistake? Uh-uh, no thanks. Too much trouble going back through all the paperwork. Besides, Justine would probably turn around and sue 'em within an inch of their life. They'd rather turn a deaf ear and write the money off."

"When was the claim paid?"

"A week ago, they said."

I stared at her for a moment, considering. "I don't know what to tell you, Ms. Dunaway . . ."

"Call me Sis. I don't go for that Ms. bull."

"All right, Sis. If you're really convinced Justine's implicated in her mother's death, of course I'll try to help. I just don't want to waste your time."

"I can appreciate that," she said.

I stirred in my seat. "Look, I'll tell you what let's do. Why don't you pay me for two hours of my time. If I don't come up with anything concrete in that period, we can have another conversation and you can decide then if you want me to proceed."

"Sixty dollars," she said.

"That's right. Two hours."

"Well, all right. I guess I can do that." She opened her tote and peeled six tens off a roll of bills she'd secured with a rubber band. I wrote out an abbreviated version of a standard contract. She said she'd be staying in town overnight and gave me the telephone number at the motel where she'd checked in. She handed me the death notice. I made sure I had her sister's full name and the exact date of her death and told her I'd be in touch.

My first stop was the Hall of Records at the Santa Teresa County Courthouse two and a half blocks away. I filled out a copy order, supplying the necessary information, and paid seven bucks in cash. An hour later, I returned to pick up the certified copy of Margery Crispin's death certificate. Cause of death was listed as a "myocardial infarction." The certificate was signed by Dr. Yee, one of the contract pathologists out at the county morgue. If Marge Crispin had been the victim of foul play, it was hard to believe Dr. Yee wouldn't have spotted it.

I swung back by the office and picked up my car, driving over to Wynington-Blake, the mortuary listed in the newspaper clipping. I asked for Mr. Sharonson, whom I'd met when I was working on another case. He was wearing a somber charcoal-gray suit, his tone of voice carefully modulated to reflect the solemnity of his work. When I mentioned Marge Crispin, a shadow crossed his face.

"You remember the woman?"

"Oh, yes," he said. He closed his mouth then, but the look he gave me was eloquent.

I wondered if funeral home employees took a loyalty oath, vowing never to divulge a single fact about the dead. I thought I'd prime the pump a bit. Men are worse gossips than women once you get 'em going. "Mrs. Crispin's sister was in my office a little while ago and she seems to think there was something. . . uh, irregular about the woman's death."

I could see Mr. Sharonson formulate his response. "I wouldn't say there was anything *irregular* about the woman's death, but there was certainly something sordid about the circumstances."

"Oh?" said I.

He lowered his voice, glancing around to make certain we couldn't be overheard. "The two were estranged. Hadn't spoken for months as I understand it. The woman died alone in a seedy hotel on lower State Street. She drank."

"Nooo," I said, conveying disapproval and disbelief.

"Oh, yes," he said. "The police picked up the body, but she wasn't identified for weeks. If it hadn't been for the article in the paper, her daughter might not have ever known."

"What article?"

"Oh, you know the one. There's that columnist for the local paper who does all those articles about the homeless. He did a write-up about the poor woman. 'Alone in Death' I think it was called. He talked about how pathetic this woman was. Apparently, when Ms. Crispin read the article, she began to suspect it might be her mother. That's when she went out there to take a look."

"Must have been a shock," I said. "The woman did die of natural causes?"

"Oh, yes."

"No evidence of trauma, foul play, anything like that?"

"No, no, no. I tended her myself and I know they ran toxicology tests. I guess at first they thought it might be acute alcohol poisoning, but it turned out to be her heart."

I quizzed him on a number of possibilities, but I couldn't come up with anything out of the ordinary. I thanked him for his time, got back in my car, and drove over to the trailer park where Justine Crispin lived.

The trailer itself had seen better days. It was moored in a dirt patch with a wooden crate for an outside step. I knocked on the door, which opened about an inch to show a short strip of round face peering out at me. "Yes?"

"Are you Justine Crispin?"

"Yes."

"I hope I'm not bothering you. My name is Kinsey Millhone. I'm an old friend of your mother's and I just heard she passed away."

The silence was cautious. "Who'd you hear that from?"

I showed her the clipping. "Someone sent me this. I couldn't believe my eyes. I didn't even know she was sick."

Justine's eyes darkened with suspicion. "When did you see her last?"

I did my best to imitate Sis Dunaway's folksy tone. "Oh, gee. Must have been last summer. I moved away in June and it was probably some time around then because I remember giving her my address. It was awfully sudden, wasn't it?"

"Her heart give out."

"Well, the poor thing, and she was such a love." I wondered if I'd laid it on too thick. Justine was staring at me like I'd come to the wrong place. "Would you happen to know if she got my last note?" I asked.

"I wouldn't know anything about that."

"Because I wasn't sure what to do about the money."

"She owed you money?"

"No, no. I owed *her* . . . which is why I wrote."

Justine hesitated. "How much?"

"Well, it wasn't much," I said, with embarrassment. "Six hundred dollars, but she was such a doll to lend it to me and then I felt so bad when I couldn't pay her back right away. I asked her if I could wait and pay her this month, but then I never heard. Now I don't know what to do."

I could sense the shift in her attitude. Greed seems to do that in record time. "You could pay it to me and I could see it went into her estate," she said helpfully.

"Oh, I don't want to put you to any trouble."

"I don't mind," she said. "You want to come in?"

"I shouldn't. You're probably busy and you've already been so nice. . . ."

"I can take a few minutes."

"Well. If you're sure," I said.

Justine held the door open and I stepped into the trailer, where I got my first clear look at her. This girl was probably thirty pounds overweight with listless brown hair pulled into an oily ponytail. Like Sis, she was decked out in a pair of jeans, with an oversize T-shirt hanging almost to her knees. It was clear big butts ran in the family. She shoved some junk aside so I could sit down on the banquette, a fancy word for the ripped plastic seat that extended along one wall in the kitchenette.

"Did she suffer much?" I asked.

"Doctor said not. He said it was quick, as far as he could tell. Her heart probably seized up and she fell down dead before she could draw a breath."

"It must have been just terrible for you."

Her cheeks flushed with guilt. "You know, her and me had a falling out."

"Really? Well, I'm sorry to hear that. Of course, she always said you two had your differences. I hope it wasn't anything serious."

"She drank. I begged her and begged her to give it up, but she wouldn't pay me no mind," Justine said.

"Did she 'go' here at home?"

She shook her head. "In a welfare hotel. Down on her luck. Drink had done her in. If only I'd known . . . if only she'd reached out."

I thought she was going to weep, but she couldn't quite manage it. I clutched her hand. "She was too proud," I said.

"I guess that's what it was. I've been thinking to make some kind of contribution to AA, or something like that. You know, in her name."

"A Marge Crispin Memorial Fund," I suggested.

"Like that, yes. I was thinking this money you're talking about might be a start."

"That's a beautiful thought. I'm going right out to the car for my checkbook so I can write you a check."

It was a relief to get out into the fresh air again. I'd never heard so much horsepuckey in all my life. Still, it hardly constituted proof she was a murderess.

I hopped in my car and headed for a pay phone, spotting one in a gas station half a block away. I pulled change out of the bottom of my handbag and dialed Sis Dunaway's motel room. She was not very happy to hear my report.

"You didn't find anything?" she said. "Are you positive?"

"Well, of course I'm not positive. All I'm saying is that so far, there's no evidence that anything's amiss. If Justine contributed to her mother's death, she was damned clever about it. I gather the autopsy didn't show a thing."

"Maybe it was some kind of poison that leaves no trace."

"Uh, Sis? I hate to tell you this, but there really isn't such a poison that I ever heard of. I know it's a common fantasy, but there's just no such thing."

Her tone turned stubborn. "But it's possible. You have to admit that. There could be such a thing. It might be from South America. . . darkest Africa, someplace tike that."

Oh, boy. We were really tripping out on this one. I squinted at the receiver. "How would Justine acquire the stuff?"

"How do I know? I'm not going to sit here and solve the whole case for you! You're the one gets paid thirty dollars an hour, not me."

"Do you want me to pursue it?"

"Not if you mean to charge me an arm and a leg!" she said. "Listen here, I'll pay sixty dollars more, but you better come up with something or I want my money back."

She hung up before I could protest. How could she get her money back when she hadn't paid this portion? I stood in the phone booth and thought about things. In spite of myself, I'll admit I was hooked. Sis Dunaway might harbor a lot of foolish ideas, but her conviction was unshakable. Add to that the fact that Justine was lying about *something* and you have the kind of situation I can't walk away from.

I drove back to the trailer park and eased my car into a shady spot just across the street. Within moments, Justine appeared in a banged-up white Pinto, trailing smoke out of the tail pipe. Following her wasn't hard. I just hung my nose out the window and kept an eye on the haze. She drove over to Milagro Street to the branch office of a savings and loan. I pulled into a parking spot a few doors down and followed her in, keeping well out of sight. She was dealing with the branch manager, who eventually walked her over to a teller and authorized the cashing of a quite large check, judging from the number of bills the teller counted out.

Justine departed moments later, clutching her handbag protectively. I would have been willing to bet she'd been cashing that insurance check. She drove back to the trailer where she made a brief stop, probably to drop the money off.

She got back in her car and drove out of the trailer park. I followed discreetly as she headed into town. She pulled into a public parking lot and I eased in after her, finding an empty slot far enough away to disguise my purposes. So far, she didn't seem to have any idea she was being tailed. I kept my distance as she cut through to State Street and walked up a block to Santa Teresa Travel. I pretended to peruse the posters in the window while I watched her chat with the travel agent sitting at a desk just inside the front door. The two transacted business, the agent handing over what apparently were prearranged tickets. Justine wrote out a check. I busied myself at a newspaper rack, extracting a paper as she came out again. She walked down State Street half a block to a hobby shop where she purchased one of life's ugliest plastic floral wreaths. Busy little lady, this one, I thought.

She emerged from the hobby shop and headed down a side street, moving into the front entrance of a beauty salon. A surreptitious glance through the window showed her, moments later, in a green plastic cape, having a long conversation with the stylist about a cut. I checked my watch. It was almost twelve-thirty. I scooted back to the travel agency and waited until I saw Justine's travel agent leave the premises for lunch. As soon as she was out of sight, I went in, glancing at the nameplate on the edge of her desk.

The blond agent across the aisle caught my eye and smiled.

"What happened to Kathleen?" I asked.

"She went out to lunch. You just missed her. Is there something I can help you with?"

"Gee, I hope so. I picked up some tickets a little while ago and now I can't find the itinerary she tucked in the envelope. Is there any way you could run me a copy real quick? I'm in a hurry and I really can't afford to wait until she gets back."

"Sure, no problem. What's the name?"

"Justine Crispin," I said.

I found the nearest public phone and dialed Sis's motel room again. "Catch this," I said. "At four o'clock, Justine takes off for Los Angeles. From there, she flies to Mexico City."

"Well, that little shit."

"It gets worse. It's one-way."

"I knew it! I just knew she was up to no good. Where is she now?"

"Getting her hair done. She went to the bank first and cashed a big check—"

"I bet it was the insurance."

"That'd be my guess."

"She's got all that money *on* her?"

"Well, no. She stopped by the trailer first and then went and picked up her plane ticket. I think she intends to stop by the cemetery and put a wreath on Marge's grave. . . . "

"I can't stand this. I just can't stand it. She's going to take all that money and make a mockery of Marge's death."

"Hey, Sis, come on. If Justine's listed as the beneficiary, there's nothing you can do."

"That's what you think. I'll make her pay for this, I swear to God I will!" Sis slammed the phone down.

I could feel my heart sink. Uh-oh. I tried to think whether I'd mentioned the name of the beauty salon. I had visions of Sis descending on Justine with a tommy gun. I loitered uneasily outside the shop, watching traffic in both directions. There was no sign of Sis. Maybe she was going to wait until Justine went out to the gravesite before she mowed her down.

At two-fifteen, Justine came out of the beauty shop and passed me on the street. She was nearly unrecognizable. Her hair had been cut and permed and it fell in soft curls around her freshly made-up face. The beautician had found ways to bring out her eyes, subtly heightening her coloring with a touch of blusher on her cheeks. She looked like a million bucks—or a hundred thousand, at any rate. She was in a jaunty mood, paying more attention to her own reflection in the passing store windows than she was to me, hovering half a block behind.

She returned to the parking lot and retrieved her Pinto, easing into the flow of traffic as it moved up State. I tucked in a few cars back, all the while scanning for some sign of Sis. I couldn't imagine what she'd try to do, but as mad as she was, I had to guess she had some scheme in the works.

Fifteen minutes later, we were turning into the trailer park, Justine leading while I lollygagged along behind. I had already used up the money Sis had authorized, but by this time I had my own stake in the outcome. For all I knew, I was going to end up protecting Justine from an assassination attempt. She stopped by the trailer just long enough to load her bags in the car and then she drove out to the Santa Teresa Memorial Park, which was out by the airport.

The cemetery was deserted, a sunny field of gravestones among flowering shrubs. When the road forked, I watched Justine wind up the lane to the right while I headed left, keeping an eye on her car, which I could see across a wide patch of grass. She parked and got out, carrying the wreath to an oblong depression in the ground where a temporary marker had been set, awaiting the permanent monument. She rested the wreath against the marker and stood there looking down. She seemed awfully exposed and I couldn't help but wish she'd duck down some to grieve. Sis was probably crouched somewhere with a knife between her teeth, ready to leap out and stab Justine in the neck.

Respects paid, Justine got back into her car and drove to the airport where she checked in for her flight. By now, I was feeling baffled. She had less than an hour before her plane was scheduled to depart and there was still no sign of Sis. If there was going to be a showdown, it was bound to happen soon. I ambled into the gift shop and inserted myself between the wall and a book rack, watching Justine through windows nearly obscured by a display of Santa Teresa T-shirts. She sat on a bench and calmly read a paperback.

What was going on here?

Sis Dunaway had seemed hell-bent on avenging Marge's death, but where was she? Had she gone to the cops? I kept one eye on the clock and one eye on Justine. Whatever Sis was up to, she had better do it quick. Finally, mere minutes before the flight was due to be called, I left the newsstand, crossed the gate area, and took a seat beside Justine. "Hi," I said. "Nice permanent. Looks good."

She glanced at me and then did a classic double take. "What are you doing here?"

"Keeping an eye on you."

"What for?"

"I thought someone should see you off. I suspect your Aunt Sis is en route, so I decided to keep you company until she gets here."

"Aunt *Sis*?" she said, incredulously.

"I gotta warn you, she's not convinced your mother had a heart attack."

"What are you talking about? Aunt Sis is dead."

I could feel myself smirk. "Yeah, sure. Since when?"

"Five years ago."

"Bullshit."

"It's not bullshit. An aneurysm burst and she dropped in her tracks."

"Come on," I scoffed.

"It's the truth," she said emphatically. By that time, she'd recovered her composure and she went on the offensive. "Where's my money? You said you'd write a check for six hundred bucks."

"Completely dead?" I asked.

The loudspeaker came on. "May I have your attention, please. United Flight 3440 for Los Angeles is now ready for boarding at Gate Five. Please have your boarding pass available and prepare for security check."

Justine began to gather up her belongings. I'd been wondering how she was going to get all that cash through the security checkpoint, but one look at her lumpy waistline and it was obvious she'd strapped on a money belt. She picked up her carry-on, her shoulder bag, her jacket, and her paperback and clopped, in spike heels, over to the line of waiting passengers.

I followed, befuddled, reviewing the entire sequence of events. It had all happened today. Within hours. It wasn't like I was suffering brain damage or memory loss. And I hadn't seen a ghost. Sis had come to my office and laid out the whole tale about Marge and Justine. She'd told me all about their relationship, Justine's history as a con, the way the two women tried to outdo each other, the insurance, Marge's death. How could a murder have gotten past Dr. Yee? Unless the woman wasn't murdered, I thought suddenly.

Oh.

Once I saw it in *that* light, it was obvious.

Justine got in line between a young man with a duffel bag and a woman toting a cranky baby. There was some delay up ahead while the ticket agent got set. The line started to move and Justine advanced a step with me right beside her.

"I understand you and your mother had quite a competitive relationship."

"What's it to you," she said. She kept her eyes averted, facing dead ahead, willing the line to move so she could get away from me.

"I understand you were always trying to get the better of each other."

"What's your point?" she said, annoyed.

I shrugged. "I figure you read the article about the unidentified dead woman in the welfare hotel. You went out to the morgue and claimed the body as your mom's. The two of you agreed to split the insurance money, but your mother got worried about a double cross, which is exactly what this is."

"You don't know what you're talking about."

The line moved up again and I stayed right next to her. "She hired me to keep an eye on you, so when I realized you were leaving town, I called her and told her what was going on. She really hit the roof and I thought she'd charge right out, but so far there's been no sign of her. . . . "

Justine showed her ticket to the agent and he motioned her on. She moved through the metal detector without setting it off.

I gave the agent a smile. "Saying good-bye to a friend," I said, and passed through the wooden arch right after she did. She was picking up the pace, anxious to reach the plane.

I was still talking, nearly jogging to keep up with her. "I couldn't figure out why she wasn't trying to stop you and then I realized what she must have done—"

"Get away from me. I don't want to talk to you."

"She took the money, Justine. There's probably nothing in the belt but old papers. She had plenty of time to make the switch while you were getting your hair done."

"Ha, ha," she said sarcastically. "Tell me another one."

I stopped in my tracks. "All right. That's all I'm gonna say. I just didn't want you to reach Mexico City and find yourself flat broke."

"Blow it out your buns," she hissed. She showed her boarding pass to the woman at the gate and passed on through. I could hear her spike heels tiptapping out of ear range.

I reversed myself, walked back through the gate area and out to the walled exterior courtyard, where I could see the planes through a windbreak of protective glass. Justine crossed the tarmac to the waiting plane, her shoulders set. I didn't think she'd heard me, but then I saw her hand stray to the waist. She walked a few more steps and then halted, dumping her belongings in a pile at her feet. She pulled her shirt up and checked the money belt. At that distance, I saw her mouth open, but it took a second for the shrieks of outrage to reach me.

Ah, well, I thought. Sometimes a mother's love is like a poison that leaves no trace. You bop along through life, thinking you've got it made, and next thing you know, you're dead.

Grafton comments: "The actual spark [for writing the story] was an article in the local paper. I know I clipped a news article about two women who claimed the body of their deceased mother, an indigent whose identity was unknown at the time her body was found in a downtown hotel. She'd been taken to the morgue and the county was on the verge of consigning her to a pauper's grave. There were some shenanigans involved and it seemed like an amusing starting point for a short mystery tale.

I clip articles weekly—filing away anything that strikes my fancy. Some clippings remain in my files for years before my Shadow finally pipes up and suggests a way to use them. I am, of course, interested in crime of any sort, legal and police procedure, climate, curious occupations, jails, prisons, firearms, and California history—all of which can play a role in the development of a mystery novel. I love the fact—naughty girl that I am—that some hard-working, underpaid journalist has done the legwork, gathering information that I then have at my disposal for the price of my daily paper."

SARA PARETSKY

When Sara Paretsky's gutsy private eye, Victoria Iphigenia "V. I." Warshawski, strode onto the mystery scene in the 1982 novel *Indemnity Only*, mystery fans with a feminist bent hailed her as resourceful gal with a social conscience. And while Paretsky detailed the sleuth's step-by-step crime solving efforts in a manner that calls to mind the classic private eye novel, she did something refreshing, too. She gave her private eye a "family" of friends who would turn up again and again in later books. Their presence in the detective's life inspires reflection on the importance of friendship and connection to a person who is pursuing a traditionally solitary career. In addition, the fact that some of these characters have colorful ethnic identities only adds pizzazz—and some mouthwatering descriptions of ethnic cooking—to the mix.

A native of Ames, Iowa, Paretsky earned a bachelor's degree from the University of Kansas. Then she went on to acquire a master's degree and Ph.D. from the University of Chicago. Since 1971, she has called Chicago home—and in her mysteries, she has made this city come alive for an international audience. Now she is recognized as one of the more important writers of regional American mysteries.

Not only was she instrumental in establishing the appeal of regional settings, but Paretsky took the mystery novel as social commentary to new levels. Her early books set the pattern. In her first book, she looks at wrongdoing in the insurance industry. In *Bitter Medicine* (1987) she spies corruption in the medical profession. She takes on child abuse and environmental pollution in *Blood Shot* (1988).

Paretsky does not limit her quest for social fair play to writing fiction. She is also a founder and a former president of Sisters in Crime, an organization that facilitates networking among female crime writers and has worked to ensure more review attention for mysteries written by women.

Like her colleagues in crime writing, Paretsky keeps attuned to the news. Earlier in this *Omnibus*, Sue Grafton tells us her story "A Poison That Leaves No Trace" was inspired by a specific newspaper article. Paretsky's story, "Photo Finish," was engendered by an onslaught of stories and photos in the press.

Paretsky told us, "I started thinking about (this story) when Princess Diana died. I thought she brought a lot of happiness to a lot of people, and I always felt sorry for her because of her complicated personal life. She seemed to be a genuinely loving and engaged mother, and I felt especially sad for her sons, who had to see the circumstances of her death become international headlines while they were trying to mourn her loss. I started imagining what a boy who adored his mother might feel about seeing her the object of every paparazzo in the world, and that became the genesis for 'Photo Finish.'"

Photo Finish

2000

I

W HEN he came into my office that July afternoon I thought I'd met him before. It was something about his smile, sweet but aloof, as if inviting and withholding at the same time. Now that I'm in the computer age I check databases before my first meeting with a new client, but whatever Hunter Davenport did hadn't made Lexis-Nexis yet. If I'd seen him before, it wasn't on the evening news.

"I'm glad you could meet me on short notice, Ms. Warshawski: I'm in town only a few days and these Chicago hotel bills mount up." He had a trace of that Southern drawl we Northerners secretly find appealing. "They warned me summer in Chicago could make Charleston feel cool, but I could hardly believe them until I got off that plane."

I shook his hand and offered him the armchair. Outside, the heat was turning sidewalks into reflecting pools, but in my windowless office all seasons and hours are alike; with air-conditioning and floor lamps on, it could have been midwinter.

"Charleston, South Carolina? Is that your home, Mr. Davenport?"

"I lived there when I was a teenager, but most of my adult life has been spent in Europe. I can't quite shake the accent, though, or a secret longing for long summer afternoons where time stops and all we do is lie in the long grass, waiting for fish to rise and drinking lemonade."

I smiled: I feel nostalgia for those same endless summers, when my friends and I kept our ears cocked for the Good Humor truck while we jumped rope.

"So what brings you to Chicago when you could be in Charleston getting just as hot, and visiting your old haunts in the bargain?"

He smiled again. "Since the grandmother who raised me died, there hasn't been anything to take me back. I'm looking for my father. Someone told me he'd retired to Chicago, but I didn't see him in any of the phone books. So I thought I'd better get an investigator. The folks at the *Herald-Star* said you were good."

That was enterprising, an out-of-towner going straight to the dailies for advice. "When did you last see him?"

"When I was eleven. When my mother died I guess he couldn't stand it. He left me at my grandmother's—my mother's mother—and took off. I never even got a postcard from him after that."

"And why do you want to find him now? After what, fifteen years?"

"A pretty good guess, Ms. Warshawski. I'm twenty-four. When my grand-mother died I started thinking I wanted more family. Also, well,—" he played with his fingers as if embarrassed, "I wondered if he didn't have a side to his story I ought to hear. I grew up listening to my granny and my aunt—her unmarried daughter who lived with her—repeat what a bad old bag of bones my old man was. They blamed him for my mama's death. But I began to see that was impossible, so I started wondering about all the rest of what they had to say about my folks. I guess every man likes to know what kind of person his own old man was—what he's got to measure himself against, so to speak."

I'm no less human than the next woman—I couldn't resist the self-deprecating smile, or the wistful yearning in his blue-grey eyes. I printed out a contract for him and told him I needed a five hundred-dollar advance. Under the floor lamp his helmet of ash-blond hair looked like spun gold; as he leaned forward to hand me five hundreds in cash I could almost imagine the money to be some conjuror's trick.

"I do accept checks and the usual credit cards," I said.

"I don't have a permanent address these days. Cash is easier for me."

It was odd, but not that odd: plenty of people who visit detectives don't want a paper trail. It just made me wonder.

His story boiled down to this: his father, also named Hunter Davenport, was a photographer, at least, he had been a photographer when young Hunter's mother died. Hunter, Senior, had been a freelance journalist in Vietnam, where my client's mother was an army nurse. The two met, married, produced young Hunter.

"That's why I lived in Europe as a child: after the war my father covered hot spots in Africa and Asia. My mother and I lived in Paris during the school year and joined him on assignment during the summer. Then she died, in a car wreck in South Africa. It had nothing to do with whatever conflict he was covering. I don't even know where he was working—when you're a kid, you don't pay attention to that kind of thing. It was just the ordinary dumb kind of wreck she could have had in Paris or Charleston. He wasn't with her, in the car with her, I mean, but my grandmother always blamed him, said if he hadn't kept her half a world away it never would have happened."

He stumbled through the words so quickly I had to lean forward to make out what he was saying. He stopped abruptly. When he spoke again it was in a slow flat voice, but his knuckles showed white where he gripped his hands against his crossed legs.

"I was with her when she died. My mother was so beautiful. You never will see a woman as beautiful as her. And when she was covered with blood—it was hard. I still see her in my dreams, that way." He took a deep breath. "It must have been hard for him, for Hunter—my—my dad—because the next thing I knew I was at school in Charleston, living with my grandmother, and I never saw him again."

"What was your mother's name? Birth name, I mean."

He'd gone away to some private world; my question brought him suddenly back to my office. "Oh. Helen. Helen—Alder."

"And why do you think your father's in Chicago?"

"The agency. The agency where he used to sell his pictures, they told me they'd last heard from him here."

I had to pry more information from him: the agency was a French bureau. First he claimed not to remember the name, but when I handed the hundreds back across the table he came up with it: Sur Place, on Boulevard St. Germaine in Paris. No, he didn't know his father's social security number. Or his date of birth: he and his mother spent so much time apart from his father that ordinary holidays and birthdays weren't times they had in common. As for where his father came from, young Hunter was similarly ignorant.

"My dad never talked to me about his childhood that I can remember. And my mother's family declared him *hors la loi*, so that—"

"Declared him ooh-la-la?"

"What? Oh, *hors la loi*—an outlaw, you know. They never talked about him."

The client was staying at the Hotel Trefoil, a tiny place on Scott Street where they unpack your luggage and hand you a hot towel when you walk in so you can wipe the day's sweat from your brow. If he could afford the Trefoil my fee wouldn't make a dent in his loose change. I told him I'd do what I could and that I'd get back to him in a few days. He thanked me with that tantalizing familiar smile.

"What do you do yourself, Mr. Davenport? I feel I should recognize you."

He looked startled. In fact, I thought he looked almost frightened, but in the pools of lamplight I couldn't be certain. Anyway, a second later he was laughing.

"I don't do anything worth recording. I'm not an actor or an Internet genius that you should know me."

He left on that note, making me wonder how he afforded the Trefoil. Perhaps his Charleston grandmother had left him money. I laid the five hundreds in a circle on my desktop and ran a marking pen over them. They weren't counterfeit, but of course fairy's gold vanishes overnight. Just in case I'd drop them at the bank on my way home.

The international operator got me the number of Sur Place, which cheered me: young Davenport had given me information so unwillingly that I'd been afraid he'd manufactured the agency's name, it was nine at night in Paris; the night operator at the photo agency didn't speak English. I think he was telling me to call tomorrow, when Monsieur Duval would be in, but I wasn't a hundred percent sure.

It was only two in Chicago, and Sherman Tucker, the photo editor at the *Herald-Star*, was at his desk taking calls. "Vic, darling, you've found a corpse and I get the first look at it."

"Not even close." Sherman has a passion for the old noir private eyes. He keeps hoping I'll behave like Race Williams or the Continental Op and start stumbling over bodies every time I walk out the front door. "Ever use a stringer named Hunter Davenport, or heard anything about him? He used to freelance in Africa but someone thinks he might have moved to Chicago."

"Hunter Davenport? I never heard of the guy but he gets more popular by the hour. You're the second person today asking for him."

"Did you refer an extremely beautiful young man to me?" I asked.

Sherman laughed. "I don't look at guys' legs, V. I. But, yeah, there was a kid in here earlier. I told him if he didn't want to take a missing person to the cops to go to you."

Sherman promised to call me if any of his staff recognized Davenport's name. I felt as though I was trailing after my own client, but I checked the city and suburban directories just to be sure. There were a lot of Davenports, but no Hunters. I frowned at my desk, then dug out the phone directory disk for the Southeast from a service I subscribe to and looked up "Alder" in Charleston, South Carolina. There weren't any. A whole bunch of Aldermans and Aldershots were listed, but no plain Alders. The client had said his granny was dead. She didn't seem to have any relatives besides young Hunter. No wonder he wanted to find his father.

I checked with the department of motor vehicles, but Hunter, Senior, didn't have a driver's license. For almost any other search I'd need a social security number or a place and date of birth or some such thing. Of course, if the guy really had retired to Chicago, it was possible he'd been born here. I looked with distaste at the hundred or so Davenports in the city, and the two hundred more scattered through the suburbs. As a last resort I'd start calling them to see if any of them had a brother or cousin named Hunter, but first I'd see what I could learn from the county.

They know me in that mausoleum on Washington, but the warmth of my greeting still depends on who's working the counter that day. I was lucky this afternoon. A middle-aged clerk who was marking time until he could take early retirement and devote himself to his homemade pie shop was on duty. I've bought desserts from him from time to time; he was willing to give me a fifteen-year stack of registers at one go.

Twenty minutes before closing, when even my friendly clerk was snarling at the citizens to hurry up and finish, I found Hunter Davenport. He had been born in 1942 at Chicago Lying-In, to Mildred and Wayland Davenport (race: white, no previous live births, home address on Cottage Grove, age of parents, twenty-seven and thirty-five respectively). If Mildred and Wayland were still alive they were ancient, and they probably had long since moved from Cottage Grove, but at least it was a place to start.

I detoured to my bank to deposit the five hundreds. As I was boarding the L at Lake Street, I thought I saw my client's gold halo in the crowd. I jumped off the train, but by the time I'd fought past the rush hour crowd behind me I couldn't see him. I finally decided it must have been a trick of light.

II

Wayland Davenport had died the same year as my client's mother. Poor Hunter, Senior, losing his wife and his father at the same time. His mother

Mildred was still alive, though, living in a shabby apartment complex in Lincolnwood. When I rang the bell we began one of those tedious conversations through the intercom, where she couldn't make out what I was saying and I kept shouting into the door mike.

"I'm too old to work," she screeched.

"Your son's work," I hollered. "His photographs. We're interested in a display—an exhibit. Africa in the 1970's through American eyes."

"You'd better go away," she finally said. "I'm not buying anything."

I ground my teeth. A woman carrying two large bags of groceries came up the walk, followed by three young children. The biggest had his own small shopping bag but the younger two had their hands free to punch each other. The woman kept muttering an ineffectual "Michael, Tania, stop it." When she tried to balance a bag on her hip while she fumbled for her keys, I took the bags and held the door. She thanked me with the same exhausted mutter she used on her children.

"I'm visiting Mildred Davenport in 4K but I'll be glad to carry your bags up for you first," I said brightly.

"Oh! Oh, thank you. Michael, let go of Tania's hair."

She was on four as well, but at the other end, and no, she didn't know Mildred, more than to recognize her. The kids kept her running all day, and Mildred never left her own apartment, except on Mondays when someone from the senior center came to take her to the store or the doctor.

"Do you know if her son is staying with her?"

"Is that who that man is? I don't like the way he looks at Tania. I told my husband it wouldn't surprise me if he was a molester, out of prison; they won't tell us who's in the building. We could be murdered here or our children abducted and would the management care? Not any more than they did the time the people in 5A were keeping goldfish in the bathtub and let it overflow into our place. And then the cats, yowling to get out. I have complained a thousand times—Tania, stop pinching—."

I was thankful when we reached her door. I dumped the bags on the floor, in the middle of a litter of Legos, Beanie babies and half-empty cereal bowls, and fled as the children's whines rose to howls.

Before leaving my office this morning I had written a short letter to Mildred Davenport, giving her the same story I had tried shouting through the intercom: I was a freelance journalist writing a book on Africa through American eyes and very much wanted to get hold of some of her son's photographs from the eighties.

At the far end of the corridor I knocked loudly on her door. After a long wait I heard a shuffling on the other side, and then movement at the peephole. I smiled in a cheery, unthreatening way.

She opened the door the width of a chain bolt, "What do you want?"

I kept smiling. "I put it in writing—I thought that might be easier than me trying to explain it through the door."

She grudgingly took the envelope from me and shut the door again. The television was turned up so loud I could hear it through the closed door. After about ten minutes she came back.

"I guess you can talk to him but he says he doesn't know what you mean, he never was in Africa."

I followed her into a living room where a fan stirred air so heavy it fell back like soup onto my hair and blouse. A television tuned to Oprah provided the only light. Furniture and stacks of newspapers were crammed so close together that it was hard to find a place to stand.

"Hunter! This here's the lady." She shouted over Oprah in a flat nasal.

A figure stirred in one of the overstuffed armchairs. In the flashes from the screen I'd mistaken him for a heap of towels or blankets. Mrs. Davenport muted the sound.

"Who you work for?" he said. "They have money for prints?"

"Gaudy Press. They have some money, but they don't throw it around." I looked around for a place to sit and finally perched on the arm of another chair. "They're especially interested in your work in the eighties. When you were in Africa."

"Never was in Africa." Hunter shot a look at his mother.

"If they want to pay you for your work," Mrs. Davenport began, but he cut her off.

"I said I never was in Africa. You don't know anything about my life away from here."

"I'm only deaf, not crazy," his mother snapped. "Why don't you see if you can make some money. Show this lady your photographs. Even if you don't have Africa you've got plenty of others."

"You go back to Oprah and the lady can go back to her publisher and tell them no sale." He took the control from his mother and restored the sound; a woman whose car had broken down on the Santa Ana Freeway had been rescued by an angel.

I moved close enough to him that I could see his frayed t-shirt and the stubble of greying hair on his chin. "Your son says you were in South Africa in 1986."

He curled his lip at me. "I don't have a son. That I know of."

"Helen Alder's son? That the two of you produced after you married in Vietnam?"

"Helen Alder? I never heard of a . . . " His voice trailed away, and then he said with a ferocious urgency that astounded me, "Where are you really from?"

"Could we go where we can hear each other?"

His mother watched suspiciously when he pushed himself up from his chair, but she stayed behind when he led me to the kitchen. The stuffy air was larded with stale dishwater. The window had a two-by-four nailed across it to keep it from opening. Sweat started to gather at the back of my neck.

"Who sent you to me?" His teeth showed, crooked and tobacco-stained, through the stubble.

"Your son."

"I don't have any children. I never married. I never was in Africa."

"What about Vietnam?" I asked.

He shot me an angry look. "And if I say, yeah, I was there, you won't believe I didn't marry this Helen whosis."

"Try me." I wanted to keep my voice affable, but standing in the musty room was hard on my back as well as my manners.

"I was a photographer. For the old *Chicago American* before it folded. I covered the war for them from Sixty-three to Sixty-nine. Sur Place bought a lot of my shots—the French were more interested in Indochina than we were. After the paper collapsed I signed on with them as a freelancer."

"Where were you in 1986? Here?"

He shook his head. "Europe. England. Sometimes New York."

I took a notepad from my handbag and started fanning my face with it. "When did you come back to Chicago? Do you work for Sur Place out of here?"

His face contorted into a sneer. "I haven't worked for anyone for a long time. My mother doesn't like me sponging off her, but she's paranoid about burglary and she thinks a man around the house, even a washed-up ex-photographer, is better than living alone. Now it's your turn. And don't give me any crap about being a freelance writer."

"Okay. I'm a private investigator. A man claiming to be Hunter Davenport, Junior, asked me to find you." I showed him my license.

His face began to look like dull putty. "Someone was pulling your leg. I don't have a son."

"Fair, very good-looking, most people would be proud to claim him."

He began to fidget violently with the utensil drawers. "Get the guy to give you a blood sample. We'll compare DNA. If his matches mine you're welcome to my whole portfolio. How'd you find me?"

I told him, county birth records followed by tracing his father, Wayland Davenport, through old phone books. Wayland had gone from Cottage Grove Avenue to Loomis, then Montrose, stair-stepping his way up the northwest side until landing at a bungalow in Lincolnwood in 1974. His widow moved into this little apartment four years ago.

"So anyone could find me," he muttered.

"And is that a problem?"

He gave an unconvincing laugh. "No one wants to find me these days, so it's no problem whatsoever. Now you've wasted your time and mine enough. Go hunt up some real mystery. Like who your client is and why he's stolen my name."

I stopped in the kitchen doorway and looked back at him. "By the way, who is Helen Alder?"

He bared his teeth, showing a broken chip on the left incisor. "The figment of your client's imagination."

I put a business card on the counter top. "Give me a call if you decide to tell me the truth about her."

As I made my way through the dim passage to the front door, someone on television was extolling a drug whose side effects included nausea, fainting and memory loss. Over the cheerful pitch, Mildred Davenport's voice rose querulously, demanding to know whether I was going to buy any of his pictures. Her son said something inaudible. The last thing I heard on my way out was her calling to him to make sure he put the chain-bolt on behind me.

When I stepped back into the sticky July heat, the back of my blouse was wet all the way across my shoulders. I smelled of stale grease. I sank into my car and turned on the air conditioner. Behind me a blue Toyota was idling, the driver lying with the seat reclining so that all I could see was the newspaper over his chest, like a character in a James Bond movie.

I made a U-turn and drove as fast as I could to the expressway. I wanted to get to the Trefoil and ask my client the same questions Hunter Davenport had put to me: who had given me those five hundred-dollar bills and why did he really want to find Hunter Davenport?

III

My client had checked into the Trefoil as Hunter Davenport, but he'd gone out early this morning and hadn't come back yet. The receptionist wouldn't tell me if young Hunter had used another name on check-in, or if he'd shown a credit card:

"Ma'am, I'm sure you must understand that I cannot possibly discuss our guests with you."

I pulled out my ID. "I'm a private investigator. Normally I don't discuss my cases any more than you discuss your guests, but when Mr. Davenport hired me he paid cash and—something I found out this morning makes me wonder whether Davenport is his name."

He shook his head. "I'm sorry, ma'am, but unless you are with the police and have legitimate grounds for an inquiry, I cannot discuss any of our guests with any outsider. Newspaper reporters have come up with such inventive ways of violating privacy that it's our ironclad rule."

"You often have celebrities here?"

"We often have guests who prize privacy. That's why they choose the Trefoil."

The Trefoil is a small boutique hotel. There wasn't any way I could hover unobtrusively in the lobby and sneak into the elevator. I wrote a note for Hunter Davenport asking him to call me as soon as he came in. When I handed it to the receptionist I managed to sneak a look at the cubbyhole where he put the envelope: five-oh-eight. It never hurts to know.

When I got to my office, my part-time assistant told me the client had called. "He said to thank you for your help but he's decided it's a needle in a haystack and not to go on looking. The five hundred can cover your fee and expenses."

I thought my jaw might crack my sternum, it dropped so far and fast. "When did he call?"

Mary Louise looked at her notes. "At one o'clock."

It was almost two now, so he'd stopped the investigation before I visited the hotel. I told Mary Louise about the case.

"Finding Hunter, Senior, was easier than I thought it would be, actually. But the guy claims he never had a kid. He even offered to do a DNA match. That might have been a bluff, but it didn't sound like it. He knows something about Helen Alder, something that got him pretty agitated, but I don't think it had anything to do with the kid."

Helen Alder's name didn't mean any more to Mary Louise than it had to me. We talked it over for a bit until Mary Louise left to pick her foster kids up from summer camp. Before she left she had me fill out an expense report and time sheet—an important reason I keep her on my payroll. I had a clean profit of a hundred-fifty. At least I could afford another call to Paris.

Although it was now nine-twenty in Europe, Monsieur Duval was indeed in, and indeed he did speak English. Certainly he remembered 'Unter Davenport, but this was a matter most strange, that I was the second person to ask for him in one month. Could it be that Davenport's fortunes were going to change, that he might once again be going to work? If so, Sur Place would like to continue to represent him: he had done very inventive work in the past.

"Do you know where he is now?" I asked.

"We think he maybe go to Chicago, but we have no direct word from him since four years now. One woman at Sur Place, she say he always talk about Chicago when he is unhappy."

So the client had gotten the Chicago information from Sur Place. "What kind of pictures did you buy from him?"

"All kinds. But of course, for our clients, for *Paris Match*, or the *Sun*, we want mostly the faces that are popular with their readers. The Monaco princesses now that Princess Diana is no more, or even Princess Diana's sons. Sometimes they like Madonna. You know, the celebrity. But by and by 'Unter, he fall more in love with what he sees in a bottle than what he sees behind the camera, and we have to tell him good-bye."

"Did he ever shoot a woman named Helen Alder?"

"'Elen Alder? 'Elen Alder? I do not know this woman. But I will look in our files. If you have e-mail I will let you know."

I gave him my details, not very hopefully. If Helen Alder had been a celebrity subject, I think even I would have heard of her. Her name had clearly meant something to Davenport, although it took a minute for it to register. Maybe they'd had some brief fling in Vietnam that he'd forgotten about. She had a kid, named him after his biological father, brought him up on the idea that she was a widow. Then the kid found out the truth and started tracking down the photographer.

It was all useless speculation. I logged on to the Web and did a search through Lexis-Nexis and a few other databases but didn't find any Helen Alders. I gave it up and turned my attention to other clients' problems.

IV

At three the next morning Davenport came forcibly back to mind when the phone hauled me out of sleep.

"Vic, why would an old drunk be clutching your business card when he was run over?" It was John McGonnigal, a Chicago police sergeant I used to do a lot of work with. I'd lost track of him when the Department transferred him from downtown to one of the far northwest precincts.

"John!" I sat up in bed, trying to scramble my wits together. "What old drunk?"

"Sixty-ish. Five-ten, five-eleven, three-day growth, chip on left incisor. Ring a bell?"

Hunter Davenport. I demanded details in exchange for a name and McGonnigal grudgingly supplied them. Hunter had been bar-hopping, as far as the cops could make out, ending up at the Last Belt on Lincoln around one a.m. A witness said a car had actually driven up on the sidewalk and hit Hunter before roaring off into the night. The few onlookers out at that hour couldn't guess at the color or make of the car, or remember the license number.

"He didn't have any ID. Just some singles wadded up in his pocket and your card. What's the story, Warshawski?"

"There is no story. Maybe he was trying to work up the nerve to invite me out for a drink. Have you talked to his mother? No, of course not, you only just learned who he was." I gave him Mildred Davenport's address. "I'll meet you there in twenty minutes."

He began a sentence with "You can leave police businesses" but I hung up before he told me where.

There's a wonderful freedom in driving the city in the pre-dawn—no one else is out and you feel as though you own the empty streets. I coasted up to Mrs. Davenport's building at the same time that McGonnigal's unmarked car arrived.

He grunted a greeting but didn't actively try to keep me from following him into the building. He had phoned Mrs. Davenport from the hospital, waking her up, confirming her nightmares about the city's dangers, but she buzzed us in. She opened her own door the width of the chain and demanded McGonnigal's ID, then caught sight of me.

"What do you know about this, young woman? Are you with the police? Hunter told me you weren't really interested in his photographs, but he's never been mixed up with any crimes, at least not that I know of."

"Can we come in, ma'am?" McGonnigal said. "We'll wake all the neighbors if we have to talk to you through the door."

She compressed her mouth in a suspicious line, but unbolted the chain. "Hunter's been like a cat on a hot brick ever since this lady came over. He's been drinking way too much for years. I warned him after Vietnam no one would keep a drunk on their payroll forever and I was right. All those glamorous places he used to visit, all those famous people he took pictures of, didn't count for anything in the end: he had to come home to his ma and the little bit of Social Security he can claim. So when this lady said maybe someone wanted to buy some of his old pictures, I thought he should talk to her."

McGonnigal stopped her to ask me about that; I muttered that I was a go-between with a possible buyer but nothing had come of it. Before he could push me further, Mrs. Davenport interrupted.

"Yesterday, after this lady left, someone started calling on the phone and hanging up. I thought maybe it was her bothering him, but all Hunter would say was he didn't know who was on the phone. Finally about eight o'clock tonight, last night I should say, the fifteenth time the phone rang, he said, I can't take this, they're going to drive me insane. And off he went.

"I knew he was going out to find a bar, like he always does when he's in trouble. I told him a million times all it gets you is a hangover and the trouble still there in the morning, but you can't talk to a drunk. But after he left, the calls kept coming. Someone who just said, Hunter, I know where you are, Hunter, and then hung up, so the last time I yelled before he could say anything, He's not here, leave me alone or I'll have the cops on you. I should have done it then and there, but how could I know they'd follow after him in the street?"

"Who could have been harassing him?" McGonnigal demanded of me.

I shook my head, bleakly, and asked Mrs. Davenport if her son ever discussed any threats from anyone overseas.

"If he had any troubles like that he never said anything to me about them. He lived away from home for thirty years and he wasn't much of a letter writer at the best of times. I don't know what he got up to, all the places he visited."

"Do you think he could have a child he never told you about?" I asked.

"With a man anything's possible, Just because he's your own boy doesn't change that." She folded her lips tightly.

McGonnigal was demanding what that was about when his mobile phone rang. He grunted into the mouthpiece a few times, then turned to Mrs. Davenport.

"Does he have any insurance? It looks like they can save him, but it's going to be expensive."

"Insurance? Where would he get insurance? He wasn't even a vet, just a war correspondent. And if they think I've got fifty thousand lying around to pay their rotten bills they can think again."

While McGonnigal relayed the news to the hospital, I wandered into the back room, looking for evidence of Davenport's work. I found a worn black zip-case under the daybed, along with his clothes and a few personal items. The case was stuffed with hundreds of prints.

McGonnigal came in and watched me go through them. Near the bottom of the stack I came on a dozen views of a woman who looked so familiar that I thought I must surely know her. Tortoiseshell combs pulled a halo of ash-blond hair away from her face and her blue-gray eyes smiled at the camera with a wistful yearning. At first I thought my leap of recognition was because she looked so much like my client. But I felt sure I knew her face, and that that was why I thought I'd known him when he came into my office.

I tried not to let McGonnigal see I'd come on anything I knew. I was zipping up the case when it fell from my hands, scattering photographs wholesale. I managed to stick a shot of the wistful woman inside my t-shirt while I was scrabbling under the daybed for the rest.

V

Sherman Tucker, the *Herald-Star's* photo editor, wasn't happy at climbing out of bed so early in the morning, but he met me at the paper. He took one look at the print I'd borrowed, and went without speaking to a cabinet where he pulled out a thick file.

"Were you brain-dead thirteen years ago? The only person photographed more back then was Princess Di."

"I was in law school," I mumbled. "My father was dying. I didn't follow the society pages."

Sherman slapped a dozen versions of the face onto the table: Lady Helen Banidore riding to hounds in Virginia, Lady Helen bringing her infant son Andrew home from the hospital, opening a charity hall, leaving a courthouse in tears after her divorce, laughing on the arm of a Marine colonel at a British embassy ball.

She had been born Lady Helen Aldershot, only child of the Earl of Revere. Revere didn't have a dime, or even a shilling, to his name, so everyone agreed it was a wonderful thing when Helen married one of the heirs to Banidore Tobacco in South Carolina. Happiest of all had been in the paparazzi who followed her, supplying the insatiable appetites in America and France for beautiful women with titles.

Even I used to read the reports that filtered from the *National Enquirer* into *People* and the daily papers after the star-studded wedding in the Revere's picturesque private chapel. After the wedding Jim Banidore and Lady Helen moved back to America, dividing their time between New York and Charleston. About the time the kid was born, the tabloids began screaming that Banidore hung out in leather bars when he was in New York. Old Mrs. Banidore tried suing the *Star* over a photo of Jim in an embrace with a man in a motorcycle bar, but the matter was quietly dropped a few months later.

If Lady Helen was disconsolate at her husband's behavior, she hid it well. She'd been a lively member of the international nightclub scene before her marriage; after Andrew's birth she took up with her old playmates. The divorce was messy—old Mrs. Banidore tried to claim Andrew wasn't even Jim's son, but the terms of the family trust apparently made it important for Jim to have a male child, so he swore an affidavit of paternity.

Lady Helen's alimony, estimated at a hundred thousand dollars a month, depended on her never breathing a word about her husband's extra-curricular activities. If she remarried of course the alimony stopped, but old Mrs. Banidore also got the family lawyers to insert a clause that gave her custody of the kid if the Banidores could prove Lady Helen was sleeping with other men.

This last clause lashed the paparazzi into a competitive frenzy. They staked out Lady Helen's apartment on the Faubourg St. Honore, they followed her skiing in the French Alps and the Canadian Rockies, they zoomed on her nude sunbathing in the Virgin Islands. When she went on safari in Kenya with Italian racer Egidio Berni as part of the group, the photographers followed in a helicopter. That was where Lady Helen died.

The *Herald-Star* hadn't paid much attention to Lady Helen, since she didn't have a natural following in Chicago, but of course they covered her death. I flipped through Sherman's files to read the front-page story.

Lady Helen's safari was spending a week at a luxury lodge, from which they took day or night trips to study animals. It sounded like fun: they even followed elephants on their nocturnal treks into mineral caves.

In deference to the divorce decree, Berni stayed in one suite, Lady Helen and young Andrew in another. One evening Berni and Lady Helen decided to go for a sunset drive. An enterprising photographer had bribed one of the guides to let him know if Lady Helen and Berni were ever alone; the helicopter caught up with the Land Rover three miles from the lodge. Berni took off, hurtling the Rover across the veldt, and smashed into a rhinoceros. He and Lady Helen were killed instantly.

Some moron brought young Andrew to the crash site, and the *Herald-Star* had used a photograph of the white-faced boy kneeling by his dead mother, cradling her head on his knees.

I would have to be brain dead not to know that was my client as a child. And I'd have to be even deader not to figure Hunter Davenport for the photographer in the chopper.

"So Andrew Banidore hired me to find one of the men who drove his mother to her death. Or who he thinks drove her to her death. And then what? Lay in wait like James Bond to—."

I stood up so fast I knocked half the photos off Sherman's table. When he squawked a protest I was already out the door. I shouted "I'll call you" over my shoulder and ran down the hall to the street.

I'd been an idiot. James Bond. The glimpse I thought I'd had of my client on the L platform two days ago. The guy in the car behind me yesterday morning. My client had tracked me while I located Hunter Davenport. When I'd found Davenport for him, my client breathed threatening messages over the

phone until Davenport fled the apartment, then chased him to Uptown where
he ran him over.

V. I. Warshawski, ace detective. Ace imbecile.

VI

The Trefoil's tiny lobby was filled with luggage and travelers. The receptionist
on duty was settling bills and handing towels and keys to joggers while jug-
gling two phones. I took a towel with a smiled thanks and slipped into the elevator behind two lean, sweat-covered men in shorts and cropped tops.

On the fifth floor I knelt in front of five-oh-eight and probed the keyhole. I
was in an agony of tension—if some other guest should come out—the maid—
if Andrew Banidore had left and a stranger lay in the bed. The guest doors had
nice sturdy old-fashioned locks, the kind that look impressive on the outside but
only have three tumblers. In another two minutes I was inside the room.

Lying there in bed, Andrew Banidore looked almost like his mother's twin.
The white-gold hair fell away from his face, which was soft with the slackness
of sleep.

"Andrew!" I called sharply from the doorway.

He stirred and turned over, but a night spent tracking his subject through
Uptown had apparently left him exhausted. I went to the bed and shook him
roughly. When his wistful blue grey eyes finally blinked open I said, "He's not
dead. Does that upset you?"

"He's not?" His voice was thick with sleep. "But I—." He woke completely
and sat up, his face white. "How did you get in here? What are you talking
about?"

"You were too tired when you got in to lock the door, I guess." I sat on the
edge of the bed. "You've got five minutes before I call the cops. Better make
good use of them."

"What are you going to tell them? How you broke into my hotel room?"

"I'm going to tell them to look for the blue Toyota that hit Hunter
Davenport early this morning. If you rented it, that'll be easy, because you had
to show someone a driver's license. If you stole it, it'll still have your fingerprints on it."

I went to the bureau and rifled through the documents on top. He was traveling on a British passport. He had a first-class ticket on Air France, with an
open return date. He had a rental agreement with one of the big chains for a
blue Toyota. His wallet held an American driver's license issued by the state of
South Carolina, a variety of credit cards, and two photos of his mother.

"Put those pictures down."

I held them between my fingers, as if poised to tear them. "You can always
get more. Most photographed woman in the world and all, there are a million
pictures of her lying around. I just saw twenty-eight of them."

"She gave those to me. I can't get more that she gave me."

He was out of bed and across the room so fast I just had time to slip the pictures into my shirt pocket. He tried to fight me for them but I was dressed and he wasn't: I stood on his left foot until he stopped punching at me.

"I'll return them when you give me a few answers. You have lived in South Carolina, and your mother was killed in a car accident in South Africa. Did you happen to tell me anything else true? Is your grandmother dead? What about all those other tobacco-smoking Banidores? You really an orphan?"

He pulled on a pair of jeans and looked at me sullenly. "I hate them all. The way they talk about her, they were so happy when she died, it was as if all their dreams came true at once. The fact that Jim died of AIDS five years after I had to go live in fucking stupid Charleston, I wasn't supposed to mention that. Poor dear Jim picked up a virus in Africa when he went out to get Andrew, they told all their friends at the country club. We should never have allowed Helen to keep the boy to begin with. Then all my he-man cousins made my life miserable claiming she was a whore and I wasn't even one of the family. As if I wanted to be related to that houseful of cretins."

"Did you kill your grandmother?"

He gave a hoarse bark of laughter. "If I'd thought of it in time. No, she died the old-fashioned way, of a stroke."

"So what made you decide to go after Davenport?"

"I always meant to. Ever since the day she died. Chasing her all over Europe. It was a game to him. She didn't have a life. She knew she'd lose me to those dammed Banidores if she ever got caught with another man and I was the one person she really loved. I was the only one she cared about losing.

"She was trying to protect our life together and he, that Davenport, he was trying to destroy it. For twenty-four hours he got a taste of what that was like, how it feels when someone knows where you are and is following you. I missed him when he snuck out of that apartment building last night, but when the lady yelled he wasn't home I found him at the bus stop. He got on a bus and I followed the bus. He got off and went into a bar, I went in behind him. But it wasn't enough he was scared. I told him who I was, what he'd done, and he tried to tell me it was a job. Just a job. He killed my mother, he ruined my life, and he thought I should slap him on the back and say, Tough luck, old sport, but a man's gotta do and all that crap.'

"That was when I couldn't take it anymore. I got into the car. He started to go back into the bar and I couldn't stand it. I just drove up on the sidewalk and—I should have gone straight to the airport and taken the first flight out, but my passport and ticket and everything were still here. Besides, I never thought you'd find out before I left this afternoon."

I leaned against the door and looked down at him. "You never thought. You are an extremely lucky guy: Hunter Davenport is going to live. But he has very expensive hospital bills and no insurance. You are going to pay every dime of those bills. If you don't, then I am suddenly going to find evidence that links you to that Toyota. The cursory washing they give it at the rental place, believe me, traces of Davenport's blood will be on it a long time. Do you understand?"

He nodded fractionally. "Now give me back my pictures."

"I want to hear you say it. I want to know that you understand what you've agreed to."

He shut his eyes. "I agree to pay Hunter Davenport's hospital bills. I agree to look after the man who killed my mother. I agree to live in hell the rest of my life."

I wanted to say something, something consoling, or maybe heartening: let it go, move on, but his face was so pinched with pain I couldn't bear to look at him. I put the snapshots on his knee and let myself out.

PETER LOVESEY

Peter Lovesey began his mystery-writing career by entering and winning a contest with the 1970 novel *Wobble to Death*. Centered on a Victorian endurance walking contest known as a "wobble," that book introduces series characters Sergeant Cribb and Constable Thackeray, who appear in several more humorous whodunits set during the Victorian Age. He also wrote another series of mysteries set in that period, featuring Albert, "Bertie," Prince of Wales, as a sleuth. The first of them is *Bertie and the Tinman: From the Memoirs of King Edward VII*, published in 1987. Lovesey does not confine his historical whodunits to the nineteenth century, however. For examples, he looks at some twentieth-century crimes in *The False Inspector Dew: A Murder Mystery Set Aboard the S.S. Mauritania, 1921* (1982) and in *Keystone* (1983).

Lovesey has also written a good number of contemporary crime novels that also succeed as novels of character. In them he explores how pressures of modern life combine with resentments and other factors to cause otherwise law-abiding individuals to perpetrate crimes. Lovesey often takes readers into familiar milieus, such as the country church and the English village, where placid appearances mask the tensions that tear people apart. These books are not humorless, but in contrast with Lovesey's historical novels, which are strong on comedy, the novels set in contemporary times are generally darker. His latest novel, *The Circle*, was published in May 2005.

Lovesey's short fiction demonstrates his command of craft and may range from humorous to edgy. His 1991 short story "The Crime of Miss Oyster Brown" is remarkable for taking a very minor transgression and showing how it can lead to major trouble. Here goodness itself is a liability for more than one character. Lovesey said he got the idea for his story when observing some items stored in his sister-in-law's home. We'll let you know what they were at the end of his story.

The Crime of Miss Oyster Brown

1991

MISS OYSTER BROWN, a devout member of the Church of England, joined passionately each Sunday in every prayer of the Morning Service—except for the general Confession, when, in all honesty, she found it difficult to class herself as a lost sheep. She was willing to believe that everyone else in church had erred and strayed. In certain cases she knew exactly how, and with whom, and she would say a prayer for them. On her own account, however, she could seldom think of anything to confess. She tried strenuously, more strenuously—dare I say it?—than you or me to lead an untainted life. She managed conspicuously well. Very occasionally, as the rest of the congregation joined in the Confession, she would own up to some trifling sin.

You may imagine what a fall from grace it was when this virtuous woman committed not merely a sin, but a crime. She lived more than half her life before it happened.

She resided in a Berkshire town with her twin sister Pearl, who was a mere three minutes her senior. Oyster and Pearl—a flamboyance in forenames that owed something to the fact that their parents had been plain John and Mary Brown. Up to the moment of birth the Browns had been led to expect one child who, if female, was to be named Pearl. In the turmoil created by a second, unscheduled, daughter, John Brown jokingly suggested naming her Oyster. Mary, bosky from morphine, seized on the name as an inspiration, a delight to the ear when said in front of dreary old Brown. Of course the charm was never so apparent to the twins, who got to dread being introduced to people. Even in infancy they were aware that their parents' friends found the names amusing. At school they were taunted as much by the teachers as the children. The names never ceased to amuse. Fifty years on, things were still said just out of earshot and laced with pretended sympathy. "Here come Pearl and Oyster, poor old ducks. Fancy being stuck with names like that."

No wonder they faced the world defiantly. In middle age they were a formidable duo, stalwarts of the choir, the Bible-reading Circle, the Townswomen's Guild and the Magistrates' Bench. Neither sister had married. They lived together in Lime Tree Avenue, in the mock-Tudor house where they were born. They were not short of money.

There are certain things people always want to know about twins, the more so in mystery stories. I can reassure the wary reader that Oyster and Pearl were not identical; Oyster was an inch taller, more sturdy in build than her sister and slower of speech. They dressed individually, Oyster as a rule in tweed skirts and check blouses that she made herself, always from the same Butterick pattern, Pearl in a variety of mail-order suits in pastel blues and greens. No one confused them. As for that other question so often asked about twins, neither sister could be characterized as "dominant." Each possessed a forceful personality by any standard. To avoid disputes they had established a household routine, a division of the duties, that worked pretty harmoniously, all things considered. Oyster did most of the cooking and the gardening, for example, and Pearl attended to the housework and paid the bills when they became due. They both enjoyed shopping, so they shared it. They did the church flowers together when their turn came, and they always ran the bottle stall at the church fête. Five vicars had held the living at St Saviour's in the twins' time as worshippers there. Each new incumbent was advised by his predecessor that Pearl and Oyster were the mainstays of the parish. Better to fall foul of the diocesan bishop himself than the Brown twins.

All of this was observed from a distance, for no one, not even a vicar making his social rounds, was allowed inside the house in Lime Tree Avenue. The twins didn't entertain, and that was final. They were polite to their neighbours without once inviting them in. When one twin was ill, the other would transport her to the surgery in a state of high fever rather than call the doctor on a visit.

It followed that people's knowledge of Pearl and Oyster was limited. No one could doubt that they lived an orderly existence; there were no complaints about undue noise, or unwashed windows or neglected paintwork. The hedge was trimmed and the garden mown. But what really bubbled and boiled behind the regularly washed net curtains—the secret passion that was to have such a dire result—was unsuspected until Oyster committed her crime.

She acted out of desperation. On the last Saturday in July, 1991, her well-ordered life suffered a seismic shock. She was parted from her twin sister. The parting was sudden, traumatic and had to be shrouded in secrecy. The prospect of anyone finding out what had occurred was unthinkable.

So for the first time in her life Oyster had no Pearl to change the light bulbs, pay the bills and check that all the doors were locked. Oyster—let it be understood—was not incapable or dim-witted. Bereft as she was, she managed tolerably well until the Friday afternoon, when she had a letter to post, a letter of surpassing importance, capable—God willing—of easing her desolation. She had agonized over it for hours. Now it was crucial that the letter caught the last post of the day. Saturday would be too late. She went to the drawer where Pearl always kept the postage stamps and—calamity—not one was left.

Stamps had always been Pearl's responsibility. To be fair, the error was Oyster's; she had written more letters than usual and gone through the supply. She should have called at the Post Office when she was doing the shopping.

It was too late. There wasn't time to get there before the last post at five-fifteen. She tried to remain calm and consider her options. It was out of the question to ask a neighbour for a stamp; she and Pearl had made it a point of honour never to be beholden to anyone else. Neither could she countenance the disgrace of despatching the letter without a stamp in the hope that it would get by, or the recipient would pay the amount due.

This left one remedy, and it was criminal.

Behind one of the Staffordshire dogs on the mantel-piece was a bank statement. She had put it there for the time being because she had been too busy to check where Pearl normally stored such things. The significant point for Oyster at this minute was not the statement, but the envelope containing it. More precisely, the top right-hand corner of the envelope, because the first class stamp had somehow escaped being cancelled.

Temptation stirred and uncoiled itself.

Oyster had never in her life steamed an unfranked stamp from an envelope and used it again. Nor, to her knowledge, had Pearl. Stamp collectors sometimes removed used specimens for their collections, but what Oyster was contemplating could in no way be confused with philately. It was against the law. Defrauding the Post Office. A crime.

There was under twenty minutes before the last collection.

I couldn't, she told herself. *I'm on the Parochial Church Council. I'm on the Bench.*

Temptation reminded her that she was due for a cup of tea in any case. She filled the kettle and pressed the switch. While waiting, watching the first wisp of steam rise from the spout, she weighed the necessity of posting the letter against the wickedness of re-using a stamp. It was not the most heinous of crimes, Temptation whispered. And once Oyster began to think about the chances of getting away with it, she was lost. The kettle sang, the steam gushed and she snatched up the envelope and jammed it against the spout. Merely, Temptation reassured her, to satisfy her curiosity as to whether stamps could be separated from envelopes by this method.

Those who believe in retribution will not be in the least surprised that the steam was deflected by the surface of the envelope and scalded three of Oyster's ringers quite severely. She cried out in pain and dropped the envelope. She ran the cold tap and plunged her hand under it. Then she wrapped the sore fingers in a piece of kitchen towel.

Her first action after that was to turn off the kettle. Her second was to pick up the envelope and test the corner of the stamp with the tip of her fingernail. It still adhered to some extent, but with extreme care she was able to ease it free, consoled that her discomfort had not been entirely without result. The minor accident failed to deter her from the crime. On the contrary, it acted like a prod from Old Nick.

There was a bottle of gum in the writing desk and she applied some to the back of the stamp, taking care not to use too much, which might have oozed out at the edges and discoloured the envelope. When she had positioned the stamp neatly on her letter, it would have passed the most rigorous inspection. She felt a wicked frisson of satisfaction at having committed an undetectable crime. Just in time, she remembered the post and had to hurry to catch it.

There we leave Miss Oyster Brown to come to terms with her conscience for a couple of days.

We meet her again on the Monday morning in the local chemist's shop. The owner and pharmacist was John Trigger, whom the Brown twins had known for getting on for thirty years, a decent, obliging man with a huge moustache who took a personal interest in his customers. In the face of strong competition from a national chain of pharmacists, John Trigger had persevered with his old-fashioned service from behind a counter, believing that some customers still preferred it to filling a wire basket themselves. But to stay in business he had been forced to diversify by offering some electrical goods.

When Oyster Brown came in and showed him three badly scalded fingers out in blisters, Trigger was sympathetic as well as willing to suggest a remedy. Understandably he enquired how Oyster had come by such a painful injury. She was expecting the question and had her answer ready, adhering to the truth as closely as a God-fearing woman should.

"An accident with the kettle."

Trigger looked genuinely alarmed. "An electric kettle? Not the one you bought here last year?"

"I didn't," said Oyster at once.

"Must have been your sister. A Steamquick. Is that what you've got?"

"Er, yes."

"If there's a fault . . . "

"I'm not here to complain, Mr Trigger. So you think this ointment will do the trick?"

"I'm sure of it. Apply it evenly, and don't attempt to pierce the blisters, will you?" John Trigger's conscience was troubling him. "This is quite a nasty scalding, Miss Brown. Where exactly did the steam come from?"

"The kettle."

"I know that. I mean was it the spout?"

"It really doesn't matter," said Oyster sharply. "It's done."

"The lid, then? Sometimes if you're holding the handle you get a rush of steam from that little slot in the lid. I expect it was that."

"I couldn't say," Oyster fudged, in the hope that it would satisfy Mr Trigger. It did not. "The reason I asked is that there may be a design fault."

"The fault was mine, I'm quite sure."

"Perhaps I ought to mention it to the manufacturers."

"Absolutely not," Oyster said in alarm. "I was careless, that's all. And now, if you'll excuse me . . ." She started backing away and then Mr Trigger ambushed her with another question.

"What does your sister say about it?"

"My sister?" From the way she spoke, she might never have had one.

"Miss Pearl."

"Oh, nothing. We haven't discussed it," Oyster truthfully stated.

"But she must have noticed your fingers."

"Er, no. How much is the ointment?"

Trigger told her and she dropped the money on the counter and almost rushed from the shop. He stared after her, bewildered.

The next time Oyster Brown was passing, Trigger took the trouble to go to the door of his shop and enquire whether the hand was any better. Clearly she wasn't overjoyed to see him. She assured him without much gratitude that the ointment was working. "It was nothing. It's going to clear up in a couple of days."

"May I see?"

She held out her hand.

Trigger agreed that it was definitely on the mend. "Keep it dry, if you possibly can. Who does the washing up?"

"What do you mean?"

"You, or your sister? It's well known that you divide the chores between you. If it's your job, I'm sure Miss Pearl won't mind taking over for a few days. If I see her, I'll suggest it myself."

Oyster reddened and said nothing.

"I was going to remark that I haven't seen her for a week or so," Trigger went on. "She isn't unwell, I hope?"

"No," said Oyster. "Not unwell."

Sensing correctly that this was not an avenue of conversation to venture along at this time, he said instead, "The Steamquick rep was in yesterday afternoon, so I mentioned what happened with your kettle."

She was outraged. "You had no business."

"Pardon me, Miss Brown, but it is my business. You were badly scalded. I can't have my customers being injured by the products I sell. The rep was very concerned, as I am. He asked if you would be so good as to bring the kettle in next time you come, so that he can check if there's a fault."

"Absolutely not," said Oyster. "I told you I haven't the slightest intention of complaining."

Trigger tried to be reasonable. "It isn't just your kettle. I've sold the same model to other customers."

"Then they'll complain if they get hurt."

"What if their children get hurt?"

She had no answer.

"If it's inconvenient to bring it in, perhaps I could call at your house."

"No," she said at once.

"I can bring a replacement. In fact, Miss Brown, I'm more than a little concerned about this whole episode. I'd like you to have another kettle with my compliments. A different model. Frankly, the modern trend is for jug kettles that couldn't possibly scald you as yours did. If you'll kindly step into the shop, I'll give you one now to take home."

The offer didn't appeal to Oyster Brown in the least. "For the last time, Mr Trigger," she said in a tight, clipped voice, "I don't require another kettle." With that, she walked away up the high street.

Trigger, from the motives he had mentioned, was not content to leave the matter there. He wasn't a churchgoer, but he believed in conducting his life on humanitarian principles. On this issue, he was resolved to be just as stubborn as she. He went back into the shop and straight to the phone. While Oyster Brown was out of the house, he would speak to Pearl Brown, the sister, and see if he could get better co-operation from her.

Nobody answered the phone.

At lunchtime, he called in to see Ted Collins, who ran the garden shop next door, and asked if he had seen anything of Pearl Brown lately.

"I had Oyster in this morning," Collins told him.

"But you haven't seen Pearl?"

"Not in my shop. Oyster does all the gardening, you know. They divide the work."

"I know."

"I can't think what came over her today. Do you know what she bought? Six bottles of Rapidrot."

"What's that?"

"It's a new product. An activator for composting. You dilute it and water your compost heap and it speeds up the process. They're doing a special promotion to launch it. Six bottles are far too much, and I tried to tell her, but she wouldn't be told."

"Those two often buy in bulk," said Trigger. "I've sold Pearl a dozen tubes of toothpaste at a go, and they must be awash with Dettol."

"They won't use six bottles of Rapidrot in twenty years," Collins pointed out. "It's concentrated stuff, and it won't keep all that well. It's sure to solidify after a time. I told her one's plenty to be going on with. She's wasted her money, obstinate old bird. I don't know what Pearl would say. Is she ill, do you think?"

"I've no idea," said Trigger, although in reality an idea was beginning to form in his brain. A disturbing idea. "Do they get on all right with each other? Daft question," he said before Collins could answer it. "They're twins. They've spent all their lives in each other's company."

For the present he dismissed the thought and gave his attention to the matter of the electric kettle. He'd already withdrawn the Steamquick kettles from sale. He got on the phone to Steamquick and had an acrimonious conversation with some little Hitler from their public relations department who insisted that thousands of the kettles had been sold and the design was faultless.

"The lady's injury isn't imagined, I can tell you," Trigger insisted.

"She must have been careless. Anyone can hurt themselves if they're not careful. People are far too ready to put the blame on the manufacturer."

"People, as you put it, are your livelihood."

There was a heavy sigh. "Send us the offending kettle, and we'll test it."

"That isn't so simple."

"Have you offered to replace it?"

The man's whole tone was so condescending that Trigger had an impulse to frighten him rigid. "She won't let the kettle out of her possession. I think she may be keeping it as evidence."

"Evidence?" There was a pause while the implication dawned. "Blimey."

On his end of the phone, Trigger permitted himself to grin.

"You mean she might take us to court over this?"

"I didn't say that—"

"Ah."

" . . . but she does know the law. She's a magistrate."

An audible gasp followed, then: "Listen, Mr, er—"

"Trigger."

"Mr Trigger. I think we'd better send someone to meet this lady and deal with the matter personally. Yes, that's what we'll do."

Trigger worked late that evening, stocktaking. He left the shop about ten-thirty. Out of curiosity he took a route home via Lime Tree Avenue and stopped the car opposite the Brown sisters' house and wound down the car window. There were lights upstairs and presently someone drew a curtain. It looked like Oyster Brown.

"Keeping an eye on your customers, Mr Trigger?" a voice close to him said.

He turned guiltily. A woman's face was six inches from his. He recognized one of his customers, Mrs Wingate. She said, "She's done that every night this week."

"Oh?"

"Something fishy's going on in there," she said. "I walk my little dog along the verge about this time every night. I live just opposite them, on this side, with the wrought-iron gates. That's Pearl's bedroom at the front. I haven't seen Pearl for a week, but every night her sister Oyster draws the curtains and leaves the light on for half an hour. What's going on, I'd like to know. If Pearl is ill, they ought to call a doctor. They won't, you know."

"That's Pearl's bedroom, you say, with the light on?"

"Yes, I often see her looking out. Not lately."

"And now Oyster switches on the light and draws the curtains?"

"And pulls them back at seven in the morning. I don't know what you think, Mr Trigger, but it looks to me as if she wants everyone to think Pearl's in there, when it's obvious she isn't."

"Why is it obvious?"

"All the windows are closed. Pearl always opens the top window wide, winter and summer."

"That is odd, now you mention it."

"I'll tell you one thing," said Mrs Wingate, regardless that she had told him several things already. "Whatever game she's up to, we won't find out. Nobody ever sets foot inside that house except the twins themselves."

At home and in bed that night, Trigger was troubled by a gruesome idea, one that he'd tried repeatedly to suppress. Suppose the worst had happened a week ago in the house in Lime Tree Avenue, his thinking ran. Suppose Pearl Brown had suffered a heart attack and died. After so many years of living in that house as if it were a fortress, was Oyster capable of dealing with the aftermath of death, calling in the doctor and the undertaker? In her shocked state, mightn't she decide that anything was preferable to having the house invaded, even if the alternative was disposing of the body herself?

How would a middle-aged woman dispose of a body? Oyster didn't drive a car. It wouldn't be easy to bury it in the garden, nor hygienic to keep it in a cupboard in the house. But if there was one thing every well-bred English lady knew about, it was gardening. Oyster was the gardener.

In time, everything rots in a compost heap. If you want to accelerate the process, you buy a preparation like Rapidrot.

Oyster Brown had purchased six bottles of the stuff. And every night she drew the curtains in her sister's bedroom to give the impression that she was there.

He shuddered.

In the fresh light of morning, John Trigger told himself that his morbid imaginings couldn't be true. They were the delusions of a tired brain. He decided to do nothing about them.

Just after eleven-thirty, a short, fat man in a dark suit arrived in the shop and announced himself as the Area Manager of Steamquick. His voice was suspiciously like the one that Trigger had found so irritating when he had phoned their head office. "I'm here about this allegedly faulty kettle," he announced.

"Miss Brown's?"

"I'm sure there's nothing wrong at all, but we're a responsible firm. We take every complaint seriously."

"You want to see the kettle? You'll be lucky."

The Steamquick man sounded smug. "That's all right. I telephoned Miss Brown this morning and offered to go to the house. She wasn't at all keen on that idea, but I was very firm with the lady, and she compromised. We're meeting here at noon. She's agreed to bring the kettle for me to inspect. I don't know why you found her so intractable."

"High noon, eh? Do you want to use my office?"

Trigger had come to a rapid decision. If Oyster was on her way to the shop, he was going out. He had two capable assistants.

This was a heaven-sent opportunity to lay his macabre theory to rest. While Oyster was away from the house in Lime Tree Avenue, he would drive there and let himself into the back garden. Mrs Wingate or any other curious neighbour watching from behind the lace curtains would have to assume he was trying to deliver something. He kept his white coat on, to reinforce the idea that he was on official business.

Quite probably, he told himself, the compost heap will turn out to be no bigger than a cowpat. The day was sunny and he felt positively cheerful as he turned up the Avenue. He checked his watch. Oyster would be making mincemeat of the Steamquick man about now. It would take her twenty minutes, at least, to walk back.

He stopped the car and got out. Nobody was about, but just in case he was being observed he walked boldly up the path to the front door and rang the bell. No one came.

Without appearing in the least furtive, he stepped around the side of the house. The back garden was in a beautiful state. Wide, well-stocked and immaculately weeded borders enclosed a finely trimmed lawn, yellow roses on a trellis and a kitchen garden beyond. Trigger took it in admiringly, and then remembered why he was there. His throat went dry. At the far end, beyond the kitchen garden, slightly obscured by some runner beans on poles, was the compost heap—as long as a coffin and more than twice as high.

The flesh on his arms prickled.

The compost heap was covered with black plastic bin-liners weighted with stones. They lay across the top, but the sides were exposed. A layer of fresh green garden refuse, perhaps half a metre in depth, was on the top. The lower part graduated in colour from a dull yellow to earth-brown. Obvious care had been taken to conserve the shape, to keep the pressure even and assist the composting process.

Trigger wasn't much of a gardener. He didn't have the time for it. He did the minimum and got rid of his garden rubbish with bonfires. Compost heaps were outside his experience, except that as a scientist he understood the principle by which they generated heat in a confined space. Once, years ago, an uncle of his had demonstrated this by pushing a bamboo cane into his heap from the top. A wisp of steam had issued from the hole as he withdrew the cane. Recalling it now, Trigger felt a wave of nausea.

He hadn't the stomach for this.

He knew now that he wasn't going to be able to walk up the garden and probe the compost heap. Disgusted with himself for being so squeamish, he turned to leave, and happened to notice that the kitchen window was ajar, which was odd, considering that Oyster was not at home. Out of interest he tried the door handle. The door was unlocked.

He said, "Anyone there?" and got no answer.

From the doorway he could see a number of unopened letters on the kitchen table. After the humiliation of turning his back on the compost heap, this was like a challenge, a chance to regain some self-respect. This at least, he was capable of doing. He stepped inside and picked up the letters. There were five, all addressed to Miss P. Brown. The postmarks dated from the beginning of the previous week.

Quite clearly Pearl had not been around to open her letters.

Then his attention was taken by an extraordinary line-up along a shelf. He counted fifteen packets of cornflakes, all open, and recalled his conversation with Ted Collins about the sisters buying in bulk. If Collins had wanted convincing, there was ample evidence here: seven bottles of decaffeinated coffee, nine jars of the same brand of marmalade and a tall stack of boxes of paper tissues. Eccentric housekeeping, to say the least. Perhaps, he reflected, it meant that the buying of six bottles of Rapidrot had not, after all, been so sinister.

Now that he was in the house, he wasn't going to leave without seeking an answer to the main mystery, the disappearance of Pearl. His mouth was no longer dry and the gooseflesh had gone from his arms. He made up his mind to go upstairs and look into the front bedroom.

On the other side of the kitchen door more extravagance was revealed. The passage from the kitchen to the stairway was lined on either side with sets of goods that must have overflowed from the kitchen. Numerous tins of cocoa, packets of sugar, pots of jam, gravy powder and other grocery items were stored as if for a siege, stacked along the skirting boards in groups of at least half a dozen. Trigger began seriously to fear for the mental health of the twins. Nobody had suspected anything like this behind the closed doors. The stacks extended halfway upstairs.

As he stepped upwards, obliged to tread close to the banisters, he was gripped by the sense of alienation that must have led to hoarding on such a scale. The staid faces that the sisters presented to the world gave no intimation of this strange compulsion. What was the mentality of people who behaved as weirdly as this?

An appalling possibility crept into Trigger's mind. Maybe the strain of so many years of appearing outwardly normal had finally caused Oyster to snap. What if the eccentricity so apparent all around him were not so harmless as it first appeared? No one could know what resentments, what jealousies lurked in this house, what mean-minded cruelties the sisters may have inflicted on each other. What if Oyster had fallen out with her sister and attacked her? She was a sturdy woman, physically capable of killing.

If she'd murdered Pearl, the compost-heap method of disposal would certainly commend itself.

Come now, he told himself. This is all speculation.

He reached the top stair and discovered that the stockpiling had extended to the landing. Toothpaste, talcum powder, shampoos and soap were stacked up in profusion. All the doors were closed. It wouldn't have surprised him if when he opened one he was knee-deep in toilet-rolls.

First he had to orientate himself. He decided that the front bedroom was to his right. He opened it cautiously and stepped in.

What happened next was swift and devastating. John Trigger heard a piercing scream. He had a sense of movement to his left and a glimpse of a figure in white. Something crashed against his head with a mighty thump, causing him to pitch forward.

About four, when the Brown twins generally stopped for tea, Oyster filled the new kettle that the Steamquick Area Manager had exchanged for the other one. She plugged it in. It was the new-fangled jug type, and she wasn't really certain if she was going to like it, but she certainly needed the cup of tea.

"I know it was wrong," she said, "and I'm going to pray for forgiveness, but I didn't expect that steaming a stamp off a letter would lead to this. I suppose it's a judgement."

"Whatever made you do such a wicked thing?" her sister Pearl asked, as she put out the cups and saucers.

"The letter had to catch the post. It was the last possible day for the Kellogg's Cornflakes competition, and I'd thought of such a wonderful slogan. The prize was a fortnight in Venice."

Pearl clicked her tongue in disapproval. "Just because I won the Birds Eye trip to the Bahamas, it didn't mean you were going to be lucky. We tried for twenty years and only ever won consolation prizes."

"It isn't really gambling, is it?" said Oyster. "It isn't like betting."

"It's all right in the Lord's eyes," Pearl told her. "It's a harmless pastime. Unfortunately we both know that people in the church wouldn't take a charitable view. They wouldn't expect us to devote so much of our time and money to competitions. That's why we have to be careful. You didn't tell anyone I was away?"

"Of course not. Nobody knows. For all they know, you were ill, if anyone noticed at all. I drew the curtains in your bedroom every night to make it look as if you were here."

"Thank you. You know I'd do the same for you."

"I might win," said Oyster. "Someone always does. I put in fifteen entries altogether, and the last one was a late inspiration."

"And as a result we have fifteen packets of cornflakes with the tops cut off," said Pearl, "They take up a lot of room."

"So do your frozen peas. I had to throw two packets away to make some room in the freezer. Anyway, I felt entitled to try. It wasn't much fun being here alone, thinking of you sunning yourself in the West Indies. To tell you the truth, I didn't really think you'd go and leave me here. It was a shock." Oyster carefully poured some hot water into the teapot to warm it. "If you want to know, I've also entered the Rapidrot Trip of a Lifetime competition. A week in San Francisco followed by a week in Sydney. I bought six bottles to have a fighting chance."

"What's Rapidrot?"

"Something for the garden." She spooned in some tea and poured on the hot water. "You must be exhausted. Did you get any sleep on the plane?"

Hardly any," said Pearl. "That's why I went straight to bed when I got in this morning." She poured milk into the teacups. "The next thing I knew was the doorbell going. I ignored it, naturally. It was one of the nastiest shocks I ever had hearing the footsteps coming up the stairs. I could tell it wasn't you. I'm just thankful that I had the candlestick to defend myself with."

"Is there any sign of life yet?"

"Well, he's breathing, but he hasn't opened his eyes, if that's what you mean. Funny, I would never have thought Mr Trigger was dangerous to women."

Oyster poured the tea. "What are we going to do if he doesn't recover? We can't have people coining into the house." Even as she was speaking, she put down the teapot and glanced out of the kitchen window towards the end of the garden. She had the answer herself.

Peter Lovesey recalls: "It's not wise or kind for a writer to draw inspiration from the secret hopes of family members. I made an exception with this story. My sister-in-law once opened a cupboard and it was stacked with cartons of chocolate-coated cornflakes. She wasn't a chocolate cornflake junkie; she was going through a phase of entering competitions. She was buying the *Competitors' Journal* and spending a lot of time thinking up slogans that would win. The house was stacked with products that offered weekends in Spain, household encyclopedias and music centres. I think she won a few times, but it did create storage problems. That was all a long time ago. Having admitted that this was the inspiration for the story, I must add that my sister-in-law bears no other resemblance to Miss Oyster Brown."

MICHAEL MALONE

Michael Malone has written everything from soap operas to screenplays to film analysis to humorous novels to a sentimental Christmas novel, but mystery readers probably know him best for crime fiction set in the North Carolina Piedmont country where he was born and now resides. He has populated the pages of his mysteries with colorful local characters who inhabit a world described as only a writer who hails from the place can depict it.

Born in Durham, North Carolina, Malone is the eldest of six children. From an early age, he became intensely interested in writing and in film. He attended Syracuse University, and then Harvard University, where he wrote a Ph.D. dissertation on archetypes and eroticism in American film. While at Harvard, Malone met Maureen Quilligan, the woman he would marry. He also began writing his first novel, *Painting the Roses Red*. Published in 1975, the book looks at the graduate school experience. His first works of fiction were strong on humor and satire, with his 1980 novel *Dingley Falls* probably receiving the most critical attention and fan feedback.

Malone made a success of writing for the soaps, serving as head writer for *One Life to Live* from 1991 to 1995. He also wrote television plays, pilots, and specials. In addition, Malone taught writing and film history at several colleges, including Yale University and Swarthmore College.

Malone's first crime novel, *Uncivil Seasons*, was published in 1983. It introduces two series characters: Lieutenant Justin Bartholomew Savile V, a homicide division head, and police chief Cudberth "Cuddy" Mangum. Both work on the police force in Hillston, North Carolina. In this first mystery, Savile's status as a member of the town's leading family helps him discover the truth in a murder case. The looming execution of an African American man is at the heart of Malone's second crime novel, *Time's Witness*, published in 1989. A serial killer must be apprehended in the 2001 novel *First Lady*. His most recent crime novel, *The Killing Club,* was published in 2005.

Set in a small town in the American South, Malone's short mystery story "Red Clay" is a stellar example of his work. Here's what he has to say about its genesis: "Red Clay began with a scene I imagined first like an old photograph. In the early sixties, a beautiful film actress, Stella Doyle, charged with murdering her husband, is led past a hostile crowd, down courthouse steps on a hot summer day in a small Southern town. A boy stands beside his father, watching the scene. This boy, Buddy Clay, the narrator, is embarrassed when his father removes his hat in deference to the woman, then defends her in front of the crowd. Obsessed by the mystery of this surprising moment,

Buddy pursues his own brief encounters with Stella over the decades as he struggles to get at the secret of his father's feelings for the former movie star, and so to understand both the kind of man his father was, and the kind of man he himself has become."

Red Clay

UP on its short slope the columned front of our courthouse was wavy in the August sun, like a courthouse in lake water. The leaves hung from maples, and the flag of North Carolina wilted flat against its metal pole. Heat sat sodden over Devereux County week by relentless week; they called the weather "dog days," after the star, Sirius, but none of us knew that. We thought they meant no dog would leave shade for street on such days—no dog except a mad one. I was ten that late August in 1959; I remembered the summer because of the long heat wave, and because of Stella Doyle.

When they pushed open the doors, the policemen and lawyers flung their arms up to their faces to block the sun and stopped there in the doorway as if the hot light were shoving them back inside. Stella Doyle came out last, a deputy on either side to walk her down to where the patrol car, orange as Halloween candles, waited to take her away until the jury could make up its mind about what had happened two months earlier out at Red Hills. It was the only house in the county big enough to have a name. It was where Stella Doyle had, maybe, shot her husband, Hugh Doyle, to death.

Excitement over Doyle's murder had swarmed through the town and stung us alive. No thrill would replace it until the assassination of John F. Kennedy. Outside the courthouse, sidewalk heat steaming up through our shoes, we stood patiently waiting to hear Mrs. Doyle found guilty. The news stood waiting, too, for she was, after all, not merely the murderer of the wealthiest man we knew; she was Stella Doyle. She was the movie star.

Papa's hand squeezed down on my shoulder and there was a tight line to his mouth as he pulled me into the crowd and said, "Listen now, Buddy, if anybody ever asks you, when you're grown, 'Did you ever see the most beautiful woman God made in your lifetime,' son, you say 'Yes, I had that luck, and her name was Stella Dora Doyle.'" His voice got louder, right there in the crowd for everybody to hear. "You tell them how her beauty was so bright, it burned back the shame they tried to heap on her head, burned it right on back to scorch their faces."

Papa spoke these strange words looking up the steps at the almost plump woman in black the deputies were holding. His arms were folded over his seersucker vest, his fingers tight on the sleeves of his shirt. People around us had turned to stare and somebody snickered.

Embarrassed for him, I whispered, "Oh, Papa, she's nothing but an old murderer. Everybody knows how she got drunk and killed Mr. Doyle. She shot him right through the head with a gun."

Papa frowned. "You don't know that."

I kept on. "Everybody says she was so bad and drunk all the time, she wouldn't let folks even live in the same house with her. She made him throw out his own mama and papa."

Papa shook his head at me. "I don't like to hear ugly gossip coming out of your mouth, all right, Buddy?"

"Yes, sir."

"She didn't kill Hugh Doyle."

"Yes, sir."

His frown scared me; it was so rare. I stepped closer and took his hand, took his stand against the rest. I had no loyalty to this woman Papa thought so beautiful. I just could never bear to be cut loose from the safety of his good opinion. I suppose that from that moment on, I felt toward Stella Doyle something of what my father felt, though in the end perhaps she meant less to me, and stood for more. Papa never had my habit of symbolizing.

The courthouse steps were wide, uneven stone slabs. As Mrs. Doyle came down, the buzzing of the crowd hushed. All together, like trained dancers, people stepped back to clear a half-circle around the orange patrol car. Newsmen shoved their cameras to the front. She was rushed down so fast that her shoe caught in the crumbling stone and she fell against one of the deputies.

"She's drunk!" hooted a woman near me, a country woman in a flowered dress belted with a strip of painted rope. She and the child she jiggled against her shoulder were puffy with the fat of poverty. "Look'it her"—the woman pointed—"look at that dress. She thinks she's still out there in Hollywood." The woman beside her nodded, squinting out from under a visor of the kind of hat pier fishermen wear. "I went and killed my husband, wouldn't no rich lawyers come running to weasel me out of the law." She slapped at a fly's buzz.

Then they were quiet and everybody else was quiet and our circle of sun-stunned eyes fixed on the woman in black, stared at the wonder of one as high as Mrs. Doyle about to be brought so low.

Holding to the stiff, tan arm of the young deputy, Mrs. Doyle reached down to check the heel of her shoe. Black shoes, black suit and purse, wide black hat—they all sinned against us by their fashionableness, blazing wealth as well as death. She stood there, arrested a moment in the hot immobility of the air, then she hurried down, rushing the two big deputies down with her, to the open door of the orange patrol car. Papa stepped forward so quickly that the gap filled with people before I could follow him. I squeezed through, fighting with my elbows, and I saw that he was holding his straw hat in one hand and offering the other hand out to the murderer. "Stella, how are you? Clayton Hayes."

As she turned, I saw the strawberry-gold hair beneath the hat; then her hand, bright with a big diamond, took away the dark glasses. I saw what Papa meant. She was beautiful. Her eyes were the color of lilacs, but darker than lilacs. And her skin held the light like the inside of a shell. She was not like other pretty women, because the difference was not one of degree. I have never seen anyone else of her kind.

"Why, Clayton! God Almighty, it's been years."

"Well, yes, a long time now, I guess," he said, and shook her hand.

She took the hand in both of hers. "You look the same as ever. Is this your boy?" she said. The violet eyes turned to me.

"Yes, this is Buddy. Ada and I have six so far, three of each."

"Six? Are we that old, Clayton?" She smiled. "They said you'd married Ada Hackney."

A deputy cleared his throat. "Sorry, Clayton, we're going to have to get going."

"Just a minute, Lonnie. Listen, Stella, I just wanted you to know I'm sorry as I can be about your losing Hugh."

Tears welled in her eyes. "He did it himself, Clayton," she said.

"I know that. I know you didn't do this." Papa nodded slowly again and again, the way he did when he was listening. "I know that. Good luck to you."

She swatted tears away. "Thank you."

"I'm telling everybody I'm sure of that."

"Clayton, thank you."

Papa nodded again, then tilted his head back to give her his slow, peaceful smile. "You call Ada and me if there's ever something we can do to help you, you hear?" She kissed his cheek and he stepped back with me into the crowd of hostile, avid faces as she entered the police car. It moved slow as the sun through the sightseers. Cameras pushed against its windows.

A sallow man biting a pipe skipped down the steps to join some other reporters next to us. "Jury sent out for food," he told them. "No telling with these yokels. Could go either way." He pulled off his jacket and balled it under his arm. "Jesus, it's hot."

A younger reporter with thin, wet hair disagreed. "They all think Hollywood's Babylon and she's the whore. Hugh Doyle was the local prince, his daddy kept the mills open in the bad times, quote unquote half the red-necks in the county. They'll fry her. For that hat if nothing else."

"Could go either way," grinned the man with the pipe. "She was born in a shack six miles from here. Hat or no hat, that makes her one of them. So what if she did shoot the guy, he was dying of cancer anyhow, for Christ's sake. Well, she never could act worth the price of a bag of popcorn, but Jesus damn she was something to look at!"

Now that Stella Doyle was gone, people felt the heat again and went back to where they could sit still in the shade until the evening breeze and wait for the jury's decision. Papa and I walked back down Main Street to our furniture store. Papa owned a butcher shop, too, but he didn't like the meat business and wasn't very good at it, so my oldest brother ran it while Papa sat among the mahogany bedroom suites and red maple dining room sets in a big rocking chair and read, or talked to friends who dropped by. The rocker was actually for sale but he had sat in it for so long now that it was just Papa's chair. Three ceiling fans stirred against the quiet, shady air while he answered my questions about Stella Doyle.

He said that she grew up Stella Dora Hibble on Route 19, in a three-room, tin-roofed little house propped off the red clay by concrete blocks—the kind of saggy-porched, pinewood house whose owners leave on display in their dirt yard, like sculptures, the broken artifacts of their aspirations and the debris of their unmendable lives: the doorless refrigerator and the rusting car, the pyre of metal and plastic that tells drivers along the highway "Dreams don't last."

Stella's mother, Dora Hibble, had believed in dreams anyhow. Dora had been a pretty girl who'd married a farmer and worked harder than she had the health for, because hard work was necessary just to keep from going under. But in the evenings Mrs. Hibble had looked at movie magazines. She had believed the romance was out there and she wanted it, if not for her, for her children. At twenty-seven, Dora Hibble died during her fifth labor. Stella was eight when she watched from the door of the bedroom as they covered her mother's face with a thin blanket. When Stella was fourteen, her father died when a machine jammed at Doyle Mills. When Stella was sixteen, Hugh Doyle, Jr., who was her age, my father's age, fell in love with her.

"Did you love her, too, Papa?"

"Oh, yes. All us boys in town were crazy about Stella Dora, one time or another. I had my attack of it, same as the rest. We were sweethearts in seventh grade. I bought a big-size Whitman's Sampler on Valentine's. I remember it cost every cent I had."

"Why were y'all crazy about her?"

"I guess you'd have to worry you'd missed out on being alive if you didn't feel that way about Stella, one time or another."

I was feeling a terrible emotion I later defined as jealousy. "But didn't you love Mama?"

"Well, now, this was before it was my luck to meet your mama."

"And you met her coming to town along the railroad track and you told your friends 'That's the girl for me and I'm going to marry her,' didn't you?"

"Yes, sir, and I was right on both counts." Papa rocked back in the big chair, his hands peaceful on the armrests.

"Was Stella Dora still crazy about you after you met Mama?"

His face crinkled into the lines of his reply laughter. "No, sir, she wasn't. She loved Hugh Doyle, minute she laid eyes on him, and he felt the same. But Stella had this notion about going off to get to be somebody in the movies. And Hugh couldn't hold her back, and I guess she couldn't get him to see what it was made her want to go off so bad either."

"What was it made her want to go?"

Papa smiled at me. "Well, I don't know, son. What makes you want to go off so bad? You're always saying you're going here, and there, 'cross the world, up to the moon. I reckon you're more like Stella than I am."

"Do you think she was wrong to want to go be in the movies?"

"No."

"You don't think she killed him?"

"No, sir, I don't."

"Somebody killed him."

"Well, Buddy, sometimes people lose hope and heart and feel like they can't go on living."

"Yeah, I know. Suicide."

Papa's shoes tapped the floor as the rocker creaked back and forth. "That's right. Now you tell me, why're you sitting in here? Why don't you ride your bike on over to the ballpark and see who's there?"

"I want to hear about Stella Doyle."

"You want to hear. Well. Let's go get us a Coca-Cola, then. I don't guess somebody's planning to show up in this heat to buy a chest of drawers they got to haul home."

"You ought to sell air conditioners, Papa. People would buy air conditioners."

"I guess so."

So Papa told me the story. Or at least his version of it. He said Hugh and Stella were meant for each other. From the beginning it seemed to the whole town a fact as natural as harvest that so much money and so much beauty belonged together, and only Hugh Doyle with his long, free, easy stride was rich enough to match the looks of Stella Dora. But even Hugh Doyle couldn't hold her. He was only halfway through the state university, where his father had told him he'd have to go before he married Stella, if he wanted a home to bring her to, when she quit her job at Coldsteam's beauty parlor and took the bus to California. She was out there for six years before Hugh broke down and went after her.

By then every girl in the county was cutting Stella's pictures out of the movie magazines and reading how she got her lucky break, how she married a big director and divorced him, and married a big star, and how that marriage broke up even quicker. Photographers traveled all the way to Thermopylae to take pictures of where she was born. People tried to tell them her house was gone, had fallen down and had been used for firewood, but they just took photographs of Reverend Ballister's house instead and said Stella had grown up in it. Before long, even local girls would go stand in front of the Ballister house like a shrine, sometimes they'd steal flowers out of the yard. The year that *Fever*, her best movie, came to the Grand Theater on Main Street, Hugh Doyle flew out to Los Angeles and won her back. He took her down to Mexico to divorce the baseball player she'd married after the big star. Then Hugh married her himself and put her on an ocean liner and took her all over the world. For a whole two years, they didn't come home to Thermopylae. Everybody in the county talked about this two-year honeymoon, and Hugh's father confessed to some friends that he was disgusted by his son's way of life.

But when the couple did come home, Hugh walked right into the mills and turned a profit. His father confessed to the same friends that he was flabbergasted Hugh had it in him. But after the father died Hugh started drinking and Stella joined him. The parties got a little wild. The fights got loud. People talked. They said he had other women. They said Stella'd been locked up in a sanatorium. They said the Doyles were breaking up.

And then one June day a maid at Red Hills, walking to work before the morning heat, fell over something that lay across a path to the stables. And it was Hugh Doyle in riding clothes with a hole torn in the side of his head. Not far from his gloved hand, the police found Stella's pistol, already too hot from the sun to touch. The cook testified that the Doyles had been fighting like cats and dogs all night long the night before, and Hugh's mother testified that he wanted to divorce Stella but she wouldn't let him, and so Stella was arrested. She said she was innocent, but it was her gun, she was his heir, and she had no alibi. Her trial lasted almost as long as that August heat wave.

A neighbor strolled past the porch, where we sat out the evening heat, waiting for the air to lift. "Jury's still out," he said. Mama waved her hand at him. She pushed herself and me in the big green wood swing that hung from two chains to the porch roof, and answered my questions about Stella Doyle. She said, "Oh, yes, they all said Stella was 'specially pretty. I never knew her to talk to myself."

"But if Papa liked her so much, why didn't y'all get invited out to their house and everything?"

"Her and your papa just went to school together, that's all. That was a long time back. The Doyles wouldn't ask folks like us over to Red Hills."

"Why not? Papa's family used to have a *whole* lot of money. That's what you said. And Papa went right up to Mrs. Doyle at the courthouse today, right in front of everybody. He told her, You let us know if there's anything we can do."

Mama chuckled the way she always did about Papa, a low ripple like a pigeon nesting, a little exasperated at having to sit still so long. "You know your papa'd offer to help out anybody he figured might be in trouble, white or black. That's just him; that's not any Stella Dora Doyle. Your papa's just a good man. You remember that, Buddy."

Goodness was Papa's stock-in-trade; it was what he had instead of money or ambition, and Mama often reminded us of it. In him she kept safe all the kindness she had never felt she could afford for herself. She, who could neither read nor write, who had stood all day in a cigarette factory from the age of nine until the morning Papa married her, was a fighter. She wanted her children to go farther than Papa had. Still, for years after he died, she would carry down from the attic the yellow mildewed ledgers where his value was recorded in more than $75,000 of out-of-date bills he had been unwilling to force people in trouble to pay. Running her sun-spotted finger down the brown wisps of names and the money they'd owed, she would sigh that proud, exasperated ripple, and shake her head over foolish, generous Papa.

Through the front parlor window I could hear my sisters practicing the theme from *The Apartment* on the piano. Someone across the street turned on a light. Then we heard the sound of Papa's shoes coming a little faster than usual down the sidewalk. He turned at the hedge, carrying the package of shiny butcher's paper in which he brought meat home every evening. "Verdict just came in!" he called out happily. "Not guilty! Jury came back about forty minutes ago. They already took her home."

Mama took the package and sat Papa down in the swing next to her. "Well, well," she said. "They let her off."

"Never ought to have come up for trial in the first place, Ada, like I told everybody all along. It's like her lawyers showed. Hugh went down to Atlanta, saw that doctor, found out he had cancer, and he took his own life. Stella never even knew he was sick."

Mama patted his knee. "Not guilty; well, well."

Papa made a noise of disgust. "Can you believe some folks out on Main Street tonight are all fired up *because* Stella got off! Adele Simpson acted downright indignant!"

Mama said, "And you're surprised?" And she shook her head with me at Papa's innocence.

Talking of the trial, my parents made one shadow along the wood floor of the porch, while inside my sisters played endless variations of "Chopsticks," the notes handed down by ghostly creators long passed away.

A few weeks later, Papa was invited to Red Hills, and he let me come along; we brought a basket of sausage biscuits Mama had made for Mrs. Doyle.

As soon as Papa drove past the wide white gate, I learned how money could change even weather. It was cooler at Red Hills, and the grass was the greenest grass in the country. A black man in a black suit let us into the house, then led us down a wide hallway of pale yellow wood into a big room shuttered against the heat. She was there in an armchair almost the color of her eyes. She wore loose-legged pants and was pouring whiskey from a bottle into a glass.

"Clayton, thanks for coming. Hello there, little Buddy. Look, I hope I didn't drag you from business."

Papa laughed. "Stella, I could stay gone a week and never miss a customer." It embarrassed me to hear him admit such failure to her.

She said she could tell I liked books, so maybe I wouldn't mind if they left me there to read while she borrowed my daddy for a little bit. There were white shelves in the room, full of books. I said I didn't mind but I did; I wanted to keep on seeing her. Even with the loose shirt soiled and rumpled over a waist she tried to hide, even with her face swollen from heat and drink and grief, she was something you wanted to look at as long as possible.

They left me alone. On the white piano were dozens of photographs of Stella Doyle in silver frames. From a big painting over the mantelpiece her remarkable eyes followed me around the room. I looked at that painting as sun deepened across it, until finally she and Papa came back. She had a tissue to her nose, a new drink in her hand. "I'm sorry, honey," she said to me. "Your daddy's been sweet letting me run on. I just needed somebody to talk to for a while about what happened to me." She kissed the top of my head and I could feel her warm lips at the part in my hair.

We followed her down the wide hall out onto the porch. "Clayton, you'll forgive a fat old souse talking your ear off and bawling like a jackass."

"No such thing, Stella."

"And you *never* thought I killed him, even when you first heard. My God, thank you."

Papa took her hand again. "You take care now," he said.

Then suddenly she was hugging herself, rocking from side to side. Words burst from her like a door flung open by wind. "I could kick him in the ass, that bastard! Why didn't he tell me? To quit, to *quit,* and use *my* gun, and just about get me strapped in the gas chamber, that goddamn bastard, and never say a word!" Her profanity must have shocked Papa as much as it did me. He never used it, much less ever heard it from a woman.

But he nodded and said, "Well, good-bye, I guess, Stella. Probably won't be seeing you again."

"Oh, Lord, Clayton, I'll be back. The world's so goddamn little."

She stood at the top of the porch, tears wet in those violet eyes that the movie magazines had loved to talk about. On her cheek a mosquito bite flamed like a slap. Holding to the big white column, she waved as we drove off into the dusty heat. Ice flew from the glass in her hand like diamonds.

Papa was right; they never met again. Papa lost his legs from diabetes, but he'd never gone much of anywhere even before that. And afterward, he was one of two places—home or the store. He'd sit in his big wood wheelchair in the furniture store, with his hands peaceful on the armrests, talking with whoever came by.

I did see Stella Doyle again; the first time in Belgium, twelve years later. I went farther than Papa.

In Bruges there are small restaurants that lean like elegant elbows on the canals and glance down at passing pleasure boats. Stella Doyle was sitting, one evening, at a table in the crook of the elbow of one of them, against an iron railing that curved its reflection in the water. She was alone there when I saw her. She stood, leaned over the rail, and slipped the ice cubes from her glass into the canal. I was in a motor launch full of tourists passing below. She waved with a smile at us and we waved back. It had been a lot of years since her last picture, but probably she waved out of habit. For the tourists motoring past, Stella in white against the dark restaurant was another snapshot of Bruges. For me, she was home and memory. I craned to look back as long as I could, and leapt from the boat at the next possible stop.

When I found the restaurant, she was yelling at a well-dressed young man who was leaning across the table, trying to soothe her in French. They appeared to be quarreling over his late arrival. All at once she hit him, her diamond flashing into his face. He filled the air with angry gestures, then turned and left, a white napkin to his cheek. I was made very shy by what I'd seen—the young man was scarcely older than I was. I stood unable to speak until her staring at me jarred me forward. I said, "Mrs. Doyle? I'm Buddy Hayes. I came out to see you at Red Hills with my father, Clayton Hayes, one time. You let me look at your books."

She sat back down and poured herself a glass of wine. "You're *that* little boy? God Almighty, how old am I? Am I a hundred yet?" Her laugh had been loosened by the wine. "Well, a Red Clay rambler, like me. How 'bout that. Sit down. What are *you* doing over here?"

I told her, as nonchalantly as I could manage, that I was traveling on college prize money, a journalism award. I wrote a prize essay about a murder trial.

"Mine?" she asked, and laughed.

A waiter, plump and flushed in his neat black suit, trotted to her side. He shook his head at the untouched plates of food. "Madame, your friend has left, then?"

Stella said, "Mister, I helped him along. And turns out, he was no friend."

The waiter then turned his eyes, sad and reproachful, to the trout on the plate.

"How about another bottle of that wine and a great big bucket of ice?" Stella asked.

The waiter kept flapping his fat quick hands around his head, entreating us to come inside. *"Les moustiques, madame!"*

"I just let them bite," she said. He went away grieved.

She was slender now, and elegantly dressed. And while her hands and throat were older, the eyes hadn't changed, nor the red-gold hair. She was still the most beautiful woman God had made in my lifetime, the woman of whom my father had said that any man who had not desired her had missed out on being alive, the one for whose honor my father had turned his back on the whole town of Thermopylae. Because of Papa, I had entered my adolescence daydreaming about fighting for Stella Doyle's honor; we had starred together in a dozen of her movies: I dazzled her jury; I cured Hugh Doyle while hiding my own noble love for his wife. And now here I sat drinking wine with her on a veranda in Bruges; me, the first Hayes ever to win a college prize, ever to get to college. Here I sat with a movie star.

She finished her cigarette, dropped it spinning down into the black canal. "You look like him," she said. "Your papa. I'm sorry to hear that about the diabetes."

"I look like him, but I don't think like him," I told her.

She tipped the wine bottle upside down in the bucket. "You want the world," she said. "Go get it, honey."

"That's what my father doesn't understand."

"He's a good man," she answered. She stood up slowly. "And I think Clayton would want me to get you to your hotel."

All the fenders of her Mercedes were crushed. She said, "When I've had a few drinks, I need a strong car between me and the rest of the cockeyed world."

The big car bounced over the moon-white street. "You know what, Buddy? Hugh Doyle gave me my first Mercedes, one morning in Paris. At breakfast. He held the keys out in his hand like a damn daffodil he'd picked in the yard. He gave me *this* goddamn thing." She waved her finger with its huge diamond. "This damn thing was tied to my big toe one Christmas morning!" And she smiled up at the stars as if Hugh Doyle were up there tying diamonds on them. "He had a beautiful grin, Buddy, but he was a son of a bitch."

The car bumped to a stop on the curb outside my little hotel. "Don't miss your train tomorrow," she said. "And you listen to me, don't go back home; go on to Rome."

"I'm not sure I have time."

She looked at me. "*Take* time. Just take it. Don't get scared, honey."

Then she put her hand in my jacket pocket and the moon came around her hair, and my heart panicked crazily, thudding against my shirt, thinking she might kiss me. But her hand went away, and all she said was, "Say hi to Clayton when you get home, all right? Even losing his legs and all, your daddy's lucky, you know that?"

I said, "I don't see how."

"Oh, I didn't either till I was a lot older than you. And had my damn in-laws trying to throw me into the gas chamber. Go to bed. So long, Red Clay."

Her silver car floated away. In my pocket, I found a large wad of French money, enough to take me to Rome, and a little ribboned box, clearly a gift she had decided not to give the angry young man in the beautiful suit who'd arrived too late. On black velvet lay a man's wristwatch, reddish gold.

It's an extremely handsome watch, and it still tells me the time.

I only went home to Thermopylae for the funerals. It was the worst of the August dog days when Papa died in the hospital bed they'd set up next to his and Mama's big four poster in their bedroom. At his grave, the clots of red clay had already dried to a dusty dull color by the time we shoveled them down upon him, friend after friend taking a turn at the shovel. The petals that fell from roses fell limp to the red earth, wilted like the crowd who stood by the grave while Reverend Ballister told us that Clayton Hayes was "a good man." Behind a cluster of Mama's family, I saw a woman in black turn away and walk down the grassy incline to a car, a Mercedes.

After the services I went driving, but I couldn't outtravel Papa in Devereux County. The man at the gas pump listed Papa's virtues as he cleaned my windshield. The woman who sold me the bottle of bourbon said she'd owed Papa $215.00 since 1944, and when she'd paid him back in 1966 he'd forgotten all about it. I drove along the highway where the foundations of tin-roofed shacks were covered now by the parking lots of minimalls; beneath the asphalt, somewhere, was Stella Doyle's birthplace. Stella Dora Hibble, Papa's first love.

Past the white gates, the Red Hills lawn was as parched as the rest of the county. Paint blistered and peeled on the big white columns. I waited a long time before the elderly black man I'd met twenty years before opened the door irritably.

I heard her voice from the shadowy hall yelling, "Jonas! Let him in."

On the white shelves the books were the same. The photos on the piano as young as ever. She frowned so strangely when I came into the room. I thought she must have been expecting someone else and didn't recognize me.

"I'm Buddy Hayes, Clayton's—"

"I know who you are."

"I saw you leaving the cemetery. . . ."

"I know you did."

I held out the bottle.

Together we finished the bourbon in memory of Papa, while shutters beat back the sun, hid some of the dirty glasses scattered on the floor, hid Stella Doyle in her lilac armchair. Cigarette burns scarred the armrests, left their marks on the oak floor. Behind her the big portrait showed Time up for the heartless bastard he is. Her hair was cropped short, and gray. Only the color of her eyes had stayed the same; they looked as remarkable as ever in the swollen face.

"I came out here to bring you something."

"What?"

I gave her the thin, cheap, yellowed envelope I'd found in Papa's desk with his special letters and papers. It was addressed in neat, cursive pencil to "Clayton." Inside was a silly Valentine card. Betty Boop popping bonbons into her pouty lips, exclaiming "Ooooh, I'm sweet on you." It was childish and lascivious at the same time, and it was signed with a lipstick blot, now brown with age, and with the name "Stella," surrounded by a heart.

I said, "He must have kept this since the seventh grade."

She nodded. "Clayton was a good man." Her cigarette fell from her ashtray onto the floor. When I came over to pick it up, she said, "Goodness is luck; like money, like looks. Clayton was lucky that way." She went to the piano and took more ice from the bucket there; one piece she rubbed around the back of her neck then dropped into her glass. She turned, the eyes wet, like lilac stars. "You know, in Hollywood, they said, '*Hibble?!* What kind of hick name is that, we can't use that!' So I said, 'Use Doyle, then.' I mean, I took Hugh's name six years before he ever came out to get me. Because I knew he'd come. The day I left Thermopylae he kept yelling at me, 'You can't have both!' He kept yelling it while the bus was pulling out. 'You can't have me and it both!' He wanted to rip my heart out for leaving, for *wanting* to go." Stella moved along the curve of the white piano to a photograph of Hugh Doyle in a white open shirt, grinning straight out at the sun. She said, "But I could have both. There were only two things I *had* to have in this little world, and one was the lead in a movie called *Fever*, and the other one was Hugh Doyle." She put the photograph down carefully. "I didn't know about the cancer till my lawyers found out he'd been to see that doctor in Atlanta. Then it was easy to get the jury to go for suicide." She smiled at me. "Well, not easy. But we turned them around. I think your papa was the only man in town who *never* thought I was guilty."

It took me a while to take it in. "Well, he sure convinced me," I said.

"I expect he convinced a lot of people. Everybody thought so much of Clayton."

"You killed your husband."

We looked at each other. I shook my head. "Why?"

She shrugged. "We had a fight. We were drunk. He was sleeping with my fucking maid. I was crazy. Lots of reasons, no reason. I sure didn't plan it."

"You sure didn't confess it either."

"What good would that have done? Hugh was dead. I wasn't about to let his snooty-assed mother shove me in the gas chamber and pocket the money."

I shook my head. "Jesus. And you've never felt a day's guilt, have you?"

Her head tilted back, smoothing her throat. The shuttered sun had fallen down the room onto the floor, and evening light did a movie fade and turned Stella Doyle into the star in the painting behind her. "Ah, baby, don't believe it," she said. The room stayed quiet.

I stood up and dropped the empty bottle in the wastebasket. I said, "Papa told me how he was in love with you."

Her laugh came warmly through the shuttered dusk. "Yes, and I guess I was sweet on him, too, boop boop dedoo."

"Yeah, Papa said no man could say he'd been alive if he'd seen you and not felt that way. I just wanted to tell you I know what he meant." I raised my hand to wave good-bye.

"Come over here," she said, and I went to her chair and she reached up and brought my head down to her and kissed me full and long on the mouth. "So long, Buddy." Slowly her hand moved down my face, the huge diamond radiant.

News came over the wire. The tabloids played with it for a few days on back pages. They had some pictures. They dug up the Hugh Doyle trial photos to put beside the old studio glossies. The dramatic death of an old movie star was worth sending a news camera down to Thermopylae, North Carolina, to get a shot of the charred ruin that had once been Red Hills. A shot of the funeral parlor and the flowers on the casket.

My sister phoned me that there was even a crowd at the coroner's inquest at the courthouse. They said Stella Doyle had died in her sleep after a cigarette set fire to her mattress. But rumors started that her body had been found at the foot of the stairs, as if she'd been trying to escape the fire but had fallen. They said she was drunk. They buried her beside Hugh Doyle in the family plot, the fanciest tomb in the Methodist cemetery, not far from where my parents were buried. Not long after she died, one of the cable networks did a night of her movies. I stayed up to watch *Fever* again.

My wife said, "Buddy, I'm sorry, but this is the biggest bunch of sentimental slop I ever saw. The whore'll sell her jewels and get the medicine and they'll beat the epidemic but she'll die to pay for her past and then the town'll see she was really a saint. Am I right?"

"You're right."

She sat down to watch awhile. "You know, I can't decide if she's a really lousy actress or a really good one. It's weird."

I said, "Actually, I think she was a much better actress than anyone gave her credit for."

My wife went to bed, but I watched through the night. I sat in Papa's old rocking chair that I'd brought north with me after his death. Finally, at dawn I turned off the set, and Stella's face disappeared into a star, and went out. The reception was awful and the screen too small. Besides, the last movie was in black and white; I couldn't see her eyes as well as I could remember the shock of their color, when she first turned toward me at the foot of the courthouse steps, that hot August day when I was ten, when my father stepped forward out of the crowd to take her hand, when her eyes were lilacs turned up to his face, and his straw hat in the summer sun was shining like a knight's helmet.

ED McBAIN

Ed McBain may be best known today as the mystery writer who created the "Eighty-seventh Precinct" novels. That series is notable for the author's portrayal of a group of series characters who interact with one another in the course of their police work. They solve crimes in a city the author calls Isola—a metropolis modeled on Manhattan. In his first book in the series, McBain sought to place equal emphasis on each of the characters in his police squad, but most readers will agree Detective Steve Carella is a standout. Other memorable characters in the series include Bert Kling, Meyer Meyer, and Lieutenant Peter Byrnes. The series is notable for its influence on later writers of police procedurals and for its portraits of the city in all its moods. The author has said he thinks of the city as a character, and of the multibook series as one long novel in which each book stands as a chapter.

Before he became a popular writer of crime novels under the McBain pen name, the author gained fame under his actual name, Evan Hunter, as the author of a mainstream novel, *The Blackboard Jungle* (1954). Based on his experiences teaching in a tough inner-city school in the Bronx and later made into a film of the same title, the poignant and powerful book became a bestseller. Also under the Hunter name, the author penned numerous novels and screenplays. Meanwhile, as McBain, he also wrote a detective series set in Florida, featuring the sleuth Matthew Hope.

Whether writing as McBain or as Hunter, the prolific author always demonstrates a command of his craft. He also has a flair for irony, which may pack the most punch in his short fiction. In his 1999 short story "Barking at Butterflies," published under the McBain moniker, he plays with two trends then *au courant* in crime writing: the focus on couples as characters and the use of pets as instigators of action. While many writers have strayed into coy portrayals of furry friends, McBain instead takes a misogynist's view of one pooch in this chiller.

The author has one remark to share about the story. "Regarding inspiration," he writes, "the love of my life, Dragica, brought to our marriage a Maltese poodle named Sasha. He's still with us, and we get along fine now."

Barking at Butterflies

1999

DAMN dog barked at everything. Sounds nobody else could hear, in the middle of the night the damn dog barked at them.

"He's protecting us," Carrie would say.

Protecting us. Damn dog weighs eight pounds soaking wet, he's what's called a Maltese poodle, he's protecting us. His name is Valletta, which is the capital of Malta. That's where the breed originated, I suppose. Some sissy Maltese nobleman must've decided he needed a yappy little lapdog that looked like a white feather duster. Little black nose. Black lips. Black button eyes. Shaggy little pip-squeak named Valletta. Who barked at everything from a fart to a butterfly. Is that someone ringing the bell? The damn dog would hurl himself at the door like a grizzly bear, yelping and growling and raising a fuss that could wake the dead in the entire county.

"He's just protecting us," Carrie would say.

Protecting us.

I hated that damn dog.

I still do.

He was Carrie's dog, you see. She rescued him from a husband-and-wife team who used to beat him when he was just a puppy—gee, I wonder why. This was two years before we got married. I used to think he was cute while she was training him. She'd say, "Sit, Valletta," and he'd walk away. She'd say, "Stay, Valletta," and he'd bark. She'd say, "Come, Valletta," and he'd take a nap. This went on for six months. He still isn't trained.

Carrie loved him to death.

As for El Mutto, the only thing on earth *he* loved was Carrie. Well, you save a person's life, he naturally feels indebted. But this went beyond mere gratitude. Whenever Carrie left the house, Valletta would lie down just inside the door, waiting for her to come home. Serve him a hot pastrami on rye, tell him, "Come, Valletta, time to eat," he'd look at me as if he'd been abandoned by the love of his life and never cared to breathe again. When he heard her car in the driveway, he'd start squealing and peeing on the rug. The minute she put her key in the lock, he jumped up in the air like a Chinese acrobat, danced and pranced on his hind legs when she opened the door, began squealing and leaping all around her until she knelt beside him and scooped him into her embrace and made comforting little sounds to him: "Yes, Valletta, yes, Mommy, what a good boy, oh, yes, what a beautiful little puppyboy."

I used to joke about cooking him.

"Maltese meatloaf is delicious," I used to tell Carrie. "We'll pluck him first, and then wash him real good, and stuff him and put him in the oven for what,

an hour? Maybe forty-five minutes, the size of him. Serve him with roast potatoes and—"

"He understands every word you say," she'd tell me.

Damn dog would just cock his head and look up at me. Pretended to be
bewildered, the canny little son of a bitch.

"Would you like to be a meatloaf?" I'd ask him.

He'd yawn.

"You'd better be a good dog or I'll sell you to a Filipino man."

"He understands you."

"You want to go home with a Filipino man?"

"Why do you talk to him that way?"

"In the Philippines they *eat* dogs, did you know that, Valletta? Dogs are a
delicacy in the Philippines. You want to go home with a Filipino man?"

"You're hurting him."

"He'll turn you into a rack of Maltese chops, would you like that, Valletta?"

"You're hurting *me*, too."

"Or some breaded Maltese cutlets, what do you say, Valletta? You want to
go to Manila?"

"Please don't, John. You know I love him."

Damn dog would rush into the bathroom after her, sit by the tub while she took
her shower, lick the water from her toes while she dried herself. Damn dog would
sit at her feet while she was peeing on the toilet. Damn dog would even sit beside
the bed whenever we made love. I asked her once to please put him out in the hall.

"I feel as if there's a *pervert* here in the bedroom watching us," I said.

"He's not watching us."

"He's sitting there *staring* at us."

"No, he's not."

"Yes, he is. It embarrasses me, him staring at my privates that way."

"Your privates? When did you start using *that* expression?"

"Ever since he started staring at it."

"He's not staring at it."

"He is. In fact, he's *glaring* at it. He doesn't like me making love to you."

"Don't be silly, John. He's just a cute little puppydog."

One day, cute little puppydog began barking at *me*.

I came in the front door, and the stupid little animal was sitting smack in the
middle of the entry, snarling and barking at me as if I were a person come to
read the gas meter.

"What?" I said.

He kept barking.

"You're barking at *me*?" I said. "This is *my* house, I *live* here, you little shit,
how *dare* you bark at me?"

"What is it, what is it?" Carrie yelled, rushing into the hallway.

"He's barking at me," I said.

"Shhh, Valletta," she said. "Don't bark at John."

He kept barking, the little well-trained bastard.

"How would you like to become a Maltese hamburger?" I asked him.

He kept barking.

I don't know when I decided to kill him.

Perhaps it was the night Carrie seated him at the dinner table with us. Until then, she'd been content to have him sitting at our feet like the despicable little beggar he was, studying every bite we took, waiting for scraps from the table.

"Go ahead," I'd say, "watch every morsel we put in our mouths. You're *not* getting fed from the table."

"Oh, John," Carrie would say.

"I can't enjoy my meal with him staring at me that way."

"He's not staring at you."

"What do you call what he's doing right this minute? Look at him! If that isn't staring, what is it?"

"I think you're obsessed with this idea of the dog staring at you."

"Maybe because he *is* staring at me."

"If he is, it's because he loves you."

"He doesn't love me, Carrie."

"Yes, he does."

"He loves *you*."

"He loves you, too, John."

"No, just you. In fact, if you want to talk about obsession, *that's* obsession. What that damn mutt feels for you is *obsession*."

"He's not a mutt, and he's not obsessed. He just wants to be part of the family. He sees us eating, he wants to join us. Come, Valletta, come sweet puppy-boy, come little Mommy, come sit with your family," she said, and hoisted him off the floor and plunked him down on a chair between us.

"I'll get your dish, sweet babypup," she said.

"Carrie," I said, "I will not have that mutt sitting at the table with us."

"He's not a mutt," she said. "He's purebred."

"Valletta," I said, "get the hell off that chair or I'll—"

He began barking.

"You mustn't raise your hand to him," Carrie said. "He was abused. He thinks you're about to hit him."

"*Hit* him?" I said. "I'm about to *kill* him!"

The dog kept barking.

And barking.

And barking.

I guess that's when I decided to do it.

October is a good time for dying.

"Come, Valletta," I said, "let's go for a walk."

He heard me say "Come," so naturally he decided to go watch television.

"Is Daddy taking you for a walk?" Carrie asked.

Daddy.

Daddy had Mr. Smith and Mr. Wesson in the pocket of his bush jacket. Daddy was going to walk little pisspot here into the woods far from the house and put a few bullets in his head and then sell his carcass to a passing Filipino man or toss it to a wayward coyote or drop it in the river. Daddy was going to tell Carrie that her prized purebred mutt had run away, naturally, when I commanded him to come. I called and called, I would tell her, but he ran and ran, and God knows where he is now.

"Don't forget his leash," Carrie called from the kitchen.

"I won't, darling."

"Be careful," she said. "Don't step on any snakes."

"Valletta will protect me," I said, and off we went.

The leaves were in full voice, brassy overhead, rasping underfoot. Valletta kept backing off on the red leather leash, stubbornly planting himself every ten feet or so into the woods, trying to turn back to the house where his beloved mistress awaited his return. I kept assuring him that we were safe here under the trees, leaves dropping gently everywhere around us. "Come, little baby-pup," I cooed, "come little woofikins, there's nothing can hurt you here in the woods."

The air was as crisp as a cleric's collar.

When we had come a far-enough distance from the house, I reached into my pocket and took out the gun. "See this, Valletta?" I said. "I am going to shoot you with this. You are never going to bark again, Valletta. You are going to be the most silent dog on earth. Do you understand, Valletta?"

He began barking.

"Quiet," I said.

He would not stop barking.

"Damn you!" I shouted. "Shut up!"

And suddenly he yanked the leash from my hands and darted away like the sneaky little sissydog he was, all white and furry against the orange and yellow and brown of the forest floor, racing like a ragged whisper through the carpet of leaves, trailing the red leash behind him like a narrow trickle of blood. I came thrashing after him. I was no more than six feet behind him when he ran into a clearing saturated with golden light. I followed him with the gun hand, aiming at him. Just as my finger tightened on the trigger, Carrie burst into the clearing from the opposite end.

"No!" she shouted, and dropped to her knees to scoop him protectively into her arms, the explosion shattering the incessant whisper of the leaves, the dog leaping into her embrace, blood flowering on her chest, oh dear God, no, I thought, oh dear sweet Jesus, no, and dropped the gun and ran to her and pressed her bleeding and still against me while the damn dumb dog barked and barked.

He has not barked since.

For him, it must seem as if she's gone someplace very far away, somewhere never even remotely perceived in his tiny Maltese mentality. In a sense this is true. In fact, I have repeated the story so often to so many people that I've come to believe it myself. I told her family and mine, I told all our friends, I even told the police, whom her brother was suspicious and vile enough to call, that I came home from work one day and she was simply gone. Not a hint that she was leaving. Not even a note. All she'd left behind was the dog. And she hadn't even bothered to feed him before her departure.

Valletta often wanders into the woods looking for her.

He circles the spot where two autumns ago her blood seeped into the earth. The area is bursting with fresh spring growth now, but he circles and sniffs the bright green shoots, searching, searching. He will never find her, of course. She is wrapped in a tarpaulin and buried deep in the woods some fifty miles north of where the three of us once lived together, Carrie and I and the dog.

There are only the two of us now.

He is all I have left to remind me of her.

He never barks and I never speak to him.

He eats when I feed him, but then he walks away from his bowl without once looking at me and falls to the floor just inside the entrance door, waiting for her return.

I can't honestly say I like him any better now that he's stopped barking. But sometimes . . .

Sometimes when he cocks his head in bewilderment to observe a floating butterfly, he looks so cute I could eat him alive.

DENNIS LEHANE

Dennis Lehane's breakout novel, *Mystic River*, brought the author a wide reading audience when it was published in 2001. Needless to say, when the 2003 film of the book was made, it only brought Lehane more acclaim. The fact that the movie is directed by Clint Eastwood, and features Sean Penn and Tim Robbins in Academy Award–winning performances, doesn't hurt matters. The book and the film called attention to Lehane as a writer whose forte is dark fiction firmly anchored in character. Characterization, setting, and plot in his books are all built on Lehane's life experience in working-class neighborhoods.

The author knows well the world of which he writes. The son of a Sears & Roebuck truck driver and a mother who processed foods for local schools, Lehane was raised in Dorchester, Massachusetts, when that neighborhood was a tightly knit, Irish Catholic, blue-collar enclave within the city of Boston. He was educated in public schools and attended two colleges before he settled down at Eckerd College in Florida. Before returning to Boston, he also worked on a master's degree at Florida International University in Miami. Back in Boston, he worked as a valet and then as a chauffeur for the Ritz hotel, occasionally working at his writing while sitting behind the wheel of a limousine, while waiting to drive customers to their destinations.

In 1994 he published his first novel, *A Drink Before the War*. The hard-edged, fast-action book introduces a pair of private eyes, Patrick Kenzie and Angela Gennaro, who appear in four more books following the first. The duo's quick repartee and courage in the face of violence makes them memorable—and they face violence often. In the Kenzie-Gennaro series, Lehane's skills at describing landscape and local venues are very evident. His writing takes readers from a treacherous rock quarry to local bars and—drawing on all the senses for his descriptions—makes those settings memorable. Lehane builds on these talents in *Mystic River* and in his 2003 novel, *Shutter Island*.

Set in South Carolina, Lehane's short story "Running Out of Dog" proves he can write about local characters who do not inhabit the author's home turf. Colorful dialogue adds to the appeal of this one. Lehane said he wrote the story to explain a strange phenomenon. "I went to college in Florida," he said, "and used to drive back and forth from Boston during breaks. For a reason no one has ever been able to explain adequately to me, I often saw dead dogs along the blue highways of South Carolina. I once did the drive with a friend and we counted ten dogs in a hundred and eighty miles. One every eighteen miles essentially. So I just started wondering about the South Carolina dog problem and that's when I came up with the story."

Running Out of Dog

THIS *thing with Blue and the dogs and Elgin Bern happened a while back, a few years after some of our boys—like Elgin Bern and Cal Sears—came back from Vietnam, and a lot of others—like Eddie Vorey and Carl Joe Carol, the Stewart cousins—didn't. We don't know how it worked in other towns, but that war put something secret in our boys who returned. Something quiet and untouchable. You sensed they knew things they'd never say, did things on the sly you'd never discover. Great card players, those boys, able to bluff with the best, let no joy show in their face no matter what they were holding.*

A small town is a hard place to keep a secret, and a small Southern town with all that heat and all those open windows is an even harder place than most. But those boys who came back from overseas, they seemed to have mastered the trick of privacy. And the way it's always been in this town, you get a sizable crop of young, hard men coming up at the same time, they sort of set the tone.

So, not long after the war, we were a quieter town, a less trusting one (or so some of us seemed to think), and that's right when tobacco money and textile money reached a sort of critical mass and created construction money and pretty soon there was talk that our small town should maybe get a little bigger, maybe build something that would bring in more tourist dollars than we'd been getting from fireworks and pecans.

That's when some folks came up with this Eden Falls idea—a big carnival-type park with roller coasters and water slides and such. Why should all those Yankees spend all their money in Florida? South Carolina had sun too. Had golf courses and grapefruit and no end of KOA campgrounds.

So now a little town called Eden was going to have Eden Falls. We were going to be on the map, people said. We were going to be in all the brochures. We were small now, people said, but just you wait. Just you wait.

And that's how things stood back then, the year Perkin and Jewel Lut's marriage hit a few bumps and Elgin Bern took up with Shelley Briggs and no one seemed able to hold on to their dogs.

The problem with dogs in Eden, South Carolina, was that the owners who bred them bred a lot of them. Or they allowed them to run free where they met up with other dogs of opposite gender and achieved the same result. This wouldn't have been so bad if Eden weren't so close to I-95, and if the dogs weren't in the habit of bolting into traffic and fucking up the bumpers of potential tourists.

The mayor, Big Bobby Vargas, went to a mayoral conference up in Beaufort, where the governor made a surprise appearance to tell everyone how pissed off he was about this dog thing. Lot of money being poured into Eden these days, the governor said, lot of steps being taken to change her image, and he for one would be goddamned if a bunch of misbehaving canines was going to mess all that up.

"Boys," he'd said, looking Big Bobby Vargas dead in the eye, "they're starting to call this state the Devil's Kennel 'cause of all them pooch corpses along the interstate. And I don't know about you all, but I don't think that's a real pretty name."

Big Bobby told Elgin and Blue he'd never heard anyone call it the Devil's Kennel in his life. Heard a lot worse, sure, but never that. Big Bobby said the governor was full of shit. But, being the governor and all, he was sort of entitled.

The dogs in Eden had been a problem going back to the twenties and a part-time breeder named J. Mallon Ellenburg who, if his arms weren't up to their elbows in the guts of the tractors and combines he repaired for a living, was usually lashing out at something—his family when they weren't quick enough, his dogs when the family was. J. Mallon Ellenburg's dogs were mixed breeds and mongrels and they ran in packs, as did their offspring, and several generations later, those packs still moved through the Eden night like wolves, their bodies stripped to muscle and gristle, tense and angry, growling in the dark at J. Mallon Ellenburg's ghost.

Big Bobby went to the trouble of measuring exactly how much of 95 crossed through Eden, and he came up with 2.8 miles. Not much really, but still an average of .74 dog a day or 4.9 dogs a week. Big Bobby wanted the rest of the state funds the governor was going to be doling out at year's end, and if that meant getting rid of five dogs a week, give or take, then that's what was going to get done.

"On the QT," he said to Elgin and Blue, "on the QT, what we going to do, boys, is set up in some trees and shoot every canine who gets within barking distance of that interstate."

Elgin didn't much like this "we" stuff. First place, Big Bobby'd said "we" that time in Double O's four years ago. This was before he'd become mayor, when he was nothing more than a county tax assessor who shot pool at Double O's every other night, same as Elgin and Blue. But one night, after Harlan and Chub Uke had roughed him up over a matter of some pocket change, and knowing that neither Elgin nor Blue was too fond of the Uke family either, Big Bobby'd said, "We going to settle those boys' asses tonight," and started running his mouth the minute the brothers entered the bar.

Time the smoke cleared, Blue had a broken hand, Harlan and Chub were curled up on the floor, and Elgin's lip was busted. Big Bobby, meanwhile, was hiding under the pool table, and Cal Sears was asking who was going to pay for the pool stick Elgin had snapped across the back of Chub's head.

So Elgin heard Mayor Big Bobby saying "we" and remembered the ten dollars it had cost him for that pool stick, and he said, "No, sir, you can count me out this particular enterprise."

Big Bobby looked disappointed. Elgin was a veteran of a foreign war, former Marine, a marksman. "Shit," Big Bobby said, "what good are you, you don't use the skills Uncle Sam spent good money teaching you?"

Elgin shrugged. "Damn, Bobby. I guess not much."

But Blue kept his hand in, as both Big Bobby and Elgin knew he would. All the job required was a guy didn't mind sitting in a tree who liked to shoot things. Hell, Blue was home.

Elgin didn't have the time to be sitting up in a tree anyway. The past few months, he'd been working like crazy after they'd broke ground at Eden Falls—mixing cement, digging postholes, draining swamp water to shore up the foundation—with the real work still to come. There'd be several more months of drilling and bilging, spreading cement like cake icing, and erecting scaffolding to erect walls to erect facades. There'd be the hump-and-grind of rolling along in the dump trucks and drill trucks, the forklifts and cranes and industrial diggers, until the constant heave and jerk of them drove up his spine or into his kidneys like a corkscrew.

Time to sit up in a tree shooting dogs? Shit. Elgin didn't have time to take a piss some days.

And then on top of all the work, he'd been seeing Drew Briggs's ex-wife, Shelley, lately. Shelley was the receptionist at Perkin Lut's Auto Emporium, and one day Elgin had brought his Impala in for a tire rotation and they'd got to talking. She'd been divorced from Drew over a year, and they waited a couple of months to show respect, but after a while they began showing up at Double O's and down at the IHOP together.

Once they drove clear to Myrtle Beach together for the weekend. People asked them what it was like, and they said, "Just like the postcards." Since the postcards never mentioned the price of a room at the Hilton, Elgin and Shelley didn't mention that all they'd done was drive up and down the beach twice before settling in a motel a bit west in Conway. Nice, though; had a color TV and one of those switches turned the bathroom into a sauna if you let the shower run. They'd started making love in the sauna, finished up on the bed with the steam coiling out from the bathroom and brushing their heels. Afterward, he pushed her hair back off her forehead and looked in her eyes and told her he could get used to this.

She said, "But wouldn't it cost a lot to install a sauna in your trailer?" then waited a full thirty seconds before she smiled.

Elgin liked that about her, the way she let him know he was still just a man after all, always would take himself too seriously, part of his nature. Letting him know she might be around to keep him apprised of that fact every time he did. Keep him from pushing a bullet into the breech of a thirty-aught-six, slamming the bolt home, firing into the flank of some wild dog.

Sometimes, when they'd shut down the site early for the day—if it had rained real heavy and the soil loosened near a foundation, or if supplies were running late—he'd drop by Lut's to see her. She'd smile as if he'd brought her flowers, say, "Caught boozing on the job again?" or some other smartass thing, but it made him feel good, as if something in his chest suddenly realized it was free to breathe.

Before Shelley, Elgin had spent a long time without a woman he could publicly acknowledge as his. He'd gone with Mae Shiller from fifteen to nineteen, but she'd gotten lonely while he was overseas, and he'd returned to find her gone from Eden, married to a boy up in South of the Border, the two of them working a corn-dog concession stand, making a tidy profit, folks said. Elgin dated some, but it took him a while to get over Mae, to get over the loss of something he'd always expected to have, the sound of her laugh and an image of her stepping naked from Cooper's Lake, her pale flesh beaded with water, having been the things that got Elgin through the jungle, through the heat, through the ticking of his own death he'd heard in his ears every night he'd been over there.

About a year after he'd come home, Jewel Lut had come to visit her mother, who still lived in the trailer park where Jewel had grown up with Elgin and Blue, where Elgin still lived. On her way out, she'd dropped by Elgin's and they'd sat out front of his trailer in some folding chairs, had a few drinks, talked about old times. He told her a bit about Vietnam, and she told him a bit about marriage. How it wasn't what you expected, how Perkin Lut might know a lot of things but he didn't know a damn sight about having fun.

There was something about Jewel Lut that sank into men's flesh the way heat did. It wasn't just that she was pretty, had a beautiful body, moved in a loose, languid way that made you picture her naked no matter what she was wearing. No, there was more to it. Jewel, never the brightest girl in town and not even the most charming, had something in her eyes that none of the women Elgin had ever met had; it was a capacity for living, for taking moments—no matter how small or inconsequential—and squeezing every last thing you could out of them. Jewel gobbled up life, dove into it like it was a cool pond cut in the shade of a mountain on the hottest day of the year.

That look in her eyes—the one that never left—said, Let's have fun, goddammit. Let's eat. Now.

She and Elgin hadn't been stupid enough to do anything that night, not even after Elgin caught that look in her eyes, saw it was directed at him, saw she wanted to eat.

Elgin knew how small Eden was, how its people loved to insinuate and pry and talk. So he and Jewel worked it out, a once-a-week thing mostly that happened down in Carlyle, at a small cabin had been in Elgin's family since before the War Between the States. There, Elgin and Jewel were free to partake of each other, squeeze and bite and swallow and inhale each other, to make love in the lake, on the porch, in the tiny kitchen.

They hardly ever talked, and when they did it was about nothing at all, really—the decline in quality of the meat at Billy's Butcher Shop, rumors that parking meters were going to be installed in front of the courthouse, if McGarrett and the rest of Five-O would ever put the cuffs on Wo Fat.

There was an unspoken understanding that he was free to date any woman he chose and that she'd never leave Perkin Lut. And that was just fine. This wasn't about love; it was about appetite.

Sometimes, Elgin would see her in town or hear Blue speak about her in that puppy-dog-love way he'd been speaking about her since high school, and he'd find himself surprised by the realization that he slept with this woman. That no one knew. That it could go on forever, if both of them remained careful, vigilant against the wrong look, the wrong tone in their voices when they spoke in public.

He couldn't entirely put his finger on what need she satisfied, only that he needed her in that lakefront cabin once a week, that it had something to do with walking out of the jungle alive, with the ticking of his own death he'd heard for a full year. Jewel was somehow reward for that, a fringe benefit. To be naked and spent with her lying atop him and seeing that look in her eyes that said she was ready to go again, ready to gobble him up like oxygen. He'd earned that by shooting at shapes in the night, pressed against those damp foxhole walls that never stayed shored up for long, only to come home to a woman who couldn't wait, who'd discarded him as easily as she would a once-favored doll she'd grown beyond, looked back upon with a wistful mix of nostalgia and disdain.

He'd always told himself that when he found the right woman, his passion for Jewel, his need for those nights at the lake, would disappear. And, truth was, since he'd been with Shelley Briggs, he and Jewel had cooled it. Shelley wasn't Perkin, he told Jewel; she'd figure it out soon enough if he left town once a week, came back with bite marks on his abdomen.

Jewel said, "Fine. We'll get back to it whenever you're ready."

Knowing there'd be a next time, even if Elgin wouldn't admit it to himself.

So Elgin, who'd been so lonely in the year after his discharge, now had two women. Sometimes, he didn't know what to think of that. When you were alone, the happiness of others boiled your insides. Beauty seemed ugly. Laughter seemed evil. The casual grazing of one lover's hand into another was enough to make you want to cut them off at the wrist. *I will never be loved*, you said. *I will never know joy.*

He wondered sometimes how Blue made it through. Blue, who'd never had a girlfriend he hadn't rented by the half hour. Who was too ugly and small and just plain weird to evoke anything in women but fear or pity. Blue, who'd been carrying a torch for Jewel Lut since long before she married Perkin and kept carrying it with a quiet fever Elgin could only occasionally identify with. Blue, he knew, saw Jewel Lut as a queen, as the only woman who existed for him in Eden, South Carolina. All because she'd been nice to him, pals with him and Elgin, back about a thousand years ago, before sex, before breasts, before Elgin or Blue had even the smallest clue what that thing between their legs was for, before Perkin Lut had come along with his daddy's money and his nice smile and his bullshit stories about how many men he'd have killed in the war if only the draft board had seen fit to let him go.

Blue figured if he was nice enough, kind enough, waited long enough—
then one day Jewel would see his decency, need to cling to it.

Elgin never bothered telling Blue that some women didn't want decency.
Some women didn't want a nice guy. Some women, and some men too, wanted
to get into a bed, turn out the lights, and feast on each other like animals until
it hurt to move.

Blue would never guess that Jewel was that kind of woman, because she was
always so sweet to him, treated him like a child really, and with every friendly
hello she gave him, every pat on the shoulder, every "What you been up to, old
bud?" Blue pushed her further and further up the pedestal he'd built in his mind.

"I seen him at the Emporium one time," Shelley told Elgin. "He just come
in for no reason anyone understood and sat reading magazines until Jewel
came in to see Perkin about something. And Blue, he just stared at her. Just
stared at her talking to Perkin in the showroom. When she finally looked back,
he stood up and left."

Elgin hated hearing about, talking about, or thinking about Jewel when he
was with Shelley. It made him feel unclean and unworthy.

"Crazy love," he said to end the subject.

"Crazy something, babe."

Nights sometimes, Elgin would sit with Shelley in front of his trailer, listen
to the cicadas hum through the scrawny pine, smell the night and the rock salt
mixed with gravel; the piña colada shampoo Shelley used made him think of
Hawaii though he'd never been, and he'd think how their love wasn't crazy
love, wasn't burning so fast and furious it'd burn itself out they weren't careful.
And that was fine with him. If he could just get his head around this Jewel Lut
thing, stop seeing her naked and waiting and looking back over her shoulder
at him in the cabin, then he could make something with Shelley. She was
worth it. She might not be able to fuck like Jewel, and, truth be told, he did-
n't laugh as much with her, but Shelley was what you aspired to. A good
woman, who'd be a good mother, who'd stick by you when times got tough.
Sometimes he'd take her hand in his and hold it for no other reason but the
doing of it. She caught him one night, some look in his eyes, maybe the way
he tilted his head to look at her small white hand in his big brown one.

She said, "Damn, Elgin, if you ain't simple sometimes." Then she came out
of her chair in a rush and straddled him, kissed him as if she were trying to
take a piece of him back with her. She said, "Baby, we ain't getting any younger.
You know?"

And he knew, somehow, at that moment why some men build families and
others shoot dogs. He just wasn't sure where he fit in the equation.

He said, "We ain't, are we?"

Blue had been Elgin's best buddy since either of them could remember, but
Elgin had been wondering about it lately. Blue'd always been a little different,

something Elgin liked, sure, but there was more to it now. Blue was the kind of guy you never knew if he was quiet because he didn't have anything to say or, because what he had to say was so horrible, he knew enough not to send it out into the atmosphere.

When they'd been kids, growing up in the trailer park, Blue used to be out at all hours because his mother was either entertaining a man or had gone out and forgotten to leave him the key. Back then, Blue had this thing for cockroaches. He'd collect them in a jar, then drop bricks on them to test their resiliency. He told Elgin once, "That's what they are—resilient. Every generation, we have to come up with new ways to kill 'em because they get immune to the poisons we had before." After a while, Blue took to dousing them in gasoline, lighting them up, seeing how resilient they were then.

Elgin's folks told him to stay away from the strange, dirty kid with the white-trash mother, but Elgin felt sorry for Blue. He was half Elgin's size even though they were the same age; you could place your thumb and forefinger around Blue's biceps and meet them on the other side. Elgin hated how Blue seemed to have only two pairs of clothes, both usually dirty, and how sometimes they'd pass his trailer together and hear the animal sounds coming from inside, the grunts and moans, the slapping of flesh. Half the time you couldn't tell if Blue's old lady was in there fucking or fighting. And always the sound of country music mingled in with all that animal noise, Blue's mother and her man of the moment listening to it on the transistor radio she'd given Blue one Christmas.

"My fucking radio," Blue said once and shook his small head, the only time Elgin ever saw him react to what went on in that trailer.

Blue was a reader—knew more about science and ecology, about anatomy and blue whales and conversion tables than anyone Elgin knew. Most everyone figured the kid for a mute—hell, he'd been held back twice in fourth grade— but with Elgin he'd sometimes chat up a storm while they puffed smokes together down at the drainage ditch behind the park. He'd talk about whales, how they bore only one child, who they were fiercely protective of, but how if another child was orphaned, a mother whale would take it as her own, protect it as fiercely as she did the one she gave birth to. He told Elgin how sharks never slept, how electrical currents worked, what a depth charge was. Elgin, never much of a talker, just sat and listened, ate it up, and waited for more.

The older they got, the more Elgin became Blue's protector, till finally, the year Blue's face exploded with acne, Elgin got in about two fights a day until there was no one left to fight. Everyone knew—they were brothers. And if Elgin didn't get you from the front, Blue was sure to take care of you from behind, like that time a can of acid fell on Roy Hubrist's arm in shop, or the time someone hit Carnell Lewis from behind with a brick, then cut his Achilles tendon with a razor while he lay out cold. Everyone knew it was Blue, even if no one actually saw him do it.

Elgin figured with Roy and Carnell, they'd had it coming. No great loss. It was since Elgin'd come back from Vietnam, though, that he'd noticed some things and kept them to himself, wondered what he was going to do the day he'd know he had to do something.

There was the owl someone had set afire and hung upside down from a telephone wire, the cats who turned up missing in the blocks that surrounded Blue's shack off Route 11. There were the small pink panties Elgin had seen sticking out from under Blue's bed one morning when he'd come to get him for some cleanup work at a site. He'd checked the missing-persons reports for days, but it hadn't come to anything, so he'd just decided Blue had picked them up himself, fed a fantasy or two. He didn't forget, though, couldn't shake the way those panties had curled upward out of the brown dust under Blue's bed, seemed to be pleading for something.

He'd never bothered asking Blue about any of this. That never worked. Blue just shut down at times like that, stared off somewhere as if something you couldn't hear was drowning out your words, something you couldn't see was taking up his line of vision. Blue, floating away on you, until you stopped cluttering up his mind with useless talk.

One Saturday, Elgin went into town with Shelley so she could get her hair done at Martha's Unisex on Main. In Martha's, as Dottie Leeds gave Shelley a shampoo and rinse, Elgin felt like he'd stumbled into a chapel of womanhood. There was Jim Hayder's teenage daughter, Sonny, getting one of those feathered cuts was growing popular these days and several older women who still wore beehives, getting them reset or plastered or whatever they did to keep them up like that. There was Joylene Covens and Lila Sims having their nails done while their husbands golfed and the black maids watched their kids, and Martha and Dottie and Esther and Gertrude and Hayley dancing and flitting, laughing and chattering among the chairs, calling everyone "Honey," and all of them—the young, the old, the rich, and Shelley—kicking back like they did this every day, knew each other more intimately than they did their husbands or children or boyfriends.

When Dottie Leeds looked up from Shelley's head and said, "Elgin, honey, can we get you a sports page or something?" the whole place burst out laughing, Shelley included. Elgin smiled though he didn't feel like it and gave them all a sheepish wave that got a bigger laugh, and he told Shelley he'd be back in a bit and left.

He headed up Main toward the town square, wondering what it was those women seemed to know so effortlessly that completely escaped him, and saw Perkin Lut walking in a circle outside Dexter Isley's Five & Dime. It was one of those days when the wet, white heat was so overpowering that unless you were in Martha's, the one place in town with central air-conditioning, most people stayed inside with their shades down and tried not to move much.

And there was Perkin Lut walking the soles of his shoes into the ground, turning in circles like a little kid trying to make himself dizzy.

Perkin and Elgin had known each other since kindergarten, but Elgin could never remember liking the man much. Perkin's old man, Mance Lut, had pretty much built Eden, and he'd spent a lot of money keeping Perkin out of the war, hid his son up in Chapel Hill, North Carolina, for so many semesters even Perkin couldn't remember what he'd majored in. A lot of men who'd gone overseas and come back hated Perkin for that, as did the families of most of the men who hadn't come back, but that wasn't Elgin's problem with Perkin. Hell, if Elgin'd had the money, he'd have stayed out of that shitty war too.

What Elgin couldn't abide was that there was something in Perkin that protected him from consequence. Something that made him look down on people who paid for their sins, who fell without a safety net to catch them.

It had happened more than once that Elgin had found himself thrusting in and out of Perkin's wife and thinking, Take that, Perkin. Take that.

But this afternoon, Perkin didn't have his salesman's smile or aloof glance. When Elgin stopped by him and said, "Hey, Perkin, how you?" Perkin looked up at him with eyes so wild they seemed about to jump out of their sockets.

"I'm not good, Elgin. Not good."

"What's the matter?"

Perkin nodded to himself several times, looked over Elgin's shoulder. "I'm fixing to do something about that."

"About what?"

"About that." Perkin's jaw gestured over Elgin's shoulder.

Elgin turned around, looked across Main and through the windows of Miller's Laundromat, saw Jewel Lut pulling her clothes from the dryer, saw Blue standing beside her, taking a pair of jeans from the pile and starting to fold. If either of them had looked up and over, they'd have seen Elgin and Perkin Lut easily enough, but Elgin knew they wouldn't. There was an air to the two of them that seemed to block out the rest of the world in that bright Laundromat as easily as it would in a dark bedroom. Blue's lips moved and Jewel laughed, flipped a T-shirt on his head.

"I'm fixing to do something right now," Perkin said.

Elgin looked at him, could see that was a lie, something Perkin was repeating to himself in hopes it would come true. Perkin was successful in business, and for more reasons than just his daddy's money, but he wasn't the kind of man who did things; he was the kind of man who had things done.

Elgin looked across the street again. Blue still had the T-shirt sitting atop his head. He said something else and Jewel covered her mouth with her hand when she laughed.

"Don't you have a washer and dryer at your house, Perkin?"

Perkin rocked back on his heels. "Washer broke. Jewel decides to come in town." He looked at Elgin. "We ain't getting along so well these days. She keeps reading those magazines, Elgin. You know the ones? Talking about liberation, leaving your bra at home, shit like that." He pointed across the street. "Your friend's a problem."

Your friend.

Elgin looked at Perkin, felt a sudden anger he couldn't completely understand, and with it a desire to say, That's my friend and he's talking to my fuck-buddy. Get it, Perkin?

Instead, he just shook his head and left Perkin there, walked across the street to the Laundromat.

Blue took the T-shirt off his head when he saw Elgin enter. A smile, half frozen on his pitted face, died as he blinked into the sunlight blaring through the windows.

Jewel said, "Hey, we got another helper!" She tossed a pair of men's briefs over Blue's head, hit Elgin in the chest with them.

"Hey, Jewel."

"Hey, Elgin. Long time." Her eyes dropped from his, settled on a towel.

Didn't seem like it at the moment to Elgin. Seemed almost as if he'd been out at the lake with her as recently as last night. He could taste her in his mouth, smell her skin damp with a light sweat.

And standing there with Blue, it also seemed like they were all three back in that trailer park, and Jewel hadn't aged a bit. Still wore her red hair long and messy, still dressed in clothes seemed to have been picked up, wrinkled, off her closet floor and nothing fancy about them in the first place, but draped over her body, they were sexier than clothes other rich women bought in New York once a year.

This afternoon, she wore a crinkly, paisley dress that might have been on the pink side once but had faded to a pasty newspaper color after years of washing. Nothing special about it, not too high up her thigh or down her chest, and loose—but something about her body made it appear like she might just ripen right out of it any second.

Elgin handed the briefs to Blue as he joined them at the folding table. For a while, none of them said anything. They picked clothes from the large pile and folded, and the only sound was Jewel whistling.

Then Jewel laughed.

"What?" Blue said.

"Aw, nothing." She shook her head. "Seems like we're just one happy family here, though, don't it?"

Blue looked stunned. He looked at Elgin. He looked at Jewel. He looked at the pair of small, light-blue socks he held in his hands, the monogram JL stitched in the cotton. He looked at Jewel again.

"Yeah," he said eventually, and Elgin heard a tremor in his voice he'd never heard before. "Yeah, it does."

Elgin looked up at one of the upper dryer doors. It had been swung out at eye level when the dryer had been emptied. The center of the door was a circle of glass, and Elgin could see Main Street reflected in it, the white posts that supported the wood awning over the Five & Dime, Perkin Lut walking in circles, his head down, heat shimmering in waves up and down Main.

The dog was green.

Blue had used some of the money Big Bobby'd paid him over the past few weeks to upgrade his target scope. The new scope was huge, twice the width of the rifle barrel, and because the days were getting shorter, it was outfitted with a light-amplification device. Elgin had used similar scopes in the jungle, and he'd never liked them, even when they'd saved his life and those of his platoon, picked up Charlie coming through the dense flora like icy gray ghosts. Night scopes— or LADs as they'd called them over there—were just plain unnatural, and Elgin always felt like he was looking through a telescope from the bottom of a lake. He had no idea where Blue would have gotten one, but hunters in Eden had been showing up with all sorts of weird Marine or army surplus shit these last few years; Elgin had even heard of a hunting party using grenades to scare up fish— blowing'em up into the boat already half cooked, all you had to do was scale 'em.

The dog was green, the highway was beige, the top of the tree line was yellow, and the trunks were the color of army fatigues.

Blue said, "What you think?"

They were up in the tree house Blue'd built. Nice wood, two lawn chairs, a tarp hanging from the branch overhead, a cooler filled with Coors. Blue'd built a railing across the front, perfect for resting your elbows when you took aim. Along the tree trunk, he'd mounted a huge klieg light plugged to a portable generator, because while it was illegal to "shine" deer, nobody'd ever said anything about shining wild dogs. Blue was definitely home.

Elgin shrugged. Just like in the jungle, he wasn't sure he was meant to see the world this way— faded to the shades and textures of old photographs. The dog, too, seemed to sense that it had stepped out of time somehow, into this seaweed circle punched through the landscape. It sniffed the air with a misshapen snout, but the rest of its body was tensed into one tight muscle, leaning forward as if it smelled prey.

Blue said, "You wanna do it?"

The stock felt hard against Elgin's shoulder. The trigger, curled under his index finger, was cold and thick, something about it that itched his finger and the back of his head simultaneously, a voice back there with the itch in his head saying, "Fire."

What you could never talk about down at the bar to people who hadn't been there, to people who wanted to know, was what it had been like firing on human beings, on those icy gray ghosts in the dark jungle. Elgin had been in fourteen battles over the course of his twelve-month tour, and he couldn't say with certainty that he'd ever killed anyone. He'd shot some of those shapes, seen them go down, but never the blood, never their eyes when the bullets hit. It had all been a cluster-fuck of swift and sudden noise and color, an explosion of white lights and tracers, green bush, red fire, screams in the night. And afterward, if it was clear, you walked into the jungle and saw the corpses, wondered if you'd hit this body or that one or any at all.

And the only thing you were sure of was that you were too fucking hot and still—this was the terrible thing, but oddly exhilarating too—deeply afraid.

Elgin lowered Blue's rifle, stared across the interstate, now the color of seashell, at the dark mint tree line. The dog was barely noticeable, a soft dark shape amid other soft dark shapes.

He said, "No, Blue, thanks," and handed him the rifle.

Blue said, "Suit yourself, buddy." He reached behind them and pulled the beaded string on the klieg light. As the white light erupted across the highway and the dog froze, blinking in the brightness, Elgin found himself wondering what the fucking point of a LAD scope was when you were just going to shine the animal anyway.

Blue swung the rifle around, leaned into the railing, and put a round in the center of the animal, right by its rib cage. The dog jerked inward, as if someone had whacked it with a bat, and as it teetered on wobbly legs, Blue pulled back on the bolt, drove it home again, and shot the dog in the head. The dog flipped over on its side, most of its skull gone, back leg kicking at the road like it was trying to ride a bicycle,

"You think Jewel Lut might, I dunno, like me?" Blue said.

Elgin cleared his throat. "Sure. She's always liked you."

"But I mean . . ." Blue shrugged, seemed embarrassed suddenly, "How about this: you think a girl like that could take to Australia?"

"Australia?"

Blue smiled at Elgin. "Australia."

"Australia?" he said again.

Blue reached back and shut off the light. "Australia. They got some wild dingoes there, buddy. Could make some real money. Jewel told me the other day how they got real nice beaches. But dingoes too. Big Bobby said people're starting to bitch about what's happening here, asking where Rover is and such, and anyway, ain't too many dogs left dumb enough to come this way anymore. Australia," he said, "they never run out of dog. Sooner or later, here, I'm gonna run out of dog."

Elgin nodded. Sooner or later, Blue would run out of dog. He wondered if Big Bobby'd thought that one through, if he had a contingency plan, if he had access to the National Guard.

"The boy's just, what you call it, zealous," Big Bobby told Elgin.

They were sitting in Phil's Barbershop on Main. Phil had gone to lunch, and Big Bobby'd drawn the shades so people'd think he was making some important decision of state.

Elgin said, "He ain't zealous, Big Bobby. He's losing it. Thinks he's in love with Jewel Lut."

"He's always thought that."

"Yeah, but now maybe he's thinking she might like him a bit too."

Big Bobby said, "How come you never call me Mayor?"

Elgin sighed.

"All right, all right. Look," Big Bobby said, picking up one of the hair-tonic botttes on Phil's counter and sniffing it, "so Blue likes his job a little bit."

Elgin said, "There's more to it and you know it."

Playing with combs now. "I do?"

"Bobby, he's got a taste for shooting things now."

"Wait." He held up a pair of fat, stubby hands. "Blue always liked to shoot things. Everyone knows that. Shit, if he wasn't so short and didn't have six or seven million little health problems, he'd a been the first guy in this town to go to The 'Nam. 'Stead, he had to sit back here while you boys had all the fun."

Calling it The 'Nam. Like Big Bobby had any idea. Calling it fun. Shit.

"Dingoes," Elgin said.

"Dingoes?"

"Dingoes. He's saying he's going to Australia to shoot dingoes."

"Do him a world of good too." Big Bobby sat back down in the barber's chair beside Elgin. "He can see the sights, that sort of thing."

"Bobby, he ain't going to Australia and you know it. Hell, Blue ain't never stepped over the county line in his life."

Big Bobby polished his belt buckle with the cuff of his sleeve. "Well, what you want me to do about it?"

"I don't know. I'm just telling you. Next time you see him, Bobby, you look in his fucking eyes."

"Yeah. What'll I see?"

Elgin turned his head, looked at him. "Nothing."

Bobby said, "He's your buddy."

Elgin thought of the small panties curling out of the dust under Blue's bed. "Yeah, but he's your problem."

Big Bobby put his hands behind his head, stretched in the chair. "Well, people getting suspicious about all the dogs disappearing, so I'm going to have to shut this operation down immediately anyway."

He wasn't getting it. "Bobby, you shut this operation down, someone's gonna get a world's worth of that nothing in Blue's eyes."

Big Bobby shrugged, a man who'd made a career out of knowing what was beyond him.

The first time Perkin Lut struck Jewel in public was at Chuck's Diner.

Elgin and Shelley were sitting just three booths away when they heard a racket of falling glasses and plates, and by the time they came out of their booth, Jewel was lying on the tile floor with shattered glass and chunks of bone china by her elbows and Perkin standing over her, his arms shaking, a look in his eyes that said he'd surprised himself as much as anyone else.

Elgin looked at Jewel, on her knees, the hem of her dress getting stained by the spilled food, and he looked away before she caught his eye, because if that happened he just might do something stupid, fuck Perkin up a couple-three ways.

"Aw, Perkin," Chuck Blade said, coming from behind the counter to help Jewel up, wiping gravy off his hands against his apron.

"We don't respect that kind of behavior 'round here, Mr. Lut," Clara Blade said. "Won't have it neither."

Chuck Blade helped Jewel to her feet, his eyes cast down at his broken plates, the half a steak lying in a soup of beans by his shoe. Jewel had a welt growing on her right cheek, turning a bright red as she placed her hand on the table for support.

"I didn't mean it," Perkin said.

Clara Blade snorted and pulled the pen from behind her ear, began itemizing the damage on a cocktail napkin.

"I didn't." Perkin noticed Elgin and Shelley. He locked eyes with Elgin, held out his hands. "I swear."

Elgin turned away and that's when he saw Blue coming through the door. He had no idea where he'd come from, though it ran through his head that Blue could have just been standing outside looking in, could have been standing there for an hour.

Like a lot of small guys, Blue had speed, and he never seemed to walk in a straight line. He moved as if he were constantly sidestepping tackles or land mines—with sudden, unpredictable pivots that left you watching the space where he'd been, instead of the place he'd ended up.

Blue didn't say anything, but Elgin could see the determination for homicide in his eyes and Perkin saw it too, backed up, and slipped on the mess on the floor and stumbled back, trying to regain his balance as Blue came past Shelley and tried to lunge past Elgin.

Elgin caught him at the waist, lifted him off the ground, and held on tight because he knew how slippery Blue could be in these situations. You'd think you had him and he'd just squirm away from you, hit somebody with a glass.

Elgin tucked his head down and headed for the door, Blue flopped over his shoulder like a bag of cement mix, Blue screaming, "You see me, Perkin? You see me? I'm a last face you see, Perkin! Real soon."

Elgin hit the open doorway, felt the night heat on his face as Blue screamed, "Jewel! You all right? Jewel?"

Blue didn't say much back at Elgin's trailer.

He tried to explain to Shelley how pure Jewel was, how hitting something that innocent was like spitting on the Bible.

Shelley didn't say anything, and after a while Blue shut up too.

Elgin just kept plying him with Beam, knowing Blue's lack of tolerance for it, and pretty soon Blue passed out on the couch, his pitted face still red with rage.

"He's never been exactly right in the head, has he?" Shelley said.

Elgin ran his hand down her bare arm, pulled her shoulder in tighter against his chest, heard Blue snoring from the front of the trailer. "No, ma'am."

She rose above him, her dark hair falling to his face, tickling the corners of his eyes. "But you've been his friend."

Elgin nodded.

She touched his cheek with her hand. "Why?"

Elgin thought about it a bit, started talking to her about the little, dirty kid and his cockroach flambés, of the animal sounds that came from his mother's trailer. The way Blue used to sit by the drainage ditch, all pulled into himself, his body tight. Elgin thought of all those roaches and cats and rabbits and dogs, and he told Shelley that he'd always thought Blue was dying, ever since he'd met him, leaking away in front of his eyes.

"Everyone dies," she said.

"Yeah." He rose up on his elbow, rested his free hand on her warm hip. "Yeah, but with most of us it's like we're growing toward something and then we die. But with Blue, it's like he ain't never grown toward nothing. He's just been dying real slowly since he was born."

She shook her head. "I'm not getting you."

He thought of the mildew that used to soak the walls in Blue's mother's trailer, of the mold and dust in Blue's shack off Route 11, of the rotting smell that had grown out of the drainage ditch when they were kids. The way Blue looked at it all—seemed to be at one with it—as if he felt a bond.

Shelley said, "Babe, what do you think about getting out of here?"

"Where?"

"I dunno. Florida. Georgia. Someplace else."

"I got a job. You too."

'You can always get construction jobs other places. Receptionist jobs too."

"We grew up here."

She nodded. "But maybe it's time to start our life somewhere else."

He said, "Let me think about it."

She tilted his chin so she was looking in his eyes. "You've *been* thinking about it."

He nodded. "Maybe I want to think about it some more."

In the morning, when they woke up, Blue was gone.

Shelley looked at the rumpled couch, over at Elgin. For a good minute they just stood there, looking from the couch to each other, the couch to each other.

An hour later, Shelley called from work, told Elgin that Perkin Lut was in his office as always, no signs of physical damage.

Elgin said, "If you see Blue . . ."

"Yeah?"

Elgin thought about it, "I dunno. Call the cops. Tell Perkin to bail out a back door. That sound right?"

"Sure."

Big Bobby came to the site later that morning, said, "I go over to Blue's place to tell him we got to end this dog thing and —"

"Did you tell him it was over?" Elgin asked.

"Let me finish. Let me explain."

"Did you tell him?"

"Let me finish." Bobby wiped his face with a handkerchief. "I was gonna tell him, but —"

"You didn't tell him."

"But Jewel Lut was there."

"What?"

Big Bobby put his hand on Elgin's elbow, led him away from the other workers. "I said Jewel was there. The two of them sitting at the kitchen table, having breakfast."

"In Blue's place?"

Big Bobby nodded. "Biggest dump I ever seen. Smells like something I-don't-know-what. But bad. And there's Jewel, pretty as can be in her summer dress and soft skin and makeup, eating Eggos and grits with Blue, big brown shiner under her eye. She smiles at me, says, 'Hey, Big Bobby,' and goes back to eating."

"And that was it?"

"How come no one ever calls me Mayor?"

"And that was it?" Elgin repeated.

"Yeah. Blue asks me to take a seat, I say I got business. He says him too."

"What's that mean?" Elgin heard his own voice, hard and sharp.

Big Bobby took a step back from it. "Hell do I know? Could mean he's going out to shoot more dog."

"So you never told him you were shutting down the operation."

Big Bobby's eyes were wide and confused. "You hear what I told you? He was in there with Jewel. Her all doll-pretty and him looking, well, ugly as usual. Whole situation was too weird. I got out."

"Blue said he had business too."

"He said he had business too," Bobby said, and walked away.

The next week, they showed up in town together a couple of times, buying some groceries, toiletries for Jewel, boxes of shells for Blue.

They never held hands or kissed or did anything romantic, but they were together, and people talked. Said, Well, of all things. And I never thought I'd see the day. How do you like that? I guess this is the day the cows actually come home.

Blue called and invited Shelley and Elgin to join them one Sunday afternoon for a late breakfast at the IHOP. Shelley begged off, said something about coming down with the flu, but Elgin went. He was curious to see where this was going, what Jewel was thinking, how she thought her hanging around Blue was going to come to anything but bad.

He could feel the eyes of the whole place on them as they ate.

"See where he hit me?" Jewel tilted her head, tucked her beautiful red hair back behind her ear. The mark on her cheekbone, in the shape of a small rain puddle, was faded yellow now, its edges roped by a sallow beige.

Elgin nodded.

"Still can't believe the son of a bitch hit me," she said, but there was no rage in her voice anymore, just a mild sense of drama, as if she'd pushed the words out of her mouth the way she believed she should say them. But the emotion she must have felt when Perkin's hand hit her face, when she fell to the floor in front of people she'd known all her life—that seemed to have faded with the mark on her cheekbone.

"Perkin Lut," she said with a snort, then laughed.

Elgin looked at Blue. He'd never seemed so . . . fluid in all the time Elgin had known him. The way he cut into his pancakes, swept them off his plate with a smooth dip of the fork tines; the swift dab of the napkin against his lips after every bite; the attentive swivel of his head whenever Jewel spoke, usually in tandem with the lifting of his coffee mug to his mouth.

This was not a Blue Elgin recognized. Except when he was handling weapons, Blue moved in jerks and spasms. Tremors rippled through his limbs and caused his fingers to drop things, his elbows and knees to move too fast, crack against solid objects. Blue's blood seemed to move too quickly through his veins, made his muscles obey his brain after a quarter-second delay and then too rapidly, as if to catch up on lost time.

But now he moved in concert, like an athlete or a jungle cat.

That's what you do to men, Jewel: you give them a confidence so total it finds their limbs.

"Perkin," Blue said, and rolled his eyes at Jewel and they both laughed.

She not as hard as he did, though.

Elgin could see the root of doubt in her eyes, could feel her loneliness in the way she fiddled with the menu, touched her cheekbone, spoke too loudly, as if she wasn't just telling Elgin and Blue how Perkin had mistreated her, but the whole IHOP as well, so people could get it straight that she wasn't the villain, and if after she returned to Perkin she had to leave him again, they'd know why.

Of course she was going back to Perkin.

Elgin could tell by the glances she gave Blue—unsure, slightly embarrassed, maybe a bit repulsed. What had begun as a nighttime ride into the unknown had turned cold and stale during the hard yellow lurch into morning.

Blue wiped his mouth, said, "Be right back," and walked to the bathroom with surer strides than Elgin had ever seen on the man.

Elgin looked at Jewel.

She gripped the handle of her coffee cup between the tips of her thumb and index finger and turned the cup in slow revolutions around the saucer, made a soft scraping noise that climbed up Elgin's spine like a termite trapped under the skin.

"You ain't sleeping with him, are you?" Elgin said quietly.

Jewel's head jerked up and she looked over her shoulder, then back at Elgin. "What? God, no. We're just . . . He's my pal. That's all. Like when we were kids."

"We ain't kids."

"I know. Don't you know I know?" She fingered the coffee cup again. "I miss you," she said softly. "I miss you. When you coming back?"

Elgin kept his voice low. "Me and Shelley, we're getting pretty serious."

She gave him a small smile that he instantly hated. It seemed to know him; it seemed like everything he was and everything he wasn't was caught in the curl of her lips. "You miss the lake, Elgin. Don't lie."

He shrugged.

"You ain't ever going to marry Shelley Briggs, have babies, be an upstanding citizen."

"Yeah? Why's that?"

"Because you got too many demons in you, boy. And they need me. They need the lake. They need to cry out every now and then."

Elgin looked down at his own coffee cup. "You going back to Perkin?"

She shook her head hard. "No way. Uh-uh. No way."

Elgin nodded, even though he knew she was lying. If Elgin's demons needed the lake, needed to be unbridled, Jewel's needed Perkin. They needed security. They needed to know the money'd never run out, that she'd never go two full days without a solid meal, like she had so many times as a child in the trailer park.

Perkin was what she saw when she looked down at her empty coffee cup, when she touched her cheek. Perkin was at their nice home with his feet up, watching a game, petting the dog, and she was in the IHOP in the middle of a Sunday when the food was at its oldest and coldest, with one guy who loved her and one who fucked her, wondering how she got there.

Blue came back to the table, moving with that new sure stride, a broad smile in the wide swing of his arms.

"How we doing?" Blue said. "Huh? How we doing?" And his lips burst into a grin so huge Elgin expected it to keep going right off the sides of his face.

Jewel left Blue's place two days later, walked into Perkin Lut's Auto Emporium and into Perkin's office, and by the time anyone went to check, they'd left through the back door, gone home for the day.

Elgin tried to get a hold of Blue for three days—called constantly, went by his shack and knocked on the door, even staked out the tree house along I-95 where he fired on the dogs.

He'd decided to break into Blue's place, was fixing to do just that, when he tried one last call from his trailer that third night and Blue answered with a strangled "Hello."

"It's me. How you doing?"

"Can't talk now."

"Come on, Blue. It's me. You okay?"

"All alone," Blue said.

"I know. I'll come by."

"You do, I'll leave."

"Blue."

"Leave me alone for a spell, Elgin. Okay?"

That night Elgin sat alone in his trailer, smoking cigarettes, staring at the walls.

Blue'd never had much of anything his whole life—not a job he enjoyed, not a woman he could consider his—and then between the dogs and Jewel Lut he'd probably thought he'd got it all at once. Hit pay dirt.

Elgin remembered the dirty little kid sitting down by the drainage ditch, hugging himself. Six, maybe seven years old, waiting to die.

You had to wonder sometimes why some people were even born. You had to wonder what kind of creature threw bodies into the world, expected them to get along when they'd been given no tools, no capacity to get any either.

In Vietnam, this fat boy, name of Woodson from South Dakota, had been the least popular guy in the platoon. He wasn't smart, he wasn't athletic, he wasn't funny, he wasn't even personable. He just was. Elgin had been running beside him one day through a sea of rice paddies, their boots making sucking sounds every step they took, and someone fired a hell of a round from the other side of the paddies, ripped Woodson's head in half so completely all Elgin saw running beside him for a few seconds was the lower half of Woodson's face. No hair, no forehead, no eyes. Just half the nose, a mouth, a chin.

Thing was, Woodson kept running, kept plunging his feet in and out of the water, making those sucking sounds, M-15 hugged to his chest, for a good eight or ten steps. Kid was dead, he's still running. Kid had no reason to hold on, but he don't know it, he keeps running.

What spark of memory, hope, or dream had kept him going?

You had to wonder.

In Elgin's dream that night, a platoon of ice-gray Vietcong rose in a straight line from the center of Cooper's Lake while Elgin was inside the cabin with Shelley and Jewel. He penetrated them both somehow, their separate torsos branching out from the same pair of hips, their four legs clamping at the small of his back, this Shelley-Jewel creature crying out for more, more, more.

And Elgin could see the VC platoon drifting in formation toward the shore, their guns pointed, their faces hidden behind thin wisps of green fog.

The Shelley-Jewel creature arched her backs on the bed below him, and Woodson and Blue stood in the corner of the room watching as their dogs padded across the floor, letting out low growls and drooling.

Shelley dissolved into Jewel as the VG platoon reached the porch steps and released their safeties all at once, the sound like the ratcheting of a thousand shotguns. Sweat exploded in Elgin's hair, poured down his body like warm rain, and the VC fired in concert, the bullets shearing the walls of the cabin, lifting the roof off into the night. Elgin looked above him at the naked night sky, the stars zipping by like tracers, the yellow moon full and mean, the shivering branches of birch trees. Jewel rose and straddled him, bit his lip, and dug her nails into his back, and the bullets danced through his hair, and then Jewel was gone, her writhing flesh having dissolved into his own.

Elgin sat naked on the bed, his arms stretched wide, waiting for the bullets to find his back, to shear his head from his body the way they'd sheared the roof from the cabin, and the yellow moon burned above him as the dogs howled and Blue and Woodson held each other in the corner of the room and wept like children as the bullets drilled holes in their faces.

Big Bobby came by the trailer late the next morning, a Sunday, and said, "Blue's a bit put out about losing his job."

"What?" Elgin sat on the edge of his bed, pulled on his socks. "You picked now—now, Bobby—to fire him?"

"It's in his eyes," Big Bobby said. "Like you said. You can see it."

Elgin had seen Big Bobby scared before, plenty of times, but now the man was trembling.

Elgin said, "Where is he?"

Blue's front door was open, hanging half down the steps from a busted hinge. Elgin said, "Blue."

"Kitchen."

He sat in his Jockeys at the table, cleaning his rifle, each shiny black piece spread in front of him on the table. Elgin's eyes watered a bit because there was a stench coming from the back of the house that he felt might strip his nostrils bare. He realized then that he'd never asked Big Bobby or Blue what they'd done with all those dead dogs.

Blue said, "Have a seat, bud. Beer in the fridge if you're thirsty."

Elgin wasn't looking in that fridge. "Lost your job, huh?"

Blue wiped the bolt with a shammy cloth. "Happens." He looked at Elgin. "Where you been lately?"

"I called you last night."

"I mean in general."

"Working."

"No, I mean at night."

"Blue, you been"—he almost said "playing house with Jewel Lut" but caught himself— "up in a fucking tree, how do you know where I been at night?"

"I don't," Blue said. "Why I'm asking."

Elgin said, "I've been at my trailer or down at Doubles, same as usual."

"With Shelley Briggs, right?"

Slowly, Elgin said, "Yeah."

"I'm just asking, buddy. I mean, when we all going to go out? You, me, your new girl."

The pits that covered Blue's face like a layer of bad meat had faded some from all those nights in the tree.

Elgin said, "Anytime you want."

Blue put down the bolt, "How 'bout right now?" He stood and walked into the bedroom just off the kitchen. "Let me just throw on some duds."

"She's working now, Blue."

"At Perkin Lut's? Hell, it's almost noon. I'll talk to Perkin about that Dodge he sold me last year, and when she's ready we'll take her out someplace nice." He came back into the kitchen wearing a soiled brown T-shirt and jeans.

"Hell," Elgin said, "I don't want the girl thinking I've got some serious love for her or something. We come by for lunch, next thing she'll expect me to drop her off in the mornings, pick her up at night."

Blue was reassembling the rifle, snapping all those shiny pieces together so fast, Elgin figured he could do it blind. He said, "Elgin, you got to show them some affection sometimes. I mean, Jesus." He pulled a thin brass bullet from his T-shirt pocket and slipped it in the breech, followed it with four more, then slid the bolt home.

"Yeah, but you know what I'm saying, bud?" Elgin watched Blue nestle the stock in the space between his left hip and ribs, let the barrel point out into the kitchen.

"I know what you're saying," Blue said. "I know. But I got to talk to Perkin about my Dodge."

"What's wrong with it?"

"What's wrong with it?" Blue turned to look at him, and the barrel swung level with Elgin's belt buckle. "What's wrong with it, it's a piece of shit, what's wrong with it, Elgin. Hell, you know that. Perkin sold me a lemon. This is the situation." He blinked. "Beer for the ride?"

Elgin had a pistol in his glove compartment. A .32. He considered it.

"Elgin?"

"Yeah?"

"Why you looking at me funny?"

"You got a rifle pointed at me, Blue. You realize that?"

Blue looked at the rifle, and its presence seemed to surprise him. He dipped it toward the floor. "Shit, man, I'm sorry. I wasn't even thinking. It feels like my arm sometimes. I forget. Man, I am sorry." He held his arms out wide, the rifle rising with them.

"Lotta things deserve to die, don't they?"

Blue smiled. "Well, I wasn't quite thinking along those lines, but now you bring it up . . ."

Elgin said, "Who deserves to die, buddy?"

Blue laughed. "You got something on your mind, don't you?" He hoisted himself up on the table, cradled the rifle in his lap. "Hell, boy, who you got? Let's start with people who take two parking spaces."

"Okay." Elgin moved the chair by the table to a position slightly behind Blue, sat in it. "Let's."

"Then there's DJs talk through the first minute of a song. Fucking Guatos coming down here these days to pick tobacco, showing no respect. Women wearing all those tight clothes, look at you like you're a pervert when you stare at what they're advertising." He wiped his forehead with his arm. "Shit."

"Who else?" Elgin said quietly.

"Okay. Okay. You got people like the ones let their dogs run wild into the highway, get themselves killed. And you got dishonest people, people who lie and sell insurance and cars and bad food. You got a lot of things. Jane Fonda."

"Sure." Elgin nodded.

Blue's face was drawn, gray. He crossed his legs over each other like he used to down at the drainage ditch. "It's all out there." He nodded and his eyelids drooped.

"Perkin Lut?" Elgin said. "He deserve to die?"

"Not just Perkin," Blue said. "Not just. Lots of people. I mean, how many you kill over in the war?"

Elgin shrugged. "I don't know."

"But some. Some. Right? Had to. I mean, that's war—someone gets on your bad side, you kill them and all their friends till they stop bothering you." His eyelids drooped again, and he yawned so deeply he shuddered when he finished.

"Maybe you should get some sleep."

Blue looked over his shoulder at him, "You think? It's been a while."

A breeze rattled the thin walls at the back of the house, pushed that thick dank smell into the kitchen again, a rotting stench that found the back of Elgin's throat and stuck there. He said, "When's the last time?"

"I slept? Hell, a while. Days maybe." Blue twisted his body so he was facing Elgin. "You ever feel like you spend your whole life waiting for it to get going?"

Elgin nodded, not positive what Blue was saying, but knowing he should agree with him. "Sure."

"It's hard," Blue said. "Hard." He leaned back on the table, stared at the brown water marks in his ceiling.

Elgin took in a long stream of that stench through his nostrils. He kept his eyes open, felt that air entering his nostrils creep past into his corneas, tear at them. The urge to close his eyes and wish it all away was as strong an urge as he'd ever felt, but he knew now was that time he'd always known was coming.

He leaned in toward Blue, reached across him, and pulled the rifle off his lap. Blue turned his head, looked at him.

"Go to sleep," Elgin said. "I'll take care of this a while. We'll go see Shelley tomorrow. Perkin Lut too."

Blue blinked. "What if I can't sleep? Huh? I've been having that problem, you know. I put my head on the pillow and I try to sleep and it won't come and soon I'm just bawling like a fucking child till I got to get up and do something."

Elgin looked at the tears that had just then sprung into Blue's eyes, the red veins split across the whites, the desperate, savage need in his face that had always been there if anyone had looked close enough, and would never, Elgin knew, be satisfied.

"I'll stick right here, buddy, I'll sit here in the kitchen and you go in and sleep."

Blue turned his head and stared up at the ceiling again. Then he slid off the table, peeled off his T-shirt, and tossed it on top of the fridge. "All right. All right. I'm gonna try." He stopped at the bedroom doorway. " 'Member—there's beer in the fridge. You be here when I wake up?"

Elgin looked at him. He was still so small, probably so thin you could still wrap your hand around his biceps, meet the fingers on the other side. He was still ugly and stupid-looking, still dying right in front of Elgin's eyes.

"I'll be here, Blue. Don't you worry."

"Good enough. Yes, sir."

Blue shut the door and Elgin heard the bedsprings grind, the rustle of pillows being arranged. He sat in the chair, with the smell of whatever decayed in the back of the house swirling around his head. The sun had hit the cheap tin roof now, heating the small house, and after a while he realized the buzzing he'd thought was in his head came from somewhere back in the house too.

He wondered if he had the strength to open the fridge. He wondered if he should call Perkin Lut's and tell Perkin to get the hell out of Eden for a bit. Maybe he'd just ask for Shelley, tell her to meet him tonight with her suitcases. They'd drive down 95 where the dogs wouldn't disturb them, drive clear to Jacksonville, Florida, before the sun came up again. See if they could outrun Blue and his tiny, dangerous wants, his dog corpses, and his smell; outrun people who took two parking spaces and telephone solicitors and Jane Fonda.

Jewel flashed through his mind then, an image of her sitting atop him, arching her back and shaking that long red hair, a look in her green eyes that said this was it, this was why we live.

He could stand up right now with this rifle in his hands, scratch the itch in the back of his head, and fire straight through the door, end what should never have been started.

He sat there staring at the door for quite a while, until he knew the exact number of places the paint had peeled in teardrop spots, and eventually he stood, went to the phone on the wall by the fridge, and dialed Perkin Lut's.

"Auto Emporium," Shelley said, and Elgin thanked God that in his present mood he hadn't gotten Glynnis Verdon, who snapped her gum and always placed him on hold, left him listening to Muzak versions of The Shirelles.

"Shelley?"

"People gonna talk, you keep calling me at work, boy."

He smiled, cradled the rifle like a baby, leaned against the wall. "How you doing?"

"Just fine, handsome. How 'bout yourself?"

Elgin turned his head, looked at the bedroom door. "I'm okay."

"Still like me?"

Elgin heard the springs creak in the bedroom, heard weight drop on the old floorboards. "Still like you."

"Well, then, it's all fine then, isn't it?"

Blue's footfalls crossed toward the bedroom door, and Elgin used his hip to push himself off the wall.

"It's all fine," he said. "I gotta go. I'll talk to you soon."

He hung up and stepped away from the wall.

"Elgin," Blue said from the other side of the door.

"Yeah, Blue?"

"I can't sleep. I just can't."

Elgin saw Woodson sloshing through the paddy, the top of his head gone. He saw the pink panties curling up from underneath Blue's bed and a shaft of sunlight hitting Shelley's face as she looked up from behind her desk at Perkin Lut's and smiled. He saw Jewel Lut dancing in the night rain by the lake and that dog lying dead on the shoulder of the interstate, kicking its leg like it was trying to ride a bicycle.

"Elgin," Blue said. "I just can't sleep. I got to do something."

"Try," Elgin said and cleared his throat.

"I just can't. I got to . . . do something, I got to go . . ." His voice cracked, and he cleared his throat. "I can't sleep."

The doorknob turned and Elgin raised the rifle, stared down the barrel.

"Sure, you can, Blue." He curled his finger around the trigger as the door opened. "Sure you can," he repeated and took a breath, held it in.

The skeleton of Eden Falls still sits on twenty-two acres of land just east of Brimmer's Point, covered in rust thick as flesh. Some say it was the levels of iodine an environmental inspector found in the groundwater that scared off the original investors. Others said it was the downswing of the state economy or the governor's failed reelection bid. Some say Eden Falls was just plain a dumb name, too biblical. And then, of course, there were plenty who claimed it was Jewel Lut's ghost scared off all the workers.

They found her body hanging from the scaffolding they'd erected by the shell of the roller coaster. She was naked and hung upside down from a rope tied around her ankles. Her throat had been cut so deep the coroner said it was a miracle her head was still attached when they found her. The coroner's assistant, man by the name of Chris Gleason, would claim when he was in his cups that the head had fallen off in the hearse as they drove down Main toward the morgue. Said he heard it cry out.

This was the same day Elgin Bern called the sheriff's office, told them he'd shot his buddy Blue, fired two rounds into him at close range, the little guy dead before he hit his kitchen floor. Elgin told the deputy he was still sitting in the kitchen, right where he'd done it a few hours before. Said to send the hearse.

Due to the fact that Perkin Lut had no real alibi for his whereabouts when Jewel passed on and owing even more to the fact there'd been some very recent and very public discord in their marriage, Perkin was arrested and brought before a grand jury, but that jury decided not to indict. Perkin and Jewel had been patching things up, after all; he'd bought her a car (at cost, but still . . .).

Besides, we all knew it was Blue had killed Jewel. Hell, the Simmons boy, a retard ate paint and tree bark, could have told you that. Once all that stuff came out about what Blue and Big Bobby'd been doing with the dogs around here, well, that just sealed it. And everyone remembered how that week she'd been separated from Perkin, you could see the dream come alive in Blue's eyes, see him allow hope into his heart for the first time in his sorry life.

And when hope comes late to a man, it's quite a dangerous thing. Hope is for the young, the children. Hope in a full-grown man —particularly one with as little acquaintanceship with it or prospect for it as Blue—well, that kind of hope burns as it dies, boils blood white, and leaves something mean behind when it's done.

Blue killed Jewel Lut.

And Elgin Bern killed Blue. And ended up doing time. Not much, due to his war record and the circumstances of who Blue was, but time just the same. Everyone knew Blue probably had it coming, was probably on his way back into town to do to Perkin or some other poor soul what he'd done to Jewel. Once a man gets that look in his eyes—that boiled look, like a dog searching out a bone who's not going to stop until he finds it—well, sometimes he has to be put down like a dog. Don't he?

And it was sad how Elgin came out of prison to find Shelley Briggs gone, moved up North with Perkin Lut of all people, who'd lost his heart for the car business after Jewel died, took to selling home electronics imported from Japan and Germany, made himself a fortune. Not long after he got out of prison, Elgin left too, no one knows where, just gone, drifting.

See, the thing is—no one wanted to convict Elgin. We all understood. We did. Blue had to go. But he'd had no weapon in his hand when Elgin, standing just nine feet away, pulled that trigger. Twice. Once we might been able to overlook, but twice, that's something else again. Elgin offered no defense, even refused a fancy lawyer's attempt to get him to claim he'd suffered something called Post Traumatic Stress Disorder, which we're hearing a lot more about these days.

"I don't have that," Elgin said. "I shot a defenseless man. That's the long and the short of it, and that's a sin."

And he was right:

In the world, case you haven't noticed, you usually pay for your sins.

And in the South, always.

JAMES CRUMLEY

If you like your fiction dark, let James Crumley serve it up to you. He's a Vietnam War vet who uses that experience—and the shadows that follow war veterans throughout their lives—to excellent advantage in his crime writing. To say he has an eye for detail and an original, but distinctly American, voice is not to say enough about the impact of his writing. Sometimes Crumley's prose hits the reader like a slap in the face, it's so hard and stunning.

Born in Three Rivers, Texas, Crumley went on to study at the Georgia Institute of Technology, Texas Arts and Industries University, and the Iowa Writers' Workshop at the University of Iowa. But he got his education in true grit and the extremes of human nature during his military service. He based his first novel, *One Count to Cadence,* on his war experience. It was published while the war still raged, in 1969.

Next, he created his first series detective, Milton Chester "Milo" Milodragovitch III. Introduced in the 1975 private eye novel *The Wrong Case,* this gumshoe is a redneck, alcoholic veteran of the Korean War, who works cases in and around Meriwether, Montana. The son of parents who committed suicide, he's a dark, haunted character whose alcoholism seems particularly explicable.

Crumley's second series detective is not a sunny character either. Chauncy Wayne "C.W." Sughrue is another redneck and alcoholic, who solves crimes in the same Montana town and seems most in his element when the violence becomes intense. He's a veteran, too, but one whose tour of duty in Vietnam was cut short when he was court-martialed for committing atrocities. The court-martial takes C.W. out of uniform, but it doesn't stop the U.S. government from enlisting his aid in infiltrating the antiwar movement. C.W. makes his first appearance in Crumley's 1978 novel, *The Last Good Kiss.*

Crumley is one of those writers whose skills at short fiction absolutely match the quality of his longer work. At just five pages long, "Hostages" is a good example. The first paragraph of this tense story of a bank robbery and its aftermath shows the author to be a master of metaphor and simile, not to mention a dab hand at painting a period piece set during the Great Depression. Later in the piece he ladles out description like some kind of addictive syrup: "Even smashed on sloe gin and laudanum, the girl's breath reminded Mabel of the soda fountain in Ogallala where her goddammed father had been the local blue-faced, morphine-addicted pharmacist."

Crumley comments, "The story is my first attempt at a period piece—I suspect my midwestern landscape came from Wright Morris and the tone from a William Humphreys story, but the rest was from my own twisted, criminal mind. And my wife's insistence on just one more draft, until the story wrote itself."

Hostages

2002

BETWEEN the hammer of the midwestern sun and the relentless sweep of the bone-dry wind, the small town of Wheatshocker seemed crushed flat and just about to blow across the plains. Long billows of dust filled the empty streets like strings of fog. Male dogs learned to squat or leaned against withered fence posts so the wind wouldn't blow them over when they lifted their legs to pee. The piss dried instantly on the sere dirt, then blew away before the dogs finished. Shadows as black as tar huddled protectively in the shallow dunes that lined the few buildings left on the main street. Most of the windowfronts were as empty as a fool's laugh, while those with glass were etched in formless shapes by the sharp, ghostly wind. The red bricks of the Farmers Bank and Trust had faded to a pallid pink, held in place by desiccated, crumbling mortar. A '32 Ford sedan idled in the bank's alley, as dusty as the rest of the heaps parked in front of the bank. A humpbacked man as small as a child sat behind the wheel, smoking a ready-roll. Only a pro would have noticed the low chortle of the reground cam in his engine. Nothing moved down the street but a mismatched team of mules slowly pulling a wagon with a large Negro in overalls and a canvas-covered bed.

The heat-stunned silence was shattered by a single gunshot. Four armed men backed out of the bank, carrying a canvas laundry bag and pushing along an old lady in a feedsack dress and a young girl in white ruffles.

"And stay down, you damn hayseeds!" the red-headed one shouted. "We've got hostages!"

The group scrambled into the sedan, the last man firing a shot into the bank's front window, then the car sped down the dusty street and around a corner after the wagon with its plodding mules. The crumbling sidewalk in front of the bank slowly filled with a group of confused customers and tellers huddled together like the survivors of a natural disaster. A red-faced man, holding a handkerchief against a bloody knot on his bald head, shoved through the crowd, and stared into the dust cloud into which the bank robbers had disappeared.

"One of you fools get that worthless old bastard out of my bank," he ordered.

"I believe the sheriff's a-dyin'," one of the tellers ventured.

"Not in *my* bank, he isn't," the banker said. "We can't afford to bury the idiot *now*."

A frail old woman with a hooked nose said to no one in particular, "I believe Mr. Baines was sweet on that poor widow woman."

"How the hell did they know to come today?" the banker muttered, his words lost on the gritty wind.

On the seventh day, Mabel had nearly slipped into an exhausted sleep when she heard the bluegum Geechi boy, Sledge, rack the slide on the sawed-off

Ithaca 12-gauge pump. The hard sound slammed through the thin walls of the farmhouse. She knew what that meant. All too well. One of the gang in the nonstop poker game downstairs had pulled a gun. Probably the red-headed prick. Absolutely against all her rules. Mabel sighed, rolled over, and kissed Baby Emma's rosebud lips. Even in her sleep, Baby Emma sucked on Mabel's tongue briefly, then nipped it with her tiny white seed-corn teeth. Mabel wanted to follow the sleepy kiss—even cupped Em's tiny, pert breasts with the rosehip nipples—but she had business to take care of. Baby Emma was twenty but easily passed for ten or eleven. The girl-child seemed built of warm and creamy vanilla scoops, and the blond ringlets curling in a tangle around her face looked like thick caramel drippings. Mabel touched her lips again, softly, not wanting to wake the young woman too quickly. Even smashed on sloe gin and laudanum, the girl's breath reminded Mabel of the soda fountain in Ogallala where her goddammed father had been the local blue-faced, morphine-addicted pharmacist. The memory made what she had to do easier. She wished she could keep the kid out of it this time—Baby Em seemed to like it too much—and she hated to lose the gimp, but they all had to go. "Get ready, sugarplum," she said, then slipped into her clothes piled on a ratty dresser.

The gang had been holed up in the sugarbeeter's house since they had taken down the Farmer's State Bank for almost sixteen thousand. That was the way she always worked. The smart ones didn't run after a job. They holed up nearby for at least two weeks. That was always the hard part, that two weeks of waiting. The easy part was finding a failing farmer with no children and a defeated wife to take them in for a price. It was 1932, and almost anybody would do anything for a price. Of course, the final payment was always a .22 short in the eye and a sack of lime in the root cellar.

As Mabel considered how to deal with this new bunch, she knew she had plenty of time to change into her grandmother clothes. The boys always seemed more likely to obey her when she looked like an old woman rather than a lush ex-whore in her mid-thirties. She gathered her thick red hair into a knot, and stuffed it under a gray wig. She bound her slightly overripe body into an old woman's girdle and a bra stuffed with sand-filled socks to make it seem as if her breasts drooped almost to her waist, all of it covered with a dress sewn from chickenfeed sacks. Her long, slim legs were sheathed in thick gray stockings, and her feet laced into ugly, thick-heeled granny shoes. In this outfit, she and Baby Em made the perfect hostages. Then Mabel added the last touches: a black straw brimless hat, ringed with cloth flowers, attached to the wig with three heavy hatpins, and a .22 Derringer up her sleeve.

Baby Em stripped butt-naked. Either she didn't like blood on her nightclothes, or she liked the warm splatter on her pale, perfect skin.

The scene downstairs was much as Mabel had imagined. The farmer and his wife, as pale as bleached bones, huddled behind the icebox, shaking so badly that the water in the melt tray shimmered as if a cold breeze were sweeping across the worn plank floorboards. A handful of cards had been scattered across the kitchen table, and several stacks of chips tumbled into piles. The largest pile was in front of Fast Freddy Okrentski, the tiny, gimp-legged humpback, who had laid down a false trail for the police and dumped the car while the gang rode out of town in the back of the farmer's wagon covered with a tarp.

The brothers, Crazy Al and Bruno Zale, the muscle, had small neat stacks of chips in front of them covered with their huge hands, hands so large they made their Smith & Wesson .38 revolvers look small. The brothers were large-jawed pug-uglies out of Nutley, New Jersey; men with the kinds of faces who, when they threatened death to the hostages, looked as if they might enjoy the feel of blood, bone chips, and brain matter dripping off their craggy smiles.

Carter Docktrey—the smooth-faced red-headed little shit from Terre Haute, who thought he led the gang, who thought he was God's gift to women, and who thought he knew how to play poker—stood in front of his overturned chair, his chip stack flat and his military Colt .45 semiautomatic pointed at Lindsey. Mabel knew that Carter's rod was mostly for show; the arrogant turd never cleaned the piece so it usually jammed after the first round.

She also knew that Lindsey, whose light blue eyes were as cool as ball bearings in a snowstorm and whose usually smooth forehead was wrinkled slightly, no more than a soft gust of wind across a still pond, was a stone killer. A single drop of sweat slipped off his bald head, over his furrowed brow, to land with a light click on his cards. His hands were under the table and more than likely had the .410 he carried strapped to his calf pointed at Carter. The little shotgun had been cut down to pistol size and loaded with tacks. To be gutshot that way ensured an endlessly painful death, so in a way she'd be doing Carter a favor. The slick little bastard hated Lindsey, who always cased and organized the jobs, because Lindsey was both smarter and calmer than Carter. So this was about them, and had little to do with Freddie the gimp, who probably was dealing seconds. He was as nimble with cards as he was with cars.

The scene was as still as a photograph. Of course, nobody had moved because Sledge stood in the corner, the Ithaca 12-gauge leveled at the table. At this range, a couple of rounds of the double-ought buckshot would have swept the room clean.

Mabel considered the scene, then, smiling, stepped behind Carter and picked up his chair. She grabbed his shoulders firmly and gently eased him into the chair. Then she took the pistol from his hand and set it in front of him.

"You're not going to be needing this, honey," she said softly, then turned to the bluegum and nodded.

Sledge returned the nod with a smile. He and Mabel had been a team since the cathouse in East Memphis where they worked had been burned down by a drunk Baptist preacher, and they went into the bank-robbing business. It had been good to them. Sledge had a small chicken farm outside Tacoma, and Mabel owned a roadhouse north of Bellingham where Canadian whiskey was easy to obtain.

Mabel turned back to Carter, rubbing his neck gently with her left hand, her right hand touching her hat. "Now what's the problem, honey?"

"Goddamned Bohunk has been dealin' seconds all night long," Carter answered.

"I can't believe that," she said, still gentle, "can't believe that any more than I can believe . . ." She paused, then her voice became hard. ". . . that you forgot what I said about no guns, you needle-dicked bug-fucking son of a bitch."

Mabel had done it wrong a couple of times in the past and had to deal with convulsions, confusion, and anger—usually, with the Derringer—so experience had taught her exactly where to put the hatpin at the base of the skull. When she tapped the thick pin with the heel of her hand, it penetrated Carter's dismal brain as easily as it might slip through a round of rat cheese. He was dead before his face hit the meager scattering of chips in front of him.

"I guess you boys will have to play four-handed, now," she said lightly as she picked up Carter's .45 off the table. "Unless you can get the farmer to change his overalls."

Then Mabel lifted the pistol casually and shot Lindsey just where his forehead became his bald pate. He went over like an acrobat. Baby Em stepped around the corner with a nickle-plated .32, pressed it against Freddie's temple, then pulled the trigger twice. She kept pulling the trigger as the gimp toppled sideways out of his chair. Crazy Al went for the piece under his jacket, but Sledge took him down with his first round at such close range that he blew Crazy Al's gun hand off at the wrist and set fire to his dirty tie. Bruno started to raise his hands as if to plead, but Sledge shot him in the face before he could open his mouth.

The sugarbeeter and his wife were shaking and weeping so hard that they had trouble dragging the bodies down to the root cellar, but Mabel kept reassuring them that the lime would destroy the bodies and that with their cut of the bank loot they could start over again in California or Oregon. The tattered couple had stopped shaking by the time they finished dumping the last sack of lime, and the tears had dried from their eyes when Mabel put the two .22 shorts into their brainpans. The couple fell on the pile as neatly as if they had planned it that way.

Sledge finished setting up the house as the women dressed for traveling. He covered the bodies with Bell jars of coal oil and phosphorus, then arranged for a fire. He laid a slow black powder fuse from the root cellar to the kitchen table, where he wrapped it around the base of a three-day candle. Then he washed the Lincoln where the gimp had hidden it in the barn, changed the local plates for real New Jersey ones, and dressed in his driver's uniform.

The guns and money were stashed in a false bottom of the trunk, an obscene amount of luggage piled on top and strapped to the back. The women were lodged in the back seat, draped in traveling dusters, big hats, and dust veils—a wealthy widow and her daughter on their way to the West Coast for a new life.

"Are we set, Mr. Sledge?" Mabel asked as he backed the large car out of the barn.

"Everything but the match, ma'am," he said.

"Well, strike the match, please," she said.

"I wish we were gonna be here to see it," Baby Em said as Sledge headed for the farmhouse. "What's gonna happen next, Momma?"

"There's a plump little bank in Ogallala right next to the drugstore," she answered. "I think we'll pay it a little visit before we go home. I know a couple of old boys in Denver who might help."

"Just no more little red-headed pricks, okay? I'd rather suck a cough drop," Baby Em said as Sledge drove out onto the section road.

"Just a blue-faced monster," Mabel said, "and he'll have plenty of cough drops, and maybe even some hard rock candy. He used to have lots of hard rock candy."

"I wanna gun in the bank next time," Baby Em whined. "Don't you?"

As the sun slipped toward the horizon, the wind paused for a moment, the dust settled, and a fire burned briefly in Mabel's eyes, a fire as brief as her sad smile.

"We don't need guns, Babydoll."

ELMORE LEONARD

Elmore Leonard is best known for writing realistic crime fiction anchored in believable dialogue. However, before he turned his talents to crime writing, he spent a decade writing western short stories, novels, and screenplays. That was during the 1950s when there were a good number of pulp magazines catering to readers with a taste for westerns. When many pulps folded during the following decade, he tried his hand at crime writing, producing his first mystery novel, *The Big Bounce*, in 1969.

Leonard credits George V. Higgins's 1972 masterwork, *The Friends of Eddie Coyle*, with influencing him profoundly. He admired Higgins's devotion to writing natural-sounding dialogue and zooming in on the point of view of an individual. Leonard tried out this approach in his 1974 novel *Fifty-Two Pick-up*, and the book put him on the map as a crime novelist.

A 1978 nonfiction assignment for the *Detroit News* led Leonard to spend two months observing day-to-day police work. Fascinated by the characters he met—including lawmen and criminals—he wrote his first book with a policeman as narrator. *City Primeval* (1980) marked another success for the author and led him to write four more novels in this vein, in quick succession: *Split Images* (1981), *Cat Chaser* (1982), *Stick*, and *La Brava*. The latter two were both published in 1983. By the time he published *Glitz* in 1985, Leonard had become the darling of literary critics and a regular on best-seller lists.

Leonard's success depends upon several factors, not the least of which is his ability to get into the heads of a wide cast of characters. His plots are satisfyingly complex but they do not dominate characterization, which is always strong in his work. He is comfortable setting his stories in a variety of cities and has a good eye for finding telling details that anchor action and atmosphere in these settings. Over the years, Leonard's flair for titling has grown. Among the most memorable are *Freaky Deaky* (1988), *Get Shorty* (1991), and *Maximum Bob* (1991).

Leonard has had a distinguished career as a writer of short stories, too. He told us one of his favorites is "When the Women Come Out to Dance." Anthologized in the 2002 volume *When the Women Come Out to Dance and Other Stories*, this tale demonstrates the author's knack for reversing expectation about character. Here dialogue does much to tell us who these people are. But actions also speak loudly here, as when the well-heeled woman of the house purchases expensive clothing for her new maid, but ignores the domestic worker's color preference entirely. In fact, this story puts a new spin on the term "malice domestic."

When the Women Come Out to Dance

2002

LOURDES became Mrs. Mahmood's personal maid when her friend Viviana quit to go to L.A. with her husband. Lourdes and Viviana were both from Cali in Colombia and had come to South Florida as mail-order brides. Lourdes' husband, Mr. Zimmer, worked for a paving contractor until his death, two years from the time they were married.

She came to the home on Ocean Drive, only a few blocks from Donald Trump's, expecting to not have a good feeling for a woman named Mrs. Mahmood, wife of Dr. Wasim Mahmood, who altered the faces and breasts of Palm Beach ladies and aspirated their areas of fat. So it surprised Lourdes the woman didn't look like a Mrs. Mahmood, and that she opened the door herself: this tall redheaded woman in a little green two-piece swimsuit, sunglasses on her nose, opened the door and said, "Lourdes, as in Our Lady of?"

"No, ma'am, Lour-des, the Spanish way to say it," and had to ask, "You have no help here to open the door?"

The redheaded Mrs. Mahmood said, "They're in the laundry room watching soaps." She said, "Come on in," and brought Lourdes into this home of marble floors, of statues and paintings that held no meaning, and out to the swimming pool, where they sat at a patio table beneath a yellow-and-white umbrella.

There were cigarettes, a silver lighter and a tall glass with only ice left in it on the table. Mrs. Mahmood lit a cigarette, a long Virginia Slim, and pushed the pack toward Lourdes, who was saying, "All I have is this, Mrs. Mahmood," Lourdes bringing a biographical data sheet, a printout, from her straw bag. She laid it before the redheaded woman showing her breasts as she leaned forward to look at the sheet.

" 'Your future wife is in the mail'?"

"From the Latina introduction list for marriage," Lourdes said. "The men who are interested see it on their computers. Is three years old, but what it tells of me is still true. Except of course my age. Now it would say thirty-five."

Mrs. Mahmood, with her wealth, her beauty products, looked no more than thirty. Her red hair was short and reminded Lourdes of the actress who used to be on TV at home, Jill St. John, with the same pale skin. She said, "That's right, you and Viviana were both mail-order brides," still looking at the sheet. "Your English is good—that's true. You don't smoke or drink."

"I drink now sometime, socially."

"You don't have e-mail."

"No, so we wrote letters to correspond, before he came to Cali, where I lived. They have parties for the men who come and we get—you know, we dress up for it."

"Look each other over."

"Yes, is how I met Mr. Zimmer in person."

"Is that what you called him?"

"I didn't call him anything."

"Mrs. Zimmer," the redheaded woman said. "How would you like to be Mrs. Mahmood?"

"I wouldn't think that was your name."

She was looking at the printout again. "You're virtuous, sensitive, hardworking, optimistic. Looking for a man who's a kind, loving person with a good job. Was that Mr. Zimmer?"

"He was okay except when he drank too much. I had to be careful what I said or it would cause him to hit me. He was strong, too, for a guy his age. He was fifty-eight."

"When you married?"

"When he died."

"I believe Viviana said he was killed?" The woman sounding like she was trying to recall whatever it was Viviana had told her. "An accident on the job?"

Lourdes believed the woman already knew about it, but said, "He was disappeared for a few days until they find his mix truck out by Hialeah, a pile of concrete by it but no reason for the truck to be here since there's no job he was pouring. So the police have the concrete broken open and find Mr. Zimmer."

"Murdered," the redheaded woman said.

"They believe so, yes, his hands tied behind him."

"The police talk to you?"

"Of course. He was my husband."

"I mean did they think you had anything to do with it."

She knew. Lourdes was sure of it.

"There was a suspicion that friends of mine here from Colombia could be the ones did it. Someone who was their enemy told this to the police."

"It have anything to do with drugs?"

The woman seeing all Colombians as drug dealers.

"My husband drove a cement truck."

"But why would anyone want to kill him?"

"Who knows?" Lourdes said. "This person who finked, he told the police I got the Colombian guys to do it because my husband was always beating me. One time he hit me so hard," Lourdes said, touching the strap of her blue sundress that was faded almost white from washing, "it separated my shoulder, the bones in here, so I couldn't work."

"Did you tell the Colombian guys he was beating you?"

"Everyone knew. Sometime Mr. Zimmer was brutal to me in public, when he was drinking."

"So maybe the Colombian guys did do it." The woman sounding like she wanted to believe it.

"I don't know," Lourdes said, and waited to see if this was the end of it. Her gaze moved out to the sunlight, to the water in the swimming pool lying still, and beyond to red bougainvillea growing against white walls. Gardeners were weeding and trimming, three of them Lourdes thought at first were Latino. No, the color of their skin was different. She said, "Those men . . ."

"Pakistanis," Mrs. Mahmood said.

"They don't seem to work too hard," Lourdes said. "I always have a garden at home, grow things to eat. Here, when I was married, I worked for Miss Olympia. She call her service 'Cleaning with Biblical Integrity.' I wasn't sure what it means, but she would say things to us from the Holy Bible. We cleaned offices in buildings in Miami. What I do here Viviana said would be different, personal to you. See to your things, keep your clothes nice?"

Straighten her dresser drawers. Clean her jewelry. Mrs. Mahmood said she kicked her shoes off in the closet, so Lourdes would see they were paired and hung in the shoe racks. Check to see what needed to be dry-cleaned. Lourdes waited as the woman stopped to think of other tasks. See to her makeup drawers in the bathroom. Lourdes would live here, have Sundays off, a half day during the week. Technically she would be an employee of Dr. Mahmood's.

Oh? Lourdes wasn't sure what that meant. Before she could ask, Mrs. Mahmood wanted to know if she was a naturalized citizen. Lourdes told her she was a permanent resident, but now had to get the papers to become a citizen.

"I say who I work for I put Dr. Wasim Mahmood?"

The redheaded wife said, "It's easier that way. You know, to handle what's taken out. But I'll see that you clear at least three-fifty a week."

Lourdes said that was very generous. "But will I be doing things also for Dr. Mahmood?"

The redheaded woman smoking her cigarette said, "What did Viviana tell you about him?"

"She say only that he didn't speak to her much."

"Viviana's a size twelve. Woz likes them young and as lean as snakes. How much do you weigh?"

"Less than one hundred twenty-five pounds."

"But not much—you may be safe. You cook?"

"Yes, of course."

"I mean for yourself. We go out or order in from restaurants. I won't go near that fucking stove and Woz knows it."

Lourdes said, "Wos?"

"Wasim. He thinks it's because I don't know how to cook, which I don't, really, but that's not the reason. The two regular maids are Filipina and speak English. In fact they have less of an accent than you. They won't give you any trouble, they look at the ground when they talk to anyone. And they leave at four, thank God. Woz always swims nude—don't ask me why, it might be a Muslim thing—so if they see him in the pool they hide in the laundry room.

Or if I put on some Southern hip-hop and they happen to walk in while I'm bouncing to Dirty South doing my aerobics, they run for the laundry room." She said without a pause, "What did Viviana say about me?"

"Oh, how nice you are, what a pleasure to work here."

"Come on—I know she told you I was a stripper."

"She say you were a dancer before, yes."

"I started out in a dump on Federal Highway, got discovered and jumped to Miami Gold on Biscayne, valet parking. I was one of the very first, outside of black chicks, to do Southern hip-hop, and I mean Dirty South raw and uncut, while the other girls are doing Limp Bizkit, even some old Bob Seeger and Bad Company—and that's okay, whatever works for you. But in the meantime I'm making more doing laptops and private gigs than any girl at the Gold and I'm twenty-seven at the time, older than any of them. Woz would come in with his buddies, all suits and ties, trying hard not to look Third World. The first time he waved a fifty at me I gave him some close-up tribal strip-hop. I said, 'Doctor, you can see better if you put your eyeballs back in your head.' He loved that kind of talk. About the fourth visit I gave him what's known as the million-dollar hand job and became Mrs. Mahmood."

She told this sitting back relaxed, smoking her Virginia Slim cigarette, Lourdes nodding, wondering at times what she was talking about, Lourdes saying "I see" in a pleasant voice when the woman paused.

Now she was saying, "His first wife stayed in Pakistan while he was here in med school. Right after he finished his residency and opened his practice, she died." The woman said, "Let's see . . . You won't have to wear a uniform unless Woz wants you to serve drinks. Once in a while he has some of his ragtop buddies over for cocktails. Now you see these guys in their Nehru outfits and hear them chattering away in Urdu. I walk in, 'Ah, Mrs. Mahmood,' in that semi-British singsongy way they speak, 'what a lovely sight you are to my eyes this evening.' Wondering if I'm the same chick he used to watch strip."

She took time to light another cigarette and Lourdes said, "Do I wear my own clothes working here?"

"At first, but I'll get you some cool outfits. What are you, about an eight?"

"My size? Yes, I believe so."

"Let's see—stand up."

Lourdes rose and moved away from the table in the direction Mrs. Mahmood waved her hand. Now the woman was staring at her. She said, "I told you his first wife died?"

"Yes, ma'am, you did."

"She burned to death."

Lourdes said, "Oh?"

But the redheaded woman didn't tell her how it happened. She smoked her cigarette and said, "Your legs are good, but you're kinda short-waisted, a bit top-heavy. But don't worry, I'll get you fixed up. What's your favorite color?"

"I always like blue, Mrs. Mahmood."

She said, "Listen, I don't want you to call me that anymore. You can say ma'am in front of Woz to get my attention, but when it's just you and I? I'd rather you called me by my own name."

"Yes?"

"It's Ginger. Well, actually it's Janeen, but all of my friends call me Ginger. The ones I have left."

Meaning, Lourdes believed, since she was married to the doctor, friends who also danced naked, or maybe even guys.

Lourdes said, "Ginger?"

"Not Yinyor. Gin-ger. Try it again."

"Gin-gar?"

"That's close. Work on it."

But she could not make herself call Mrs. Mahmood Ginger. Not yet. Not during the first few weeks. Not on the shopping trip to Worth Avenue where Mrs. Mahmood knew everyone, all the salesgirls, and some of them did call her Ginger. She picked out for Lourdes casual summer dresses that cost hundreds of dollars each and some things from Resort Wear saying, "This is cute," and would hand it to the salesgirl to put aside, never asking Lourdes her opinion, if she liked the clothes or not. She did, but wished some of them were blue. Everything was yellow or yellow and white or white with yellow. She didn't have to wear a uniform, no, but now she matched the yellow-and-white patio, the cushions, the umbrellas, feeling herself part of the décor, invisible.

Sitting out here in the evening several times a week when the doctor didn't come home, Mrs. Mahmood trying hard to make it seem they were friends, Mrs. Mahmood serving daiquiris in round crystal goblets, waiting on her personal maid. It was nice to be treated this way and it would continue, Lourdes believed, until Mrs. Mahmood finally came out and said what was on her mind, what she wanted Lourdes to do for her.

The work was nothing, keep the woman's clothes in order, water the houseplants, fix lunch for herself—and the maids, once they came in the kitchen sniffing her spicy seafood dishes. Lourdes had no trouble talking to them. They looked right at her face telling her things. Why they avoided Dr. Mahmood. Because he would ask very personal questions about their sexual lives. Why they thought Mrs. Mahmood was crazy. Because of the way she danced in just her underwear.

And in the evening the woman of the house would tell Lourdes of being bored with her life, not able to invite her friends in because Woz didn't approve of them.

"What do I do? I hang out. I listen to music. I discuss soap operas with the gook maids. Melda stops me. 'Oh, missus, come quick.' They're in the laundry room watching *As the World Turns*. She goes, 'Dick follows Nikki to where she is to meet Ryder, and it look like he was going to hurt her. But Ryder came there in time to save Nikki from a violent Dick.'"

Mrs. Mahmood would tell a story like that and look at her without an expression on her face, waiting for Lourdes to smile or laugh. But what was funny about the story?

"What do I do?" was the question she asked most. "I exist, I have no life."

"You go shopping."

"That's all."

"You play golf."

"You've gotta be kidding."

"You go out with your husband."

"To an Indian restaurant and I listen to him talk to the manager. How many times since you've been here has he come home in the evening? He has a girl-friend," the good-looking redheaded woman said. "He's with her all the time. Her or another one, and doesn't care that I know. He's rubbing it in my face. All guys fool around at least once in a while. Woz and his buddies live for it. It's accepted over there, where they're from. A guy gets tired of his wife in Pakistan? He burns her to death. Or has it done. I'm not kidding, he tells everyone her *dupatta* caught fire from the stove."

Lourdes said, "Ah, that's why you don't cook."

"Among other reasons. Woz's from Rawalpindi, a town where forty women a *month* show up at the hospital with terrible burns. If the woman survives. . . . Are you listening to me?"

Lourdes was sipping her daiquiri. "Yes, of course."

"If she doesn't die, she lives in shame because her husband, this prick who tried to burn her to death, kicked her out of the fucking house. And he gets away with it. Pakistan, India, thousands of women are burned every year 'cause their husbands are tired of them, or they didn't come up with a big enough dowry."

"You say the first wife was burn to death."

"Once he could afford white women—like, what would he need her for?"

"You afraid he's going to burn you?"

"It's what they do, their custom. And you know what's ironic? Woz comes here to be a plastic surgeon, but over in Pakistan, where all these women are going around disfigured? There are no plastic surgeons to speak of." She said, "Some of them get acid thrown in their face." She said, "I made the biggest mistake of my life marrying a guy from a different culture, a towelhead."

Lourdes said, "Why did you?"

She gestured. "This . . ." Meaning the house and all that went with it.

"So you have what you want."

"I won't if I leave him."

"Maybe in the divorce he let you keep the house."

"It's in the prenup, I get zip. And at thirty-two I'm back stripping on Federal Highway, or working in one of those topless doughnut places. You have tits, at least you can get a job. Woz's favorite, I'd come out in a nurse's uni-form, peel everything off but the perky little cap?" The woman's mind moving to this without pausing. "Woz said the first time he saw the act he wanted to hire me. I'd be the first topless surgical nurse."

Lourdes imagined this woman dancing naked, men watching her, and thought of Miss Olympia warning the cleaning women with her Biblical Integrity: no singing or dancing around while cleaning the offices, or they might catch the eye of men working late. She made it sound as if they were lying in wait. "Read the Book of Judges," Miss Olympia said, "the twenty-first verse." It was about men waiting for women, the daughters of Shiloh, to come out to dance so they could take them, force the women to be their wives. Lourdes knew of cleaning women who sang while they worked, but not ones who danced. She wondered what it would be like to dance naked in front of men.

"You don't want to be with him," Lourdes said, "but you want to live in this house."

"There it is," the woman who didn't look at all like a Mrs. Mahmood said.

Lourdes sipped her daiquiri, put the glass down and reached for the pack of Virginia Slims on the table.

"May I try one of these?"

"Help yourself."

She lit the cigarette, sucking hard to get a good draw. She said, "I use to smoke. The way you do it made me want to smoke again. Even the way you hold the cigarette."

Lourdes believed the woman was very close to telling what she was thinking about. Still, it was not something easy to talk about with another person, even for a woman who danced naked. Lourdes decided this evening to help her.

She said, "How would you feel if a load of wet concrete fell on your husband?"

Then wondered, sitting in the silence, not looking at the woman, if she had spoken too soon.

The redheaded woman said, "The way it happened to Mr. Zimmer? How did you feel?"

"I accepted it," Lourdes said, "with a feeling of relief, knowing I wouldn't be beaten no more."

"Were you ever happy with him?"

"Not for one day."

"You picked him, you must've had some idea."

"He picked me. At the party in Cali? There were seven Colombian girls for each American. I didn't think I would be chosen. We married . . . In two years I had my green card and was tired of him hitting me."

The redheaded Mrs. Mahmood said, "You took a lot of shit, didn't you?" and paused this time before saying, "How much does a load of concrete cost these days?"

Lourdes, without pausing, said, "Thirty thousand."

Mrs. Mahmood said, "Jesus Christ," but was composed, sitting back in her yellow cushions. She said, "You were ready. Viviana told you the situation and you decided to go for it."

"I think it was you hired me," Lourdes said, "because of Mr. Zimmer—you so interested in what happen to him. Also I could tell, from the first day we sat here, you don't care for your husband."

"You can understand why, can't you? I'm scared to death of catching on fire. He lights a cigar, I watch him like a fucking hawk."

Giving herself a reason, an excuse.

"We don't need to talk about him," Lourdes said. "You pay the money, all of it before, and we don't speak of this again. You don't pay, we still never speak of it."

"The Colombian guys have to have it all up front?"

"The what guys?"

"The concrete guys."

"You don't know what kind of guys they are. What if it looks like an accident and you say oh, they didn't do nothing, he fell off his boat."

"Woz doesn't have a boat."

"Or his car was hit by a truck. You understand? You not going to know anything before."

"I suppose they want cash."

"Of course."

"I can't go to the bank and draw that much."

"Then we forget it."

Lourdes waited while the woman thought about it smoking her Virginia Slim, both of them smoking, until Mrs. Mahmood said, "If I give you close to twenty thousand in cash, today, right now, you still want to forget it?"

Now Lourdes had to stop and think for a moment.

"You have that much in the house?"

"My getaway money," Mrs. Mahmood said, "in case I ever have to leave in a hurry. What I socked away in tips getting guys to spot their pants and that's the deal, twenty grand. You want it or not? You don't, you might as well leave, I don't need you anymore."

So far in the few weeks she was here, Lourdes had met Dr. Mahmood face-to-face with reason to speak to him only twice. The first time, when he came in the kitchen and asked her to prepare his breakfast, the smoked snook, a fish he ate cold with tea and whole wheat toast. He asked her to have some of the snook if she wished, saying it wasn't as good as kippers but would do. Lourdes tried a piece; it was full of bones but she told him yes, it was good. They spoke of different kinds of fish from the ocean they liked and he seemed to be a pleasant, reasonable man.

The second time Lourdes was with him face-to-face he startled her, coming out of the swimming pool naked as she was watering the plants on the patio. He called to her to bring him his towel from the chair. When she came with it he said, "You were waiting for me?"

"No, sir, I didn't see you."

As he dried his face and his head, the hair so short it appeared shaved, she stared at his skin, at his round belly and his strange black penis, Lourdes looking up then as he lowered the towel.

He said, "You are a widow?" She nodded yes and he said, "When you married, you were a virgin?"

She hesitated, but then answered because she was telling a doctor, "No, sir."

"It wasn't important to your husband."

"I don't think so."

"Would you see an advantage in again being a virgin?"

She had to think—it wasn't something ever in her mind before—but didn't want to make the doctor wait, so she said, "No, not at my age."

The doctor said, "I can restore it if you wish."

"Make me a virgin?"

"Surgically, a few sutures down there in the tender dark. It's becoming popular in the Orient with girls entering marriage. Also for prostitutes. They can charge much more, often thousands of dollars for that one night." He said, "I'm thinking of offering the procedure. Should you change your mind, wish me to examine you, I could do it in your room."

Dr. Mahmood's manner, and the way he looked at her that time, made Lourdes feel like taking her clothes off.

He didn't come home the night Lourdes and Mrs. Mahmood got down to business. Or the next night. The morning of the following day, two men from the Palm Beach County sheriff's office came to the house. They showed Lourdes their identification and asked to see Mrs. Mahmood.

She was upstairs in her bedroom trying on a black dress, looking at herself in the full-length mirror and then at Lourdes' reflection appearing behind her.

"The police are here," Lourdes said.

Mrs. Mahmood nodded and said, "What do you think?" turning to pose in the dress, the skirt quite short.

Lourdes read the story in the newspaper that said Dr. Wasim Mahmood, prominent etc., etc., had suffered gunshot wounds during an apparent carjacking on Flagler near Currie Park and was pronounced dead on arrival at Good Samaritan. His Mercedes was found abandoned on the street in Delray Beach.

Mrs. Mahmood left the house in her black dress. Later, she phoned to tell Lourdes she had identified the body, spent time with the police, who had no clues, nothing at all to go on, then stopped by a funeral home and arranged to have Woz cremated without delay. She said, "What do you think?"

"About what?" Lourdes said.

"Having the fucker burned."

She said she was stopping to see friends and wouldn't be home until late.

One A.M., following an informal evening of drinks with old friends, Mrs. Mahmood came into the kitchen from the garage and began to lose her glow.

What was going on here?

Rum and mixes on the counter, limes, a bowl of ice. A Latin beat coming from the patio. She followed the sound to a ring of burning candles, to Lourdes in a green swimsuit moving in one place to the beat, hands raised, Lourdes grinding her hips in a subtle way.

The two guys at the table smoking cigarettes saw Mrs. Mahmood, but made no move to get up.

Now Lourdes turned from them and saw her, Lourdes smiling a little as she said, "How you doing? You look like you feeling no pain."

"You have my suit on," Mrs. Mahmood said.

"I put on my yellow one," Lourdes said, still moving in that subtle way, "and took it off. I don't wear yellow no more, so I borrow one of yours. Is okay, isn' it?"

Mrs. Mahmood said, "What's going on?"

"This is *cumbia*, Colombian music for when you want to celebrate. For a wedding, a funeral, anything you want. The candles are part of it. *Cumbia*, you should always light candles."

Mrs. Mahmood said, "Yeah, but what is going on?"

"We having a party for you, Ginger. The Colombian guys come to see you dance."

IAN RANKIN

When he created John Rebus of the Edinburgh CID in the 1987 novel *Knots and Crosses,* there was "in Scotland, no tradition for the crime writer, no rules for the crime writer to live up to," Edinburgh author Ian Rankin said. He felt he had free rein, and he used it to look at the underside of a city known to tourists for its prominent castle and annual arts festival. Hardly a review was written about the Rebus series that did not employ the words "dark" and "gritty." But there is humor—albeit black humor—in Rankin's books, as well.

By the time Rankin wrote *Knots and Crosses,* he had already written award-winning poetry and three mainstream novels. He had occupied himself as a student at Edinburgh University, sung with a band called The Dancing Pigs, and worked as a swineherd, too. Intending to write a kind of retelling of the *Dr. Jekyll and Mr. Hyde* story, he did not see *Knots and Crosses* as a crime novel and was surprised to win a mystery-reading audience. No doubt, those who love crime stories were intrigued by Rebus—who is, after all, named for a picture puzzle—and by the author's noir-style outlook on his city. But he embraced the genre more consciously and enthusiastically in his following books. He also became a popular spokesperson for Scottish crime writing, and was dubbed, by American writer James Ellroy, "the King of tartan noir." This kind of categorization is attention-getting, but what will be more lasting is Rankin's reputation for writing the satisfyingly introspective police procedural, set in the dark environs of a well-drawn city.

Under his own name, Rankin also wrote a spy novel, *The Watchman,* published in 1990. That same year saw publication of a mainstream novel set in the United States, *Westwind.* He has also written thrillers as Jack Harvey.

Rankin recalls his fascination with a huge funfair in Kirkcaldy near Fife. He remembers "a coming together of dodge 'ems and ghosts trains and penny arcades, stretched along the sea-front. It seemed to go on for miles—especially when I was a young kid. I wasn't the adventurous sort—no gravity-defying rides for me. I stuck to the slot machines and dodge 'ems. However, there would also be one or two palm-readers, working out of small caravans. These were oases of calm amid the noise and confusion. There were always chalkboards outside, advertising the worth of the palm-reader. I was never allowed to go in, and always a bit tentative anyway.

To me, those caravans represented secret knowledge, something I'd never have access to. Using a Gypsy Rose Lee–type character in my novel *Witch Hunt* got me interested again, and the result was 'The Hanged Man'."

The Hanged Man

2002

THE killer wandered through the fairground.

It was a traveling fair, and this was its first night in Kirkcaldy. It was a Thursday evening in April. The fair wouldn't get really busy until the weekend, by which time it would be missing one of its minor, if well-established, attractions.

He'd already made one reconnaissance past the small white caravan with its chalkboard outside. Pinned to the board were a couple of faded letters from satisfied customers. A double-step led to the bead curtain. The door was tied open with baling twine. He didn't think there was anyone in there with her. If there was, she'd have closed the door. But all the same, he wanted to be careful. "Care" was his byword.

He called himself a killer. Which was to say that if anyone had asked him what he did for a living, he wouldn't have used any other term. He knew some in the profession thought "assassin" had a more glamorous ring to it. He'd looked it up in a dictionary, found it was to do with some old religious sect and derived from an Arabic word meaning "eater of hashish." He didn't believe in drugs himself; not so much as a half of lager before the job.

Some people preferred to call it a "hit," which made them "hit men." But he didn't *hit* people; he killed them stone dead. And there were other, more obscure euphemisms, but the bottom line was, he was a killer. And for today, the fair was his place of work, his hunting ground.

Not that it had taken a magic ball to find the subject. She'd be in that caravan right now, waiting for a punter. He'd give it ten more minutes, just so he could be sure she wasn't with someone—not a punter necessarily; maybe sharing a cuppa with a fellow traveler. Ten minutes: If no one came out or went in, he'd make himself her next and final customer.

Of course, if she was a real fortuneteller, she'd know he was coming and would have hightailed it out of town. But he thought she was here. He knew she was.

He pretended to watch three youths on the firing range. They made the elementary mistake of aiming along the barrel. The sights, of course, had been skewed; probably the barrel, too. And if they thought they were going to dislodge one of the moving targets by hitting it . . . well, best think again. Those targets would be weighted, reinforced. The odds were always on the side of the showman.

The fair stretched along the waterfront. There was a stiff breeze making some of the wooden structures creak. People pushed hair out of their eyes, or tucked chins into the collars of their jackets. The place wasn't busy, but it was busy enough. He didn't stand out, nothing memorable about him at all. His jeans, lumberjack shirt, and trainers were work clothes: At home he preferred a bit more style. But he was a long way from home today. His base was on the west coast, just down the Clyde from Glasgow. He didn't know anything about Fife at all. Kirkcaldy, what little he'd seen of it, wouldn't be lingering in his memory. He'd been to towns all over Scotland and the north of England. In his mind they formed a geography of violence. In Carlisle he'd used a knife, making it look like a drunken Saturday brawl. In Peterhead it had been a blow to the head and strangulation, with orders that the body shouldn't ever be found—a grand and a half to a fishing-boat captain had seen to that. In Airdrie, Arbroath, Ardrossan . . . he didn't always kill. Sometimes all that was needed was a brutal and public message. In those cases he became the postman, delivering the message to order.

He moved from the shooting range to another stall, where children tried to attach hoops to the prizes on a carousel. They were faring little better than their elders next door. No surprise, with most of the prizes oh-so-slightly exceeding the circumference of each hoop. When he checked his watch, he was surprised to find that the ten minutes had passed. A final look around, and he climbed the steps, tapped at the open door, and parted the bead curtain.

"Come in, love," she said. Gypsy Rosa, the sign outside called her. Palms read, your fortune foretold. Yet here she was, waiting for him.

"Close the door," she instructed. He saw that the twine holding it open was looped over a bent nail. He loosed it, and closed the door. The curtains were shut—which was ideal for his purpose—and, lacking any light from outside, the interior glowed from the half-dozen candles spaced around it. The surfaces had been draped with lengths of cheap black cloth. There was a black cloth over the table, too, with patterns of sun and moon embroidered into it. And there she sat, gesturing for him to squeeze his large frame into the banquette opposite. He nodded. He smiled. He looked at her.

She was middle-aged, her face lined and rouged. She'd been a looker in younger days, he could see that, but scarlet lipstick now made her mouth look too large and moist. She wore black muslin over her head, a gold band holding it in place. Her costume looked authentic enough: black lace, red silk, with astrological signs sewn into the arms. On the table sat a crystal ball, covered for now with a white handkerchief. The red fingernails of one hand tapped against a tarot deck. She asked him his name.

"Is that necessary?" he asked.

She shrugged. "It helps sometimes." They were like blind dates alone in a restaurant, the world outside ceasing to matter. Her eyes twinkled in the candlelight.

"My name's Mort," he told her.

She repeated the name, seeming amused by it.

"Short for Morton. My father was born there."

"It's also the French for death," she added.

"I didn't know," he lied.

She was smiling. "There's a lot you don't know, Mort. That's why you're here. A palm reading, is it?"

"What else do you offer?"

"The ball." She nodded toward it. "The cards."

He asked which she would recommend. In turn, she asked if this was his first visit to a psychic healer—that's what she called herself, "a psychic healer": "Because I heal souls," she added by way of explanation.

"I'm not sure I need healing," he argued.

"Oh, my dear, we all need some kind of healing. We're none of us *whole*. Look at you, for example."

He straightened in his chair, becoming aware for the first time that she was holding his right hand, palm upward, her fingers stroking his knuckles. She looked down at the palm, frowned a little in concentration.

"You're a visitor, aren't you, dear?"

"Yes."

"Here on business, I'd say."

"Yes." He was studying the palm with her, as though trying to read its foreign words.

"Mmm." She began running the tip of one finger down the well-defined lines which crisscrossed his palm. "Not ticklish?" she chuckled. He allowed her the briefest of smiles. Looking at her face, he noticed it seemed softer than it had when he'd first entered the caravan. He revised her age downward, felt slight pressure as she seemed to squeeze his hand, as if acknowledging the compliment.

"Doing all right for yourself, though," she informed him. "I mean, moneywise; no problems there. No, dear, your problems all stem from your particular line of work."

"My work?"

"You're not as relaxed about it as you used to be. Time was, you wouldn't have considered doing anything else. Easy money. But it doesn't feel like that anymore, does it?"

It felt warm in the caravan, stuffy, with no air getting in and all those candles burning. There was the metal weight pressed to his groin, the weight he'd always found so reassuring in times past. He told himself she was using cheap psychology. His accent wasn't local; he wore no wedding ring; his hands were clean and manicured. You could tell a lot about someone from such details.

"Shouldn't we agree on a price first?" he asked.

"Why should we do that, dear? I'm not a prostitute, am I?" He felt his ears reddening. "And besides, you can afford it, we both know you can. What's the point of letting money get in the way?" She was holding his hand in an ever tighter grip. She had strength, this one: He'd bear that in mind when the time came. He wouldn't play around, wouldn't string out her suffering. A quick squeeze of the trigger.

"I get the feeling," she said, "you're wondering why you're here. Would that be right?"

"I know exactly why I'm here."

"What? Here with me? Or here on this planet, living the life you've chosen?"

"Either . . . both." He spoke a little too quickly, could feel his pulse rate rising. He had to get it down again, had to be calm when the time came. Part of him said, *Do it now.* But another part said, *Hear her out.* He wriggled, trying to get comfortable.

"What I meant, though," she went on, "is you're not sure anymore why you do what you do. You've started to ask questions." She looked up at him. "The line of business you're in, I get the feeling you're just supposed to do what you're told. Is that right?" He nodded. "No talking back, no questions asked. You just do your work and wait for payday."

"I get paid upfront."

"Aren't you the lucky one?" She chuckled again. "But the money's not enough, is it? It can never recompense for not being happy or fulfilled."

"I could have got that from my girlfriend's *Cosmopolitan*."

She smiled, then clapped her hands. "I'd like to try you with the cards. Are you game?"

"Is that what this is—a game?"

"You have your fun with words, dear. Euphemisms, that's all words are."

He tried not to gasp: It was as if she'd read his mind from earlier—all those euphemisms for "killer." She wasn't paying him any heed, was busy shuffling the outsized tarot deck. She asked him to touch the deck three times. Then she laid out the top three cards.

"Ah," she said, her fingers caressing the first one. "*Le soleil.* It means, the sun."

"I know what it means," he snapped.

She made a pout with her lips. "I thought you didn't know any French."

He was stuck for a moment. "There's a picture of the sun right there on the card," he said finally.

She nodded slowly. His breathing had quickened again.

"Second card," she said. "Death himself. *La mort.* Interesting that the French give it the feminine gender."

He looked at the picture of the skeleton. It was grinning, doing a little jig. On the ground beside it sat a lantern and an hourglass. The candle in the lantern had been snuffed out; the sand in the hourglass had all fallen through.

"Don't worry," she said, "it doesn't always portend a death."

"That's a relief," he said with a smile.

"The final card is intriguing—the hanged man. It can signify many things." She lifted it up so he could see it.

"And the three together?" he asked, curious now.

She held her hands as if in prayer. "I'm not sure," she said at last. "An unusual conjunction, to be sure."

"Death and the hanged man: a suicide maybe?"

She shrugged.

"Is the sex important? I mean, the fact that it is a man?"

She shook her head.

He licked his lips. "Maybe the ball would help," he suggested.

She looked at him, her eyes reflecting light from the candles. "You might be right." And she smiled. "Shall we?" As if they were but children, and the crystal ball little more than an illicit dare.

As she pulled the small glass globe toward them, he shifted again. The pistol barrel was chafing his thigh. He rubbed his jacket pocket, the one containing the silencer. He would have to hit her first, just to quiet her while he fitted the silencer to the gun.

Slowly, she lifted the handkerchief from the ball, as if raising the curtain on some miniaturized stage show. She leaned forward, peering into the glass, giving him a view of creped cleavage. Her hands flitted over the ball, not quite touching it. Had he been a gerontophile, there would have been a hint of the erotic to the act.

"Don't you go thinking that!" she snapped. Then, seeing the startled look on his face, she winked. "The ball often makes things clearer."

"What was I thinking?" he blurted out.

"You want me to say it out loud?"

He shook his head, looked into the ball, saw her face reflected there, stretched and distorted. And floating somewhere within was his own face, too, surrounded by licking flames.

"What do you see?" he asked, needing to know now.

"I see a man who is asking why he is here. One person has the answer, but he has yet to ask this person. He is worried about the thing he must do— rightly worried, in my opinion."

She looked up at him again. Her eyes were the color of polished oak. Tiny veins of blood seemed to pulse in the whites. He jerked back in his seat.

"You know, don't you?"

"Of course I know, Mort."

He nearly overturned the table as he got to his feet, pulling the gun from his waistband. "How?" he asked. "Who told you?"

She shook her head, not looking at the gun, apparently not interested in it. "It would happen one day. The moment you walked in, I felt it was you."

"You're not afraid." It was a statement rather than a question.

"Of course I'm afraid." But she didn't look it. "And a little sad, too."

He had the silencer out of his pocket, but was having trouble coordinating his hands. He'd practiced a hundred times in the dark and had never had this trouble before. He'd had victims like her, though: the ones who accepted, who were maybe even a little grateful,

"You know who wants you dead?" he asked.

She nodded. "I think so. I may have gotten the odd fortune wrong, but I've made precious few enemies in my life."

"He's a rich man."

"Very rich," she conceded. "Not all of it honest money. And I'm sure he's well used to getting what he wants." She slid the ball away, brought out the cards again, and began shuffling them. "So ask me your question,"

He was screwing the silencer onto the end of the barrel. The pistol was loaded, he only had to slide the safety off. He licked his lips again. So hot in here, so dry . . .

"Why?" he asked. "Why does he want a fortuneteller dead?"

She got up, made to open the curtains.

"No," he commanded, pointing the gun at her, sliding off the safety. "Keep them closed."

"Afraid to shoot me in daylight?" When he didn't answer, she pulled open one curtain, then blew out the candles. He kept the pistol trained on her: a head shot, quick and always fatal. "I'll tell you," she said, sliding into her seat again. She motioned for him to sit. After a moment's hesitation, he did so, the pistol steady in his right hand. Wisps of smoke from the extinguished candles rose either side of her.

"We were young when we met," she began. "I was already working in a fairground—not this one. One night, he decided there had been enough of a courtship." She looked deep into his eyes, his own oak-colored eyes. "Oh yes, he's used to getting what he wants. You know what I'm saying?" she went on quietly. "There was no question of consent. I tried to have the baby in secret, but it's hard to keep secrets from a man like him, a man with money, someone people fear. My baby was stolen from me. I began traveling then, and I've been traveling ever since. But always with my ear to the ground, always hearing things." Her eyes were liquid now. "You see, I knew a time would come when my baby would grow old enough to begin asking questions. And I knew the baby's father would not want the truth to come out." She reached out a shaking hand, reached past the gun to touch his cheek. "I just didn't think he'd be so cruel."

"Cruel?"

"So cruel as to send his own son—our son—to do his killing."

He shot to his feet again, banged his fists against the wall of the caravan. Rested his head there and screwed shut his eyes, the oak-colored eyes—mirrors of her own—which had told her all she'd needed to know. He'd left the pistol on the table. She lifted it, surprised by its weight, and turned it in her hand.

"I'll kill him," he groaned. "I swear, I'll kill him for this."

With a smile, she slid the safety catch on, placed the gun back on the table. When he turned back to her, blinking away tears, she looked quite calm, almost serene, as if her faith in him had been rewarded at last. In her hand, she was holding a tarot card.

The hanged man.

"It will need to look like an accident," she said. "Either that or suicide."

Outside, the screams of frightened children: waltzers and big wheel and ghost train. One of his hands fell lightly on hers, the other reaching for his pistol.

"Mother," he said, with all the tenderness his parched soul could muster.

CATHERINE AIRD

Catherine Aird is the pseudonym for Kinn Hamilton McIntosh, an English crime writer whose career has spanned nearly four decades. Aird is the author of a long-running series of detective novels centered on the work of Inspector C. D. "Seedy" Sloane, who solves crimes in the fictional county of Calleshire. Leavened with humor and witty observations about human nature, Aird's mysteries fit into the "cozy" category, but like so many of the best works in that school of writing, they often deliver more serious messages. Aird frequently sets her work in milieus and in the context of events that have been used effectively by earlier writers—the cathedral close, the country house, the garden maze, the village fete are examples—but she always keeps her point of view firmly anchored in the contemporary. As a result, she avoids writing dated or unrealistic fiction while still succeeding at winning readers who are nostalgic for the classic English way of life.

Aird was born and educated in Yorkshire. Her dream of becoming a physician was cut short when, while a young woman, she developed a life-threatening illness. Bedridden for several years, she recovered and became the manager and medical dispenser for her father's medical practice in Sturry, near Canterbury, where she still lives. Aird is an active member of village and parish committees, undertaking much voluntary work, and she has written several works of local history and *son et lumière* productions under the McIntosh name. Aird served as an editor of *The Oxford Companion to Crime & Mystery Writing* (1999), and she was chair of the British Crime Writers Association, an organization that presented her with a Lifetime Achievement Award.

Aird's short story "The Holly and the Poison Ivy" is published for the first time in *A New Omnibus of Crime*. Here we see an excellent example of the author's playfulness with conventions of the genre—notably the delivery of a deadly meal to one diner under the eyes of a family gathered around the table for a Christmas dinner. Characters' personalities are made memorable with an economy of words, and much is learned through bantering conversation. There's even the question of whether or not the butler (inadvertently) did it.

Aird comments, "There is a long tradition of crime short stories being set around Christmas-time, often set in the past, too. As I also enjoy writing about the edges of my own early memory, I combined the two in 'The Holly and the Poison Ivy.' The solving of the mystery hangs on a scientific fact. I would, though, have presented a very strange sight to anyone seeing me trying to demonstrate it to myself before I wrote about it."

The Holly and the Poison Ivy

2005

"So who's coming for Christmas dinner, then, Mum?" asked Joshua. "Friends, foes, or family?"

"Neighbors," said his mother.

Both her children groaned. Her parents-in-law politely said nothing.

Libby Hawkins smiled around the dining table at them all. "Besides, the family are here already—except Daddy, of course." Her husband's business activities presently lay in a distant land whose national holidays—and Holy Days—did not fall in the month of December.

"Which neighbors?" demanded her son.

"The Viponds . . . ," began Libby Hawkins.

"Oh, no," protested Joshua. "I can't stand him and his old jokes. I've heard them all a hundred times before. If not two hundred."

"The Bentleys . . . ," continued Libby serenely.

"He's so boring," said her daughter, Clare, "and I don't like her."

"Mr. Vipond does," remarked Joshua.

"Joshua," remonstrated his mother, "you shouldn't say things like that."

"Mrs. Bentley's a man-eater," insisted her son unrepentantly. "Even the milkman runs away from her, and the postman won't knock. Ever. If he's got a parcel, he just leaves it on the doorstep and scarpers."

"What we've all got to remember," said Libby Hawkins, "is that she's not a nut-eater." She turned to her mother-in-law. "Melissa Bentley's got an allergy to nuts so we shan't be having chestnut stuffing in the turkey."

"We didn't have any of those in my young days," said the old lady.

"What, no chestnut stuffing, Grandma?" said Joshua. "What a shame."

"No allergies," said his grandmother briskly. "Tell me, is Mr. Vipond's devotion to Mrs. Bentley reciprocated?"

"No," said Libby Hawkins, aware that the elderly were less reticent than the young and even more difficult to divert.

Joshua snorted. "She's got her claws into someone else, that's why. . . ."

Libby shot her son a warning glance.

"Who else is coming?" asked Clare into the silence.

"All right," sighed Libby. "If you must know, the Hellaby-Lumbs."

There were concerted moans from both her son and daughter.

"What have we done to deserve it?" asked Joshua histrionically, turning in appeal to his grandmother. "I couldn't have led a better life if I'd tried, now could I, Granny?"

"That I wouldn't know, Joshua," she said with gentle irony, "would I?"

"Rumors would have reached you for sure if I hadn't," he said gloomily. "Bound to have done."

"It's not what we've done to deserve it," pointed out Libby Hawkins. "It's what they're going to do for us. The Viponds have asked the whole family round for Boxing Day, and the Bentleys are having open house for the entire neighborhood on Christmas Eve."

"And the Hellaby-Lumbs?" asked Clare a little breathlessly.

"Don't tell her, Mummy," interrupted Joshua. "I bet it'll be the biggest bash of the lot. They're show-offs with attitude and too much money."

"New Year's Eve," said Libby mildly. "With some musical group or other playing."

"Which group?" asked Clare urgently. "Oh, Mummy, which group?"

"I don't know, darling. You'll have to ask them yourself."

Joshua Hawkins was silent for a while and then he murmured something to his grandmother that the rest of the family could not hear.

"It's rude to whisper," said Clare.

"You, Joshua," declared the old lady, suddenly sitting up very straight, "have been reading too many murder stories. That's your trouble."

"No, I haven't," said Joshua Hawkins.

"Murder stories," carried on his grandmother. "You've always got your nose buried in one."

"All I said, Granny, was that it would be quite fun to have a really old-fashioned Christmas this year. That's all."

"And what I am saying," insisted Arabella Hawkins firmly "is that the way you found out what you are pleased to imagine an old-fashioned Christmas was really like has been by reading all those Golden Age detective stories."

Joshua, as befitted the youth he was, considered this allegation carefully. "Well," he admitted, "I suppose you could say I wouldn't have known much about butlers otherwise."

"There you are, then."

"Although," admitted Joshua, "I must say that I still don't understand exactly what it was that butlers did. . . ."

"Damned if I ever knew myself," remarked his grandfather from the other side of the dining table. "A cushy number, if you ask me."

"Everything," said Mrs. Arabella Hawkins unexpectedly, her stern expression melting with sudden warmth. "Butlers did everything."

"I've always suspected that the Admirable Crichton wasn't all fiction," murmured Libby Hawkins drily. The presence in the house of her two elderly parents-in-law—to say nothing of the absence of her husband—in what was arguably the busiest week of the whole year was not a great help when it came to making preparations for the festive season. But everyone was trying to make the best of it in their own way.

"If we were to have a really old-fashioned Christmas," went on Joshua persuasively, "I could be the butler. That would really be fun and I wouldn't have to sit down with everyone either."

With wry detachment Libby Hawkins watched her son maneuvering them all into compliance with his wishes. One fine day Joshua was going to make a great salesman—one fine day, that is, when he had finished his education and could get a job: any job at all. At the moment, though, she realized that he was just a very bored young man who was doing his best to inject a little interest into a family Christmas made duller by his father's absence abroad. And, of course, to avoid sitting in his place at the head of the table on the day itself.

Joshua was saying innocently, "The butler must have done something to earn his oats, granddad."

"He saw to the drink, of course," said old Bertram Hawkins.

"In more ways than one, I expect," grinned Joshua, adding with mock solemnity, "Human nature doesn't change."

"And the cigars . . . all that sort of thing," Bertram Hawkins waved a hand.

"Ugh!" exclaimed Clare at once. "This house is a 'no smoking zone.' We're not having cigars here, are we, Mummy?"

Libby nodded absently in agreement. Her daughter was a born proselytizer: where she would end up was anyone's guess at the moment. At least Clare herself wasn't smoking anything—anything, that is, as far as she knew, added Libby mentally, her fingers crossed. That alone was something to be truly thankful for these days.

"And the silver," Arabella Hawkins reminded them all. "The butler always looked after the silver. He cleaned it and kept it in the safe in his pantry— you've heard about butlers' pantries and butlers' sinks, surely, haven't you, Joshua?"

Joshua, who had not thought about cleaning the silver, protested, "That wasn't man's work, surely."

"Sexist," said Clare promptly.

"Libby, dear," Mrs. Hawkins leaned forward. "What happened to that big old silver salver that we gave you?"

"It's in the att– . . . it's upstairs," Libby quickly amended her response. "I'll bring it down and Joshua can give it a good polish." A polish of any sort was something the salver hadn't had in years, but this was not the moment to say so.

"I'm sure that the maids would have laid the table anyway," insisted Joshua. "Clare can do that . . . and bring the food in here from the kitchen."

"Oh, she can, can she?" responded that young woman spiritedly. "Well, let me tell you, brother of mine, that . . ."

"But you'll have to be the maid," said Joshua unanswerably, "because there isn't anyone else."

"There aren't as many maids about as there used to be," remarked old Arabella Hawkins with deliberate ambiguity. She patted a stray wave of her white hair back into position. "Not these days."

"You can say that again, Granny," retorted Joshua, with a wicked grin. "Speaking for myself, I can only say that I haven't met many."

"The butler would see to all the napery, too," went on Arabella Hawkins, leaving everyone—but particularly Joshua—unsure whether he knew what she meant.

Her mother-in-law's circle, decided Libby silently, had probably used coded speech where Joshua's generation dealt in *double entendre*. She sat back and relaxed while her son had it explained to him that "napery" meant all the household table linen.

"Education isn't everything," remarked Clare, who hadn't yet decided whether she wanted to go to college or not. "Besides, we can't have a murder here at Christmas."

"Why not?" asked Joshua—as she had known he would.

"Because," said Clare, "though you can be the butler and I can be the maid, we haven't got a library for the body to be found in, that's why."

"We're not having a murder, darling," murmured Libby. "Just an old-fashioned Christmas."

"I don't see not having a library as an insuperable obstacle," began Joshua.

Libby decided against rising to this and said with the skill born of long maternal practice in diversionary tactics, "Don't forget that there's that lovely big white tablecloth which Granny gave us. I always keep it specially for Christmas."

"That belonged to my grandmother," said Arabella Hawkins complacently. "You don't see real linen like that these days."

Libby Hawkins made a mental note to see that the tablecloth was properly ironed in time, although exactly when she would do that, she wasn't sure. Her gaze drifted to the old-fashioned mirror hanging over the dining room sideboard. That, too, had come from her parents-in-law's old house, but it, at least, required nothing more than a gentle wipe before being garlanded with holly and ivy for the festive season.

"I do wish so many of the napkins hadn't disappeared over the years, Libby, dear," her mother-in-law was saying. "It was the laundry, you know."

"Paper napkins will do just as well," said Libby, thinking that it wouldn't be long before "laundry" was nearly as archaic a word as "butler." "They're so pretty these days."

"Tell me," enquired Arabella Hawkins, "will the gentleman in whom you say Melissa Bentley has got her claws be with us at Christmas, too?"

"Yes. It's Mr. Hellaby-Lumb, poor fish," said Joshua.

"Ah," remarked Arabella Hawkins. "How interesting."

"Anything else, Granny, that you can remember?" asked Clare. "About Christmas in the old days, I mean."

A reminiscent look came over Arabella Hawkins's lined face. "Lots of lovely things to eat but best of all were the Elvas plums."

Libby made a mental note to lay in a supply of crystallized fruit.

"But what I really remember about the Christmases when I was young was how lovely the dinner table looked." She gave a sweet smile. "And, Joshua . . ."

"Yes, Granny?"

"That was the butler's job."

Clare made a face at him.

"What made it so beautiful?" asked Libby swiftly.

"The epergne," said the old lady.

"All right, Granny," said Joshua. "I surrender. What's an epergne?"

"A table center with lots of little dishes hanging from it with pretty things to eat in them—bon-bons and chocolates . . ."

Libby mentally added sugared almonds to her shopping list. Melissa Bentley needn't eat them.

"And," continued her mother-in-law, well back in her own childhood now, "the epergne would have been decorated all over with trailing ivy. That looked really lovely against the white cloth."

Libby relaxed. There was ivy in the garden and she and Clare could do something pretty with it round the old silver candelabrum, another gift that had been relegated to the attic. It really wasn't any wonder that silver had gone so out of fashion—cleaning that, too, would keep Joshua busy.

"And when I was a lad," contributed Bertram Hawkins, "they used something called smilax on the table center instead." He grinned. "Got you there, haven't I, Joshua? We didn't have any murders but I bet you don't know what smilax is."

"Sounds like a patent medicine, Grandpa."

"A climbing species of asparagus that people used to use for decoration." He sat back in his chair. "And no, you didn't eat it."

In the end the smilax was about the only feature that was missing from the table on Christmas Day. Libby had enhanced the effect of the candelabrum and its red candles by placing it on the large silver salver retrieved from the back of the attic and polished back into brightness. She had draped the substitute epergne with ivy and Clare had contrived to hang a little dish of sweetmeats from each branch. Her mother-in-law, pleased, pronounced it as good an epergne as she had seen in years.

Joshua, bustling about with a corkscrew, had paused to admire it, too. "I like the mirror effect of the salver."

"Stop slacking, Narcissus," commanded Clare, "and give me a hand with these side-plates instead of admiring your own reflection."

"I don't have a reflection," said Joshua. "I'm a vampire."

By evening all was ready. Joshua answered the front door with aplomb, announced the guests with considerable *empressement* and dispensed the drinks before withdrawing to collapse, helpless with laughter, behind the kitchen door.

"Don't!" pleaded Clare. "I'm sure I'm going to giggle when I go in. I can't help it."

"Mr. Hellaby-Lumb liked it when I called him 'sir,'" said Joshua.

"I'll bet."

He grinned. "But I could tell that Mrs. Bentley didn't care one little bit for the way I called her 'madam.'"

"Joshua, you are awful."

"Mr. Vipond can't take his eyes off her but she's trying to get her claws into Mr. Hellaby-Lumb, the poor fish."

"Well," said Clare with the unconscious realism of the young, "he is the one with the money."

"Money isn't everything."

"Want to bet?" she said, starting off in the direction of the dining room with the soup. "Just light the candles, will you, and then you can tell everyone that dinner is served."

Libby Hawkins picked up her soupspoon and relaxed. Joshua and Clare were clearly enjoying acting in their new roles, and the guests had entered into the Christmas spirit with evident relish.

"Are they open to offers of work?" asked Gordon Hellaby-Lumb jovially as they reached the coffee stage. "They're as good as those professionals we've got lined up for New Year's Eve, aren't they, my dear?"

Mrs. Hellaby-Lumb gave a remote smile, her eyes not leaving Melissa Bentley. That lady had devoted her evening to chatting up Mr. Hellaby-Lumb. And Mr. Vipond had spent all his time making sheep's eyes at Mrs. Bentley— to her obvious enjoyment and in spite of the equally apparent misgivings of Mrs. Vipond.

The boring Mr. Bentley, sitting between Mrs. Vipond and Mrs. Hellaby-Lumb, had been dull but courteously attentive to both while studiously appearing not to notice his wife's outrageous flirting with Gordon Hellaby-Lumb and her occasional titillating encouragement of Paul Vipond. Melissa Bentley was sitting between her two admirers, almost invisible from her husband, and was clearly enjoying herself mightily behind the shelter of the epergne. At the head of the table Bertram Hawkins was taking pleasure from watching his grandchildren milking what fun they could from acting as butler and parlormaid. What Arabella Hawkins was thinking was anyone's guess. Her shrewd old eyes were darting about, watching everyone, and missing nothing.

This was just as well. Her observations were to prove very helpful when she came to describe the evening again and again to Detective Inspector Sloan, head of the tiny Criminal Investigation Department of the Berebury Police Force. This was after the sudden death of Melissa Bentley from an acute anaphylactic reaction to nuts.

"She drank some coffee, Inspector," said Arabella Hawkins, "just a sip, I should say . . . then she started to complain that her mouth and throat were burning."

The detective inspector nodded.

"And almost immediately after that her hands and face started to swell. This was before she collapsed, of course. She was dead before the ambulance arrived." Arabella Hawkins did not sound too disturbed at this. It was Libby and the children who were too distraught to be comforted.

They still had to be questioned, though.

"If," said Detective Inspector Sloan patiently to Joshua, "we might go through everything once more. . . ."

"Like I said," repeated Joshua for the fourth or fifth time, "Clare made the coffee in the kitchen and brought it through to the dining room."

"And?"

"And she stood the pot over there." He waved a hand in the direction of the sideboard under the big mirror. "The coffee cups were there already. And there wasn't anything in them then," he added defiantly.

"What were you doing at the time?" Detective Inspector Sloan wasn't completely *au fait* himself with the arcane duties of Joshua's temporary office but he did not say so. "Were you still butlering?"

"Putting the nuts and crystallized fruit on the table . . ." Joshua said dully. "With the dates and the figs."

"Then?"

"Clare poured out the coffee and I passed the cups down the table to everyone."

"You didn't hand them round yourself?"

"No. I just took them from Clare and put them on the table." He looked at the policeman and said belligerently, "I know that's not the right thing to do but Clare and I were only doing this for a lark. We hadn't ever done it before."

"What about the cream?" asked Sloan, pointing to a jug.

"I passed it down after the coffee, with the sugar." Joshua scowled. "And, no, I didn't put anything in the cups except coffee."

"Quite so." Detective Inspector Sloan didn't for one moment suppose that he had. As the policeman saw it, any motive for handing a fatal dose of nuts to Melissa Bentley lay between Mrs. Vipond and Mrs. Hellaby-Lumb, with her husband, Paul Bentley, also well in the running. The man might well be as dull as everyone said he was, but even so, to Sloan's more experienced eye he didn't have the look of a *mari complaisant:* more one of a vengeful man suppressing great anger. "Then what?"

"Mr. Vipond accidentally put some cream in a coffee that Mrs. Bentley wanted black."

"And?" Detective Inspector Sloan didn't think that old aphorism about always killing the thing you loved applied to Mr. Vipond, but he couldn't be overlooked.

"So Mrs. Bentley passed the cup back across the table—round that candlestick thing to her husband who does take cream in his coffee and someone else passed a black coffee back for her instead through—or, rather, round—the centerpiece." He gulped. "I think that must have been the one that Mrs. Bentley had—the one that had the nut in it."

So did Detective Inspector Sloan. The fingerprint people weren't prepared to commit themselves. The elegant little eggshell handles of the hastily cleared coffee cups had been singularly unrevealing in this respect. "Who handed it to her?"

Joshua suddenly looked defenseless. "I don't know for sure. It was difficult to see across the table from where I was standing what with all that ivy trailing round and anyway I was still pouring the coffee. All I saw for sure when I looked down from my side of the table was a hand with a cup in it reflected in the silver salver coming out from under all the ivy."

"Man's or woman's?"

"Woman's." That, at least, he was sure about.

"Right or left?"

He paused for thought. "Left from where I saw it reflected on the salver—that means it would have been her right, doesn't it?"

The inspector didn't answer this. "Wedding ring?" he asked instead.

"I couldn't see that because there was a cup in her hand."

Clare had only seen things through the mirror above the sideboard. She stood in front of it now and tried to explain. "I heard them talking about Mrs. Bentley having cream in her coffee when she didn't like it." She gave a little shiver. "It reminded me of Cecily Cardew putting sugar in Gwendolen Fairfax's tea just because she didn't want it in *The Importance of Being Earnest*, Inspector."

"Really, miss?" In his book there were even more important things than being earnest. There was being right in the important matter of murder. "Now, suppose you tell me exactly what you saw in your mirror. . . ." Sloan went and stood beside Clare, both of them facing the sideboard and the great mirror above it.

Mrs. Vipond, Mr. Bentley, and Mrs. Hellaby-Lumb, all sitting on the side of the table opposite Melissa Bentley, had been uniformly vague about what they had and hadn't seen. In fact, they had reminded Detective Inspector Sloan of nothing so much as the three monkeys who saw no evil, heard no evil, and spoke no evil. And weren't going to, either. In one way or another Melissa Bentley's behavior had been a threat to all three.

"I just saw a hand passing over a cup of coffee that was going across the table, Inspector," said Clare, still very shaken and tearful. "I had my back to the table, getting the cups ready for Joshua, like we are now, and I was rather in the way of the reflection of the person themselves so I didn't see who it was." Mr. Vipond and Mr. Hellaby-Lumb on the other side of the table had declared that they had not noticed anything at all, being busy with passing more cups round. The adult Hawkinses had similarly noticed nothing.

"Left or right hand?" he asked Clare patiently.

Clare raised her own hand in front of the mirror. "My right, so her left," she said promptly, "because it would be a mirror-image, wouldn't it?"

Detective Inspector Sloan left her standing in front of the mirror while he went back to the table and sat where Mrs. Hellaby-Lumb had been sitting. He advanced his own right hand across the table.

"No, Inspector," said Clare. "Your other hand."

Obligingly, he put out his left hand.

"That's right. That's the one I saw."

He turned to Joshua and asked him to stand where he had been earlier, looking down at the reflection in the salver. Sloan put out his own hand again.

"Tell me again which hand you saw come round from the other side of the table in the salver."

"A left hand," he said promptly. "Her right, I suppose."

Detective Inspector Sloan shook his head.

"We can't both be right," wailed Clare, dismayed.

He smiled benignly. "Oh, yes, you can."

"Someone's going to get away with murder," muttered Joshua, who suddenly discovered that he minded about this.

"No, they aren't," said the Inspector. "Two witnesses should be enough for any prosecution."

"But what about us?" stammered Joshua. "We don't agree."

"We saw different hands," said Clare starting to cry again.

"The lawyers will make mincemeat of either Clare or me," said Joshua, feeling suddenly less grown-up than he liked.

His sister shivered. "Of both of us, I expect."

Detective Inspector Sloan explained himself. "If a mirror is parallel to an image it reverses it from left to right."

"That's right," agreed Clare eagerly. "Like the mirror on the wall."

The policeman nodded. "But when the mirror is at ninety degrees to the image . . ."

"As the salver was," agreed Joshua, greatly puzzled. "It was flat on the table."

"And you saw the image while you were standing up."

"True, but . . ."

"When it reverses the image top to bottom instead of right to left," finished Detective Inspector Sloan. "You both saw the same hand over the coffee cup— Mrs. Hellaby-Lumb's left one. Mrs. Vipond would only have been able to get her right one into that position by leaning across Mr. Bentley."

Clare swallowed as her natural realism reasserted itself. "I suppose you could say Mrs. Hellaby-Lumb had the most to lose. . . ."

"She had means, motive, and opportunity," said Joshua, recovering some of his aplomb. "And you have two witnesses." Turning politely to the police inspector, he resumed his butler mode and asked, "Will that be all, sir?"

"Yes, thank you, Hawkins," said Detective Inspector Sloan, entering into the spirit of things. "For the time being, anyway."

JEFFERY DEAVER

Jeffery Deaver did not have to turn to crime writing to make a living. He had already worked as a journalist, folksinger, and attorney when he began turning out thrillers. His first book, *Manhattan Is My Beat* (1988), uses the multi-layered approach the author employs to great advantage in much of his following work. Here a young punk who works in a video store tries to solve the murder of her favorite customer, a man who repeatedly rented the same movie. Art and reality overlap as the punk, who calls herself Rune, seeks answers to the killing in the film itself.

Rune aspires to be a filmmaker and solves more crimes in two more novels, *Death of a Blue Movie Star* (1990) and *Hard News* (1991). After writing these books, Deaver produced five more thrillers featuring a variety of characters who find themselves in terrible jeopardy. Perhaps the most tense of them is the 1995 novel *A Maiden's Grave*, in which an escaped murderer takes hostage a busload of deaf girls.

If these books were thrillers, Deaver's next book, *The Bone Collector* (1997), is a chiller. It is also notable because it introduces Lincoln Rhyme, a quadriplegic sleuth who pits his brainpower against a serial killer in a beat-the-clock effort to understand the puzzling clues that the killer leaves. Unable to move any part of his body except his finger, Rhyme must rely on the physical work of Amy Sachs, a green new cop who must cut her teeth on this grisly case. The book was made into a film starring Denzel Washington and Angelina Jolie.

Deaver went on to write more Lincoln Rhyme books and some titles apart from that series, including the 2004 novel *Garden of Beasts*, which is set in Nazi Germany, and the 2005 novel *The Twelfth Card*, in which Rhyme and Sachs pursue a hit man who targets a schoolgirl and leaves the eponymous twelfth card of the tarot deck—the one depicting The Hanged Man—at the scene of a crime. He also published an anthology, *Twisted: Collected Stories of Jeffery Deaver, Volume I*, in 2003.

The following short story is printed for the first time in this *Omnibus*. Deaver told us, " 'Copycat' is first and foremost a short story with what I hope is a spine-jarring twist. But it's also a look at a writer's confrontation with his or her fiction. To what extent does a writer have a responsibility to society to write about crime or refrain from writing about it? Of course there's more to this lofty premise than there seems to be."

Copycat

2002

I

DETECTIVE Quentin Altman rocked back, his chair squealing with the tell-tale caw of aging government furniture, and eyed the narrow, jittery man sitting across from him. "Go on," the cop said.

"So I check out this book from the library. Just for the fun of it. I never do that, just read a book for the fun of it. I mean, *never*. I don't get much time off, you know."

Altman hadn't known this but he could certainly have deduced it. Wallace Gordon was the Greenville *Tribune*'s sole crime reporter and must've spent sixty, seventy hours a week banging out copy, to judge by the number of stories appearing under his byline every day.

"And I'm reading along and—"

"What is it you're reading?"

"A novel—a murder mystery. I'll get to that. . . . I'm reading along and I'm irritated," the reporter continued, "because somebody'd circled some passages. In a *library* book."

Altman grunted distractedly. He was head of Homicide in a burgh with a small-town name but big-city crime statistics. The fifty-something detective was busy and he didn't have much time for reporters with crackpot theories. There were twenty-two folders of current cases on his desk and here Wallace was delivering some elliptical message about defaced books.

"I don't pay much attention at first but I go back and reread one of the circled paragraphs. It jogs my memory. Anyway, I checked the morgue—"

"Morgue?" Altman frowned, rubbing his wiry red hair, which showed not a strand of gray.

"*Our* morgue, not yours. In the newspaper office. All the old stories."

"Got it. How 'bout getting to the point?"

"I found the articles about the Kimberly Banning murder."

Quentin Altman grew more attentive. Twenty-eight-year-old Kimberly had been strangled to death eight months ago. The murder occurred two weeks after a similar killing—of a young female grad student. The two deaths appeared to be the work of the same person but there were few forensic leads and no motive that anyone could determine. The cases prompted a taskforce investigation but eventually the suspects were cleared and the case grew cold.

Tall and gaunt, with tendons and veins rising from his pale skin, reporter Wallace tried—usually unsuccessfully—to tone down his intimidating physique and face with brown tweed jackets, corduroy slacks and pastel shirts. He asked the cop, "You remember how the whole town was paranoid after the first girl was killed? And how everybody was double locking their doors and never letting strangers into their houses?"

Altman nodded.

"Well, look at this." The reporter pulled latex gloves out of his pocket and put them on.

"Why the gloves, Wallace?"

The man ignored the question and dug a book out of his battered briefcase. Altman got a look at the title. *Two Deaths in a Small Town.* He'd never heard of it.

"This was published six months *before* the first killing." He opened the book to a yellow Post-it tab and pushed it forward. "Read those paragraphs." The detective pulled on his CVS drugstore glasses and leaned forward.

The Hunter knew that now that he'd killed once, the town would be more alert than ever. Its soul would be edgier, its collective nerves would be as tense as an animal trap's blue-steel spring. Women would not stroll the streets alone and those who did would be looking around constantly, alert for any risk. Only a fool would let a stranger into her house and the Hunter did not enjoy killing fools.

So on Tuesday night he waited until bedtime—11:00 p.m.—and then slipped onto Maple Street. There, he doused a parked convertible's roof with gasoline and ignited the pungent, amber liquid. A huge whoosh. . . . He hid in the bushes and, hypnotized by the tornado of flames and ebony smoke swirling into the night sky above the dying car, he waited. In ten minutes behemoths of fire trucks roared up the street, their wailing sirens drawing people from their homes to find out what the excitement might be.

Among those on the sidewalk was a young, demure blonde with a heart-shaped face, Clara Steading. This was the woman the Hunter knew he had to possess—possess completely. She was love incarnate, Amore herself, she was Beauty, she was Passion. . . . And she was also completely ignorant of her role as the object of his demented desire. Clara shivered in her bathrobe, standing on the sidewalk, along with a clutch of chattery neighbors, as they watched the firemen extinguish the blaze and offered words of sympathy to the dismayed owner of the car, who lived a few doors away.

Finally the onlookers grew bored, or repulsed by the bitter smell of the burnt rubber and plastic, and they returned to their beds or their late-night snacks or their mind-numbing TV. But their vigilance didn't flag; the moment they stepped inside, every one of them locked their doors and windows carefully—to make certain that the strangler would not wreak his carnage in their homes.

Though in Clara Steading's case, her diligence in securing the deadbolt and chains had a somewhat different effect: locking the Hunter inside with her.

"Jesus," Altman muttered. "That's just what happened in the Kimberly Banning case, how the perp got inside. He set fire to a car."

"A convertible," Wallace added. "And then I went back and found some passages that'd been marked. One of them was about how the killer had stalked his victim by pretending to work for the city and trimming the plants in a park across from her apartment."

This was just how the first victim of the Greenville Strangler, the pretty grad student, had been stalked.

Wallace point out several other passages, marked with asterisks. There were margin notes too. One said, "Check this one out. Important." Another jotting was "Used distraction." And: "Disposing of body. Note this."

"So the killer's a copycat," Altman murmured. "He used the novel for research."

Which meant that there could be evidence in the book that might lead to the perp: fingerprints, ink, handwriting. Hence, the reporter's *CSI* gloves.

Altman stared at the melodramatic dust jacket on the novel—a drawing of a man's silhouette peering into the window of a house. The detective pulled on his own latex gloves and slipped the book into an evidence envelope. He nodded at the reporter and said a heartfelt, "Thanks. We haven't had a lead on this one in over eight months."

Walking into the office next to his—that of his assistant, a young crew-cut detective named Josh Randall—he instructed the man to take the book to the county lab for analysis. When he returned, Wallace was still sitting expectantly in the hard chair across from Altman's desk.

Altman wasn't surprised he hadn't left. "And the quid pro quo?" the detective asked. "For your good deed?"

"I want an exclusive. What else?"

"I figured."

Altman didn't mind this in theory; cold cases were bad for the department's image and solving cold cases was good for a cop's career. Not to mention that there was still a killer out there. He'd never liked Wallace, though, who always seemed a little out of control in a spooky way and was as irritating as most crusaders usually are.

"Okay, you've got an exclusive," Altman said. "I'll keep you posted." He rose, then paused. Waited for Wallace to leave.

"Oh, I'm not going anywhere, my friend."

"This's an official investigation—"

"And it wouldn't've been one without me. I want to write this one from the inside out. Tell my readers how a homicide investigation works from your point of view."

Quentin Altman argued some more but in the end he gave in, feeling he had no choice. "All right. But just don't get in my way. You do that, you're out of here."

"Wouldn't think of it." Wallace frowned an eerie look into his long, toothy face. "I might even be helpful." Maybe it was a joke but there was nothing humorous about the delivery. He then looked up at the detective. "So whatta we do next?"

"Well, *you're* going to cool your heels. *I'm* going to review the case file."

"But—"

"Relax, Wallace. Investigations take time. Sit back, take your jacket off. Enjoy our wonderful coffee."

Wallace glanced at the closet that served as the police station's canteen. He rolled his eyes and the ominous tone of earlier was replaced with a laugh. "Funny. I didn't know they still made instant."

The detective winked and ambled down the hall on his aching bones.

II

Quentin Altman hadn't run the Greenville Strangler case.

He'd worked on it some—the whole department'd had a piece of the case—but the officer in charge had been Bob Fletcher, a sergeant who'd been on the force forever. Fletcher, who'd never remarried after his wife left him some years before and was childless, had devoted his life to his job after the divorce and seemed to take his inability to solve the Strangler case hard; the soft-spoken man had actually given up a senior spot in Homicide and transferred to Robbery. Altman was now glad for the sergeant's sake that there was a chance to nail the killer who'd eluded him.

Altman wandered down to Robbery with the news about the novel and to see if Fletcher knew anything about it. The sergeant, though, was out in the field at the moment and so Altman left a message and then dove into the cluttered and oppressively hot records room. He found the Strangler files easily; the folders sported red stripes on the side, a harsh reminder that, while this might've been a cold case, it was still very much open.

Returning to his office, he sat back, sipping the, yeah, disgusting instant coffee, and read the file, trying to ignore Wallace's incessant scribbling on his steno pad, the scratchy noise irritatingly audible throughout the office. The events of the murders were well documented. The perp had broken into two women's apartments and strangled them. There'd been no rape, sexual molestation or postmortem mutilation. Neither woman had ever been stalked or threatened by former boyfriends and, though Kimberly had recently purchased some condoms, none of her friends knew that she'd been dating. The other victim, Becky Winthrop, her family said, hadn't dated for over a year.

Sergeant Fletcher had carried out a by-the-book investigation but most killings of this sort, without witnesses, motive, or significant trace found at the scene, are generally not solved without the help of an informant—often a friend or acquaintance of the perp. But, despite extensive press coverage of the investigation and pleas on TV by the mayor and Fletcher, no one had come forward with any information about possible suspects.

An hour later, just as he closed the useless file, Altman's phone rang. The documents department had blown up images of the handwriting and was prepared to compare these to any samplers found elsewhere, though until such specimens were found the officers could do nothing.

The techs had also checked for any impression evidence—to see if the killer had written something on, say, a Post-it note on top of one of the pages—but found nothing.

A ninhydrin analysis revealed a total of nearly two hundred latent fingerprints on the three pages on which the marked paragraphs appeared and another eighty on the jacket. Unfortunately many of them were old and only fragments. Technicians had located a few that were clear enough to be identified and had run them through the FBI's integrated automated fingerprint identification system in West Virginia. But all the results had come back negative.

The cover of the book, wrapped in print-friendly cellophane, yielded close to four hundred prints but they too were mostly smudges and fragments. IAFIS had provided no positive IDs for these either.

Frustrated, Altman thanked the technician and hung up.

"So what was that about?" Wallace asked, looking eagerly at the sheet of paper in front of Altman, which contained both notes on the conversation he'd just had—and a series of compulsive doodles.

He explained to the reporter about the forensic results.

"So no leads," Wallace summarized and jotted a note, leaving the irritated detective to wonder why the reporter'd actually found it necessary to write this observation down.

As he gazed at the reporter an idea occurred to Altman and he stood up abruptly. "Let's go."

"Where?"

"Your crime scene."

"Mine?" Wallace asked, scrabbling to follow the detective as he strode out the door.

III

The library near Gordon Wallace's apartment, where he'd checked out the novel *Two Deaths in a Small Town,* was a branch in the Three Pines neighborhood of Greenville, so named because legend had it that three trees in a park here had miraculously survived the fire of 1829, which had destroyed the rest of the town. It was a nice area, populated mostly by businessmen, professionals, and educators; the college was nearby (the same school where the first Strangler victim had been a student).

Altman followed Wallace inside and the reporter found the head of the branch, introduced her to the detective. Mrs. McGiver was a trim woman dressed in stylish gray; she looked more like a senior executive with a high-tech company than a librarian.

The detective explained how they suspected the book had been used by a copycat as a model for the killings. Shock registered on the woman's face as she realized that the Strangler was somebody who'd been to her library. Perhaps he was even someone she knew.

"I'd like a list of everybody who checked out that book." Altman had considered the possibility that the killer might not have checked it out but had merely looked through it here, in the library itself. But that meant he'd have to underline the passages in public and risk drawing the attention of librarians or patrons. He concluded that the only safe way for the Strangler to do his homework was at home.

"I'll see what I can find," she said.

Altman had thought that it might take days to pull together this information but Mrs. McGiver was back in minutes. Altman felt his gut churning with excitement as he gazed at the sheets of paper in her hand, relishing the sensations of the thrill of the hunt and pleasure at finding a fruitful lead.

But as he flipped through the sheets, he frowned. Every one of the thirty or so people checking out *Two Deaths* had done so recently—within the last six months. They needed the names of those who'd checked it out *before* the killings eight months ago. He explained this to her.

"Oh, but we don't have records that far back. Normally we would, but about six months ago our computer was vandalized."

"Vandalized?"

She nodded, frowning. "Somebody poured battery acid or something into the hard drives. Ruined them and destroyed all our records. The backup too. Somebody from your department handled the case. I don't remember who."

Wallace said, "I didn't hear about it."

"They never found who did it. It was very troubling but more of an inconvenience than anything. Imagine if he'd decided to destroy the books themselves."

Altman caught Wallace's eye. "Dead end," the cop angrily. Then he asked the librarian, "How 'bout the names of everybody who had a library card then? Were their names in the computer too?"

She nodded. "Prior to six months ago, they're gone too. I'm sorry."

Forcing a smile onto his face, he thanked the librarian and walked to the doorway. But he stopped so suddenly that Wallace nearly slammed into his back.

"What?" the reporter asked.

Altman ignored him and hurried back to the main desk, calling out, "Mrs. McGiver! Hold up there! I need you to find out something for me."

Drawing glares and a couple of harsh *shhhh*'s from readers.

IV

The author of *Two Deaths in a Small Town*, Andrew M. Carter, lived in Hampton Station, near Albany, about two hours away from Greenville.

Mrs. McGiver's copy of *Who's Who in Contemporary Mystery Writing* didn't include street addresses or phone numbers, but Altman called the DMV and they tracked down the specifics.

The idea that occurred to Altman as he was leaving the library was that Carter might've gotten a fan letter from the Strangler. Maybe he'd written to express some admiration, maybe he'd asked for more information or how the author had done his research. If there was such a letter the county forensic handwriting expert could easily link the notation with the fan, who—if they were lucky—might have signed his real name to the letter and included his address.

Mentally crossing his fingers he placed a call to the author. A woman answered. "Hello?"

"I'm Detective Altman with the Greenville Police Department," he said. "I'd like to speak to Andrew Carter."

"I'm his wife," she said. "He's not available." The matter-of-fact tone in her voice suggested that this was her knee-jerk response to all such calls.

"When will he be available?"

"This is about the murders, isn't it?"

"That's right, ma'am."

A hesitation. "The thing is. . . ." Her voice lowered and Altman suspected that her unavailable husband was in a nearby room. "He hasn't been well."

"I'm sorry," Altman said. "Is it serious?"

"You bet it's serious," she said angrily. "When the news got out that Andy's book, you know, inspired somebody to kill those girls he got real depressed. He cut himself off from everybody. He stopped writing." She hesitated. "He stopped *everything*. He just gave up."

"Must've been difficult, Mrs. Carter," Altman said sympathetically, reflecting that reporter Wallace wasn't the first person to wonder if the novel had inspired a copycat.

"You have no idea. I told him it was just a coincidence—those women getting killed like he wrote in the book. Just a weird coincidence. But these reporters and, well, *everybody*, friends, neighbors. . . . They kept yammering on and on about how Andy was to blame."

Altman supposed she wasn't going to like the fact he'd found proof that her husband's book had probably been the model for the killings.

She continued, "He's been getting better lately. Anything about the case could set him back."

"I do understand that, ma'am, but you have to see my situation. We've got a possibility of catching the killer and your husband could be real helpful. . . ."

The sound on the other end of the line grew muffled and Altman could hear her talking to someone else.

Quentin Altman wasn't surprised when she said, "My husband just got back. I'll put him on."

"Hello?" came a soft, uneasy voice. "This's Andy Carter."

Altman identified himself.

"Were you the policeman I talked to a while back?"

"Me? No. That might've been the case detective. Sergeant Bob Fletcher."

"Right. That was the name."

So Fletcher *had* talked to the author. There was no reference in the case file that he recalled. He must've missed it. He reiterated to Carter what he'd told the author's wife and the man said immediately, "I can't help you. And frankly, I don't *want* to. . . . This's been the worst time of my life."

"I appreciate that, sir. But that killer's still free. And—"

"But I don't *know* anything. I mean, what could I possible tell you that—"

"We may have a sample of the killer's handwriting—we found some notes in a copy of your book that make us think he might've written them. And we'd like to compare it to any letters from fans you might've received."

There was a long pause. Finally the author whispered, "So he *did* use my book as a model."

In a kind voice Altman said, "It's looking that way, Mr. Carter. The underlined passages are the ones that fit the M.O. of the two murders. I'm afraid they're identical."

Altman heard nothing for a moment then he asked, "Sir, are you all right?"

The author cleared his throat. "I'm sorry. I can't help you. I just. . . . It'd be too much for me."

Quentin Altman often told young officers who worked for him that a detective's most important trait is persistence. He said in an even voice, "You're the only one who can help us trace the book back to the killer. He destroyed the library computer so we don't have the names of who checked out your book. There's no match on the fingerprints either. . . . I want to catch this man real bad. And I suspect you do too, Mr. Carter. Don't you, now?"

There was no response. Finally the faint voice continued, "Do you know that *strangers* sent me clippings about the killings? Perfect strangers. Hundreds of them. They blamed *me*. They called my book a 'blueprint for murder.' I had to go into the hospital for a month afterwards, I was so depressed. . . . I *caused* those murders! Don't you understand that?"

Altman looked up at Wallace and shook his head.

The reporter gestured for the phone. Altman figured, Why not?

"Mr. Carter, there's a person here I'm going to put on the line. I'd like him to have a word with you."

"Who?"

The cop handed the receiver over and sat back, listening to the one-sided conversation.

"Hello, Mr. Carter." The reporter's gaunt frame hunched over the phone and he gripped the receiver in astonishingly long, strong fingers. "You don't know me. My name is Wallace Gordon. I'm a fan of your book—I loved it. I'm a reporter for the *Tribune* here in Greenville. . . . I got that. I understand how you feel—my colleagues step over a lot of lines. But I don't operate that way. And I know you're reluctant to get involved here. I'm sure you've been through a tough time but let me just say one thing: I'm no talented novelist like you— I'm just a hack journalist—but I *am* a writer and if I have any important belief in my life it's in the freedom to write whatever moves us. Now. . . . No, please, Mr. Carter, let me finish. I heard that you stopped writing after the murders. . . . Well, you and your talent were as much a victim of those crimes as those women were. You exercised your God-given right to express yourself and a terrible accident happened. That's how I'd look at this madman: an act of God. You can't do anything about those women. But you can help yourself and your family to move on. . . . And there's something else to consider: You're in a position to make sure nobody else ever gets hurt by this guy again."

Altman lifted an impressed eyebrow at the reporter's sales pitch. Wallace held the receiver to his ear for a moment, listening. Finally he nodded and glanced at Altman. "He wants to talk to you."

Altman took the phone. "Yessir?"

"What exactly would you want me to do?" came the tentative voice through phone.

"All I need is to go through the fan mail you got about the book."

A bitter laugh. "Hate mail, you mean. That's mostly what I got.

"Whatever you received. We're mostly interested in handwritten letters, so we can match physical evidence. But any emails you got, we'd like to see too."

A pause. Was he going to balk? Then the detective heard the man say, "It'll take me a day or two. I kind of stopped. . . . Well, let me just say things haven't been too organized around my office lately."

"That's fine." Altman gave the author the directions to the police station and told him to wear kitchen gloves and handle the handwritten letters by the edges to make sure he didn't mess up the fingerprints.

"All right," Carter said sullenly.

Altman wondered if he'd really come. He started to tell the author how much he appreciated the help but after a moment he realized that the man had hung up and he was listening to dead air.

V

Andy Clark did indeed make the journey to Greenville.

He turned out not to resemble either a sinister artist or a glitzy celebrity but rather any one of the hundreds of white, middle-aged men who populated this region of the Northeast. Thick, graying hair, neatly trimmed. A slight paunch (much slighter than Altman's own, thanks to the cop's fondness for his wife's casseroles). His outfit wasn't an arm-patch sports jacket or any other authorial garb, but an L. L. Bean windbreaker, Polo shirt, and corduroy slacks.

It had been two days since Altman had spoken to Carter. The man now stood uneasily in the cop's office, taking the coffee that the young detective Josh Randall offered and nodding greetings to the cops and to Gordon Wallace. Carter slipped off his windbreaker, tossing it on an unoccupied chair. The author's only moment of ill ease in this meeting was when he glanced on Altman's desk and blinked as he saw the case file that was headed, *Banning, Kimberly—Homicide #13-04.* A brief look of dismay filled his face. Quentin Altman was grateful that he'd had the foresight to slip the crime scene photos of the victim's body to the bottom of the folder.

They made small talk for a minute or two and then Altman nodded at a large white envelope in the author's hand. "You find some letters you think might be helpful?"

"Helpful?" Carter asked, rubbing his red eyes. "I don't know. You'll have to decide that." He handed the envelope to the detective.

Altman opened it envelope and, donning latex gloves, pulled out what must've been about two hundred or so sheets.

The detective led the men into the department conference room and spread the letters out on the table. Randall joined them.

Some of them were typed or printed out from a computer—but these were signed, offering a small sample of the correspondent's handwriting. Some were written in cursive, some in block letters. They were on many different types and sizes of paper and colors of ink or pencil. Crayons too.

For an hour the men, each wearing rubber gloves, pored over the letters. Altman could understand the author's dismay. Many of them were truly vicious. Finally he divided them into several piles. First, the email, none of which seemed to have been written by potential killers. Second were the hand-written letters that seemed like the typical innocent opinions of readers. None of these asked for details about how he'd researched the novel or seemed in any way incriminating, though some were angry and some were disturbingly personal ("Come and see us in Sioux City if your in town and the wife and me will treat you to our special full body massage outside on the deck behind our trailer.")

"Ick," said young officer Randall.

The final pile, Altman explained, "included letters that were reasonable and calm and cautious. . . . Just like the Strangler. See, he's an organized offender. He's not going to give anything away by ranting. If he has any questions he's going to ask them politely and carefully—he'll want some detail but not too much; that'd arouse suspicion." Altman gathered up this stack—about ten letters—placed them in an evidence envelope and handed them to the young detective. "Over to the county lab, stat."

A man stuck his head in the door—Detective Bob Fletcher. The even-keeled sergeant introduced himself to Carter. "We never met but I spoke to you on the phone about the case," the cop said.

"I remember." They shook hands.

Fletcher nodded at Altman, smiling ruefully. "He's a better cop than me. I never thought that the killer might've tried to write you."

The sergeant, it turned out, had contacted Carter not about fan mail but to ask if the author'd based the story on any previous true crimes, thinking there might be a connection between them and the Strangler murders. It had been a good idea but Carter had explained that the plot for *Two Deaths* was a product of his imagination.

The sergeant's eyes took in the stacks of letters. "Any luck?" he asked.

"We'll have to see what the lab finds." Altman then nodded toward the author. "But I have to say that Mr. Carter here's been a huge help. We'd be stymied for sure, it wasn't for him."

Appraising Carter carefully, Fletcher said, "I have to admit I never got a chance to read your book but I always wanted to meet you. An honest-to-God famous author. Don't think I've ever shook one's hand before."

Carter gave an embarrassed laugh. "Not very famous to look at my sales figures."

"Well, all I know is my girlfriend read your book and she said it was the best thriller she'd read in years."

Carter said, "I appreciate that. Is she around town? I could autograph her copy."

"Oh," Fletcher said hesitantly, "well, we're not going out any more. She left the area. But thanks for the offer." He headed back to Robbery.

There was now nothing to do but wait for the lab results to come back so Wallace suggested coffee at Starbucks. The men wandered down the street, ordered, and sat sipping the drinks, as Wallace pumped Carter for information about breaking into fiction writing, and Altman simply enjoyed the feel of the hot sun on his face.

The men's recess ended abruptly, though, fifteen minutes later when Altman's cell phone rang.

"Detective," came the enthusiastic voice of his youthful assistant, Josh Randall, "we've got a match! The handwriting in one of Mr. Carter's fan letters matches the notes in the margins of the book. The ink's the same too."

The detective said, "Please tell me there's a name and address on the letter."

"You bet there is. Howard Desmond's his name. And his place is over in Warwick." A small town twenty minutes from the sites of both of the Greenville Strangler's attacks.

The detective told his assistant to pull together as much information on Desmond as he could. He snapped the phone shut and, grinning, announced. "We've found him. We've got our copycat."

VI

But, as it turned out, they didn't have him at all.

At least not the flesh-and-blood suspect.

Single, 42-year-old Howard Desmond, a veterinary technician, had skipped town six months before, leaving in a huge hurry. One day he'd called his landlord and announced that he was moving. He'd left virtually overnight, abandoning everything in the apartment but his valuables. There was no forwarding address. Altman had hoped to go through whatever he'd left behind but the landlord explained that he'd sold everything to make up for the lost rent. What didn't sell he'd thrown out. The detective called the state public records department to see if they had any information about him.

Altman spoke to the vet in whose clinic Desmond had worked and the doctor's report was similar to the landlord's. In April Desmond had called and quit his job, effective immediately, saying only that he was moving to Oregon to take care of his elderly grandmother. He'd never called back with a forwarding address for his last check, as he said he would.

The vet described Desmond as quiet and affectionate to the animals in his care but with little patience for people.

Altman contacted the authorities in Oregon and found no record of any Howard Desmonds in the DMV files or on the property or income tax rolls. A bit more digging revealed that all of Desmond's grandparents—his parents too—had died years before; the story about the move to Oregon was apparently a complete lie.

The few relatives the detective could track down confirmed that he'd just disappeared and they didn't know where he might be. They echoed his boss's assessment, describing the man as intelligent but a recluse, one who—significantly—loved to read and often lost himself in novels, appropriately for a killer who took his homicidal inspiration from a book.

"What'd his letter to Andy say?" Wallace asked.

With an okaying nod from Altman, Randall handed it to the reporter, who then summarized out loud. "He asks how Mr. Carter did the research for his book. What were the sources he used? How did he learn about the most efficient way a murderer would kill someone? And he's curious about the mental makeup of a killer. Why did some people find it easy to kill while others couldn't possibly hurt anyone?"

Altman shook his head. "No clue as to where he might've gone. We'll get his name into NCIC and VICAP but, hell, he could be anywhere. South America, Europe, Singapore. . . ."

Since Bob Fletcher's Robbery Division would've handled the vandalism at the Greenville library's Three Pines Branch, which they now knew Desmond was responsible for, Altman sent Randall to ask the sergeant if he'd found any leads as part of the investigation that would be helpful.

The other men found themselves staring at Desmond's fan letter as if it were a corpse at a wake, silence surrounding them.

Altman's phone rang and he took the call. It was the county clerk, who explained that Desmond owned a small vacation home about sixty miles from Greenville, on the shores of Lake Muskegon, tucked into the backwater, piney wilderness.

"You think he's hiding out there?" Wallace asked.

"I say we go find out. Even if he's hightailed it out of the state, though, there could be some leads there as to where he did go. Maybe airline receipts or something, notes, phone message on an answering machine."

Wallace grabbed his jacket and his reporter's notebook. "Let's go."

"No, no, no," Quentin Altman said firmly. "You get an exclusive. You don't get to go into the line of fire."

"Nice of you to think of me," Wallace said sourly.

"Basically I just don't want to get sued by your newspaper if Desmond decides to use you for target practice."

The reporter gave a scowl and dropped down into an officer chair.

Josh Randall returned to report that Sergeant Bob Fletcher had no helpful information in the library vandalism case.

But Altman said, "Doesn't matter. We've got a better lead. Suit up, Josh."

"Where're we going?"

"For a ride in the country. What else on a nice fall day like this?"

VII

Lake Muskegon was a large but shallow body of water bordered by willow, tall grass, and ugly pine. Altman didn't know the place well. He'd brought his family here for a couple of picnics over the years and he and Bob Fletcher had come to the lake once on a half-hearted fishing expedition, of which Altman had only vague memories: gray, drizzly weather and a nearly empty creel at the end of the day.

As he and Randall drove north through the increasingly deserted landscape he briefed the young man. "Now, I'm ninety-nine percent sure Desmond's not here. But what we're going to do first is clear the house—I mean closet by closet—and then I want you stationed in the front to keep an eye out while I look for evidence. Okay?"

"Sure, boss."

They passed Desmond's overgrown driveway and pulled off the road, then eased into a thick tangle of forsythia stalks.

Together, the men cautiously made their way down the weedy drive toward the "vacation house," a dignified term for the tiny, shabby cottage sitting in a three-foot-high sea of grass and brush. A path had been beaten through the foliage—somebody had been here recently—but it might not have been Desmond; Altman had been a teenager once himself and knew that nothing attracts adolescent attention like a deserted house.

They drew their weapons and Altman pounded on the door, calling, "Police. Open up."

Silence.

He hesitated a moment, adjusted the grip on his gun and kicked the door in.

Filled with cheap, dust-covered furniture, buzzing with stuporous fall flies, the place appeared deserted. They checked the four small rooms carefully and found no sign of Desmond. Outside, they glanced in the window of the garage and saw that it was empty. Then Altman sent Randall to the front of the driveway to hide in the bushes and report anybody's approach.

He then returned to the house and began to search, wondering just how hot the cold case was about to become.

VIII

Two hundred yards from the driveway that led to Howard Desmond's cottage a battered, ten-year-old Toyota pulled onto the shoulder of Route 207 and then eased into the woods, out of sight of any drivers along the road.

A man got out and, satisfied that his car was well hidden, squinted into the forest, getting his bearings. He noticed the line of the brown lake to his left and figured the vacation house was in the ten-o'clock position ahead of him. Through dense underbrush like this it would take him about fifteen minutes to get to the place, he estimated.

That'd make the time pretty tight. He'd have to move as quickly as he could and still keep the noise to a minimum.

The man started forward but then stopped suddenly and patted his pocket. He'd been in such a hurry to get to the house he couldn't remember if he'd taken what he wanted from the glove compartment. But, yes, he had it with him.

Hunched over and picking his way carefully to avoid stepping on noisy branches, Gordon Wallace continued on toward the cabin where, he hoped, Detective Altman was lost in police work and would be utterly oblivious to his furtive approach.

IX

The search of the house revealed virtually nothing that would indicate that Desmond had been here recently—or where the man might now be. Quentin Altman found some bills and cancelled checks. But the address on them was Desmond's apartment in Warwick.

He decided to check the garage, thinking he might come across something helpful the killer had tossed out of the car and forgotten about—maybe a sheet containing directions or a map or receipt.

Altman discovered something far more interesting than evidence, though; he found Howard Desmond himself.

That is to say, his corpse.

The moment Altman opened the old-fashioned double doors of the garage he detected the smell of decaying flesh. He knew where it had to be coming from: a large coal bin in the back. Steeling himself, he flipped up the lid.

The mostly skeletal remains of a man about six feet tall were inside, lying on his back, fully clothed. He'd been dead about six months—just around the time Desmond disappeared, Altman recalled.

DNA would tell for certain if this was the vet tech but Altman discovered the man's wallet in his hip pocket and, sure enough, the driver's license inside was Desmond's. DNA or dental records would tell for certain.

The man's skull was shattered; the cause of death was probably trauma to the head by a blunt object. There was no weapon in the bin itself but after a careful examination of the garage he found a heavy mallet wrapped in a rag and hidden in the bottom of a trash filled oil drum. There were some hairs adhering to the mallet that resembled Desmond's. Altman set the tool on a workbench, wondering what the hell was going on.

Somebody had murdered the Strangler. Who? And why? Revenge?

But then Altman did one of the things he did best—let his mind run free. Too many detectives get an idea into their heads and can't see past their initial conclusions. Altman, though, always fought against this tendency and he now asked himself: But what if Desmond *wasn't* the Strangler?

They knew for certain that he was the one who'd underlined the passages in the library's copy of *Two Deaths in a Small Town*. But what if he'd done so *after* the killings? The letter Desmond had written to Carter was undated. Maybe— just like the reporter Gordon Wallace himself had done—he'd read the book after the murders and been struck by the similarity. He'd started to investigate the crime himself and the Strangler had found out and murdered him.

But then who was the killer?

Just like Gordon Wallace had done. . . .

Altman felt another little tap in his far-ranging mind as fragments of facts lined up for him to consider—facts that all had to do with the reporter. For instance, Wallace was physically imposing, abrasive, temperamental. At times he could be threatening, scary. He was obsessed with crime and he knew police and forensic procedures better than most cops, which also meant that he knew how to antici- pate investigators' moves (He'd sure blustered his way right into the middle of the reopened case just the other day, Altman reflected.) Wallace owned a Motorola police scanner and would've been able to listen in on calls about the victims. His apartment was a few blocks from the college where the first victim was killed.

The detective considered: Let's say that Desmond had read the passages, become suspicious and circled them, then made a few phone calls to find out more about the case. He might've called Wallace, who, as the *Tribune*'s crime reporter, would be a logical source for more information.

Desmond had met with the reporter, who'd then killed him and hid the body here.

Impossible. . . . Why, for instance, would Gordon have brought the book to the police's attention?

Maybe to preempt suspicion?

Altman returned to the disgusting, impromptu crypt once again to search it more carefully, trying to unearth some answers.

X

Gordon Wallace caught a glimpse of Altman in the garage.

The reporter had crept up to a spot only thirty feet away and was hiding behind a bush. The detective wasn't paying any attention to who might be outside, apparently relying on Josh Randall to alert him to intruders. The young detective was at the head of the driveway, a good 200 feet away, his back to the garage.

Breathing heavily in the autumn heat, the reporter started through the grass in a crouch. He stopped beside the building and glanced into the side window fast, noting that Altman was standing over a coal bin in the rear of the garage, squinting at something in his hand.

Perfect, Wallace thought and, reaching into his pocket, eased to the open doorway, where his aim would be completely unobstructed.

XI

The detective had found something in Desmond's wallet and was staring at it—a business card—when he heard the snap of a twig behind him and, alarmed, turned.

A silhouette of a figure was standing in the doorway. He seemed to be holding his hands at chest level.

Blinded by the glare, Altman gasped, "Who're—?"

A huge flash filled the room.

The detective stumbled backward, groping for his pistol.

"Damn," came a voice he recognized.

Altman squinted against the back lighting. "Wallace! You goddamn son of a bitch! What the hell're you doing here?"

The reporter scowled and held up the camera in his hand, looking just as unhappy as Altman. "I was trying to get a candid of you on the job. But you turned around. You ruined it."

"*I* ruined it? I told you not to come. You can't—"

"I've got a first amendment right to be here," the man snapped. "Freedom of the press."

"And I've got a right to throw your ass in jail. This's a crime scene."

"Well, that's why I want the pictures," he said petulantly. Then he frowned. "What's that smell?" The camera sagged and the reporter started to breathe in shallow gasps. He looked queasy.

"It's Desmond. Somebody murdered him. He's in the coal bin."

"Murdered *him*? So he's not the killer?"

Altman lifted his radio and barked to Randall, "We've got visitors back here."

"What?"

"We're in the garage."

The young officer showed up a moment later, trotting fast. A disdainful look at Wallace. "Where the hell did you come from?"

"How'd you let him get past?" Altman snapped.

"Not his fault," the reporter said, shivering at the smell. "I parked up the road. How 'bout we get some fresh air?"

Angry, Altman took perverse pleasure in the reporter's discomfort. "I oughta throw you in jail."

Wallace held his breath and started for the coal bin, raising the camera.

"Don't even think about it," Altman growled and pulled the reporter away.

"Who did it?" Randall asked, nodding at the body.

Altman didn't share that for a moment he'd actually suspected Wallace Gordon himself. Just before the photo op incident he'd found a stunning clue as to who Desmond's—and the two women's killer—probably was. He held up a business card. "I found this on the body."

On the card was written, "Detective Sergeant Robert Fletcher, Greenville Police Department."

"Bob?" Randall whispered in shock.

"I don't want to believe it," Altman muttered slowly, "but back at the office he didn't let on he even knew about Desmond, let alone that they'd met at some point."

"True."

"And," he continued, nodding at the mallet, "Bob does all that metal work—his hobby, remember? That could be one of his."

Randall looked uneasily at the murder weapon.

Altman's heart pounded furiously at the betrayal. He now speculated about what had happened. Fletcher bobbled the case intentionally—because *he* was the killer, probably destroying any evidence that led to him. A loner, a history of short, difficult relationships, obsessed with violence and military history and artifacts and hunting. . . . He'd lied to them about not about reading *Two Deaths* and *had* used it as a model to kill those women. Then—*after* the killings—Desmond happened to read the book too, underlined the passages and, being a good citizen, contacted case officer Fletcher, who was none other than the killer himself. The sergeant murdered him, dumped the body here and then destroyed the library's computer. Of course, he never made any effort to pursue the vandalism investigation.

Alarmed, Quentin Altman had another thought. He turned to the reporter. "Where was Fletcher when you left the office? Did you see him at the station?" The detective's hand strayed to his pistol as he looked around the tall grass, wondering if the sergeant had followed him here and intended to kill them as well. Fletcher was a crack rifle shot.

But Randall replied, "He was in the conference room with Andy Carter."

No! Altman realized that they weren't the only ones at risk; the author was a witness too—and therefore a potential victim of Fletcher's. Altman grabbed his cell phone and called the central dispatcher. He asked for Carter.

"He's not here, sir," the woman said.

"What?"

"It was getting late so he decided to get a hotel room for the night."

"Which one's he staying at?"

"I think it's the Sutton Inn."

"You have the number?"

"I do, sure. But he's not there right now."

"Where is he?"

"He went out to dinner. I don't know where but if you need to get in touch with him you can call Bob Fletcher's phone. They were going together."

XII

Twenty minutes from town, driving at twice the posted limit.

Altman tried again to call Fletcher but the sergeant wasn't answering. There wasn't much Altman could do except try to reason with the sergeant, have him give himself up, plead with him not to kill Carter too. He prayed that the cop hadn't already done so.

Another try. Still no answer.

He skidded the squad car through the intersection at Route 202, nearly sideswiping one of the dairy tankers that were ubiquitous in these parts.

"Okay, that was exciting," Randall whispered, removing his sweaty palm from the dashboard as the truck's horn brayed in angry protest behind them.

Altman was about to call Fletcher's phone again when a voice clattered over the car's radio, "All units. Reports of shots fired on Route 128 just west of Ralph's grocery. Repeat, shots fired. All units respond."

"You think that's them?"

"We're three minutes away. We're about to find out." Altman called in their position and then pushed the accelerator to the floor; they broke into three-digit speed.

After a brief, harrowing ride, the squad car crested a hill. Randall called breathlessly, "Look!"

Altman could see Bob Fletcher's Police Interceptor half on, half off the road. He skidded to a stop nearby and the two officers jumped out, Wallace's car—which'd been hitching an illegal ride on their light bar and siren, braked to a stop fifty feet behind them. The reporter too jumped out, ignoring the detective's shout to stay back.

Altman felt Randall grip his arm. The young officer was pointing at the shoulder about fifty feet away. In the dim light they could just make out the form of Andrew Carter lying face down in a patch of bloody dirt.

Oh, goddamnit! They weren't in time; the sergeant had added the author to the list of his victims.

Crouching beside the car, Altman whispered to Randall, "Head up the road that way. Look out for Fletcher. He's someplace close."

Scanning the bushes, in a crouch, Altman ran toward the author's body. As he did he happened to glance to his left and gasped. There was Bob Fletcher on the ground, holding a sheriff's department shotgun.

He shouted to Randall, "Look out!" And dropped flat. But as he swung the gun toward Fletcher he noted that the sergeant wasn't moving. The detective hit the man with his flashlight beam. Fletcher's eyes were glazed over and there was blood on his chest.

Wallace was crouching over Carter. The reporter called, "He's alive!"

The detective rose, pulled the scattergun out of Fletcher's lifeless hands and trotted over to the author. Fletcher had shot him and he was unconscious.

"Andy, stay with us!" Altman called, pressing his hand onto the bloody wound in the author's belly. Over the crest of the road the detective could see the flashing lights and hear sirens, growing steadily louder. He leaned down and whispered into the man's ear, "Hang in there! You'll be all right, you'll be all right, you'll be all right. . . ."

XIII

His book had saved his life, the author was explaining with a laugh that turned into a wince.

It was the next morning, and Quentin Altman and Carter's wife—a handsome, middle-aged blonde—were standing at his bedside in Greenville Hospital. Fletcher's bullet had missed vital organs but had snapped a rib and the author was in major pain despite the happy pills he'd been given.

Carter told them what had happened last evening: "Fletcher says let's go to dinner—he knew some good barbecue place in the country. We were driving along this deserted road and I was talking about *Two Deaths* and said that this was just the sort of road I had in mind when I wrote that scene where the Hunter was stalking the first victim after he sees her at McDonalds. Then, Fletcher said that *he* pictured that road being in cornfields, not forests."

"But he said he hadn't read the book," Altman said.

"Exactly. . . . He realized he'd screwed up. He got real quiet for a minute, and I was thinking something's wrong. I was even going to jump out of the car. But then he pulls his gun out and I grab it but he still shoots me. I reach over with my foot and slam on the brake. We go off the road and he slams his head into the window or something. I grab the gun and roll out of the car. I'm heading for the bushes to hide in but I see him getting the shotgun from the trunk. He starts toward me and I shoot him." He shook his head. "Man, if it hadn't been for the book, what he said about it, I never would've known what he was going to do."

Since Altman was involved in the incident, the investigation of the shooting went to another detective, who reported that the forensics bore out Carter's story. There was GSR—gunshot residue—on Fletcher's hand, which meant he'd fired the pistol, and a bullet with Carter's blood on it embedded in the cruiser passenger door. Evidence also proved that Fletcher was indeed the Greenville Strangler. The sergeant's fingerprints were all over the mallet and a search of the sergeant's house revealed several items—stockings and lingerie—that had been taken from the homes of the victims. Murdering Howard Desmond and trying to murder Andy Carter—well, those had been to cover up his original crimes. But what had been the sergeant's motive for killing the two women in Greenville? Maybe the anger at being left by his wife had boiled over. Maybe he'd had a secret affair with one of the victims, which had turned sour, and he'd decided to stage her death as a random act of violence. Maybe some day an answer would come to light.

Or maybe, Altman reflected, unlike in a mystery novel, they'd never know what had driven the man to step over the edge into the dark world of the killers he'd once hunted.

It was then that Wallace Gordon loped into the hospital room "Hot off the presses." He handed a copy of the *Tribune* to Carter. On the front page was Wallace's story about the solving of the Greenville Strangler case.

"Keep that," Wallace said. "A souvenir."

Thanking him, Carter's wife folded the paper up and set it aside with the stiff gesture of someone who has no interest in memorabilia about a difficult episode in one's life.

Quentin Altman walked to the door and, just as he was about to leave, paused. He turned back. "Oh, one thing, Andy—how's that book of yours end? Do the police ever find the Hunter?"

Carter caught himself as he was about to answer. The author gave a grin. "You know, detective—you want to find that out, I'm afraid you're just going to have to buy yourself a copy."

XIV

Several days later Andrew Carter slipped out of his bed, where he'd lain, wide-awake, for the past three hours. It was two A.M.

He glanced at the quiescent form of his sleeping wife and—with the help of his cane—limped to the his closet, where he found and pulled on an old pair of faded jeans, sneakers and a Boston University sweatshirt—his good-luck writing clothes, which he hadn't donned in well over a year.

Still in pain from the gunshot, he walked slowly down the hall to his office and went inside, turning on the light. Sitting at his desk, he clicked on his computer and stared at the screen for a long moment.

Then suddenly he began to write. His keyboarding was clumsy at first, his fingers jabbing two keys at once or missing the intended one altogether. Still, as the hours passed, his skill as a typist returned and soon the words were pouring from his mind onto the screen flawlessly and fast.

By the time the sky began to glow with pink-gray light and a morning bird's cell-phone trill sounded from the crisp holly bush outside his window he'd finished the story completely—thirty-nine double-spaced pages.

He moved the cursor to the top of the document, thought about an appropriate title and typed: *Copycat*.

Then Andy Carter sat back in his comfortable chair and carefully read his work from start to finish.

The story opened with a reporter finding a suspense novel that contained several circled passages, which were strikingly similar to two real-life murders that had occurred earlier. The reporter takes the book to a detective, who concludes that the man who circled the paragraphs is the perpetrator, a copycat inspired by the novel to kill.

Reviving the case, the detective enlists the aid of the novel's author, who reluctantly agrees to help and brings the police some fan letters, one of which leads to the suspected killer.

But when the police track the suspect to his summer home they find that *he's* been murdered too. He wasn't the killer at all but had presumably circled the passages only because he, like the reporter, was struck by the similarity between the novel and the real-life crimes.

Then the detective gets a big shock: On the fan's body he finds clues that prove that a local police sergeant is the real killer. The author, who happens to be with this very officer at that moment, is nearly killed but manages to wrestle gun away and shoot the cop in self-defense.

Case closed.

Or so it seems. . . .

But Andy Carter hadn't ended the story there. He added yet another twist. Readers learn at the very end that the sergeant was innocent. He'd been set up as a fall guy by the real Strangler.

Who happened to be the author himself.

Racked by writer's block after his first novel was published, unable to follow it up with another, the author had descended into madness. Desperate and demented, he came to believe that he might jumpstart his writing by actually re-enacting scenes from his novel so he stalked and strangled two women, exactly as his fictional villain had done.

The murders hadn't revived his ability to write, however, and he slumped further into depression. And then, even more troubling, he heard from the fan who'd grown suspicious about the similarities between certain passages in the novel and the real crimes. The author had no choice: he met with the fan at his lakeside cottage and beat him to death, hiding the body in the garage and covering up the disappearance by pretending to be the fan and telling his boss and landlord that he was leaving town unexpectedly.

The author believed he was safe. But his contentment didn't last. Enter the reporter who'd found the underlined passages, and the investigation started anew; the police called, asking him for fan letters. The author knew the only way to be safe was to give the police a scapegoat. So he agreed to meet with the police—but in fact he'd arrived in town a day before his planned meeting with the detective. He broke into the police sergeant's house, planted some incriminating clothing he'd taken from the dead women's houses and stole one of the cop's mallets and a business card. He then went out to the dead fan's lake house, where he'd hidden the body, and used the tool to crush the skull of the decomposed body and hid the mallet, along with some of the dead man's hairs, in an oil drum. The card he slipped into the wallet. The next day he showed up at the police station with the fan letter that led to the cottage—and ultimately to the sergeant.

The author, who'd asked the unsuspecting sergeant to drive to dinner, grabbed his gun, made him stop the car and get out. Then he shot him, rested the pistol near the dead cop's hands and fired it into the woods to get gunshot residue on the man's finger (writers know as much about forensics as most cops). The author had gotten the shotgun from the trunk, left it with the sergeant and then climbed back into the squad car, where he'd taken a deep breath and shot himself in the belly—as superficially as he could.

He'd then crawled onto the road to wait for a passing car to come to their aid.

The police bought the entire story.

In the final scene the author returned home to try to resume his writing, having literally gotten away with murder.

Carter now finished rereading the story, his heart thumping hard with pride and excitement. True, it needed polishing but, considering that he hadn't written a word for more than a year, it was a glorious accomplishment.

He was a writer once again.

The only problem was that he couldn't publish the story. He couldn't even *show* it to a soul.

For the simple reason, of course, that it wasn't fiction; every word was true. Andy Carter himself was the homicidal author.

Still, he thought, as he erased the entire story from his computer, publishing it didn't matter one bit. The important thing was that by writing it he'd managed to kill his writer's block as ruthlessly and efficiently as he'd murdered Bob Fletcher and Howard Desmond and the two women in Greenville. And, even better, he knew too how to make sure that he'd never be blocked again: From now on he'd give up fiction and pursue what he'd realized he was destined to write: true crime.

What a perfect solution this was! He'd never want for ideas again; TV news, magazines and the papers would provide dozens of story leads he could choose from.

And, he reflected, limping downstairs to make a pot of coffee, if it turned out that there were no crimes that particularly interested him . . . well, Andy Carter knew that he was fully capable of taking matters into his own hands and whipping up a bit of inspiration all by himself.

ALEXANDER McCALL SMITH

Alexander McCall Smith's charmingly quirky detective fiction found an international audience through word of mouth. First published by Polygon, an imprint of Edinburgh University Press, in 1998, Smith's first mystery is titled after an enterprise founded by Mma. Precious Ramotswe: *The No. I Ladies' Detective Agency.* Located at the bottom of a hill in the dusty Botswana countryside, the agency's work depends upon the common sense and uncommon insights of its founding private eye. If the site of the detective agency is something novel in detective fiction, that's not all that's notable here. Smith has Ramotswe set out to solve several puzzles in one book, and he makes her memorable as a woman of large, "traditionally built" stature.

Smith had already written two more books in the series when Anchor Books bought the first and introduced it to a wider audience. He went on to write more mysteries, and in 2004 he introduced another female sleuth, Elizabeth Dalhousie, in *The Sunday Philosophy Club,* set in Edinburgh, Scotland.

Smith is well acquainted with the worlds where he sets his fiction. He was born in Rhodesia (now known as Zimbabwe), Africa, and educated there and at the University of Edinburgh, where he took the position of a professor of medical law. He worked to establish a law school in Botswana and has served in several high-level posts examining bioethics. He has written books and journal articles on medical and legal topics, and he is also the author of light children's books. He plays the bassoon in a group he cofounded—The Really Terrible Orchestra—based in Edinburgh, where he now resides.

Set in Swaziland, Smith's poignant story "He Loved to Go for Drives with His Father" was written especially for *A New Omnibus of Crime.* Like the works in the Ramotswe series, it is strong on description of the African scene. Meanwhile, characters' fates, which are balanced on a delicate crucible, are tipped toward tragedy when one throws ethics to the winds.

Smith recalled: "I lived for six months in Swaziland back in 1980. I found myself intrigued by the country, which is a small land-locked kingdom in southern Africa. When I lived there I was sure that one day I would write about the place, and indeed I have written several short stories set there, but this is the first time that one has featured the Uncle Charlie Hotel. In those days it was a remarkable place, complete with its amazing mural. I do not know whether it is still standing.

I always thought that in Manzini, where the story is set, there would be many small and concealed dramas. I thought that there might well be a feeling of desperation there—particularly amongst those from elsewhere who had to live there for their job. In many respects it was Somerset Maugham territory, an ideal setting for a story of a crime that would not be too serious but which would lock people into a claustrophobic togetherness."

He Loved to Go for Drives with His Father

2005

I

This took place some time ago, in a country called Swaziland, a small land-locked kingdom in southern Africa. It is a country of great beauty, rising from a swathe of low country in the south to highlands in the northwest. When viewed from a distance, these northern hills seem impossibly blue, fading into the sky as gently as mist shades into the contours of the land. Along the east side of the country there is a range of mountains, the Lebombo Mountains, from the ridge of which one may look down into Mozambique below, and beyond that, when conditions are right, to a line of blue which is the Indian Ocean.

At that time, which was in the nineteen fifties, the country was a British protectorate, presided over by a Paramount Chief, Sobhuza II, who was later to be referred to as the king. He was a man of considerable wisdom, much admired by his people, who were an offshoot of the Zulu nation and who were proud of their heritage.

The Paramount Chief lived in a sprawl of buildings between the two main towns of the country, Mbabane, which was the capital, and Manzini, which was close to the airstrip and the few factories which the country had. The Paramount Chief's place was at the foot of a small group of hills which was sacred to the Swazi nation, being the place where leaders were traditionally buried in caves, wrapped in the hides of their finest oxen. Nobody was allowed to scale these hills except on the occasion of a royal burial or similar ceremony.

II

There was a Scottish doctor who took up a post as government medical offi-cer in Manzini. He was based at the hospital there—a rambling collection of buildings next door to a hotel called the Uncle Charlie Hotel. This hotel, which had a bar and a long veranda, also boasted a dining room in which a striking mural had been painted. This mural showed a great African lake, with palm trees and mopani forests about its edges. Giraffe and zebra were depicted moving across savanna. Nobody paid much attention to this mural, which had been painted as a shallow strip around the top of the walls, just below the ceil-ing, but every now and then a visitor who saw its merits would stand and stare at it. Such people said that for some reason the mural made them sad. "It shows the beauty of Africa distilled," said one such visitor. "And it shows us what is being lost."

382

The doctor had been allocated a house in the town, close to the tennis courts. It was a good house, commensurate with his position in the community, and it boasted a particularly attractive garden. The previous medical officer, who had been a bachelor, had spent all his spare time in the garden and had stocked it colorfully and imaginatively. He had been particularly fond of bougainvillea, which grew in profusion along the side of the house and around the kitchen garden. The local man who helped him in the garden did not like the bougainvillea, which he said attracted snakes. Nor did he like that doctor's collection of aloes, which he said were poisonous, and which he hoped would die of neglect. But aloes thrive on neglect, and they continued to grow.

The new doctor appreciated the garden but did not take a strong interest in it. He enjoyed playing chess, and he would sit for hours on the verandah, working out chess problems using a set made by Italian prisoners of war. His wife, who was not interested in chess, was a keen member of the tennis club. She was a strong player and would give lessons to any of the other tennis-playing wives who were eager to improve their game. She never played with her husband, who said that he found tennis a dull game after the first few services had been knocked over the net.

After chess, the doctor's other passion was cars. He was something of an amateur mechanic, and he would sometimes spend the whole weekend tinkering with the engine of the old green Pontiac which he had bought in Cape Town and driven all the way up to Swaziland. This car was his pride and joy until it was badly damaged in an accident on the road that ran from Manzini to Mbabane. This was a notoriously dangerous road, with its hairpin bends, and numerous vehicles had simply dropped over the edge, careering down through the undergrowth until they came to a ruinous halt against a tree or a granite boulder. In the accident which destroyed the doctor's car, neither he nor his wife was seriously hurt, although they were both shaken by the event.

"I don't want to drive anywhere at night in this country," said the doctor's wife to one of her tennis partners. "It's just too dangerous."

III

After the loss of his green Pontiac, the doctor was obliged to buy a much less interesting car, a Volkswagen, which, although reliable and well suited to the country's unpaved roads, was dull to drive. The engine was not very powerful, and the doctor liked to be able to accelerate more quickly in order to pass trucks. Trucks, particularly the large cattle trucks, threw up a large cloud of dust behind them, and the doctor hated having to drive in that. But there was not a very wide choice of cars in Swaziland at that time, and the doctor could not lay his hands on anything more interesting.

Some months after the doctor's road accident, the manager of the Uncle Charlie Hotel went off to Johannesburg for a weekend. This man was a thin-faced Englishman whose wife had left him because she could not bear what she described as the boredom of living in a colonial backwater like Swaziland. She had gone to Nairobi, where she had a cousin, and where she soon met and married a wealthy farmer. The manager of the Uncle Charlie Hotel was philosophical about this. "She never loved me, anyway," he said. People who heard him talk this way were shocked into silence. It was difficult to know what to say in the face of such a personal revelation.

When he went off to Johannesburg for his weekend, the doctor's wife said: "Poor man, he deserves a bit of fun after putting up with that flighty woman. Let's hope he meets somebody in Johannesburg."

The hotel manager did not meet somebody in Johannesburg, but he did come back with a different car from the one in which he had set off. This was a Mercedes-Benz, which, although not new, was a car of considerable character and charm. It had beige leather seats and a marvellous wooden steering wheel. It was one of the most striking cars in the whole country, and it was even said that the Paramount Chief had seen it on the road and asked whose it was and had expressed a desire to have a car like that at some point.

Everybody talked about this new Mercedes-Benz. It stood parked in front of the Uncle Charlie Hotel, where one of the junior waiters was detailed to wash and polish it every day, paying particular attention to the shiny chrome bumpers and the silver three-point symbol at the top of the radiator.

The doctor was particularly taken with this car. A few days after its arrival, he was seen by somebody in the dining room of the hotel to pull up beside it in his Volkswagen, get out, and peer through the window, like a schoolboy. And some time after that he was heard to say to the hospital pharmacist, "I'd kill for a car like that. I really would."

The doctor's wife was indifferent to vehicles of any sort. "Men are ridiculous," she observed at the tennis club one afternoon. "They love those bits of machinery as if they were . . . as if they were women. It's ridiculous."

"I'd prefer my husband to have a love affair with a car than another woman," said one of the other tennis players.

"That's true," said the doctor's wife. "But I still wish that men would just grow up. They're so immature."

IV

When the wife of the manager of the Uncle Charlie Hotel had gone off to Kenya, she had left behind a child. This was a boy of seven, who suffered from a condition that had seriously affected brain development. This boy could walk unaided, but could not utter more than a few words. But he was not troublesome. He did not scream or wail, as can happen with some of these distressing conditions. He merely gazed out of the window and pointed at birds and animals which attracted his attention. He took particular pleasure in looking at cattle and would make a mooing sound in imitation as he watched them. The manager of the Uncle Charlie Hotel would drive his son out in the Mercedes-Benz at the end of the working day and take him for a short spin along the Siteki road, slowing down when they came to cattle grazing at the side of the road. Then they would drive back before it got dark, which happens so suddenly in those latitudes. One minute it will be light and the next the sun will have disappeared behind the hills and the night will be filled with the screech and chirrup of nocturnal insects.

The boy loved the Mercedes-Benz. He would stand beside it for hours, looking into its gleaming paintwork as if it were a mirror.

V

Six months after the manager had gone to Johannesburg to fetch the car, there was an awful row one morning at the Uncle Charlie Hotel. The Mercedes-Benz, which had been parked at the front of the hotel overnight, was missing from its place. The manager called the police immediately, and the police inspector himself came over within twenty minutes in his gray Land Rover.

"Car theft," said the inspector. "It happens, you know. It'll be over the border by now, I'm afraid, probably taken into South Africa, although it might have been spirited up to Lourenço Marques. I'm very sorry about this, but I fear that's that. Have you got the chassis number, by the way?"

The manager did not have the number. He had bought the car in a private sale, and he had not been given proper registration documents. So there was no record of this vital piece of information.

"Then it will not be possible for us to get the cooperation of the people over the border," said the police inspector. "We wouldn't be able to prove that it was stolen, even if they found it."

The manager of the Uncle Charlie Hotel swore violently when he received this news. This did not please the police inspector, who told him to watch his tongue. "I understand how you feel," he said. "But you don't swear like that in front of me. Understand?"

Everybody sympathized with the manager over his loss.

"It's a terribly sad thing," said one of the members of the tennis club. "He used to take that boy of his for those runs up on the Siteki Road. I saw them. It was rather touching, I thought, with that little boy sitting there looking out of the side and smiling in that way of his. Poignant really."

"The insurance will pay up," said another.

"Maybe. But you can't replace those cars just like that."

"True. You can't."

VI

The doctor's wife was aware of the fact that her husband was working on a project with his friend Ed, a mechanic who had a small garage on a dirt road that led to the Umbeluzi River. She had met this man once before and did not like him. There was something about his eyes which made her uncomfortable. The whites of his eyes looked yellow.

"Fatty deposits in the eyes," said the doctor. "His cholesterol is out of control."

"I still don't like him," she said.

The doctor had shrugged. He did not like some of the women at the tennis club, but did not think it helpful to say so. "We're fiddling about with an engine," he explained. "It's an old Rover and we're stripping it right down and reboring it. Complicated stuff. But Ed's good at that sort of thing and he's teaching me a lot."

She said nothing to this. She was not interested in that sort of thing and she did not mind if that is how he wanted to spend his spare time. It was better than drinking, which is what a lot of people did in the evenings, out of sheer boredom.

Then one evening the doctor announced to her that he had managed to acquire a new car through Ed. It was a Mercedes-Benz, he said, and he was sure that she would like it. It was the same model as the one which had belonged to the manager of the Uncle Charlie Hotel, but it was a different color. The manager's car had been red; this one was black.

"How much did it cost?'" she asked. "Was it expensive?"

The doctor hesitated for a moment—just a moment. "No," he said. "It was a very good bargain."

He brought the car back to the house the following evening. He parked it front of the verandah and invited her to inspect it.

"It runs beautifully," he said. "I'll take you up to Mbabane in it if you like. We could go right now."

"No thanks," she said. "I don't want to travel at night. And you shouldn't either, or this one will end up down the hill like the Pontiac."

VII

The manager of the Uncle Charlie Hotel was astonished when he saw the doctor driving around in the Mercedes-Benz. "It's the same model as mine was," he said. "Different color. But otherwise the same. He's lucky to get a car like that."

He asked he doctor one day whether he would mind if he had a look at his new car. "I'm pretty envious of you, doc," he said. "You know I had one just the same as that. I know how nice they are to drive. Lovely cars."

"Yes," said the doctor. He did not seem to be enthusiastic about showing the car to the manager, but he could hardly refuse. He drove it around one Saturday afternoon and let the manager sit behind the wheel.

"Lovely workmanship," said the manager, caressing the steering wheel. "Beautiful."

"Built to last," said the doctor. "I loved that old Pontiac of mine, but this is in a different league."

"Take good care of it," said the manager, ruefully. "These things get stolen. And I suppose it's pretty easy to whip them away and then repaint them."

The doctor nodded. "I'll be careful," he said. "I put it away in my garage at nights, you know. That's the safest thing to do. And when I take it to the hospital, I park it right outside the main entrance where the porter can keep an eye on it."

"Very wise," said the manager. He fingered he steering wheel again, as if making contact with an old friend—an old friend who had been lost and was much regretted.

VIII

The doctor's wife left the household finances to her husband, who was good with accounts. She did not have a head for figures and simply drew on the housekeeping money that they kept in a small lock-up cupboard in the doctor's study. But one afternoon she was in the study, looking for an envelope, when she came across a file of bank statements. She decided, out of idle curiosity, to look at the statement which covered the last three months of transactions. There were regular withdrawals for obvious purposes: the payment of the account at the general store, the payment of the insurance premiums, and so on. That was all unexceptional. But then it occurred to her that it was strange that there was no payment for the new car. The money from the sale of the Volkswagen had been paid in, but nothing had gone out to pay for its replacement.

She reflected on her discovery that afternoon, and it suddenly occurred to her that the only explanation was that the car had cost him nothing. And then, while she was standing on the verandah, looking out at a frangipani tree, the thought struck her: her husband must have stolen the car, taken it to Ed's, and repainted it. All he would have had to pay for was the paint, with perhaps a small amount for Ed's time and connivance. He could have managed to pay that out of his normal pin money.

She stood quite still for a while, trying to reach another, less disturbing conclusion; but she could not. She went out into the garden and walked about in the cool of the late afternoon. She stopped and looked at a bed of Namaqualand daisies that had been planted by the previous doctor. She sought another answer in the flowers, but there was none to be had. It appalled her to think that she lived with a man who was prepared to do that. But then she thought: do I really know him all that well? He never talks to me about the things that really move him. He never does that. He is a stranger in so many ways. Men were a different continent, she thought; distant, unpredictable. Perhaps I should not be surprised.

Then she debated with herself what she should do. She could not tell the manager of the Uncle Charlie Hotel that they had his car. She could not bear the shame that would follow. She imagined what they would say at the tennis club, what would be said behind her back. It would be intolerable to be the subject of such gossip. She would rather die that be disgraced in that way.

She would have to punish him herself, she thought. She would have to show him that he could not get away with a crime like that. She would be the agent of justice.

IX

The doctor's wife was not a keen driver, but she did occasionally drive the Mercedes-Benz to the tennis club or into town to buy meat and vegetables. Now she said to the doctor, "I'd like to drive up to Mbabane some time next week to visit Jennifer. She's not been well and I want to catch up with her."

He said, "That's fine. I'll get one of the hospital drivers to pick me up. You take the car."

She went off that day. She drove up towards Mbabane and stopped near the top of the long incline, near a place where the road bent sharply. She got out to stretch her legs and looked down over the edge. The ground fell away sharply, down to a stand of eucalyptus trees far below. She heard the sound of their leaves in the wind, a sound that drifted up on the warm afternoon air. It was a beautiful country, she thought. There was so much beauty in Africa, but such wickedness too.

She returned to the car. The road was deserted, and so there was nobody to see her drive very slowly to the very edge of the road and then get out. She leaned against the car, the engine of which was still idling. She pushed, and very slowly it moved forward and then, in a sudden lurch, slipped over the edge. There was a crumbling of sand and dust from the edge of the road and a sound of crushing metal and the breaking of small trees. She watched as the car went down, turned over, and broke into flames. She leant down, picked up a handful of dust, and rubbed it into her face and hair. Then she tore her dress, and scratched at her arm with a stick until a small, bright line of blood appeared.

X

The doctor said to her, "I'm so glad that you weren't hurt. It's you I care about. I don't care about the car."

She said, "You don't care about the car? Are you sure about that?"

He shook his head. "No. Human life is more important than a machine. The important thing is that you weren't hurt. Well, hurt a tiny bit, but not much."

She was silent for a moment. Then she said, "You don't care about the car?" She paused, then, quite softly, as if remarking on something unimportant, she said, "Well, I suppose it wasn't really your car in the first place, was it?"

The doctor said nothing. They had been sitting on the verandah and he now rose to his feet and walked over to peer at one of the bougainvillea bushes that had twisted itself around one of the verandah pillars. Then he looked back at her. She saw that his face was drawn, aghast, uncomprehending.

"That poor little boy," she said. "He loved to go for drives with his father."

CREDITS

INDEX